# CHE

## THE LIFE, DEATH, AND AFTERLIFE OF A REVOLUTIONARY

edited by **JOSEPH HART**

BASIC
BOOKS

A Member of the Perseus Books Group
New York

Compilation © 2003 by Joseph Hart
Photographs © by Gianfranco Gorgoni

Originally published by Thunder's Mouth Press in 2003
Published in 2008 by Basic Books,
A Member of the Perseus Books Group

Books published by Basic Books are available at special discounts
for bulk purchases in the United States by corporations, institutions,
and other organizations. For more information, please contact the
Special Markets Department at the Perseus Books Group, 2300
Chestnut Street, Suite 200, Philadelphia, PA 19103, or call (800)
255-1514, or e-mail special.markets@perseusbooks.com.

Designed by Pauline Neuwirth, Neuwirth & Associates, Inc.

A CIP catalog record for this book is available
from the Library of Congress.

ISBN-13: 978-1-56025-519-2
ISBN-10: 1-56025-519-6
10 9 8 7 6 5 4

# CONTENTS

# PUBLISHER'S NOTE

The table of contents includes dates, not of composition, but of the source publication. The publication history of writings by and about Ernesto Che Guevara in the United States tells its own story, one merely outlined by the contents of this anthology. No work of this kind can pretend to be comprehensive. Nevertheless, certain omissions are regretted. Constraints of time and, especially, money prevented us from securing permission to reprint many essays that would add dimension to the necessarily fragmentary portrait attempted here. Ocean Press, of Melbourne, Australia, representing its own interests and those of Aleida March, denied permission to reprint Che's essay on political sovereignty and economic independence, and peremptorily threatened us with "legal proceedings." Noble comrades! Those words do not belong to you. History will not absolve you; it will forget you.

Many thanks to all contributors and to all who granted permission to reprint. Thanks to Gianfranco Gorgoni for the photographs and to Shawneric Hachey, without whom this can't be done.

# PART

## one
# VAGABOND

". . . we'd lean on the rail and look out over the vast sea, gleaming greeny-white, side by side but each lost in his own thoughts. . . . There we discovered that our vocation, our true vocation, was to roam the highways and waterways of the world for ever."

**—ERNESTO CHE GUEVARA, 1952**

**(24 YEARS OLD)**

from
# THE MAKING OF A REVOLUTIONARY
# A MEMOIR OF THE YOUNG GUEVARA
## DOLORES MOYANO MARTIN

*NEW YORK TIMES*

AUGUST 18, 1968

Ernesto Che Guevara's death at the hands of Bolivian troops last October enhanced a legend that began when he was Fidel Castro's right-hand man in Cuba. This memoir, by a childhood friend in Argentina, describes some of the events and influences that helped shape him as a revolutionary. The author, now living in Washington, has drawn primarily upon her personal journals, and correspondence with mutual friends.

I N 1932, BECAUSE of 4-year-old Ernesto Guevara's asthma, his family moved from humid Buenos Aires to Alta Gracia in the mountains of Córdoba, where the air is dry and sharp and the sky as blue and cloudless as a postcard. In 1941, the Guevaras rented a row house around the block from ours in the city of Córdoba. There were then five children: Ernesto, the oldest, followed by Celia, Roberto, Ana Maria and Juan Martin, or Patatín, the baby. Although Ernesto never acquired a Córdoban accent and was easily identifiable as not native to the province, Córdoba became his hometown. Even after the family moved back to Buenos Aires in 1948, they returned to spend their summers in the mountains.

Córdoba, which Ernesto once described as "this flat city of my loves," is known as *La Docta*, "The Scholarly." Though now a thriving industrial city, it was then a university town with a church in every block, full of students, priests and nuns. The magnificent baroque cathedral, like a gray elephant, faced the main plaza with its general on horse-back, under whose shadow little Indian-looking conscripts in Nazi-style helmets made advances to the pinafored maids on errands. Across the plaza was the Royal Cinema, where the children of the oligarchy were shown American war movies with the love scenes heavily censored by the Catholic Action. In the cafes, anticlerical liberals met to talk politics with Spanish Republicans and other anti-Fascist European exiles. A city of bookstores, religious processions, student demonstrations and military parades; a city gentle, dull, almost torpid on the surface but simmering with tensions.

With an insignificant middle class, little industry and an omnipotent and omnipresent church, Córdoba was still a feudal city in many ways. At the top of the social pyramid there were a minuscule grand oligarchy, living in splendor; a middle oligarchy, without private planes and polo fields but with plenty of other consolations, and an impoverished oligarchy, which the Guevaras joined. In the last group appearances were kept up by endless financial acrobatics.

THE GUEVARAS WERE part of the Buenos Aires upper class, and until the loss of the family's considerable fortune had lived very well indeed. Ernesto Sr. is a cousin of Alberto Gainza Paz, the editor of that bastion of conservatism the Buenos Aires daily La Prensa. Young Ernesto once mentioned, not without pride, that he was a descendant of one of the colonial viceroys of the River Plate, roughly the Argentine equivalent of having had an ancestor on the Mayflower.

Unlike the rest of the impoverished oligarchy, the Guevaras made no bones about being poor. This unconventional admission and their cartdidly Bohemian ways incensed the genteel. As someone said of the Irish—and the Lynch side of the Guevara family was Irish—in their house the inevitable never happened, only the unexpected. Mealtimes were not fixed; one just ate when one felt hungry. You were free to ride your bicycle from the street through the living room into their backyard. In the house, one could hardly see the furniture for the books and magazines piled high everywhere. One of my earliest memories of Ernesto is of him in bed, his head shaved like a convict, and wearing striped pajamas, which gave him the look of a concentration camp inmate.

Ernesto's mother, Celia, had the same wickedly teasing streak as her son. Passionate and truthful, she could be exceedingly stubborn. Ernesto Sr., a civil engineer and practicing architect, was an immensely likable man who exuded warmth and vitality. He spoke in a booming voice, and was rather absent-minded. Occasionally, he sent the children on errands which he had forgotten by the time they returned.

The Guevaras kept their house wide open to everybody and this delighted the neighborhood children. In fact, they encouraged their own children to be as democratic as possible and to bring anyone they wished for a visit. Workers, mechanics, caddies, newsboys, people from all walks of life would meet to socialize with the Guevaras' upper-class friends. Both parents shared an aristocratic contempt for bourgeois formalities and undoubtedly enjoyed shocking some of their more conventional friends who would arrive only to be formally introduced to the corner newsboy.

IN MOST LATIN American cities, especially in the provinces, the poor and the rich live side by side. There are no ghettos in this feudal society, where somehow physical immediacy does not affect the enormous social distances. Our neighborhood was typical in this respect. On one block there would be a row of neat houses, flowers growing in their backyards, mestizo maids hosing down the clouds of dust from unpaved streets, while the children rode tricycles and bicycles on the sidewalks. The next block would be empty of houses, but not of people. In these empty square blocks, called *baldios*, and in squalor and fifth, lived the poor in shacks made of cardboard and tin.

Ernesto's house on Chile Street faced one of the worst *baldios* in the neighborhood. One of our pastimes was to sit on the curb of the safe side of the street and watch the goings—on in the *baldio*. There was the coughing woman in black who would nurse her baby under a *paraiso* tree and spit phlegm over his head. There was the dwarfish 12-year-old called Quico who had the wide-open eyebrowless and lashless look of a Flemish painting. "For one sucker, Quico will show you his tongue. It's white," we would inform a new friend. "No kidding." And for one sucker you could see the furrowed tongue, white from either disease or malnutrition, protruding from the hairless, impassive face, after which Quico would dart back into his *baldio* hole.

But the most frightening of the *baldio* people was the man with the dogs. A nightmare out of Goya, he lived with three or four mangy and abused dogs in one of the darker and deeper hovels of the *baldio*. The man had lost both his legs and had fashioned himself a wooden cart which the dogs pulled downtown every morning, while he held the reins and whipped them. Some said he went to a church downtown and sat outside begging; others claimed he sold lottery tickets. Because the dogs had a difficult time pulling the weight over the rim of the *baldio* hole, their whines always preceded the apparition of the man's face—contorted into red, sputtering anger.

One day, a group of us children, including Ernesto, who was busy working on his bike, were standing on the street playing when the racket of the dogs was heard. As the man emerged over the rim, a bunch of laughing *baldio* kids began throwing stones at him and calling him names. Ernesto, the only one from our side of the street on familiar terms with the *baldio* gang, told them to stop it, and immediately the barefoot children ran back into their holes. The man pulled the reins and came to a full stop in front of us. Without saying a word, yet with a hatred so glacial that it made us shiver, he looked us over, especially Ernesto. In his icy silence, he was telling us to save our good gestures, to keep our good intentions. It was not those barefoot kids who were his enemies. It was us. Then, in his usual cloud of dust and whining dogs, the man vanished.

Ernesto's whole life was a crossing of that street of his childhood. A crossing into the forbidden world of the man with the dogs—and the woman with the goats in Bolivia. The last entry in his guerrilla diary speaks of giving 50 pesos to an old woman with goats "with orders not to say a word but with little faith that she will keep her promise." Who was that old woman of the goats? Atropos, the hag of fate, who held the thread of his life and betrayed him? Or one of those peasants of whom he wrote: "They are as impenetrable as rocks. You speak to them, but in the depths of their eyes you note they do not believe you."

AS A CHILD, Ernesto was a natural leader. Friends told me how, when the family lived in Alta Gracia, on the Córdoba mountains, Ernesto, then about 7 or 8 years old, was the leader of a gang of kids, golf-course caddies and the sons of peons who worked in the nearby hills. He would often challenge the children of the local gentility and sons of well-off families vacationing in Alta Gracia to a soccer match. Ernesto's proletarian team would win decisively, and the losers would go home weeping to mamma, with Ernesto and his gang taunting them.

He enjoyed nothing more than shocking his well-behaved, less adventurous schoolmates, although he was always an excellent student. (His memory was so good that he could glance at the lesson during recess and get an A in class.) I remember one story that made the rounds among our friends. We had been told that ink and chalk were poisonous and never to put either in our mouths. When some over-conscientious classmate warned Ernesto of the peril, he replied that it was rubbish. "Watch," he said, setting up the chalk and inkwell the way a Latin-American worker might do his *café au lait* at breakfast when preparing to dip bread in it. Dipping the chalk into the ink, Ernesto bit off a good chunk and, as he chewed it, remarked: "Not bad, not bad." Then he took a sip of ink, drying his mouth with the blotter. As he walked about after his meal, several horrified 8-year-olds followed him, anxiously waiting for the coma to begin.

Another friend recalled Ernesto at 13 or so, walking on a very high, narrow fence, with sharp cane stubs on either side, on which, had he fallen, he could have been impaled. As Castro said of him in his memorial speech: "In all the time we knew him he displayed an extraordinary lack of fear, an absolute disregard for danger, a constant readiness . . . to do the most difficult and dangerous things . . . No one was ever . . . certain that he would adopt even minimum precautions." He never lost his enthusiasm for sports, especially violent sports, though sometimes, because of his terrible asthma, he had to be carried from a rugby field half-unconscious.

Nevertheless, Ernesto's defiance of death, his apparently Hemingwaylike courting of danger, was not impetuous and exhibitionist thrill-seeking. When he did something dangerous or forbidden, whether eating chalk or walking on a fence, he did it to find out whether or not it could be done, and if it could, which was the best way to do it. The underlying attitude was intellectual, the overriding motive experimental. Ernesto was not a show-off or a thrill-seeker as a child, but a tireless and unconventional experimenter.

One of his few compromises with his asthma was that, unlike most of his peers, he did not start smoking. He also did not drink, not because he disapproved of it, but simply because he did not like it. He much preferred to drink the traditional Argentine maté

(Paraguayan tea), which he could sip endlessly from a gourd. He was remarkably frugal in his eating habits, sometimes seeming to live on a vegetable diet. He never learned to dance, possibly because he had a tin ear. We would beg him to sing "The March of St. Lawrence"— a simple-minded tune which all Argentine schoolchildren know by heart, comparable to "Yankee Doodle" in catchiness. Ernesto's wildly off-key rendition invariably broke up the house.

AS A YOUNG man, Ernesto had an infallible detector for the phony. In fact, all the Guevara family were great debunkers. Once they sensed any pomposity, pedantry or pretense in some poor soul, they would tease mercilessly until the victim fled. Ernesto was a masterful leader of these attacks. In my early adolescence, I took my reading very seriously and was especially fond of the Spanish-Arab mystics. After one comment on the subject which Ernesto overheard, he leaned forward in his chair, asking with great interest:

"How was that? Hey, everybody, listen to this: Do any of you clods know about Arab mystics and—what was it?—Manichaean dualism?" His Córdoban accent, imitating mine, was getting a little bit more pronounced, but I was so flattered by his attention that I disregarded the danger signals. Very proud, I said: "The lover and the mystic in St. John's poetry have this double vision. The inner eye and the outward eye, the lover-mystic sees both ways and the Arab poet's line goes, 'O, shame, shame. . . . ' "

At that point, and in an exaggerated Córdoban accent, Ernesto recited a profane couplet about a one-eyed nun and a cross-eyed saint. Everybody laughed and the score, as always, read: Guevaras, 1; Visitors, 0.

IN HIS LATE teens, Ernesto amazed all of us by going into business. With his friend Carlitos Figueroa, he began manufacturing an insecticide which they called *Vendavál* (Strong Wind). This they did with an effective, if outlandish, mixture of chemicals and talcum powder, which they packaged themselves and sold to hardware stores. Another business scheme Ernesto and Carlitos organized was selling shoes. They decided that they would buy shoes at auctions—where they were not paired off—for a minimum price, collate the pairs, and sell them at a profit. Either they could not match the shoes or find buyers for the leftovers, because in the end Ernesto had a considerable supply of unmatched shoes and occasionally would show up at a party wearing different sizes.

The fact that Ernesto not only paid no attention to his clothes, but tried his best to look unfashionable was a favorite topic of conversation among our friends. One has to know the mentality of the provincial oligarchy to appreciate the remarkable effect of Ernesto's appearance. Terribly clothes-conscious, all the boys we knew put a great deal of effort and money into obtaining the latest fads: cowboy boots, blue jeans, Italian shirts, British pullovers, etc., back then in the early fifties. Ernesto's favorite piece of clothing in those days was a nylon shirt, originally white but gray from use, which he wore constantly and called *La Semanera*, claiming he washed it once a week. His trousers would be wide, floppy and, once, I recall, held up by a piece of clothesline.

With Ernesto's entrance into a party, all conversation would cease, while everybody tried to appear nonchalant and unimpressed. Ernesto, enjoying himself hugely and perfectly aware of the sensation he was creating, would be in complete command. Mysteriously, instead of his being embarrassed by all of us, it always worked the other way around.

AT ANY SOCIAL gathering, the directness, the candor, the mocking quality of his opinions made his presence dangerous. When Ernesto came to dinner at my family's, we would wait for the worst to happen with a mixture of dread and delight. One night, my supremely Anglophilic relatives were discussing Churchill. In that house his name was invoked with the same reverence that Queen Victoria received in the India of the eighteen-eighties. As each elderly member of the family contributed his favorite anecdote of the man, Ernesto listened with undisguised amusement. Then, at the first lull in the conversation, he interjected: "Churchill? Bah! He was just another politician." During the uproar that followed, one of my uncles, well-known for his self-restraint, jumped up from his chair and stomped out. Ernesto was anticipating the temper of the present generation, to whom Churchill, an obsolete and slightly pompous figure out of the last century, hardly seems relevant to the issues of the age.

My father's cousins, the Ferreyras, were members of the grand oligarchy of Córdoba. They owned an enormous Edwardian château, in the city and a large ranch at Malagueño. The ranch included two polo fields, tennis courts, swimming pools, Arabian stallions, and a feudal village of workers for the family's limestone quarries. The family visited the village church every Sunday for mass, worshiping in a separate alcove to the right of the altar with its own separate entrance and private communion rail, away from the mass of workers. In many ways, Malagueño exemplified everything Ernesto despised. Yet, unpredictable as always, Ernesto had fallen madly in love with the princess of this little empire, my cousin Chichina Ferreyra, an extraordinarily beautiful and charming girl who, to the dismay of her parents, was equally fascinated by Ernesto. It would have been difficult to conceive two more opposite poles than Chichina and Ernesto. Family opposition to him was fierce. Doomed from the start, touched with the magic aura of the impossible, their stormy courtship nevertheless was touched with comic episodes.

I remember his decision to learn to drive while riding in the family's car with Chichina at the wheel one day in 1950 or 1951. Grabbing Chichina by the waist, he opened the door, pushed her out onto the sidewalk and slid behind the wheel. Down the avenue went the Plymouth, the engine coughing, gears grinding, stopping, jumping and starting again with Ernesto at the wheel like a man possessed, or, as Chichina put it. "Just like Mr. Toad with his new motorcar in 'The Wind in the Willows.'"

ERNESTO'S CAREFREE APPEARANCE, the disarray of his clothes were deceptive. Underneath was no self-indulgent hippie escapism, but an implacable will to discipline and an extraordinarily methodical streak. (A Cuban exile who had worked with him in the Bank of Cuba said, "Nobody realizes that Che was what in the United States we would call a 'first-rate executive.' Every day he would clear his desk of all incoming papers and be very thorough and organized about the business of the day, even if his working schedule was somewhat eccentric." He started working at 2 P.M. and quit about 3 A.M.)

Yet, despite all that intensity, he had such control that I do not recall his ever losing his temper. Ernesto's control is difficult to explain. He kept very tight rein over his feelings, yet he was never cold. On the contrary, his presence was always intense, vital, radiating the taut intensity of a feline: exquisite control over enormous energy. Even his eyes were at once very penetrating, intent, yet very serene.

A writer who knew him wrote that Ernesto "spoke with that utter sobriety which sometimes masks immense apocalyptic visions."

Among the evidence captured in Bolivia and exhibited by the Organization of American States in Washington was Ernesto's personal copy of Régis Debray's "Revolution in the Revolution." At one point, Debray criticizes one of Ernesto's bold tactics in the Sierra Maestra. Evidently miffed by this criticism, Ernesto had scribbled on the margin: "To climb Mount Everest is a premature aspiration also, until you learn the way—the learning, that is the action."

The Mt. Everest reference is a recurring symbol. Mario Monje, the former head of the Bolivian Communist party, recalled it. In his fateful interview with Ernesto, held in eastern Bolivia in December, 1966, Monje refused the party's support and told Ernesto that without that support he and his guerrillas were doomed. To this, Ernesto replied: "My failure will not mean that victory was not possible. There were many failures in the attempts to climb Mt. Everest and it was finally conquered."

BECAUSE OF HIS coolness, his detachment, his control, Ernesto was a superb debater. However, there was one argument which could make him almost angry. I became aware of this after one long discussion we had about Nietzsche and the validity of Christ as "Saviour of the poor." Needless to say, Ernesto shared Nietzsche's opinion that Christ as a revolutionary leader had been a flop. Some of us were quite taken by the unorthodox Christianity of writers like Renan, Unamuno, Kierkegaard and Dostoevski. I remember mentioning them in the course of our argument and Ernesto's scoffing: "Rubbish! Sentimental nonsense. Nothing. Look, when it comes to meaningful action those guys are full of hot air. In fact, if Christ himself stood in my way I, like Nietzsche, would not hesitate to step on him like a squishy worm." And with his foot, he ground an imaginary Jesus worm into dust.

The closest Ernesto came to anger was over the Christian rejection of violence as a moral alternative. To him this constituted the height of hypocritical evasion and criminal complicity. In his eyes, this attitude had served to perpetuate a system which itself had institutionalized violence of the gradual, installment-plan variety. He once said that if he had to choose between a soldier and a priest, the soldier would be the lesser of two evils.

Notwithstanding his distrust of piety and meekness, Ernesto greatly admired Gandhi. In his early 20's, his bible was not any of Marx's works but a heavily annotated copy of Nehru's "The Discovery of India." As far as any of his friends can remember, he had no connections with any left-wing political organization, group or trend, whether Socialist, Marxist or Communist. In fact, he was extremely suspicious of all political groups. He once implied that he did not see much difference between any political party and organizations such as labor, the church, the army and business.

His strongest political emotion was a deep-seated hostility toward the United States. In his eyes, the twin evils in Latin America were the native oligarchies and the United States. The only things he liked about this country were its poets and novelists; I never heard him say one good thing about anything else. He would disconcert both nationalists and Communists by being anti-American without subscribing to either of their points of view. With much bad luck, since my mother was American, I would often rally to the defense of the United States. I was never able to convince him that United States foreign policy was, more often than not, the bumbling creature of ignorance and error rather than the well-designed strategy of a sinister cabal. He was convinced of the existence of these dark princes of power and evil who directed every United States move abroad. Because of the United States, he was skeptical about the nonviolent way of Gandhi and Nehru for Latin America.

He was always ready to discuss the question of violence as a means, an instrument. What was it? When should one use it? Why should one use it? I recall an argument he had with my cousins concerning the rules of the game in street-fighting. "What was a fair fight? How did one fight fairly?" were the questions being asked. Ernesto dismissed the lot of them. "Nonsense," he said, adding that in the first place he would never get involved in a fist fight or a street fight. However, he emphasized, should he decide to fight it would only be a fight to the kill, and then "the hell with all your silly gentleman's rules of fair fighting." In such a fight he would use every dirty trick available.

Reminiscing about Ernesto in the Cuban press, his friend Alberto Granados, a biochemist, recalled another illuminating anecdote. In 1943, when Granados was arrested along with other Córdoba University students for participating in an anti-Government demonstration, Ernesto went to visit him in jail. Granados asked the 15-year-old Ernesto to organize the high-school students to demonstrate against the arrest of the university students. Ernesto astonished his older friend by replying: "Hell, Alberto, go out on the streets to have the cops beating us with nightsticks? Out of the question. I go out to demonstrate only if they give me a gun." One had to aim for victory.

As he once put it in a letter to a friend: "A victory without [?? 40]margin does not convince me. In this I am like Perón." In 1951, he explained in another letter: "*Yes* or *no* have been made for people like me. . . . I have the capacity to use these terms in fundamental decisions." One of the more fundamental decisions he made later in his life was that in Latin America there could not be any change without violence and bloodshed.

Characteristically, however, he was not humorless about this position. When he met my sister in New York while paying an official visit to the United Nations in 1964, she told him of meeting the Mexican writer Carlos Fuentes. Ernesto nodded. "Ah, yes, Fuentes," he said, "*la izquierda atinada* [the cautious left]." My sister asked, "What do you mean by that?" and Ernesto replied, "Don't you know? We are the *izquierda agitada* [the agitated left] and Fuentes the *izquierda atinada*."

AN ENDLESS SOURCE of bewilderment to all of his friends was the speed with which Ernesto could slip from severity and cold detachment into a humorous, tender and intimate mood, and vice versa. One of our aunts would tell us, "He's a Gemini, that's why." The humorous, tender, self-deprecating side of Ernesto was irresistible. With all his intellectual arrogance, he was surprisingly lacking in vanity. In this sense, Ernesto was altogether different from Castro, according to Cubans who have known both men.

Ernesto could really laugh at himself. He once wrote that people who became his friends went through three stages: "The first is one of bedazzlement generally due to the fact that he [the prospective friend] never has heard so much nonsense expressed with so much self-confidence in a friendly chat. The second stage is one of stagnation. Discovering that many of the originalities are nothing but clichés developed on another plane outside of the static morality of our society, the [prospective] friend becomes tired. If his ennui is such that he does not vanish entirely, one enters the more or less longer period of the third stage, also known as real friendship." Ernesto, who could be so cold, ruthless and cutting with people he did not like, was a man of deep and lasting friendships. He would make immediate contact with children by never talking down to them. I remember his trying to fix a broken toy and discussing it with the child as though it were a broken watch or something just as important, which of course it was to the child. He also never talked down to the servants.

A militant young Spanish Communist lived in our block. The contrast between this young man's and Ernesto's attitudes toward the poor was revealing. When the young Spaniard came to our house, he would make a special point—directed at my parents, no doubt—of first marching straight into the kitchen to greet the servants. Unaware of their wry smiles, he would hand our semiliterate servants a couple of abstruse Communist pamphlets. When Ernesto came to visit, if he happened to see one of the old women servants who appeared to be in a mood to chat, he would approach her, ask her for a maté, and sit quietly by her sipping it as if he had always lived in that kitchen. If the old maid was in a downcast mood, complaining of her rheumatism, Ernesto would discuss the ailment and its various cures. If she was in a joking mood, he would kid her along. Never patronizing or condescending, after the maté he would get up and leave as naturally as he had arrived. All our servants adored him.

When my father was killed in an automobile accident, Ernesto, to my surprise—because he was not the least bound by conventions such as paying visits of condolence—came to see me at the house where I was staying, and where he was not especially welcome. Unlike most people at the time, he was very direct and looked me in the eye, asking simply: "Are you going to be all right, kid?" I answered: Yes. After surveying the crowd sitting around me in silent disapproval, he left. He later told somebody: "That bunch of drooling phonies was not doing her any good." He was right.

During summer vacations at the end of high school, Ernesto would bicycle to spend a few days at a time at a leper hospital in San Francisco, about 125 miles from Córdoba, where Alberto Granados was working. A friend recalled asking Ernesto what he did in the leper hospital. Ernesto replied that, among other things, he read to the lepers. The friend wanted to know whether he read them "Patoruzú," Ernesto's favorite comic strip. Ernesto replied no, he was reading Goethe to them at the time.

A great reader like his parents, Ernesto enjoyed reciting poetry. At the parties of the Spanish Republican exiles who were living in Córdoba and were members of the Guevaras' circle of friends, and especially after the third glass of wine, everybody would recite the great Spanish Republican poets Lorca, Machado and Alberti. All of us, including Ernesto, grew up with their poems ringing in our ears. Another favorite of his was the Chilean Pablo Neruda, and in translation he liked Walt Whitman, Robert Frost and Baudelaire.

WHEN ERNESTO FINISHED high school in November, 1946, most of his friends thought he would go on to study engineering, because of his facility in mathematics. Instead, early in 1947, he entered the Medical School of the University of Buenos Aires.

Of his choice he wrote in a letter: "I am determined to finish but not to incarcerate myself in the ridiculous medical profession. . . . Those six or seven years lost in the study of a career are the most monstrous interest which society exacts from its future *taitas* [crooked leaders] because they coincide with the most beautiful years of our lives." He took off a couple of months in 1951 to sail to Patagonia as a ship's doctor (or more precisely, male nurse), and upon his return he began making plans for a grand tour of Latin America in company with Granados. But he promised his mother that, then, he would go back to Buenos Aires to obtain his medical degree. Eventually, there were two grand tours.

ERNESTO LEFT ON the first in January, 1952, when he was 23, on a beat-up motorcycle which he and Granados had fixed up. That summer, he came to Miramar, on the Buenos Aires seashore, to say goodby to Chichina, announcing his intention of crossing the Andes on the motorcycle. We all laughed in disbelief: Crossing the Andes on *that?* It seemed impossible. (They accomplished the feat, although the motorcycle collapsed after the crossing and they had to walk and hitchhike for the rest of the trip.)

As a farewell gift, Ernesto gave Chichina a puppy which had traveled under his jacket and which he christened in English Come-Back. The puppy, which according to Ernesto was a German shepherd police dog, grew into a delightful mongrel, the joy of the whole family. Uncle Horacio called him "my secret-police dog."

From Chile, Ernesto and Granados traveled to Peru, working their way as dishwashers load carriers, sailors, cabin boys and doctors. They learned to do anything from peeling potatoes to curing the sick, and in the process they got to know firsthand what it means to be poor and to have to work for a living in Latin America.

While in Peru they met a doctor who told them about a leper colony in San Pablo, on the Amazon River, in the province of Loreto. Both Ernesto and Granados, always interested in leprosy, went to live at the colony and almost started a revolution by fraternizing with the lepers. The colony doctors were extremely cautious in avoiding any physical contact with the patients; they ate with gloves, wore face masks and took the patients' temperature with a thermometer attached to a long stick. Not Ernesto and Granados, who organized a psychotherapy program for the inmates with soccer matches, excursions, monkey hunts and visits to jungle Indians. These efforts endeared the two young Argentines to the lepers. At their departure in June, the lepers built them a Kon-Tiki style raft made of balsa wood and cane which they christened Mambo-Tango. There was a big farewell ceremony at which the lepers read speeches and sang songs to the accompaniment of a saxophone.

ON THEIR UNLIKELY craft, Ernesto and Granados sailed down the Amazon to Leticia, a port where the frontiers of Brazil, Peru and Colombia join. At that time Ernesto wrote: "I became enamored of the Amazon . . . even though monkey meat is no delicacy." He also wrote his family. "If you don't hear from me in another year, go find my shrunken head in a U.S. museum."

In Leticia they entered a soccer match and won free tickets to Bogotá. From there, they traveled to Venezuela, where Granados accepted a permanent position in the clinical laboratory of a leper hospital. Ernesto decided to return to Argentina and fulfill the promise he had made his mother to get his medical degree. It was assumed by both friends that after his graduation, Ernesto would eventually join Granados and settle to work at the leper colony in Venezuela.

Ernesto, always nearly broke, found a seat aboard a plane belonging to some relatives or friends, equipped for the transport of race horses and scheduled to fly to Buenos Aires after delivering some horses to Miami. Except for his brief stay in New York to deliver a speech at the U.N. in 1964, this was his only real visit to the United States. He spent several weeks with one of my cousins who was then a student at the University of Miami. Remembering all our arguments about this country, I groaned when I heard he was at Miami. I knew how this visit must have confirmed all his preconceptions about the United States: that this was a garish, money-grubbing, vulgar nation which discriminated against its Negroes and ignored its poor. The worst of the North and the South, Miami was probably the spot in the United States most uncongenial to him.

Ernesto returned to Buenos Aires in October, 1952, and graduated as a doctor the next March. Between those two events, in January, 1953, he paid us his second, and final farewell visit at the old family house in Malagueño. He came especially to see Chichina, now for the last time.

In July, 1953, he was scheduled to leave on another tour of South America, and eventually to join Granados at the leper colony in Venezuela. But this second tour took him instead to the Sierra Maestra and to Cuba.

From Buenos Aires he traveled on a milk train to Bolivia, where he was little impressed by the revolution of Victor Paz Estenssoro, then in full swing. He characterized it with a medical term, saying that it was not a revolution but a "revulsive," an agent which diverts a disease from one afflicted part of the body to another. Although social conditions in Latin America infuriated him, he was profoundly skeptical of political solutions, especially those advocated by liberal reformers. In Bolivia, he worked for a short while at the Agrarian Reform office but soon left to go to the Oriente (eastern Bolivia—where he would die 14 years later). For a time he took charge of the leper colony of Los Negros near Santa Cruz.

From Bolivia he again traveled through Peru and the Amazon basin to Tolima in Colombia where he was a witness to that incredible Latin American phenomenon the Colombian *violencia*—a partisan war in the rural back-lands which took a toll of more than 300,000 lives over a 10-year period, frequently including the most savage and psychotic mutilations of women and children. From there he made his way to Central America.

WHILE HE WAS walking through Central America, a group of young Argentines offered him a ride to San José, Costa Rica. There, in a cafe, he met a group of Cuban student exiles. The Cubans were loudly recounting their now-famous attack on the Moncada barracks, led by Fidel that July 26. After listening with his usual skepticism to the Cubans' euphoric account, Ernesto asked the young men: "Now that you have told us Moncada, how about telling us a Western?" (A favorite pastime among Latin American schoolboys is telling one another movie plots). At the time it appeared fantastic to Ernesto that that handful of kids had actually defied an army barracks.

His friend Ricardo Rojo, the Argentine lawyer who had traveled with him to San José, persuaded him to postpone joining his old friend Granados at the leper colony in Venezuela, and to join him in a visit to Guatemala. They arrived there in January, 1954.

In Guatemala City, Ernesto lived in a boarding house full of Peruvian Apristas and other Latin-American exiles, near the Quinta Avenida. He was the only one of the boarders who did not take the Arbenz regime too seriously. Joking about the weakness of the Government structure, with tireless irony he punched holes in the enthusiasm of the pro-Arbenz boarders. More interested in exploring the Petén and its Maya ruins—he had long been fascinated by pre-Columbian archaelogy—Ernesto departed, leaving his friend to argue about Guatemalan politics. At the time, rumors of American intervention were in the air, and the plot to depose Arbenz was being hatched in the Guatemalan Army by Col. Carlos Castillo Armas and his followers.

The coup took place after one of Ernesto's trips to the Petén. Finally aware of the extent of American intervention and the hopelessness of the Arbenz regime—the "petty-bourgeois reformers" whom he had so often mocked—the sarcastic medico, the uncommitted and unimpressed spectator changed. According to friends, he became so furious at the role of the United States that he immediately tried to organize a resistance. Ironically, the U.S. intervention accomplished what the entire spectrum of the Latin-American left had failed to do: to convert this detached skeptic into a political activist.

The doctor died and the guerrilla leader was born there in Guatemala City in June, 1954. Ernesto, then 26 years old, began organizing blue-collar and white-collar brigades which he deployed at strategic points throughout the city. For three days he did not sleep. Word of his activities began to spread: An Argentine *loco* was making trouble, running all over town organizing a resistance movement.

The Argentine chargé d'affaires, Nicasio Sánchez Toranzo, worried that Ernesto would be in danger once Castillo Armas took over, searched for him all over Guatemala City. When he found and spoke to Guevara, Ernesto was amazed: "I did not know I was so important!" Sánchez Toranzo advised him to give up his hopeless resistance and to take immediate refuge in the Argentine Embassy. Reluctantly, Ernesto agreed, Sánchez Toranzo provided him with a safe conduct to travel to Mexico City. There he met the Castro brothers, and. . . .

CHE

# from **THE MOTORCYCLE DIARIES**
## ERNESTO CHE GUEVARA

1995

### the experts

C HILEAN HOSPITALITY, AS I never get tired of saying, is one of the things which make travelling in our neighbouring country so enjoyable. And we enjoyed it to the full, as only we know how. I awoke lazily under the bedclothes, weighing up the value of a good bed and calculating the calorie content of the previous night's meal. I went over recent events in my mind: La Poderosa's treacherous puncture which left us stranded on the road in the rain; the generous help of Raúl, owner of the bed in which we were now sleeping; and the interview we gave to *El Austral* in Temuco. Raúl was a veterinary student, not a very serious one it seemed, and owned a truck into which he had hoisted our poor old bike and brought us to this quiet town in the middle of Chile. Truth to tell, our friend might at some moment have wished he'd never met us, since we gave him a bad night's sleep, but he'd dug his own grave by bragging about the money he spent on women and inviting us for a night out at a 'cabaret'; all at his expense, naturally. This led to an animated discussion which went on for hours and was why we prolonged our stay in the land of Pablo Neruda. In the end, of course, came the inevitable problem which meant we had to postpone the visit to that very interesting place of entertainment, but to compensate we got bed and board. At one in the morning, there we were cool as you please devouring everything on the table, which was quite a lot, and some more that arrived later. Then we appropriated our host's bed since his father was being transferred to Santiago and there was not much furniture left in the house.

Alberto, dead to the world, was defying the morning sun to penetrate his slumber, while I began dressing slowly, a task which wasn't very difficult because the difference between our night wear and day wear consisted, generally, of shoes. The newspaper had a generous number of pages, unlike our own poor stunted dailies, but I was only interested in one piece of local news which I found in large type in section two: TWO ARGENTINE LEPROLOGY EXPERTS TOUR SOUTH AMERICA BY MOTORBIKE. And then in smaller type: 'They are in Temuco and want to visit Rapa-Nui.'

This was our audacity in a nutshell. We, the experts, key figures in the field of leprology in the Americas, with vast experience, having treated three thousand patients, familiar with all the important centres on the continent and their sanitary conditions, had deigned to visit this picturesque, melancholy little town. We assumed they would fully appreciate our respect for the town, but we didn't really know. Soon the whole family had gathered round the article and all the other items in the paper were treated with Olympian contempt. And so, basking in their admiration, we said goodbye to these people of whom we remember nothing, not even their name.

We had asked permission to leave the bike in the garage of a man who lived on the outskirts and we now made our way there, no longer just a pair of reasonably likeable bums with a bike in tow. No, we were now '*the experts*', and that's how we were treated. We spent the day fixing the bike and a little dark maid kept coming up with edible treats. At five o'clock, after a sumptuous 'snack' laid on by our host, we said goodbye to Temuco and headed north.

■ ■ ■

## difficulties increase

OUR DEPARTURE FROM Temuco went without a hitch until we were outside town when we noticed the back tyre had a puncture and we had to stop and fix it. We worked hard but no sooner had we put the spare on than we saw it was going down; it had a puncture too. It looked as though we'd have to spend the night in the open as there was no question of mending it at that time of night. However, we weren't just anybody now, we were the experts; we soon found a railway worker who took us to his house where we were treated like kings.

Early next morning we took the inner tubes and tyre to the garage to get some bits of metal removed and the tyre patched again. It was nearly sunset when we finally left, but first we were invited to a typical Chilean meal: tripe and another similar dish, all very spicy, washed down with a delicious rough wine. As usual, Chilean hospitality left us legless.[1]

Naturally we didn't get very far, and less than eighty kilometres on we stopped for the night at a forest warden's who expected a tip. Since it didn't materialize he didn't give us breakfast next morning, so we set off in a bad mood intending to light a fire and make some maté as soon as we'd done a few kilometres. We'd gone a little way and I was looking out for a place to stop when, without warning, the bike suddenly veered sideways and threw us off. Alberto and I, unhurt, examined the bike and found one of the steering columns broken and, even more serious, the gearbox was smashed. It was impossible to go on. All we could do was wait patiently for an obliging lorry to take us to the next town.

A car going the other way stopped and its occupants got out to see what had happened and offer their services. They said whatever two such eminent scientists needed, they would be only too pleased to help. 'I recognized you straight away from the photo in the paper,' said one. But there was nothing we wanted, except a lorry going the other way. We thanked them and had settled down for our habitual maté when the owner of a nearby shack rushed over and invited us in, and we downed a couple of litres in his kitchen. We were introduced to his *charango*, a musical instrument made with three or four wires about two metres

---

[1]The phrase in Spanish is: 'left us halfway between San Juan and Mendoza', which are Argentina's largest wine-producing provinces.

long stretched tightly over two empty tins fixed to a board. The musician has a kind of metal knuckle-duster with which he plucks the strings producing a sound like a toy guitar. Around twelve a van came along and, after much pleading, the driver agreed to take us to the next town, Lautaro. We managed to get space in the best garage in the area and someone to do the soldering, a friendly little guy called Luna who took us home for lunch a couple of times. We divided our time between working on the bike and cadging something to eat in the homes of the many curiosity seekers who came to see us at the garage. Right next door was a German family, or one of German origin, who treated us handsomely. We slept in the local barracks.

The bike was more or less mended and we were all set to leave the following day, so we decided to let our hair down with some of our new pals who invited us for a few drinks. Chilean wine is very good and I was downing it at an amazing rate, so by the time we went on to the village dance I felt ready for anything. It was a very cosy evening and we kept filling our bellies and minds with wine. One of the mechanics from the garage, a particularly nice guy, asked me to dance with his wife because he'd been mixing his drinks and was the worse for wear. His wife was pretty randy and obviously in the mood, and I, full of Chilean wine, took her by the hand to lead her outside. She followed me docilely but then realized her husband was watching and changed her mind. I was in no state to listen to reason and we had a bit of a barney in the middle of the dance floor, resulting in me pulling her towards one of the doors with everybody watching. She tried to kick me and as I was pulling her she lost her balance and went crashing to the floor. As we were running towards the village, pursued by a swarm of enraged dancers, Alberto lamented all the wine her husband might have bought us.

### the end of the road for la poderosa ii

WE GOT UP early to put the finishing touches to the bike and flee what was no longer a very hospitable spot for us, but not before accepting a final invitation to lunch from the family next to the garage.

Alberto had a premonition and didn't want to drive, so I took the controls. We did quite a few kilometres before stopping to fix the gearbox. Not much further on, as we went round a tight bend at quite a speed, the screw came off the back brake, a cow's head appeared round the bend, then lots more, and I clutched the hand brake which, soldered in an elementary fashion, broke too. For a moment I saw nothing but the shapes of cattle flashing by on all sides, while poor Poderosa gathered speed down the steep hill. By an absolute miracle, all we touched was the leg of the last cow. In the distance there was a river which seemed to be beckoning us with terrifying certainty. I steered the bike on to the side of the road and it flew up the two-metre bank, ending up lodged between two rocks, but we were unhurt.

Still reaping the benefit of the letter of recommendation from the press, we were put up by some Germans who treated us very well. During the night I had a bad case of the runs and, not wanting to leave a souvenir in the pot under my bed, I positioned myself at the window and delivered up the contents of my aching guts to the darkness beyond. The next morning I looked out to see the effect and saw that two metres below was a large tin roof with peaches on it drying in the sun; the spectacle added by me was impressive. We beat a speedy retreat.

Although at first the accident hadn't seemed important, it was now clear that we had underestimated it. The bike did strange things every time it had to go uphill. We began the climb to Malleco where there is a railway bridge the Chileans say is the highest in the Americas. The bike packed it in halfway up and we wasted the whole day waiting for some charitable soul in the form of a lorry to take us to the top. We slept in the town of Cullipulli (after the lift materialized) and left early, expecting catastrophe. On the first steep hill—one of many on that road—La Poderosa finally gave up the ghost. A lorry took us to Los Angeles where we left her in the fire station and slept at the house of a Chilean army lieutenant who seemed very grateful for the way he'd been treated in Argentina and couldn't do enough to please us. It was our last day as 'motorized bums'; the next stage, as 'non-motorized bums', looked like being more difficult.

## la gioconda's smile

THIS WAS A new stage in our adventure. We were used to attracting idle attention with our strange garb and the prosaic figure of La Poderosa II, whose asthmatic wheezing aroused pity in our hosts. All the same, we had been, so to speak, gentlemen of the road. We'd belonged to a time-honoured aristocracy of wayfarers, bearing our degrees as visiting cards to impress people. Not any more. Now we were just two tramps with packs on our backs, and the grime of the road encrusted in our overalls, shadows of our former aristocratic selves. The lorry driver had dropped us in the upper part of the city, on the way in, and we wearily dragged our packs down the streets, followed by the amused or indifferent glances of passersby. In the distance, boats glimmered enticingly in the harbour while the sea, black and welcoming, cried out to us with a grey smell which swelled our nostrils. We bought bread—bread which seemed so expensive at the time but proved cheap as we ventured further north—and kept walking downhill. Alberto was obviously tired, and although I tried not to show it. I was just as weary, so when we found a lorry park we besieged the attendant with gruesome details of the hardships we had suffered on the long hard road from Santiago. He let us sleep on some boards, accompanied by parasites whose name ends in hominis, but at least we had a roof over our heads. Single-mindedly we set about falling asleep. News of our arrival, however, had reached the ears of a fellow-countryman in a scruffy little caff next to the lorry park, and he wanted to meet us. Meeting in Chile means hospitality and neither of us was in a position to turn down this manna from heaven. Our compatriot proved to be deeply imbued with the spirit of the sisterland and was completely pie-eyed. I hadn't eaten fish for ages, and the wine was so delicious, and our host so attentive . . . anyway, we ate well and he invited us to his house the following day.

La Gioconda opened its doors early and we brewed our maté, chatting to the owner who was very interested in our journey. After that, we went off to explore the city. Valparaíso is very picturesque. Built overlooking a large bay, as it grew it clambered up the hills which sweep down to the sea. Its strange corrugated-iron architecture, arranged on a series of tiers linked by winding flights of steps and funiculars, has its madhouse museum beauty heightened by the contrast of different-coloured houses mingling with the leaden blue of the bay. As if patiently dissecting, we pry into dirty stairways and dark recesses, talking to the swarms of beggars; we plumb the city's depths, the miasmas to which we are drawn. Our dilated nostrils inhale the poverty with sadistic intensity.

We went to the ships down at the docks to see if any were going to Easter Island but the news wasn't very encouraging: no boats were going there in the next six months. We got some vague details about flights which left once a month.

Easter Island! Our imaginations soar, then stop and circle around: 'Over there, having a white "boyfriend" is an honour'; 'You don't have to work, the women do everything—you just eat, sleep and keep them happy.' This wonderful place where the weather is ideal, the women ideal, the food ideal, the work ideal (in its blissful non-existence). Who cares if we stay there a year, who cares about studying, work, family, etc.? In a shop window an enormous lobster winks at us, and from his bed of lettuce his whole body tells us, 'I'm from Easter Island, where the weather is ideal, the women ideal . . . '

We were waiting patiently in the doorway of La Gioconda for our compatriot to show up, when the owner invited us in out of the sun and treated us to one of his magnificent lunches of fried fish and watery soup. We never heard from the Argentine again while we were in Valparaíso, but we became great friends with the owner of the bar. He was a strange sort of guy, indolent and enormously generous to all the odds and sods who turned up, but he made normal customers pay through the nose for the rubbish he sold in his place. We didn't pay a cent the whole time we were there and he lavished hospitality on us. 'Today it's your turn, tomorrow it'll be mine' was his favourite saying; not very original but very effective.

We tried to contact the doctors from Petrohué, but back at work with no time to waste, they never agreed to meet us formally. At least we knew more or less where they were. That afternoon we went separate ways: Alberto following up the doctors while I went to see an old woman with asthma, a customer at La Gioconda. The poor thing was in an awful state, breathing the smell of stale sweat and dirty feet that filled her room, mixed with the dust from a couple of armchairs, the only luxuries in her house. As well as asthma, she had a bad heart. It is in cases like this, when a doctor knows he is powerless in such circumstances, that he longs for change; a change which would prevent the injustice of a system in which until a month ago this poor old woman had had to earn her living as a waitress, wheezing and panting but facing life with dignity. In these circumstances people in poor families who can't pay their way are surrounded by an atmosphere of barely disguised acrimony; they stop being father, mother, sister or brother and become a purely negative factor in the struggle for life and, by extension, a source of bitterness for the healthy members of the community who resent their illness as if it were a personal insult to those who have to support them. It is then, at the end, for people whose horizons never reach beyond tomorrow, that we see the profound tragedy which circumscribes the life of the proletariat the world over. In these dying eyes there is a humble appeal for forgiveness and also, often, a desperate plea for solace which is lost in the void, just as their body will soon be lost in the vast mystery surrounding us. How long this present order, based on an absurd idea of caste, will last I can't say, but it's time governments spent less time publicizing their own virtues and more money, much more money, funding socially useful projects. There wasn't much I could do for the sick woman. I simply advised her on her diet and prescribed a diuretic and some asthma pills. I had a few dramamine tablets left and I gave them to her. As I went out, I was followed by the old dear's fawning words and the family's indifferent gaze.

Alberto had tracked down the doctor. We had to be at the hospital at nine the following morning. Meanwhile, in La Gioconda's grubby room which serves as kitchen, restaurant, laundry room, dining room and piss-house for sundry cats and dogs, a motley crew of people had gathered: the owner, with his homespun philosophy; Doña Carolina, a helpful old dear who was deaf but left our maté kettle as good as new; a drunk, feeble-minded Mapuche indian who looked like a criminal; two more or less normal clients; and the star of the gathering — Doña Rosita, who was off her rocker. The conversation centred on a macabre event which Rosita had witnessed; it appeared she'd been the only one to see a man with a large knife flaying her poor neighbour.

'Didn't your neighbour scream, Doña Rosita?'

'Of course she screamed, he was skinning her alive! And not only that, afterwards he took her down to the sea and dragged her to the water's edge so the sea would take her away. To hear that woman scream, señor, was heart rending, you should've seen it.'

'Why didn't you tell the police, Rosita?'

'What for? Don't you remember when your cousin was flayed? I went to report it and they told me I was crazy, and if I didn't stop inventing things they'd lock me up, imagine that. No, I'm not telling that lot anything any more.'

The conversation turned to 'God's Messenger', a local man who uses the powers the Lord gave him to cure deafness, dumbness, paralysis, etc., and passes the plate round afterwards. The business seems no worse than any other. The pamphlets are extraordinary and so is people's gullibility, but they quite happily make fun of the things Doña Rosita sees.

The reception from the doctors wasn't over-friendly, but we got what we wanted: an introduction to Molinas Luco, Mayor of Valparaíso. We took our leave with all the required formality and went to the Town Hall. Our scruffy appearance didn't impress the man at the desk, but he'd had orders to let us in. The secretary showed us the copy of a letter replying to ours, explaining that our project was impossible since the only ship to Easter Island had left and there wasn't another for a year. We were ushered into the sumptuous office of Dr Molinas Luco, who received us very cordially. He gave the impression, however, of being in a play and was very careful with his diction. He only became enthusiastic when he talked about Easter Island, which he had wrested from the English by proving it belonged to Chile. He recommended we keep up with events and promised to take us next year. 'I may not be here exactly, but I'm still President of the Friends of Easter Island Society,' he said, a tacit admission of González Videla's forthcoming electoral defeat. As we went out, the man at the desk told us to take our dog with us, and to our amazement showed us a puppy which had relieved itself on the lobby carpet and was gnawing a chair leg. The dog had probably followed us, attracted by our hobo look, and the doorman had imagined it was just another accessory of our outlandish attire. Anyway, the poor animal, deprived of the bond linking him to us, got a good kick up the bum and was thrown out howling. Still, it was good to know that some living thing's wellbeing depended on our patronage.

We were determined to avoid the desert in the North of Chile by going by sea, so we went round the shipping companies trying to get a free passage to one of the northern ports. In one of them, the captain promised to take us if the maritime authorities gave us permission to work our passage. The reply was negative, of course, and we were back at square one. Alberto suddenly informed me of his heroic decision: we'd sneak on to the boat and hide in the hold. It would be best to do it at night, persuade the sailor on duty and see what happened. We fetched our bags, clearly too many, for this particular plan. After saying goodbye with great regret to our friends, we went through the main gates of the port and, burning our boats, set off on our maritime adventure.

# stowaways

WE GOT THROUGH customs with no trouble and headed boldly for our target. The boat we'd chosen, the *San Antonio*, was the centre of feverish activity in the port but, because it was small, it didn't need to come right alongside the quay for the cranes to reach it, so there was a gap of several metres between it and the docks. We had no option but to wait until the boat moved closer before going on board, and we sat on our bundles waiting philosophically for a suitable moment. At midnight, with a change of shift, the boat was brought alongside, but the harbour master, an unfriendly looking fellow, stood squarely on the gangplank checking the men. We'd made friends with the crane driver in the meantime and he advised us to wait for a better moment because the guy was a real bastard. So we began a long wait which lasted all night, keeping warm in the crane, an ancient contraption which ran on steam. The sun came up and we were still with our bundles on the dock. Our hopes of getting aboard had almost vanished when the captain turned up with a ramp which had been being mended, and the *San Antonio* was now permanently connected to dry land. So, given the thumbs up by the crane driver, we slipped on board with no trouble at all and locked ourselves and our bags in a toilet in the officers' quarters. From then on, all we had to do was say in a nasal voice 'Can't come in' or 'Occupied', on the half dozen or so times someone tried to use it.

It was midday and the boat had just sailed, but our good mood was disappearing fast because the toilet, apparently blocked for some time, stank to high heaven and it was incredibly hot. By one o'clock, Alberto had brought up the entire contents of his stomach, and at five in the afternoon, absolutely starving and with no land in sight, we presented ourselves to the captain as stowaways. He was quite surprised to see us again, and in these circumstances, but so as not to let on he knew us in front of the other officers, he winked and thundered: 'D'you think all you have to do to travel is to jump on the first boat you come across? Haven't you thought of the consequences?' The truth is we hadn't given them a moment's thought.

He called the steward and told him to give us work and something to eat. We cheerfully gobbled down our rations, but when I learned I had to clean the famous toilet, the food stuck in my throat. As I went below protesting between clenched teeth, followed by the smirking Alberto, who had been assigned to peeling potatoes, I confess I was tempted to forget everything written about the rules of friendship and ask to change jobs. There's no justice! He adds a fair portion to the accumulated muck and I have to clean it up!

After we'd dutifully done our chores, the captain summoned us again. This time he advised us not to mention our previous meeting, that he'd make sure nothing happened when we got to Antofagasta, where the boat was headed. He gave us the cabin belonging to an officer on leave, and invited us to play canasta and have a drink or two. After a rejuvenating sleep, we got up and gave credence to the saying 'New brooms sweep clean'. We set to work energetically, determined to earn the price of our passage with interest. However, by midday we thought we were overdoing it and by late afternoon we were definitely convinced we were the most inveterate pair of lay-abouts ever. We wanted to get a good sleep, ready for work the next day, not to mention washing our dirty clothes, but the captain invited us to play cards again and that put paid to our good intentions.

It took the steward, an unpleasant type, about an hour to get us up and working. My job was to clean the decks with kerosene; it took me all day and I still hadn't finished. Alberto, cunning bastard, still in the kitchen, ate more and better, not being too fussy about what he was shovelling into his stomach.

At night, after the exhausting games of canasta, we'd lean on the rail and look out over the vast sea, gleaming greeny-white, side by side but each lost in his own thoughts, on his own flight towards the stratosphere of dreams. There we discovered that our vocation, our true vocation, was to roam the highways and waterways of the world for ever. Always curious, investigating everything we set eyes on, sniffing into nooks and crannies; but always detached, not putting down roots anywhere, not staying long enough to discover what lay beneath things: the surface was enough. While all the sentimental nonsense the sea inspires drifted through our conversation, the lights of Antofagasta began to wink in the distance, to the north-east. It was the end of our adventure as stowaways, or at least the end of this adventure, since our boat was going back to Valparaíso.

### this time, failure

I CAN SEE him now, clear as day: the drunken captain, likewise all his officers and the moustachioed owner of the vessel alongside, their coarse gestures the product of bad wine. And the raucous laughter as they recounted our odyssey. 'They're tigers, you know, bet they're on your boat now, you'll find out when you're out at sea.' The captain must have let slip to his friend this or some similar phrase. We didn't know that, of course; an hour before sailing we were comfortably installed, buried in tons of sweet-smelling melons, stuffing ourselves silly. We were just saying how great sailors were since one of them had helped us get on board and hide in such a good place, when we heard an angry voice, and a moustache, larger than life, emerged from who knows where and plunged us into the depths of confusion. A long line of melon skins, scraped clean, was floating away in indian file on the calm sea. What followed was ignominious. The sailor told us afterwards, 'I'd have got him off the scent, lads, but he saw the melons and it seems he went into a "batten down the hatches, don't let anyone escape" routine. And well,' (he was sort of embarrassed) 'you shouldn't have eaten all that melon, lads!'

One of our friends from the *San Antonio* summed up his exquisite philosophy of life with elegant words: 'You're up shit creek because you're such shits. Why don't you stop shitting about and shit off back to your shitty country.'[2] So that's more or less what we did; we picked up our bags and set off for Chuquicamata, the famous copper mine.

But not straight away. We had to wait a day for permission from the authorities to visit the mine and meanwhile got the appropriate send-off from enthusiastic Bacchanalian sailors.

Lying in the meagre shade of two lamp-posts on the arid road leading to the mines, we spent a good part of the day yelling things at each other every now and again from one post to another, until we spied the asthmatic shape of the van which took us halfway, to a town called Baquedano.

There we made friends with a married couple, Chilean workers who were Communists.[3] In the light of a candle, drinking maté and eating a piece of bread and cheese, the man's shrunken features struck a mysterious, tragic note. In simple but expressive language he told us about his three months in prison, his starving wife who followed him with exemplary loyalty, his children left in the care of a kindly

[2]'Shit' has been used instead of the very common Chilean expletive *huevos* (balls). The original reads: '*Están a la hueva de puro huevones. ¿Por qué no se dejan de huevadas y se van a huevear a su huevona tierra?*'
[3]The Chilean Communist Party was proscribed and many militants persecuted under the so-called Law for the Defence of Democracy (1948–58).

neighbour, his fruitless pilgrimage in search of work and his comrades who had mysteriously disappeared and were said to be somewhere at the bottom of the sea.

The couple, numb with cold, huddling together in the desert night, were a living symbol of the proletariat the world over. They didn't have a single miserable blanket to sleep under, so we gave them one of ours and Alberto and I wrapped the other round us as best we could. It was one of the coldest nights I've ever spent; but also one which made me feel a little closer to this strange, for me anyway, human species.

At eight the next morning we got a lorry to take us to the town of Chuquicamata. We said goodbye to the couple who were heading for the sulphur mines in the mountains where the weather is so bad and conditions so hard that you don't need a work permit and nobody asks what your politics are. The only thing that counts is the enthusiasm with which the worker ruins his health for a few meagre crumbs.

Although by now we could barely make out the couple in the distance, the man's singularly determined face stayed with us and we remembered his simple invitation: 'Come, comrades, come and eat with us. I'm a vagrant too,' which showed he basically despised our aimless travelling as parasitical.

It's really upsetting to think they use repressive measures against people like these. Leaving aside the question of whether or not 'Communist vermin' are dangerous for a society's health, what had burgeoned in him was nothing more than the natural desire for a better life, a protest against persistent hunger transformed into a love for this strange doctrine, whose real meaning he could never grasp but, translated into 'bread for the poor', was something he understood and, more importantly, that filled him with hope.

The bosses, the blond, efficient, arrogant managers, told us in primitive Spanish: 'This isn't a tourist town. I'll get a guide to give you a half-hour tour round the mine and then please be good enough to leave, we have a lot of work to do.' A strike was in the offing. Yet the guide, the Yankee bosses' faithful lapdog, told us: 'Stupid gringos, they lose thousands of *pesos* every day in a strike so as not to give a poor worker a couple of extra *centavos*. That'll be over when our General Ibañez comes to power.'[4] And a foreman-poet: 'These famous terraces enable every scrap of copper to be mined. People like you ask me lots

[4]Calos Ibañez del Campo was President of Chile from 1952 to 1958. He was a populist, who promised to legalize the Communist Party if elected.

of technical questions but I'm rarely asked how many lives it has cost. I don't know the answer, doctors, but thank you for asking.'

Cold efficiency and impotent resentment go hand in hand in the big mine, linked despite the hatred by the common need to survive, on the one side, and to speculate on the other . . . maybe one day, some miner will joyfully take up his pick and go and poison his lungs with a smile. They say that's what it's like over there, where the red blaze dazzling the world comes from. So they say. I don't know.

## chuquicamata

CHUQUICAMATA IS LIKE a scene from a modern play. You can't say it lacks beauty, but it's a beauty which is imposing, charmless and cold. As you approach the mine, the whole landscape creates a feeling of suffocation on the plain. There is one point at which, after two hundred kilometres, the slight greeny hue of the town of Calama interrupting the monotonous grey is greeted with a joy which as an oasis in the desert it richly deserves. And what a desert! The weather observatory at Moctezuma, near 'Chuqui', calls it the driest in the world. The mountains, devoid of a single blade of grass in the nitrate soil, defenceless against the attack of wind and water, display their grey backbone, prematurely aged in the battle with the elements, their wrinkles belying their real geological age. And how many of the mountains surrounding their famous brother hide similar riches deep in their bowels, awaiting the arid arms of the mechanical shovels to devour their entrails, spiced with the inevitable human lives—the lives of the poor unsung heroes of this battle, who die miserable deaths in one of the thousand traps nature sets to defend its treasures, when all they want is to earn their daily bread.

Chuquicamata is essentially a great copper mountain with twenty-metre-high terraces cut into its enormous sides, from where the extracted mineral is easily transported by rail. The unique formation of the vein means that extraction is all open cast, allowing large-scale exploitation of the ore-body which grades 1 per cent copper per ton of ore. The mountain is dynamited every morning and huge mechanical shovels load the material on to rail wagons on which it is taken to the grinder to be crushed. This crushing consists of three stages which turn the raw material into medium-sized gravel. It is then put in a sulphuric acid solution which extracts the copper in the form of sulphate, also forming a copper chloride, which turns into ferrous chloride when it comes into contact with old iron. From there the liquid is taken to the so-called 'green house' where the copper sulphate solution is put into huge baths and submitted to a current of thirty volts for a week which brings about the electrolysis of the salt: the copper sticks to the thin sheets of the same metal, which have previously been formed in other baths with stronger solutions. After five or six days, the sheets are ready for the smelter; the solution has lost eight to ten grammes of sulphate per litre and is enriched with new quantities of the ground material. The sheets are then placed in furnaces which, after twelve hours smelting at two thousand degrees centigrade, produce 350-pound ingots. Every night forty-five wagons in convoy take over twenty tons of copper each down to Antofagasta, the result of a day's work.

This is a crude summary of the manufacturing process which employs a floating population of three thousand souls in Chuquicamata; but this process only extracts oxide ore. The Chile Exploration Company is building another plant to exploit the sulphate ore. This plant, the biggest of its kind in the world, has two 96-metre-high chimneys and will take almost all future production, while the old plant will be slowly phased out since the oxide ore is about to run out. There is already an enormous stockpile of raw material to feed the new smelter and it will start being processed in 1954 when the plant is opened.

Chile produces 20 per cent of all the world's copper, and copper has become vitally important in these uncertain times of potential conflict because it is an essential component of various types of weapons of destruction. Hence, an economico-political battle is being waged in Chile between a coalition of nationalist and left-wing groupings which advocate nationalizing the mines, and those who, in the cause of free enterprise, prefer a well-run mine (even in foreign hands) to possibly less efficient management by the state. Serious accusations have been made in Congress against the companies currently exploiting the concessions, symptomatic of the climate of nationalist aspiration which surrounds copper production.

Whatever the outcome of the battle, it would be as well not to forget the lesson taught by the mines' graveyards, which contain but a fraction of the enormous number of people devoured by cave-ins, silicosis and the mountain's infernal climate.

# through central peru

OUR JOURNEY CONTINUED much the same, with us eating now and again when some charitable soul took pity on our poverty. Even so, we never ate much and things got worse when that evening we were told there was a landslide up ahead and we would have to spend the night in a village called Anco. We set off again early, back in our lorry, but not far up the road we reached the landslide and had to spend the day there, famished yet curious, watching the workmen dynamite the huge boulders which had fallen across the road. For every labourer, there were at least five officious foremen, shouting their mouths off and hindering the others, who were not exactly a hive of industry either.

We tried to stave off our hunger by going down for a swim in the river, but the water was too icy to stay in for long and you might say neither of us stands the cold very well. In the end, after another of our sob stories, one man gave us some corn on the cob and another a cow's heart and some innards. A lady lent us a pot but just as we'd begun making our meal, the workmen cleared the road and the line of lorries began to move. The lady reclaimed her pot and we had to eat the corn raw and keep the uncooked meat. To add to our misery, a terrible rainstorm turned the road into a dangerous mudbath and it was nearly dark. The lorries on the far side of the avalanche came through first because there was only room for one at a time, then it was our turn. We were near the head of a long queue, but the differential on the first lorry broke when the tractor helping the manoeuvre pushed too hard, and we were all stuck again. Eventually, a jeep with a winch on the front came down the hill and heaved the lorry to the side of the road so we could all pass. The lorry drove through the night, and as usual we'd go from quite sheltered valleys on to those freezing Peruvian pampas where the icy wind cut straight through our sodden clothes. Alberto and I huddled together, our teeth chattering, taking turns to stretch out our legs to stop them getting cramp. By now, our hunger was a strange feeling no longer in one particular place but all over our bodies, making us edgy and bad tempered.

In Huancayo, where we arrived as dawn was breaking, we walked the fifteen blocks between where the lorry dropped us and the Civil Guard post, our usual stopover. We bought bread, made maté and were starting to unpack the famous heart and innards but hadn't even got the fire going when a lorry offered to take us to Oxapampa. Our interest in the place lay in the fact that the mother of a friend of ours in Argentina lived there, or so we thought. We were hoping she would assuage our hunger for a few days and perhaps offer us a *sol* or two. So we left Huancayo again without even seeing it, driven on by the call of our empty stomachs.

The first part of the journey, passing through several villages, was fine, but at six in the evening we began a dangerous descent down a road hardly wide enough for one vehicle at a time. Traffic was normally restricted to one way only each day, but this particular day was for some reason or other an exception, and lorries passing each other, with much yelling, manoeuvring and rear wheels hanging over the edge of seemingly bottomless precipices, was not exactly a reassuring sight. Alberto and I crouched, one at each corner of the lorry, ready to leap off if the need arose, but the indians travelling with us didn't move so much as an inch. Our fears were justified, however, since a fair number of crosses line this stretch of the mountainside, marking the exploits of less fortunate colleagues among the drivers. And every lorry that fell took its terrible human cargo two hundred metres down the abyss, where a fast-flowing torrent put paid to any tiny chance of survival. According to the locals, all those who've gone over the edge have been killed, with not a single injured survivor to tell the tale.

Luckily, on this occasion nothing untoward happened and we arrived at about ten at night in a village called La Merced. It was situated in a low-lying, tropical area and looked like a typical jungle village. Yet another charitable soul offered us a bed and a hefty meal. The food was included at the last moment when the man came to see if we were comfortable and we didn't have time to hide the peel of some oranges we had picked to calm our hunger pangs.

At the Civil Guard post we weren't very happy to learn that lorries didn't have to stop to be registered. That made it hard for us to hitch. While we were there, we heard two people, reporting a murder; they were the victim's son and a volatile mulatto who claimed to be an intimate friend of the dead man. The whole thing had happened mysteriously some days earlier, and the prime suspect was an indian whose photo the two men had brought. The sergeant showed it to us, saying, 'Look, gentlemen, the classic example of a murderer.' We agreed enthusiastically, but when we got outside I asked Alberto, 'Who's the murderer?' And he thought the same as I did, that the mulatto looked more likely than the indian.

During the long hours waiting for our lift, we made friends with someone who said he could arrange everything at no cost to us. He did in fact talk to a lorry driver, who agreed to take us. After we'd climbed aboard, we found he had merely arranged for us to pay five *soles* less than the twenty the driver usually charged. When we pleaded that we were completely broke, which was very close to the truth, he promised to pay. He was as good as his word, and, when we arrived, took us home for the night into the bargain. Although wider than the previous one, the road was still narrow, but it was pretty and wound through forest or tropical fruit plantations: bananas, papayas and others. It was up and down all the way to Oxapampa, which was a thousand metres above sea level, our destination and the end of the highway.

In the lorry with us was the mulatto who had reported the murder. During one of our stops he bought us a meal, lecturing us on coffee, papaya and black slaves in Peru, of whom his grandfather had been one. He said this quite openly but it was clear he was ashamed of it. In any case, Alberto and I agreed to exonerate him from any blame for the murder of his friend.

## our hopes are dashed

TO OUR DISGUST, we learned next morning that our friend in Buenos Aires had given us the wrong information and his mother had not lived in Oxapampa for quite some time. A brother-in-law did live there, though, and he had to take on our dead weight. The reception was magnificent and we had a slap-up meal, but we realized we were welcome only out of traditional Peruvian hospitality. We decided to ignore anything but direct marching orders, as we had absolutely no money and a legacy of several days' hunger, and could eat only in the home of our reluctant friends.

We had a wonderful day; swimming in the river, free of care, good food and lots of it, delicious coffee. But all good things come to an end and by the evening of the second day, the engineer—because our 'host' was an engineer—came up with a solution that was not only effective but cheap: a highways inspector had offered to take us all the way to Lima. We were delighted since the panorama looked bleak there and we wanted to get to the capital to try our luck, so we fell for it, hook, line and sinker.

That night we climbed into the back of a pick-up truck which, after a downpour which soaked us to the skin, left us at two in the morning in San Ramón, less than halfway to Lima. The driver told us to wait while he changed vehicles and left his assistant with us to allay any suspicions. Ten minutes later he too disappeared off to buy cigarettes, and this pair of Argentine wiseguys breakfasted at five in the morning on the bitter realization that we had been fooled all along the line. I hope the driver gets his come-uppance . . . (I had a gut feeling about it, but he seemed such a nice guy that we believed everything . . . even the change of vehicle.) Shortly before dawn, we came across a couple of drunks and did our brilliant 'anniversary' routine. It goes like this:

1. One of us says something in a loud voice immediately identifying us as Argentine, something with a *che* in it and other typical expressions and pronunciation. The victim asks where we're from and we strike up a conversation.
2. We begin our tale of woe but don't make too much of it, all the while staring into the distance.
3. Then I butt in and ask what the date is. Someone says it and Alberto sighs and says: 'What a coincidence, it was exactly a year ago.' The victim asks what was a year ago, and we reply that was when we started out on our trip.
4. Alberto, who is much more brazen than me, then heaves a tremendous sigh and says, 'Shame we're in such dire straits, we won't be able to celebrate' (he says this as a kind of aside to me). The victim immediately offers to pay, we pretend to refuse for a while saying we can't possibly pay him back, etc., then finally we accept.
5. After the first drink, I adamantly refuse another and Alberto makes fun of me. Our host gets annoyed and insists, I keep refusing but I won't say why. The victim keeps asking until I confess, rather shamefacedly, that in Argentina it's the custom to eat when we drink. Just how much we eat depends on what we think we can get away with, but the technique never fails.

We tried it again in San Ramón and as usual we helped down an enormous amount of drink with something more solid. All morning we lay by the riverbank, a lovely spot, but our aesthetic perception of it was hampered by terrifying visions of all kinds of delicious food. Near by, the tempting roundness of oranges poked over a fence. Our feast was fierce but sad, however, because one minute our stomachs felt full and acidy and the next we had pangs of gnawing hunger again.

We were so famished we decided to shake off any vestiges of shame and head straight for the local hospital. This time it was Alberto who was strangely embarrassed and it was up to me to intone the following diplomatically worded speech:

'Doctor' (we found one in the hospital), 'I'm a medical student, my friend is a biochemist. We are both Argentine and we're hungry. We want to eat.' The poor doctor was so astonished by this frontal attack that he bought us a meal in the restaurant where he usually ate. We were brazen.

Without even thanking him because Alberto felt ashamed, we set about finding another lorry, which we eventually did. We were now on our way to Lima, comfortably installed in the driver's cab. He even bought us coffees from time to time.

We were climbing the narrow mountain road which had so terrified us on the way in and the driver was cheerfully telling us the history of every roadside cross we passed, when all of a sudden he hit an enormous pothole in the middle of the road which any fool could have seen. We began to think he didn't know how to drive at all, but simple logic told us this could not be true, because on this road anyone but an experienced driver would have gone over the edge long ago. With tact and patience, Alberto slowly dragged the truth out of him. The man had had an accident which, according to him, had affected his eyesight, which was why he hit potholes. We tried to make him see how dangerous it was, not only for him but also for the people with him. The driver was adamant: it was his job, he was very well paid by a boss who never asked *how* he got to places, only *if* he got there. Besides, his driving licence had cost a lot of money because of the big bribe he'd had to pay for it.

The owner of the lorry got on further down the road. He was willing to take us to Lima but I, who was up top, had to hide when we came to police checkpoints because they weren't allowed to take passengers on goods vehicles like this one. The owner turned out to be a good bloke too and bought us food all the way to Lima. Before that, however, we went through La Oroya, a mining town we would have liked to visit but couldn't because we didn't stop. La Oroya is about four thousand metres above sea level, and you can tell how harsh life is in the mine just from looking at it. Its tall chimneys belched out black smoke which covered everything in soot, and the faces of the miners in the streets were also impregnated with that age-old sadness of smoke which covers everything in a unifying monotonous grey, a perfect accompaniment to the grey mountain days. While it was still light, we crossed the highest point on the road, at 4,853 metres above sea level. The cold was intense even in the daytime. Wrapped in my travelling blanket, I stared out at the landscape on all sides, reciting all kinds of verses, lulled by the roar of the lorry engine.

That night we slept just outside the city, and early the next day we were in Lima.

## city of the viceroys

WE HAD REACHED the end of one of the most important stages of our journey, we hadn't a cent and practically no chance of making any money in the short term, but we were happy.

Lima is an attractive city which has already buried its colonial past (at least compared to Cuzco) behind new houses. Its reputation as a beautiful city is not justified, but it has very nice residential suburbs, broad avenues and exceedingly pleasant resorts along the coast. Wide roads take the inhabitants of Lima to the port of Callao in just a few minutes. The port is not especially interesting (all ports seem built to a standard design) except for the fort, the scene of many battles. Standing beside the enormous walls we marvelled at Lord Cochrane's feat when, at the head of his South American sailors, he attacked and took this bastion of resistance in one of the most glorious episodes in the history of the liberation of South America.

The most memorable part of Lima is the centre of the city around its magnificent cathedral, so different from the monolithic mass of Cuzco, where the *conquistadores* crudely celebrated their own grandeur. In Lima, on the other hand, the art is more stylized, you might almost say effeminate: its towers are tall and slender, perhaps the most slender of all the cathedral towers in the Spanish colonies. The most sumptuous work is not in wood carving as in Cuzco, but in gold. The naves are light and airy, compared to the dark, hostile caverns of the Inca capital. The paintings are also light, almost cheery, done by schools which came after the hermetic mestizos who painted their saints with a dark, fettered rage. The church façades and altars demonstrate the complete range of Churrigueresque art in their love of gold. It was because of this vast wealth that the aristocracy resisted the armies of America up to the very last. Lima is the perfect example of a Peru which has never emerged from its feudal, colonial state. It is still waiting for the blood of a truly liberating revolution.

But the corner of this aristocratic city we liked best, and where we often went to relive our impressions of Machu Picchu, was the Archaeological and Anthropological Museum. Created by a scholar of pure indian blood, Don Julio Tello, it contains extraordinarily valuable collections, reflecting whole cultures.

It is not all that similar to Córdoba, but it has that same look of a colonial, or rather provincial, city. We went to the consulate to get our letters and, after reading them, went to try our luck with an introduction we had for a penpusher at the Foreign Office who, needless to say, gave us short shrift. We went from one police station to another—in one we even got a plate of rice—and in the afternoon we went to see Dr Hugo Pesce, the expert in leprology, who was amazingly friendly for someone so famous. He got us beds in a leper hospital and invited us to dinner that night. He turned out to be fascinating to talk to. We left very late.

We also got up late and had breakfast. Nobody had been told to feed us so we decided to walk down to Callao and visit the port. It was hard work because being 1 May there was no public transport and we had to do the whole fourteen kilometres on foot. There is nothing special to see in Callao. There weren't even any Argentine boats. Cheekier than ever, we scrounged a bit of food at a barracks and then hoofed it back to Lima where we ate at Dr Pesce's house again. He told us stories about different types of leprosy.

The next morning we went to the Archaeological and Anthropological Museum. Magnificent, but we didn't have time to see the whole of it. In the afternoon we were given a guided tour of the leper hospital[5] by Dr Molina who, apart from being a leprologist, is apparently a magnificent thoracic surgeon. Then it was off to dinner at Dr Pesce's again.

The whole of Saturday morning was wasted in the centre trying to

[5]The Hospital de Guía.

change fifty Swedish *krone*; we finally managed after a lot of hassle. Then we spent the afternoon in the laboratory, which wasn't much to write home about, in fact it left a lot to be desired. The bibliographic records, on the other hand, were excellent, clearly and methodically organized and very comprehensive. Dr Pesce's for dinner, of course, and we had the usual really animated chat.

Sunday was a big day for us. It was our first time at a bullfight and although it was what they call a *novillada*, that is, poor quality bulls and toreadors, we were very excited; so much so that I had trouble concentrating on one of Tello's books I was reading that morning in the library. We arrived just as the bullfight was starting and as we went in a novice toreador was killing the bull, but not by the usual *coup de grâce* method. The result was that the bull lay on the ground in agony for about ten minutes while the toreador tried to finish it off and the public booed. The third bull produced considerable excitement when it spectacularly gored the toreador and tossed him in the air, but that was all. The fiesta ended with the inglorious death of the sixth bull. I don't see any art in it. Courage, to a certain extent; skill, not much; excitement, relative. All in all, it depends what there is to do on a Sunday.

On Monday morning we went to the museum again, then to Dr Pesce's house in the evening. That night we met a Dr Valenza, a professor of psychiatry, another good talker who told us war stories and other anecdotes: "The other day I went to our local cinema to see a film with Cantinflas. Everyone was laughing but I didn't understand a thing. I wasn't alone though, no one else understood anything either. So, why do they laugh? They're really laughing at themselves, they were all laughing at a part of themselves. We're a young country, with no tradition, no education, barely discovered. So they were laughing at all the defects of our infant civilization . . . But has North America grown up, despite its skyscrapers, its cars, its luxuries? Has it matured? No, the differences are superficial, not fundamental, all America is alike in this. Watching Cantinflas, I understood Panamericanism!'

Tuesday was no different in terms of museums, but at three in the afternoon we went to see Dr Pesce and he gave Alberto a white suit and me a jacket of the same colour. Everyone agrees we look almost human. The rest of the day wasn't important.

Several days have passed and we are raring to be off, but we still don't know exactly when we're leaving. We should have left two days ago, but the lorry taking us is still here. The various aspects of our journey are all going well. As far as extending our knowledge is concerned, we've been to museums and libraries. The only really useful one is Dr Tello's Archaeological and Anthropological Museum. From the scientific point of view, leprosy that is, we have met Dr Pesce; the others are just disciples of his and are a long way off producing anything of note. There are no biochemists in Peru, so specialist doctors do the laboratory work and Alberto talked to some of them to give them contacts in Buenos Aires. He got on well with two of them but the third . . . The trouble was that Alberto introduced himself as Dr Granado, leprosy specialist, etc., and they took him for a medical doctor. So this twit he was talking to came out with: 'No, we don't have biochemists here. There's a law prohibiting doctors from opening chemists' shops, so we don't let pharmacists meddle in things they don't understand.' Alberto was ready to explode so I nudged him in the ribs and he calmed down.

Although it was very simple, one of the things which affected us most in Lima was the send-off we got from the hospital patients. They collected 100.50 *soles*, which they presented to us with a very grandiloquent letter. Afterwards some of them came up personally and some had tears in their eyes as they thanked us for coming, spending time with them, accepting their presents, sitting listening to football on the radio with them. If anything were to make us seriously specialize in leprosy, it would be the affection the patients show us wherever we go.

As a city, Lima doesn't live up to its long tradition as a viceregal seat, but its residential suburbs are attractive and its new streets nice and wide too. One interesting detail was the police presence surrounding the Colombian embassy. No less than fifty policemen, uniformed and plainclothed, do permanent guard duty round the whole block.

The first day of our journey out of Lima was uneventful. We saw the road to La Oroya but the rest we did during the night, arriving at Cerro de Pasco at dawn. We travelled with the Becerra brothers, called Cambalache, Camba for short. They were good blokes, especially the eldest one. We drove the whole day, descending into warmer climes, and the headache and general nausea I'd had since Ticlio, at 4,853 metres the highest point above sea level, started to subside. Just past Huánuco and nearing Tingo María, the front left axle broke but luckily the wheel got stuck in the mudguard so we didn't turn over. We had to spend the night there and I wanted to give myself an injection but as luck would have it the syringe broke.

The next day went by boringly and asthmatically, but that evening took a fortunate turn for Alberto and me when he mentioned in a melancholy voice that we'd been on the road for exactly six months. That was the signal for the *pisco* to flow. By the third bottle, Alberto tottered to his feet and abandoning a little monkey he was holding disappeared from the scene. Camba junior carried on for another half bottle, and collapsed right there.

The next morning we left in a hurry, before the owner was awake, because we hadn't paid the bill and the Cambas were short of money because of the axle. We drove the whole day until we finally had to stop at one of those road-closed barriers the army puts up when it rains.

Off again the next day and another halt at a barrier. They didn't let the caravan move on until the late afternoon and it was stopped again at a town called Nescuilla, our target for the day.

The road was still closed the next day, so we went to the army post to ask for grub. We set off in the afternoon, taking with us a wounded soldier, which would get us through the army road blocks. And in fact, a few kilometres further on, when other lorries were being stopped, we were allowed through to Pucallpa where we arrived after dark. Camba junior bought us a meal and as a goodbye we drank four bottles of wine which made him all sentimental and he swore eternal love. He then paid for a hotel room for us.

The main problem now was getting to Iquitos; so we buckled down to the task. Our first target was the mayor, a certain Cohen, who we were told was Jewish but a good sort; there was no doubt he was Jewish, the problem was finding out if he was a good sort. He palmed us off on the shipping agents, who then palmed us off on the captain, who received us well enough and promised, as a huge concession, to charge us a third-class fare and let us travel first class. Not happy with this, we went to see the commander of the garrison who said he could do nothing for us. Then his deputy, after a hideous interrogation in which he showed how stupid he was, promised to help.

That afternoon we went swimming in the River Ucayali which looks rather like the Upper Paraná. We came across the deputy who said he'd got a really interesting deal for us: as a special favour to him, the captain had agreed to charge us a third-class fare and put us in first class, big deal.

In the place where we were swimming, there were a pair of strangely shaped fish which the locals call *bufeo*. The story goes that they eat men, rape women and thousands of weird things like that. It is apparently a river dolphin which has, among other strange characteristics, genitals like a woman's, so the indians use it as a substitute, but they have to kill the animal when they've finished coitus because a contraction in the genital area stops the penis coming out. In the evening we tackled the always dismal task of asking our colleagues at the hospital for lodging. The welcome was, naturally, frosty, and we would have been shown the door had our passivity not won the day and we got two beds on which to lay our weary bones.

## as an afterthought[6]

THE STARS STREAKED the night sky with light in that little mountain town, and the silence and the cold dematerialized the darkness. It was — I don't really know how to explain it — as if all solid substances were spirited away in the ethereal space around us, denying our individuality and submerging us, rigid, in the immense blackness. There was not a single cloud to give the space perspective by blocking a portion of the starry sky. Only at a few metres from me did the dim light of a lamp fade the darkness around it.

The man's face was lost in the shadow; all I could see were the two sparks of his eyes and the white of his four front teeth. I still don't know whether it was the atmosphere or the man's personality which prepared me for the revelation, but I'd heard those same arguments many times from different people and they had made no impression on me. The speaker was, in fact, a very interesting man. Fleeing the knife of dogmatism in a European country as a young man, he had tasted fear (one of the few experiences that make you value life) and then, wandering from country to country, clocking up thousands of adventures, he had ended up in this isolated region waiting patiently for the great moment to arrive.

After the introductory trivialities and niceties, when the conversation was faltering and we were about to go our separate ways, he let slip, with that cheeky laugh of his, accentuating the disparity of his four front incisors: 'The future belongs to the people and gradually or suddenly they will take power, here and all over the world.

---

[6]Apparently written after Ernesto got home, it is not clear in which country and when this episode took place.

'The problem is,' he went on, 'that the people need to be educated and they can't do that before taking power, only after. They can only learn by their own mistakes, and these will be very serious and will cost many innocent lives. Or maybe not, maybe those lives are not innocent because they'll belong to those who commit the huge sin *contra natura*; in other words, they lack the ability to adapt. All of them, all those who can't adapt—you and I, for instance—will die cursing the power which they helped bring about with often enormous sacrifices. Revolution is impersonal, so it will take their lives and even use their memory as an example or as an instrument to control the young people coming after them. My sin is greater because I, more subtle or more experienced, call it what you like, will die knowing that my sacrifice stems only from a stubbornness which symbolizes our rotten crumbling civilization. I also know—and this won't change the course of history or your personal impression of me—that you will die with your fist clenched and your jaw tense, the perfect manifestation of hatred and struggle, because you aren't a symbol (some inanimate example), you are an authentic member of the society to be destroyed; the spirit of the beehive speaks through your mouth and moves through your actions. You are as useful as I am, but you don't realize how useful your contribution is to the society that sacrifices you.'

I saw his teeth and the playful grin with which he foretold history, I felt his handshake and, like a distant murmur, his conventional goodbye. The night, which folded away as his words touched it, closed in around me again, enveloping me within it. Despite what he said, I now knew . . . I knew that when the great guiding spirit cleaves humanity into two antagonistic halves, I will be with the people. And I know it because I see it imprinted on the night that I, the eclectic dissector of doctrines and psychoanalyst of dogmas, howling like a man possessed, will assail the barricades and trenches, will stain my weapon with blood and, consumed with rage, will slaughter any enemy I lay hands on. And then, as if an immense weariness were consuming my recent exhilaration, I see myself being sacrificed to the authentic revolution, the great leveller of individual will, pronouncing the exemplary *mea culpa*. I feel my nostrils dilate, savouring the acrid smell of gunpowder and blood, of the enemy's death; I brace my body, ready for combat, and prepare myself to be a sacred precinct within which the bestial howl of the victorious proletariat can resound with new vigour and new hope.

# from **BACK ON THE ROAD**

## ERNESTO CHE GUEVARA

### 2001

**T**HE SUN SHONE timidly on our backs as we walked through the bare hills of La Quiaca. I mentally went over the most recent events: my departure, with so many people and a few tears thrown in; the strange looks of the people in second class at the sight of so many fine clothes, leather coats, etc. saying goodbye to a couple of odd-looking snobs loaded down with baggage. My helper's name has changed: Alberto is now called Calica.[1] But the trip is the same: two separate wills moving out through the American continent, not knowing the exact aim of their quest nor in which direction lies their objective.

A grey mist around the bare hills gives a special shade and tone to the countryside. Opposite us a trickling stream separates Argentina from the territory of Bolivia. The two flags face each other across a tiny little railway bridge, the Bolivian new and brightly coloured, the

---

[1] He recalls his friend Alberto Granado, who accompanied him on his first trip around Latin America, and refers to Carlos Ferrer (Calica), his companion on this second trip that began on 7 July 1953. (All the notes in this diary are supplied by the Archivo Personal del Che.)

other old, dirty and faded, as if it has begun to understand the poverty of its symbolism.

We get chatting with some policemen who tell us that one of their colleagues is a Cordoban from Alta Gracia, the town of our childhood. He turns out to be Tiqui Vidora, one of the children I used to play with. A strange rediscovery in this northern corner of Argentina.

An unrelenting headache plus my asthma was forcing me to slow down. So we spent three exceptionally boring days in the village there before setting off for La Paz. When we said we were travelling second class, this immediately caused people to lose interest in our journey. But here as elsewhere, they did find it important that a good tip might be forthcoming.

Now we are in Bolivia and on our way, after a superficial inspection by the Argentine and Chilean customs.

From Villazón the train struggles on north through completely dry hills, gorges and tracks. Green is a forbidden colour.

The train's appetite picks up again on the arid plains, where saltpetre begins to put in an appearance. But then night falls and everything is lost in the gradually spreading grip of the cold. We have a cabin now, but in spite of the extra blankets and everything a faint chill enters our bones.

The next morning our boots are frozen and we have an uncomfortable sensation in our feet. The water is iced up in the toilets and even in our carafes.

Dishevelled and with unwashed faces, we feel ill at ease as we make our way to the dining car.

But the faces of our fellow-travellers make us feel much more relaxed.

At 4.00 in the afternoon the train arrives in the La Paz gap. A small but very beautiful city lies scattered about the rugged background terrain, with the perpetually snow-covered figure of Mount Illimani as its sentinel. The last few kilometres take more than an hour to complete. The train seems to be passing by the side of La Paz, when it turns back and continues its descent.

It is Saturday afternoon and the people recommended to us are very difficult to find, so we spend our time changing and removing the grime left from our journey.

On Sunday we start looking for the people recommended to us and making contact with the Argentine community.

La Paz is the Shanghai of the Americas. The widest range of adventurers of all nationalities vegetate and prosper in the midst of a colourful mestiza city that is leading the country to its destiny. The "well-to-do", refined people are shocked at what has been happening and complain bitterly about the new importance conferred on Indians and mestizos, but in all of them I thought I could detect a spark of nationalist enthusiasm for some of what the government has done.

No one denies that it is necessary to end the state of affairs symbolized by the power of the three tin-mine bosses, and young people think this has been a step forward in the struggle to make people and wealth more equal.

On the evening of 15 July there was a torchlight procession. It was long and boring as a demonstration, but interesting because the way people expressed their support was by firing off a Mauser or a "Piripipi", the wonderful repeater rifle.

The next day, guilds, high schools and trade unions marched past in a parade that never seemed to end, making the Mausers sing out rather often. After a certain number of paces, one of the leaders of the quasi-companies into which the parade was divided would always shout out: "Comrades from such and such a union, long live La Paz, long live American independence, long live Bolivia! Glory to the early martyrs for independence, glory to Pedro Domingo Murillo, glory to Guzmán, glory to Villaroel!" The recitation was given in a tired voice, suitably framed by a monotonous choral accompaniment. It was a picturesque but not virile demonstration. The weary gait and the general lack of enthusiasm robbed it of vital energy; what was missing, said those in the know, were the energetic faces of the miners.

Another day we took a lorry to Las Yungas. At the start we climbed up to 4,600 metres at a place called The Summit, then slowly came down a cliff road with a steep drop nearly always to our side. We spent two magnificent days in Las Yungas, although we could have done with two women to add the necessary erotic touch to the greenery surrounding us on all sides. On the lush slopes that fell protected by a cloudy sky down to a river many hundred metres below, there was scattered cultivation of coconut palms with their typically ringed trunks, banana trees looking at a distance like green shoots spiralling out from the forest, orange and other citrus trees, and coffee trees reddened with their fruit. Some variety was introduced by the stunted form of a papaya tree, which is a little reminiscent of the static shape of a llama or of other tropical fruits and trees.

On one patch of land a farm was being used as a school by Salesian priests, one of whom, a German, showed us round with great courtesy. Fruits and vegetables were being carefully grown there in large quantities. We did not see the children (they were at a class), but when he spoke of similar farms in Argentina and Peru I remembered the indignant words of a teacher I once knew: "As a Mexican educationalist said, they are the only place in the world where animals are treated better than people." I did not say anything in reply. But the Indian continues to be an animal for the white mind, especially for Europeans, whichever holy order they belong to.

We did the return journey in the van of some guys who had spent the weekend in the same hotel. We looked rather strange by the time we reached La Paz, but it was quick and fairly comfortable.

La Paz, naive and simple like a girl from the provinces, proudly shows off its wonderful buildings. We visited its new edifices, the pocket university whose terraces tower over the whole city, the municipal library, and so on.

The extraordinary beauty of Mount Illimani spreads its soft glow, with a halo of snow that nature has given it for all eternity. It is in the twilight hours that the solitary peak is at its most solemn and imposing.

There is a man here from an hidalgo family in Tucumán who reminds me of the mountain's august serenity. Exiled from Argentina, he has become the central focus of the Argentine community in La Paz, which looks on him as a leader and a friend. His political ideas have long been antiquated everywhere in the world, but he keeps them apart from the proletarian hurricane that has broken loose on our warring planet. He holds out his friendly hand to any Argentine, without asking who he is or why he has come. And over us poor mortals radiates his august serenity, his patriarchal, everlasting protection.[2]

We are left stranded waiting for things to change and become clearer; we shall see what happens on the 2nd. But something sinuous and big-bellied has crossed my path. We shall see . . .

We have at last visited Bolsa Negra. We took the road south up to a height of some 5,000 metres, then descended to the valley at the bottom of which are the mine management and (on one of its slopes) the actual seam.

[2]The name of the person in question is Isaías Nogués.

It is an imposing spectacle. To the back stands Illimani, serene and majestic; to the front, snow-white Mururata; and in front of us, the mine buildings looking like glasses of something that has been thrown from the hillside and remained here at the whim of the irregular terrain. An enormous variety of dark hues shoots the mountain with colour. The silence of the still mine assails even those who, like us, are not familiar with its language.

The reception is cordial; they give us lodging and then we sleep.

The next morning, a Sunday, we went with one of the engineers to a natural lake fed by one of Mururata's glaciers. In the evening we visited the mill where wolfram is obtained from the ore produced in the mine.

In brief, the process is as follows. The rock from the mine is divided into three: one part with a 70 per cent extractable deposit; another part with some wolfram, but in lesser quantity; and a layer containing nothing, which is thrown on to a rubbish heap. The second category goes to the mill on a wire rail or cableway, as they call it in Bolivia; there it is tipped out and sent for pounding into smaller pieces, after which another mill further reduces its size; it is then passed through water several times so that the metal is separated out as a fine dust.

The head of the mill, a very competent man called Señor Tenza, has planned a series of changes that will result in higher output and better exploitation of the mineral.

The next day we visited the gallery. Carrying the waterproof bags we had been given, as well as a carbide lamp and a pair of rubber boots, we entered the dark unsettling atmosphere of the mine. We spent two or three hours checking buffers, seeing seams disappear into the depths of the mountain, climbing through narrow hatches to a different layer, hearing the din of wagon-loads sent down to be picked up at another level, watching the pneumatic drills prepare holes for the load.

But the mine could not be heard throbbing. It lacked the energy of the workers who daily tear their load of materials from the earth, but who were in La Paz defending the Revolution on this 2nd of August, the Day of the Indian and of the Agrarian Reform.

The miners arrived in the evening, stony-faced and wearing coloured plastic helmets that made them look like warriors from other lands.

The spectacle of their impassive faces held our interest as the mountain echoed back the sound of unloading and the valley made the lorry carrying them seem smaller than it was.

Bolsa Negra can go on producing for another five years under present conditions. Then it will come to a standstill unless a gallery several thousand metres long is linked up with the seam. Such a gallery is planned. Nowadays this is the only thing that keeps Bolivia going; it is a mineral that the Americans will buy and the government has ordered production to be stepped up. A 30 per cent increase has been achieved thanks to the intelligence and tenacity of the engineers in charge. Doctor Revilla was very kindly waiting to invite us into his home.

We took advantage of a lorry and set off back at 4.00. Having spent the night in a small town called Palca, we arrived in La Paz early the next day.

Now we are waiting for a [?][3] to be on our way.

Gustavo Torlincheri is a great artist-photographer. In addition to a public exhibition and some pictures in his private collection, we had a chance to see his manner of working. A simple technique, completely subordinate to methodical composition, results in photos of remarkable quality. We went with him on an Andean Club trip from La Paz which took in Chacoltoya and then the water outlets belonging to the electricity company that supplies La Paz.

Another day I went to the Ministry of Peasant Affairs, where they treated me with the utmost courtesy. It is a strange place: masses of Indians from various groups in the Altiplano wait their turn to be given an audience. Each group, dressed in typical costume, has a leader or indoctrinator who speaks to them in their own native language. When they go in, the employees sprinkle them with DDT.

Finally everything was ready for our departure. Each of us had his amorous connection to leave behind. My farewell was at a more intellectual level, without the sweetness, but I think there is something between us—between her and me.

The last evening was one of libations at Nogués's house—so many that I forgot my camera there. Amid great confusion, Calica left alone for Copacabana, while I stayed on another day and used it to sleep and to retrieve my camera.

After a very beautiful trip along the lake, I crossed La Bolsa at Taqueria and arrived in Copacabana. We stayed in the best hotel there and hired a boat to take us across the next day to Isla del Sol.

[3]Word illegible.

They woke us at 5.00 in the morning and we set off for the island. The wind was very poor, so I had to do some rowing.

We reached the island at 11.00 and visited an Inca site. Later I found out there were other ruins, so we forced the boatman to go to them. It was interesting, especially the scratching around among the ruins. We found some relics there, including an idol representing a woman who nearly fulfilled my dreams. The boatman showed no eagerness to return, but we persuaded him to set sail. He made a complete hash of things, however, and we had to spend the night in a wretched little room with straw for a mattress.

We rowed back the next morning, making hard work of it because of our state of tiredness. We wasted the day sleeping and resting, then made up our minds to leave by mule the next morning. But we thought better of it and decided instead to leave it until the afternoon. I booked us on a lorry, but it left before we arrived with our bags, so we were stuck until we finally managed to get there in a van. Then our odyssey began, as we had to walk two kilometres with our heavy luggage on our backs. We eventually got hold of a couple of porters and, with a lot of laughing and cursing, reached the place where we were due to stay. One of the Indians, whom we called Túpac-Amaru, looked a sorry sight: each time he sat down to rest, he was unable to get up again without our help. We slept like a log.

The next day we were unpleasantly surprised to find that the policeman was not in his office, so we watched the lorries leave without being able to do anything. The day passed in total boredom.

The next day, comfortably installed in a "Couchette", we headed along the lake towards Puno.[4] Near the lake some *tolora* were blossoming, which we had not seen since Taquira. On reaching Puno, I had two of my books confiscated at the last customs post: *El hombre en la Unión Soviética*, and a Ministry of Peasant Affairs publication, which they loudly accused of being "Red, Red, Red". After some banter with the main policeman I agreed to look for a copy of the publication in Lima. We slept in a little hotel near the railway station.

When we were about to climb with all our luggage into our second-class compartment, a secret policeman suggested with an air of intrigue that we go into first class and travel free to Cuzco with the badges

[4]Ernesto's stay in Bolivia lasted for more than a month, although the exact dates do not appear in his passport. But from a letter to his mother from Cuzco dated 22 August 1953 (reproduced below), we know that he left La Paz on 7 August.

belonging to two of them. Of course we agreed to this and had ourselves a comfortable ride, giving the two guys what the second-class tickets would have cost.

That night, when we reached the station in Cuzco, one of them disappeared, leaving his badge in my possession. We stayed in a little dump of a hotel and had a good night's sleep.

The next day we went to check our passports and met a secret policeman who asked us in the professional sort of way they have where the badge was that I had had the night before. I explained what had happened and handed over the badge. We spent all the rest of the day visiting churches, and the next day as well. We have now seen all the most important things in Cuzco, if a little superficially, and are waiting for an Argentine lady to change some of our money into sols so that we can go to Machu-Picchu and have a look round.

We've got our sols, but only 600 for 1,000 pesos. I don't know how much this was down to the Argentine woman, because the agent did not put in an appearance. Anyway, for the moment we are safe from hunger.

*Letter to his mother*

Cuzco, 22 [August 1953]

You supply the epigraph, mum.

It has again been a great pleasure for me and I almost feel like a rich man, but the effect is different this time. Alberto has put on a show with talk about marrying Inca princesses and regaining empires. Calica keeps cursing the filth and, whenever he treads on one of the innumerable turds lining the streets, he looks at his dirty shoes instead of at the sky or a cathedral outlined in space. He does not smell the intangible and evocative matter of which Cuzco is made, but only the odour of stew and excrement. It's a question of temperament.

All this apparent incoherence—I'm going, I went, I didn't go, etc.—corresponded to the necessity that they should think us to be outside Bolivia, for a revolt was expected at any moment and we had the earnest intention to stay and see it at close range. To our disappointment it did not happen, and all we saw were displays of strength by a government which, despite everything I am told, seems to be solid enough.

I had half a mind to go and work in a mine, but I was not

willing to stay more than one month and as I was offered a minimum of three I didn't stick to the idea.

Later we went to the shores of Lake Titicaca or Copacabana and spent a day on the Isla del Sol, the famous sanctuary of Inca times. In a cemetery there, I fulfilled one of my dearest wishes as an explorer when I came across a statuette of a woman the size of a little finger, though an idol all the same, which was made of the Incas' famous *chompi* alloy.

On reaching the frontier, we had to walk two kilometres without any transport and for one kilometre it fell to me to carry my suitcase filled with books, which felt like a ton of bricks. The two of us plus a couple of labourers were completely flaked out by the time we arrived.

At Puno there was a hell of a row with the customs people, because they confiscated a Bolivian book of mine saying it was "red". There was no way of persuading them that these were scientific publications.

I don't tell you of my future life because I don't know anything about it, not even how things will go in Venezuela. But we have now got the visa through an intermediary [ . . . ]; as to the immediate future, I can tell you that I haven't changed my mind about the US$10,000, that I may do another trip in Latin America, only this time in a North-South direction with Alberto, and that maybe it will be in a helicopter. Then Europe and then it becomes unclear.

During these days of waiting, we have exhausted the supply of churches and other places of interest in Cuzco. Again I have in my head a motet of altars, large paintings and pulpits.

The pulpit in the Church of San Francisco impressed me by its simplicity and serenity, in contrast to the overelaborate style dominant in nearly all the colonial structures.

Belén has its towers, but the radiant white of the two bell towers here produces a shock in comparison with the dark hues of the old nave.

My little Inca statue, newly named Martha, is genuine and made of *tunyana*, the alloy used by the Incas. One of the museum staff told me so. It's a pity that we find the vessel fragments, which set the tone of that former civilization, are strange to our eyes. We have been eating better since the payment.

Machu-Picchu does not disappoint; I don't know how many times I can go on admiring it. But those grey clouds, those violet and other-coloured peaks against which the grey ruins stand out so clearly, are one of the most wonderful sights I can imagine.

Don Solo received us very well and charged us for only half the costs of our stay. But despite Calica's enthusiasm for this place, I still miss Alberto's company. The way in which our characters were so suited to each other is becoming more obvious to me here in Machu-Picchu.

Back to Cuzco, to have a look round a church and wait for the departure of a lorry. Our hopes crumble one by one, as the days pass and the pesos or sols grow fewer. We had already got just the lorry we needed and the bags were all loaded when a hell of a row broke out over a couple of pounds in weight that we didn't have. We might have come to a deal if we had been willing to compromise a little, but as it was we were left stranded until the next day, Saturday, and our first calculations indicate that it would have been 40 sols more expensive than on the bus.

Here in Cuzco we got to know a spiritualist medium. It was like this. As we were talking with the Argentine woman and Pacheco, the Peruvian engineer, they began to speak about spiritualism. We had to make an effort not to laugh, but we put a serious face on it and the next day they took us to meet him. The guy reported seeing some peculiar lights—in our cases, the green light of sympathy and the light of egoism in Calica, and the dark green of adaptability in me. Then he asked me if I had something in my stomach, because he saw the glow dimming inside me. This left me wondering, as my stomach was in fact grumbling because of the Peruvian peas and the tinned food. A pity I was unable to have a session with the medium.

Cuzco is already a long way behind us. We reached Lima after a seemingly endless three-day journey by bus. From Abacoy the road followed the ever narrower gorges of the River Abancoy for a whole day. We bathed in a little pool that hardly covered us, and the water was so cold that I did not enjoy it.

The journey was becoming interminable. The poultry had soiled the whole area beneath which we were seated, and an unbearable smell of duck created an atmosphere so thick you could have cut it with a knife. After a few punctures that made the journey drag on even longer, we finally reached Lima and slept like a log in a little dump of a hotel.

On the bus we got to know a French explorer whose boat had sunk on the Apurimac. The current had swept away a companion of his who, though he originally described her as a teacher, turned out to have been a student who ran away from her parents' home and did not know the first thing about anything. The guy is going to have a hard time.

I WENT TO visit Dr Pesce and the people from the leprosarium.[5] They all received me most cordially.

Nine days have passed in Lima, but we have not been to see anything extraordinary because of various engagements with friends. We have got fixed up at a university canteen, though, which charges 1.30 a meal. It's a perfect arrangement for us.

Zoraida Boluarte invited us round to her place. From there we went to see the famous 3-D at a cinema. It doesn't seem at all revolutionary to me and the films are the same as before. The real fun came later, when we ran into a couple of policemen who turned everything upside down and took us off to the police station. After spending a few hours there, we were released and told to come back the next day — that is, today. We shall see.

The business with the police didn't come to anything. After a mild interrogation and a few apologies, they let us go. The next day they called us back to ask us about a couple who had kidnapped a boy and bore some resemblance to the Roy couple in La Paz.

The days followed each other without our having the chance to do anything new. The only event of any importance was our change of residence, which has enabled us to live completely gratis.

The new house has worked out magnificently. We were invited to a party, and although I couldn't go because of my asthma it was an opportunity for Calica to get sozzled again.

We had one of those nice thorough chats with Dr Pesce in which he speaks with such assurance about such varied subjects.

We can be almost sure about the tickets for Tumbes, which are being arranged by a brother of Señora de Peirano. We are waiting here, with virtually nothing more to see in Lima.

The spineless days keep passing, and our own inertia helps to ensure

[5]Leprosorio De Guia. Both Dr Pesce and Zoraida Boluarte had offered him support and friendship during his first trip in Latin America, so he immediately visited them when he returned to Lima.

that we stay in this city longer than we wished. Maybe the question of the tickets will be resolved tomorrow, Monday, so that a final date can be set for our departure. The Pasos have shown up, saying that they have good work prospects here.

We are almost on our way. We have a last few minutes to look at dreamy Lima: its churches may be filled with magnificence inside, but in my view their exteriors do not have the august sobriety of the Cuzco temples. The cathedral has a series of Passion scenes of great artistic value, which give the impression of being by a painter from the Dutch school. But I don't like its nave, or its stylistically amorphous exterior, which looks as it if was built in a period of transition when Spain's martial fury was on the wane and a love of ease and luxury was beginning to take over. San Pedro has a number of valuable paintings, but its interior doesn't please me either.

We bumped into Rojo, who had been through the same tribulations as ourselves but with the additional problem of the books he was carrying. He is heading for Guayaquil and we will meet up there.

By way of farewell to Lima we saw *Gran concierto*, a Russian film dangerously similar to North American ones, but of better quality because of its colour and its musical fidelity. The farewell to the sick was pretty emotional. I'm thinking of writing something about it.

# PART

## two
# ON THE ROAD
# TO REVOLUTION

"I can't say, even approximately, at what moment I stopped reasoning
and acquired something like faith, because the road was quite long and
there was a lot of turning back."

—ERNESTO CHE GUEVARA, 1954

# LETTERS

## ERNESTO CHE GUEVARA

from **BACK ON THE ROAD**

2001

*Letter to his mother*

Guayaquil [21 October 1953]

I am writing you this letter (who knows when you'll read it) about my new position as a total adventurer. A lot of water has flowed under the bridge since my last epistolary news.

Here is the gist. As we were travelling along—Calica, García (one of our acquisitions) and I—we felt a little homesick for the beloved country. We said how good it must be for the two members of the group who had managed to leave for Panama, and we commented on the tremendous interview with that XX, that guardian angel who said to me what I will tell you later. The fact is that García, as if in passing, let out an invitation for us to go with them to Guatemala, and I was in the right kind of mood to take it up. Calica promised to give his answer the next day and it was "yes," so that there were four new candidates for Yankee opprobrium. But then the tribulations began at the consulates, with daily laments for the missing visa to Panama, and after various ups and downs (both factual and psychological) he seemed to change his mind to "no". Your masterly suit, pearl of your dreams, died a heroic death in a second-hand shop, and the same happened to all the unnecessary items in my luggage, which has now shrunk considerably for the benefit (I fondly hope) of the economic stability of our trio.[1]

What this means is that if a captain who is a semi-friend of ours agrees to do the necessary, García and I will be able to travel to Panama, and then the combined efforts of those who reach Guatemala, plus those from Panama, will take in tow the straggler left behind as security for the existing debts. If the captain in question fouls it up, the same two buddies will head towards Colombia, again leaving the security here, and then set off for Guatemala in whatever the Almighty unwarily places within their reach.

Guayaquil, 24 [October]. After much toing and froing and quite a lot of calls, plus a discreet bribe, we have the visa to Panama. We leave tomorrow, Sunday, and will be there on the 29th or 30th. I have written this rapidly at the consulate.

Ernesto

*Letter to his mother*

My dear mother,[2]

Don't think that my opening words are to keep Father happy; there really are signs that something is getting better and that my prospects are not so desperate at an economic level. I tell things tragically when that is the truth, and I assumed that Father considered me tough enough to endure whatever came my way, but if you prefer fairy tales I'll make up some very nice ones. In the days of silence my life has developed as follows. I went with a rucksack and a briefcase, half walking, half hitching, half (shame!) paying for shelter out of $10 that the government itself had given me. I reached El Salvador and the police confiscated some books I had brought from Guatemala, but I got through, obtained a visa (the right one this time) to enter Guatemala again, and went off to see the ruins left behind by some Mexi-

---

[1] The trio consisted of Gualo García, Andrews Herrero and Ernesto, since Calica had left for Venezuela.

[2] This letter may date from the end of April 1954.

cans, a branch of the Tlascaltecas, who once came south to conquer from their centre in Mexico and remained here until the arrival of the Spanish. The ruins are in no way comparable to the Mayan structures, still less the Incan. Then I spent a few days on the beach while awaiting a decision about the visa I had requested in order to visit some splendid ruins in Honduras. I slept in my bag on the seashore and no longer kept the strictest diet, but the healthiness of this life kept me in perfect shape — except for some blisters from the sun. I made friends with some guys who, as always in Central America, were travelling on alcohol, and, using the extrovertedness that comes with alcohol, I gave them a bit of my Guatemalan propaganda and recited some verses with a strong Colorado flavour. The upshot was that we all ended up in the police station, but they let us go after some advice from an important-looking officer to sing to the roses in the evening, and other jolly things like that. I preferred to vanish with a sonnet to thin air. The Hondurans refused me a visa just because I had residence in Guatemala, although I hardly need tell you of my good intention to see something of a strike that has broken out there and is supported by 25 per cent of the whole working population (a high figure anywhere, but especially in a country where there is no right to strike and only underground trade unions). The fruit company is in a fury, and of course Dulles and the CIA want to intervene in Guatemala because of its terrible crime in buying weapons from wherever it wishes (the United States has not sold it a single cartridge for some time now). [ . . . ]

Of course, I didn't consider the possibility of remaining there. I came back along half-abandoned roads with a big hole in my wallet, as a dollar isn't worth much more than a mango and you don't get anything great for 20. One day I walked nearly 50 kilometres (that would be lying but it was a lot), and after many days I came to the fruit company hospital where there are some small but beautiful ruins. Here I became completely convinced of what my American identity had refused to be convinced of namely, that our forefathers were Asiatic (tell Father they will soon be demanding his paternal authority). Some bas-reliefs are the Buddha in person and — in all their characteristics — just like those of the old Hindu civilizations. It is a beautiful place, so beautiful that I committed the crime of Silvestre Bonard against my stomach and spent a dollar and a bit on some rolls of film and the hire of a camera. Then I begged some grub at the hospital, but I couldn't fill my bag with it more than half way up. I didn't have enough left to pay the train fare to Guatemala City, so I headed for Puerto Barrios and found some work there unloading barrels of tar at 2.63 for twelve hours' rock-hard labour, in a place where the mosquitoes swarm angrily in fabulous quantities. I ended up with my hands a mess and my back even worse, but nevertheless feeling quite happy. I worked from 6.00 in the evening till 6.00 in the morning and slept in an abandoned house on the seashore. Then I headed for Guatemala City and here I am with better prospects than before. [ . . . ]

(my writing is not sloppy on purpose, but the result of four Cubans arguing next to me). [ . . . ]

The next will be calmer. I'll send you news if there is any. A hug for everyone.

### Letter to his mother April 1954

Mother,

As you see, I didn't go to El Petén. The son of a bitch who was supposed to sign me up made me wait a month and then told me it wasn't on. [ . . . ]

I'd already presented him with a list of medicines, instruments and the rest, and had become strong on diagnosis of the main tropical diseases in the area. Of course this will be useful to me anyway, especially as I now have a chance of working for the fruit company in a banana-growing area.

What I don't want to miss is a visit to the ruins of El Petén. There is a wonderful city there, Tical, and a much less important one, Piedras Negras, where the art of the Mayas nevertheless reached an extraordinary level. The museum here has a lintel which, though completely broken, is a genuine work of art in world terms.

My old Peruvian friends lacked a feeling for the tropics, so they weren't able to do anything similar; besides they didn't have the easy-to-work limestone that you find in these parts. I am more and more happy to have left. My medical culture is not increasing greatly, and I am absorbing other knowledge that interests me much more.[ . . . ]

I would like to pay them a visit, but I have no idea when or how. To speak of plans in my situation would be to tell of a hastily assembled dream. Anyway if I get the job at the fruit company, and only then, I intend to concentrate on settling the debts I have here and the ones I left there, to buy myself the camera, to visit El Petén, and to take myself off north in Olympic style—that is, north to Mexico.

I'm glad you have such a high opinion of me. Anyway it would be very difficult for anthropology to be my sole occupation in my mature years. It seems to me rather paradoxical that the lodestar of my life could be the study of what is now dead beyond recall. I am sure of two things. First, if I reach the genuinely creative period of life around the age of 35, my exclusive occupation, or anyway my main one, will be nuclear physics, genetics or another area that combines some of the most interesting parts of subjects with which I am familiar. Second, the American continent will be the theatre of my adventures much more than I would previously have thought; I really think I have grown to understand it and I feel American as distinct from any other people on earth. Naturally I shall visit the rest of the world. [ . . . ]

There's little I can say of my daily life that would interest you. In the morning I go to the health department and work a few hours at the laboratory; in the afternoon I go and study at a library or museum; in the evening I read medicine or something else, write a letter finally, and attend to domestic tasks. I drink *mate* when there is any, and I engage in endless discussions with the comrade Hilda Gadea, an *aprista*[3] whom I try to persuade in my gentle way to leave that dump of a party. She has a heart of platinum, at least. Her help is felt in everything to do with my daily life (beginning with the *pensión*).

DAYS HAVE PASSED in which things have and have not happened. I have a firm promise of a job as assistant to a medical practitioner. I returned my dollar. I again visited Obdulio Barthe, the Paraguayan, who told me off for the way I was behaving and admitted that he thought I was an agent from the Argentine embassy. In fact I learnt

[3]That is: a member of APRA.

that this, or something like it, is a widespread suspicion. But the Honduran leader Ventura Ramos doesn't think so. As the row with Mrs Horst is still continuing, I smuggle myself in once a day and sleep in the room of Ñico the Cuban, who kills himself laughing all day without doing anything much. Ñico leaves on Monday, so then I'll move to the room of a Guatemalan friend called Coca. A Cuban who sings tangos sleeps in the same room as Ñico; he invited me to hike south with him down to Venezuela, and I'd go if it weren't for the job they've promised me. They say they'll give me the residence permit and Zochinson has moved to become head of immigration.[ . . . ]

Once more the days pass without anything new. I am at the *pensión* sharing with the Cuban songbird, now that Ñico has left for Mexico. I go one day after another about the job, but there's nothing. Now they've told me to leave it for this week, and I don't really know what to do. I don't know whether the comrades are still set on my not getting something or not. Not much news comes from Buenos Aires. Helena is leaving for an unknown destination and I've stopped looking, but she will take me to the house of an aunt who'll give me lunch. She'll also speak to the minister over the phone. I have a good old attack of asthma, brought on by what I've been eating the last few days. I hope it will pass if I go on a strict diet for three days.

*Letter to his mother 10 May 1954*

Mother,

[ . . . ]

I think of the future with pleasant feelings; my residence permit is going ahead, if slowly, as is the way in these parts. I reckon that in a month from now I'll be able to go to the cinema without being trailed by some good-natured fellow. I have been promised something that I think I've already told Father about, and I've also mentioned my plans to him rather perfunctorily. I've decided to leave this *pensión* on the 15th and sleep in the open air in a bag I've inherited from a compatriot who was passing through. Like that I'll be able to see all the places I want, except for El Petén because the rainy season makes it impossible to go there. I'll be able to go up a volcano, as I've wanted for a long time to see the tonsils of Mother Earth (what a nice image). This is the land of the volcanoes, and there are some to suit everyone's taste. My own tastes are simple — neither too high nor too active. I could become very rich in Guatemala, but by the low method of ratifying my title, opening a clinic and specializing in allergies (it's full of telltale colleagues here). To do that would be the most horrible betrayal of the two I's struggling inside me: the socialist and the traveller. [ . . . ]

*Letter to his mother 20 June 1954*
Dear Mother,

This letter will reach you a little after your birthday, which you will perhaps spend a little uneasily on my account. Let me tell you that although there is nothing to fear at the moment, the same cannot be said of the future — although personally I have the sense of being inviolable (inviolable is not the right word but perhaps my subconscious played a trick on me). The situation may be summarized as follows.

Five or six days ago the first pirate aircraft from Honduras flew over Guatemala, without doing anything. On the next and the following days they bombed a number of military installations in Guatemala, and two days ago a warplane machine-gunned the lower parts of the city and killed a girl of two. The incident served to unite all Guatemalans behind their government and all those who, like myself, came here attracted by the country. At the same time, mercenary troops led by an ex-colonel who was dismissed from the army some time ago for treason left Tegucigalpa, the capital of Honduras, and crossed the frontier quite deeply into Guatemala. The government, acting with great caution so that the United States could not declare Guatemala the aggressor, limited itself to protesting to Tegucigalpa and sending all the information to the Security Council of the United Nations; it allowed the attacking forces to advance sufficiently so that there would not be any so-called border incidents. Colonel Arbenz has got guts, there's no doubt about that, and is prepared to die at his post if necessary. His latest speech did no more than reaffirm this fact, which we all knew already, and spread calm in the country. The danger does not come from the small number of troops that have entered the country so far, nor from the warplanes that have bombed civilian homes and machine-gunned a number of people; the danger lies in how the gringos (in this case the Yankees) are manipulating their stooges at the

United Nations, since even a vague declaration would be of great help to the attackers. The Yankees have finally dropped the good-guy mask that Roosevelt gave them and are now committing outrages in these parts. If things reach the point where it is necessary to fight planes and modern troops sent by the fruit company or the USA, then that is what will be done. The people's spirits are very high, and the shameless attacks, together with the lies in the international press, have united behind the government all those who used to be politically indifferent. There is a real climate of struggle. I myself have been assigned to emergency medical service and have also enrolled in the youth brigades to receive military instruction for any eventuality. I don't think the big explosion will come, but we shall see after the meeting of the Security Council, which is scheduled, I think, for tomorrow. Anyway, by the time this letter arrives, you will know what is to be expected.

For the rest, there's not much news. As the Argentine embassy has not been functioning these days, I haven't had any news since a letter from Beatriz and another from you last week.

I have been told they are on the point of giving me the job at the Health Department, but the offices have been busy with all the commotion and it seemed a little unwise to go bothering them about my little job when they are involved with much more important things.

Well, Mother, I hope you had the happiest birthday possible after this troubled year. I'll send news as soon as I can. Chau,

The minister came here today, Saturday, 26 June, while I was away seeing Hilda; she gave me a lot of stick because I was thinking of asking him to send me to the front. [ . . . ]

A terrible cold shower has fallen on all those who admire Guatemala. On the night of Sunday, 27 June, President Arbenz unexpectedly announced that he was resigning. He publicly denounced the fruit company and the United States as being directly behind all the bombing and strafing of the civilian population.

An English merchant ship has been bombed and sunk in the port of San José, and the bombing continues. At this moment Arbenz has announced his decision to place the command in the hands of Colonel Carlos Enrique Díaz. He said that he was motivated by his desire to save the October revolution and to stop the North Americans from coming to this land as masters. Colonel Díaz said nothing in his speech. The PDR and PRG both expressed their agreement and called on their members to cooperate with the new government. The other two parties, the PRN and PGT,[4] said nothing. I went to sleep with a feeling of frustration about what has happened. I had again spoken to the Health Ministry and asked to be sent to the front. Now I don't know what to do. We'll see what today brings.

*Letter to his mother 7 August 1954*
Dear Mother,
[ . . . ]
There's nothing more to tell you about my life in Guatemala, as its rhythm is that of any Yankee colonial dictatorship. I've settled my affairs here and am hurrying away to Mexico. [ . . . ]

*Letter to his parents August 1954*
Dear Mother and Father,
[ . . . ]
I took refuge in the Argentine embassy, where they treated me very well, but I was not on the official list of those given asylum. Now the whole torment is over and I'm thinking of going on to Mexico sometime soon—but write to me here until further notice. [ . . . ]

You sent too much clothing, in my view, and spent too much on me; I'll be almost "flashy". But I don't think I deserve it (and there are certainly no signs that I'll change soon); not all the clothes will be useful because my big motto is little luggage, strong legs and the stomach of a fakir. Give my friendly greetings to the gang from Guatemala; I urge you to treat the guys who end up there as well as possible.

When all this calms down and things take on a new rhythm, I'll write to you in a more concise way. Hugs to you all from your first-born. I ask you to forgive me for the scares and to forget about me. What comes always falls from the skies. No one dies of hunger in America—nor in Europe, I guess.

[4]PGT: the Guatemalan Labour Party.

Chau, Ernesto

*Letter to Tita Infante Guatemala City, August 1954*
Dear Tita,

I don't know when you will receive this letter, or even whether you will receive it, since now everything depends on the final destination of the bearer. This is why I won't give you any account of how things have gone here; my only aim was to introduce the bearer [ . . . ], a student of medicine who has chosen Argentina as his country for the duration of his exile from Guatemala. The bearer belonged to one of the bourgeois parties that cooperated loyally with Arbenz until his fall and concerned himself with the fate of the semi-exiled Argentines in these parts. For all these reasons I would like you to help this friend by giving him advice whenever necessary [ . . . ]; he will naturally be disoriented, as people are the first time they run around in the pampas.

I won't say anything about myself because it will be easy for me to write to you again before this introduction comes into your hands. In any case, let me say that I am continuing my voluntary exile and heading for Mexico, from where I'll make the great leap to Europe and, if possible, China.

Until it materializes somewhere in the world, here is an affectionate embrace by letter from your friend,
Ernesto

■ ■ ■

*Letter to his mother*
My dear Mother,

It's true, I've been quite lazy about writing, but the culprit, as always, has been Mister Money. The final part of the economically wretched year of 1954—a part which treated me well—coincides with the end of my chronic hunger. I have an editing job at Agencia Latina for 700 pesos a month, which gives me enough to live on and has the additional advantage that it keeps me busy for only three hours three times a week. This allows me to spend the whole morning at the hospital, where I am making swellings with the Pisani method. [ . . . ]

I am still doing the photography, but also spending time on more important matters such as my "studies" and some odd little things that have come up here. There's not much money left over, but I hope to make 2,000 this December and, with a little help from fate, we'll do a bit of photography at the end of the coming year (at the beginning, I meant). Contrary to what you might think, I'm no worse than most photographers and the best in my group of friends—although in that group you need have only one eye to win the crown.

My immediate plan is to spend six months or so in Mexico (which I find interesting and like a lot), and during that time to apply in passing, as it were, for a visa to see "the children of the great power", as Arévalo calls them. If I get it I'll go there; if not, I'll see what more definite things turn up. Nor have I rejected the idea of seeing what is happening behind the Iron Curtain. As you see, nothing new since before.

As for scientific matters, I have a lot of enthusiasm and am profiting from this because it won't last. I am doing two research projects and may start on a third—all in connection with allergy—and although it goes very slowly I am collecting material for a little book that will appear (if ever) in a couple of years under the pretentious title "The Function of the Doctor in Latin America". I can speak as something of an authority on the subject, given that, although I don't know much medicine, I do have Latin America sized up. Of course, there is no more than a general plan of work and three or four chapters, but more than enough time.

As to the changes in my thinking which, as you see it, are becoming sharper, I assure you that they won't last long. There are two ways of arriving at what you so much fear: a positive way of direct persuasion, and a negative way of complete disenchantment. I arrived by the second way, but immediately convinced myself that it was necessary to continue by the first. The manner in which the gringos treat the American continent (remember that the gringos are Yankees) aroused my growing indignation, but at the same time I studied the theoretical explanation for what they do and found that it was scientific. Then came Guatemala and all those things that are hard to relate; I saw how the whole object of someone's enthusiasm can weaken as a result of what those gentlemen decide, how a new balance sheet of red guilt and crime was being concocted, and how the Guatemalan traitors were themselves helping to spread all that in order to beg some scraps in the new order of things. I can't say, even approximately, at what moment I stopped reasoning and acquired something like faith, because the road was quite long and there was a lot of turning back. [ . . . ]

*Letter to his mother 24 September 1955*
Dear Mother,

This time my fears have come true, or so it seems, and the enemy you have hated for so many years has fallen. Here the reactions did not take long to appear: all the daily papers and foreign despatches jubilantly reported the fall of the murky dictator; the North Americans breathed with relief about the 425 million dollars they can now extract from Argentina; the bishop of Mexico City showed his satisfaction at Perón's downfall; and all the right-wing Catholics I have known in this country were also visibly content. But not my friends and I. We all followed with natural anxiety the fate of the Peronist government and the threats by the Navy to shell Buenos Aires. Perón fell as people of his ilk do fall, without the posthumous dignity of Vargas or the energetic denunciations of Arbenz, who called a spade a spade and named those guilty of aggression.

Here, progressives have described the Argentine denouement as "another victory for the dollar, the sword and the cross".

I know that today you will be overjoyed, that you will be breathing the air of freedom. [ . . . ]

Not long ago, I said in another letter to you that the military would not hand over power to civilians unless its caste domination was guaranteed. As things stand now, it will only hand over power to a government springing from the Democratic Party, or from one of the recently formed Social-Christian parties, which I imagine to be where [ . . . ] is active, that future member of the Chamber of Deputies and perhaps, eventually, leader of the yet to be founded Argentinist Party.

You will be able to say anywhere whatever it takes your fancy to say, with the absolute impunity that comes from being a member of the class in power, although I hope for your sake that you are the black sheep in the flock. I confess to you quite frankly that Perón's fall has greatly embittered me, not on his account but because of what it means for the Americas. For however much you hate the idea, and however much it has been forced to give way in the recent period, Argentina was the champion of all of us who think that the enemy is in the north. To me, who lived through Guatemala's bitter hours, what happened in Argentina was a copy at a distance; and when I saw that, together with the loyal news (odd to call it that), the voice of Córdoba was to be heard—a city theoretically occupied—I began to lose any clear picture of the situation. Afterwards everything happened in exactly the same way: the president resigned, a junta began to negotiate from a position of resistance and then collapsed, a military man came to the fore with a little naval officer by his side (the only detail added since Guatemala); then Cardinal Copello proudly spoke to the nation, calculating how his business would prosper under the new regime; the whole of the world's press—on this side of the world—launched its utterly familiar yells; the junta refused to give Perón a passport but declared freedom for one and all. People such as yourself will think you can see the dawning of a new day; I assure you that Frondizi no longer sees it, since in the event that the Radicals come out on top it won't be he who achieves it but, with the blessing of the military, Yadarola, Santander or someone else serving the interests of the Yankees and the clergy. Perhaps at first you won't see the violence, because it will be exercised in a circle far from your own. [ . . . ]

In time the Communist Party will be put out of circulation, and perhaps a day will come when even Papa feels that he made a mistake. Who knows what will meanwhile have become of your wandering son. Perhaps he will have decided to set up shop in his native country (the only one possible), or to begin a life of real struggle. [ . . . ]

Perhaps one of the bullets so common in the Caribbean will put an end to my days (this is neither idle talk nor a concrete possibility: it's just that a lot of bullets fly around in these parts). Perhaps I'll simply keep wandering long enough to complete a solid education and to take the pleasures I have awarded myself for this life, before seriously devoting myself to the pursuit of my ideal. Things develop with tremendous speed, and no one can predict where they will be next year and why.

.I don't know if you got the formal announcement of my marriage and the arrival of an heir—from Beatriz's letter it would seem not. In that case, I officially inform you of it, so that you can tell other people the news; I am married to Hilda Gadea and we will soon be having a child. I received the papers from Beatriz; they interest me a lot. I would like some correspondence about the events of the last few days, and above all a weekly copy of *Nuestra Palabra*.[5]

Chau

Kisses to all the family, and greetings from Hilda.

*Letter to his mother Mexico City, 15 July 1956*[6]

[Mother: I have received your letter. It sounds as if you were going through a pretty bad depression. It contains much wisdom and many things I didn't know about you.]

I am not Christ or a philanthropist, Mother; I'm the complete opposite of Christ, and philanthropy doesn't seem to me [ . . . ].[7] I fight for the things in which I believe, with the weapons in my reach, and I try to leave the other lying flat instead of letting myself be nailed to a cross or whatever. As to the hunger strike, you are quite wrong. We started two: on the first occasion, they released 21 of the 24 they were holding; on the second, they announced that they would release Fidel Castro tomorrow, the head of the Movement. If this happens as they said, there would be just two of us left behind bars. I don't want you to think, as Hilda suggests, that the two of us left have been sacrificed; we are simply the two whose papers are in [bad] order, so we cannot avail ourselves of the resources that our comrades have used. My plans are to leave for the closest country that will give me asylum—not so easy, given the inter-American reputation they have stuck on me—and from there to be prepared for whenever my services are necessary. I'll say again that I won't be able to write for a fairly long time.

[5]The official paper of the Argentine Communist Party.
[6]A copy of the original is in "Che" 's Personal Archives; a few corrections and amplifications have been added in square brackets.
[7]Word illegible.

What [really] gets me down is your lack of understanding for all this and your advice about moderation, egoism, and so on: in other words, the most execrable qualities an individual can have. Not only am I not moderate now, I shall try never to be. And if I ever detect in myself that the sacred flame has given way to a timid votive flicker, the least I can then do is vomit over my own shit. As to your appeal for moderate egoism, that is, for common lily-livered individualism (the qualities of XX), I must tell you that I have done a lot to wipe him out—I mean, not exactly that unfamiliar spineless type, but the other bohemian type, unconcerned about his neighbour and imbued with a sense of self-sufficiency deriving from an awareness (mistaken or not) of my own strength. During these prison days and the period of training that preceded them, I have identified totally with my comrades in the cause. I remember a phrase that once seemed to me idiotic or at least bizarre, referring to such a total identification among the members of a fighting body that the very concept of the "I" disappeared and gave way to the concept of the "we". It was a Communist morality and may, of course, appear to be a doctrinaire exaggeration, but in reality it was (and is) a beautiful thing to be able to feel that stirring of "we".

(The stains are not tears of blood but tomato juice.)

You are profoundly mistaken in believing that great inventions or works of art arise out of moderation or "moderate egoism". Any great work requires passion, and the revolution requires passion and audacity in large doses—things that humanity as a whole does have. Another odd thing is your repeated mention of God the Father; I hope you are not returning to the fold of your youth. I should also warn you that the series of SOSs are a waste of time: Petit got the wind up, while Lezica dodged the issue and gave Hilda (who went there against against my orders) a sermon on the obligations of political asylum. Raúl Lynch behaved well, from a distance, and Pavilla Nervo said that they were different ministries. They could all help, but on condition that I renounce my ideals. I don't think that you would prefer a son who is alive but a Barabbas to one who died somewhere fulfilling what he took to be his duty. The [attempts to give] assistance do no more than cause trouble for them and for myself.

[But you have some clever ideas (at least to my way of thinking), and the best of them is the business of the interplanetary rocket—a word I would like.] Moreover, it is true that, after I have set wrongs [right] in Cuba, I'll go somewhere else and it is also true that I'd be really done for if I were shut up in some bureaucratic office or allergy clinic. When all is said and done, though, it seems to me that this pain—the pain of a mother entering old age who wants her son alive—is a feeling that should be respected, a feeling that I have a duty to heed and actually want to heed. I would like to see you, not only to comfort you but to comfort myself for my sporadic and unconfessable yearnings.

Mother, I kiss you and promise to be with you if there is nothing new. Your son,

el Che


*Letter to his mother Mexico City, 15 [probably November 1956]*
Dear Mother,

Still here in Mexico, I am answering your last letters. I can't give you much news about my life, because I am only doing a little gymnastics and reading a huge amount (especially the things you can imagine). I see Hilda some weekends.

I've given up trying to get my case resolved through legal channels, so my residence in Mexico will be only temporary. In any event, Hilda is going with the little girl to spend New Year with her family. She'll be there for a month, then we'll see what happens. My long-term aim is to see something of Europe, if possible to live there, but that is getting more and more difficult. With the kind of illness I have, it seems to keep getting worse and is shaken off only in the grave.

I had a project for my life which involved ten years of wandering, then some years of medical studies and, if any time was left, the great adventure of physics.

Now that is all over. The only clear thing is that the ten years of wandering look like being more (unless unforeseen circumstances put an end to all wandering), but it will be very different from the kind I imagined. Now, when I get to a new country, it won't be to look around and visit museums or ruins, but also (because that still interests me) to join the people's struggle.

I have read the latest news from Argentina about the refusal to grant legal status to three new parties and the left-overs of what the CP used to have. Unexpected as it is, this measure is less symptomatic than everything that has been happening for some time in Argentina. All its actions display such a clear tendency— to favour one caste or class—that there can be no mistake or confusion. That class is the national landowning class, allied, as always, with foreign investors.

If I say these rather sharp things to you, it is a case of "bashing you because I love you". Now comes a hug, one of my last from Mexico. And since I am issuing admonitions, here is a final one: the mother of the Maceos complained of no longer having any sons to offer to Cuba. I won't ask so much of you—only that my price, or the price of seeing me, should not be something that is against your convictions or that might make you regret it one day.

Chau

*Letter to his mother (approximately October 1956)*
Dear Mama,

Your prickly son, a mean one at that, is not a good-for-nothing; he is like Paul Muni was when he said what he said in that voice full of pathos and moved off amid darkening shadows and specially composed music.[8] My current occupation means I am always on the go, here today, there tomorrow—which is why I haven't been to see my relatives. (I confess that, as far as tastes go, I would probably have more in common with a whale than with a bourgeois married couple employed at worthy institutions that I would wipe from the face of the earth if it was given to me to do so. I don't want you to think that this is a simple aversion on my part; it is a basic distrust. Lezica has shown that we speak different languages and have no points of contact.) I have given you this explanation in brackets because, after what I wrote, I thought you would imagine that I was in the process of becoming a bourgeois; so, being too lazy to start again and remove the paragraph, I embarked on a lengthy explanation that strikes me as rather unconvincing. Full stop, new paragraph.

In a month's time Hilda will go to visit her family in Peru, profiting from the fact that she is no longer a political criminal but a

[8]The reference is to the film *I Am a Fugitive from a Chain Gang*, in which Paul Muni played the leading role.

somewhat misguided representative of the worthy anti-Communist party, the APRA. I am in the process of changing the order of priorities in my studies. Previously I devoted myself for better or worse to medicine, and spent my spare time informally studying Saint Karl. The new stage in my life requires me to change the order: now Saint Karl comes first; he is the axis and will remain so for however many years the spheroid has room for me on its outer mantle; medicine is a more or less trivial diversion, except for one small area on which I am thinking of writing more than one substantive study—the kind that makes the bookshop cellars tremble beneath its weight. As you will remember—and if you don't, I'll remind you—I was set on editing a book on the function of the doctor, and so on. Well, I only managed to finish a couple of chapters, which smack of a *Bodies and Souls*-type of newspaper serial—just badly written and displaying at every step complete ignorance of the real heart of the matter; and so I decided to study. Moreover, I had to come up with a number of conclusions and therefore set aside my essentially adventurist approach. I decided first to carry out the main tasks, to rush at the order of things with a shield on my arm (a complete fantasy), and then, if the windmills did not break my nut, to sit down and write.

I owe Celia the letter of praise that I will write after this if I have enough time. The others are in debt to me because I have the last word with everyone, even with Beatriz. Tell her that the papers are getting through fine and giving me a very good picture of all the wonderful deeds of the government. I have carefully cut things out from them, following the example set by my pater, and Hilda has undertaken to follow the example set by her mater. A kiss for everyone, with all the right additions and a reply (negative or positive, but anyway convincing) about the Guatemalan.

Now all that remains is the final part of the speech, referring to the man, which might be entitled: "What next?" Next comes the tough part, the part I have never shunned and always enjoyed. The sky has not darkened, the constellations have not fallen apart, nor have there been floods or hurricanes of extreme severity; the signs are good. They augur victory. But if they are wrong—and in the end even the gods can be wrong—I think that I'll be able to say like a poet you don't know: "I shall carry beneath the earth only the sorrow of an unfinished song." To avoid pre-mortem pathos, this letter will appear when things are really getting hot, and then you will know that your son, in a sun-drenched land of the Americas, is cursing himself for not having studied enough surgery to help a wounded man, and cursing the Mexican government that did not let him perfect his already respectable marksmanship so that he could knock over puppets with greater agility. The struggle will be with our backs to the wall, as in the hymns, until victory or death.

Again kisses, with all the affection of a farewell that refuses to be total.

Your son

*Letter to his friend Tita Infante [approximately November 1956]*
Dear Tita,

It's so long since I wrote to you last that I have lost the confidence which comes from regular communication (I am sure you won't understand much of my letter—I'll explain everything little by little).

First, my little Indian girl is already nine months old, quite cute, very lively, and so on.

The second and main thing is that, a while ago now, some Cuban revolutionaries asked me to help the movement with my medical "knowledge" and I accepted—because you should know the kind of work I like. I went to a ranch in the mountains to organize the physical training, to vaccinate the soldiers, etc., but I got unlucky and the police rounded everyone up. As I was not OK with my papers, I ate up a couple of months in prison; the only problem was that they stole my typewriter, among other trifles—which is the reason for this handwritten missive. Then the interior ministry made the big mistake of believing my word of honour as a gentleman and released me on condition that I leave the country within ten days. It's three months since then and I'm still around, though in hiding and without any prospects in Mexico. I'm just waiting to see what happens with the Revolution: if things go well, I'll head for Cuba; if not, I'll start looking for a country where I can camp down. This year may be a disaster in my life, but there have already been so many that it doesn't frighten me or bother me a lot.

Of course, all the scientific projects have gone to the devil and now I'm an avid reader only of Charlie and Freddie[9] and others like them. I forgot to mention that when they arrested me they found various pamphlets in Russian, as well as a card issued by the Institute for Mexican-Russian Exchange, where I had been studying the language in connection with the problem of conditioned reflexes.

Maybe it would interest you to know that my married life has almost completely broken down, and will break down for good next month when my wife goes to visit her family in Peru, from which she has been separated for the past eight years. The break-up has left a certain bitterness, because she was a loyal comrade and her revolutionary conduct was irreproachable during my forced vacations, but our minds were too far apart and I live with this anarchic spirit that dreams of new horizons as soon as I have "the cross of your arms and the land of your soul", as old Pablo said.[10]

I'll say good-bye. Don't write until you get my next letter, which will have more news or at least a settled address.

As always, a fond hug from your friend

Ernesto

[10]The reference is to Pablo Neruda's poem *Una canción desesperada*.

[9]Karl Marx and Friedrich Engels.

# THE CARIBBEAN STORM
## RICARDO ROJO

from *MY FRIEND CHE*

1968

"We must grow tough, but without ever losing our tenderness."

—*CHE GUEVARA, 1967*

INCE JUNE 17, 1952—when agrarian reform was proclaimed—
Guatemala had been the major testing ground for Latin American revolution, a more significant model than the Bolivian revolution. Its importance sprang from a basic distinction between the two movements: in Bolivia, the land to be distributed belonged to the big creole landowners, and in Guatemala it belonged to U.S. corporations with powerful political influence.

Between 1821, when its independence was declared, and 1944, when the process of national revolution began, Guatemala had had only two constitutionally elected governments. Continual seizure of power and joint control by the landowning class and foreign capital marked its history. Servitude, obscurantism, and miserable living conditions were the disheartening issues of this system. At the time of the agrarian revolution, eight out of every ten inhabitants went without shoes, and seven out of every ten were illiterate. The country's feudal lords, in league with American capitalists, hypocritically lamented the consequences of this situation and falsely blamed it on the fact that half of Guatemala's population was Indian—despite the fact that most Guatemalan Indians descended from the Mayas, whose civilization was anything but unimpressive. Thus, the system that despoiled an entire nation convinced it with propaganda that its own inhabitants were the cause of its ills. By undermining national morale and encouraging resignation and fatalism, the alliance between the country's magnates and foreign millionaires could drain the wealth from the land indefinitely.

In 1944 a coalition of young army officers and intellectuals with vague vauge projects for reform took over the government. They started with no ambitious plan for the future, but with the realization that Guatemala was bogged down in a desperate existence and, as a people, had squandered its inheritance. The Mayas knew how to write, they painted beautifully, and they carved stone sculptures and worked in ceramics. The codices, temples, and archeological fragments scattered throughout the country attested to the quality of Mayan civilization. Spanish and capitalist colonizations had destroyed the best products of that civilization. They had plunged the Indian population into poverty and ignorance, although retaining important elements of social and historical cohesion. But for the young officers and intellectuals in 1944, a new period was opening, and theirs was an attempt to save half the population of Guatemala and integrate it into a national state.

The purpose of most of the government's new measures was recognition of the Indians as citizens with the same rights as the white descendants of European settlers. One after the other the pillars of the old order were pulled down—especially servitude and the system of private loans to the Indians. On the whole these reforms were supported by the majority of those who had any voice in the matter.

But the fact remained that any modification of the social status quo was bound to affect the economic privileges of the more than one thousand landowners who held over half of the country's best lands. The biggest of these was the United Fruit Company, the famous American banana monopoly. In 1953 the Guatemalan government expropriated almost four hundred thousand acres of the United Fruit's land; the company, seeing the handwriting on the wall, started in motion its gigantic and well entrenched machinery of pressure and threats, and thereupon the U.S. State Department intervened and vehemently defended the company's position.

Until now, the revolution's path had followed an almost straight line.

To accomplish the goal the President had implied in his definition —
"*Socialists, because we live in the twentieth century, but not material-
ist socialists. Man is not just a stomach. We believe that, above all, he
hungers for his dignity*" — the revolutionaries needed to study the economic reforms with care. They might believe in good faith that man's
stomach was *not* the main thing, but they could see for themselves,
day after day, that for the big economic interests the stomach *was* the
main thing.

In the slow evolution that took place between 1944 and 1953, during which time many had dropped out along the way, the revolutionaries had learned a number of things in actual practice that were not
explained in their books. And yet there were many other things they
didn't understand until it was too late: for one, that professional soldiers grow discouraged with a revolution in a much shorter time than
it takes the Indian masses to develop enthusiasm for it.

But in November 1953, when Valdovinos and I reached the port
of San José, the atmosphere in Guatemala was ostensibly enthusiastic. It was only after a few days that you noticed the tension running
through the conversations in the cafés and the little knots of people
with fear in their voices when referring to the friction between the government and the United Fruit Company.

We had decided to continue our trip after twenty days in Panama,
waiting in vain for Guevara and Gualo García. Panama was boiling
from the humid heat and fierce anti-American feelings. The temperature seemed to rise with the political passions, and the political passions grew hotter as the thermometer rose. The thought that neither
the climate nor the political situation could be changed made our contact with both unbearable; after three weeks we resolved to leave.

I was traveling under a unique Argentine passport — officially it was
only good for a single trip to Guatemala, the country that had given
me political asylum. Really a safe-conduct, it had determined my destination, and to a degree my itinerary, from the start; and of course it
ultimately placed me at the disposition of the Guatemalan authorities. Accordingly, the day after I set foot in the capital, I went to the
Department of Foreign Affairs to let them know I was there. Raúl
Oseguada, the Chancellor, was a teacher who had studied in
Argentina, as had Arévalo. But unlike him, he had moved around in
bohemian student circles and had participated in Buenos Aires night
life. He had earned his living in Argentina as a musician, playing the

guitar in dance hall orchestras, and he retained a fond, nostalgic memory of those years.

Chancellor Osegueda was our protector. He paid our keep in a modest boarding house near Quinta Avenida, and he introduced us to the official and political world of Guatemala.

It was a very busy world, but if examined closely, it was obvious that the regime was stuck in a quagmire of personal ambitions disguised as ideological differences. This struck us as a curious and original phenomenon: since all the different parties maintained that they were revolutionary, you had what seemed to be a multi-party democracy with everyone trying to conduct a revolution at once. Coming from Argentina, which was governed by a strong president backed by a solid party that wasn't partial to lobbying, we found Guatemala a notable contrast. The phenomenon became so obvious that it was impossible to ignore it. Only time would tell whether or not the system could support a revolutionary process.

About this time we heard that two Argentine brothers, driving from the United States to Buenos Aires in a '46 Ford, had arrived in Guatemala. The older one, Walter Beveraggi Allende, was professor of Political Economy at Boston University and had been involved in an international scandal of such proportions that Peron had finally taken away his Argentine citizenship, an action without precedent in Argentina and almost unheard of in Latin America. He was now crossing borders with an affidavit given him by the U.S. State Department, perhaps in acknowledgement of his position as professor at an American university. The younger brother, Domingo Beveraggi Allende, had escaped to Uruguay without papers and was traveling on a Uruguayan identity card on which it was stated that he was a citizen of Argentina. Naturally, we had to meet these two in some part of the world.

At this point my companion, Valdovinos, who had married a young Panamanian aristocrat after a fast courtship, decided to give up the adventure and join his wife, waiting for him in Panama. I joined the traveling brothers, with my safe-conduct pass.

Ours must have been one of the most suspicious-looking sets of identity papers ever assembled in Central America. Presented together they were enough to alarm any official, and that's exactly what happened with the consul of El Salvador, an obstinate man who looked us up and down, shaking his head. Chancellor Osegueda had to convince him that our visit to his country had a "cultural purpose."

My plan was to go back and look for Guevara and Gualo García, whom I imagined to be tied up by some administrative tangle with the authorities in Panama. There were moments when I was afraid they hadn't even been able to get on the ship that was to take them out of Ecuador.

Since the Allende brothers were heading south, I joined them, and we began a difficult trip through the "Banana Republics," as they are called by the American press. The rainy season had started, and some stretches of the highway, the only one we could take, were flooded over. All commercial traffic was behind schedule, and many truck drivers had decided to put off their trips until the rains ended. We passed through El Salvador and on December 16 arrived at El Amatillo, on the border of Honduras; we crossed without stopping. We entered Nicaragua at Madriz, where Somoza's national guard registered our entry on December 18, 1953. We went on to Managua, and from there to Rivas, a small colonial city, where everyone we questioned agreed that we shouldn't continue south. The rains were washing out sections of the road and it was practically impossible to pass.

But my friends put the Ford on the road again and the sensible advice of the local people was lost behind us.

About ten miles from Rivas an impenetrable curtain of rain made us begin to doubt whether we'd ever make it to Piedra Blanca, the entrance to Costa Rica.

We went on, our nerves understandably strained, trying to make out the road as it proceeded through the thickest jungle in Central America. Suddenly, we made out two forms thrashing through the mud. No doubt about it; two men were coming toward us, plodding with great difficulty along the side of the road. We made up our minds to ask them about the condition of the road ahead. Just then, the air cleared enough to let us see their faces.

Ernesto Guevara and Gualo García, bags slung over their shoulders, soaked to the bone, water and sweat pouring down their faces, looked at us through the rain.

"Stop!" I yelled. My shout was heard by the driver, who pulled up, and by the walkers, who also stopped.

We threw our arms around one another, and my friends in the Ford were introduced with very little ceremony, considering the circumstances. Guevara and García gave us a hair-raising description of the road. The water had swept away embankments and bridges, and the only vehicle they had met in the last six hours was ours.

We decided that the whole group should return to Rivas. Guevara and I were delighted. We couldn't stop talking about our experiences since separating in Guayaquil, and kept interrupting this recital to make plans to return to Guatemala.

I learned that from Panama, where they had been taken by the Great White Fleet, they had continued to Costa Rica, sometimes in Mack trucks and sometimes on foot. They had been in an accident. A truck in which they were riding overturned, landing heavily in the side ditch. Guevara was thrown with great force from his unstable perch on some fruit crates and hit the ground hard. More than ten days later the muscles and tendons of his left forearm were still sore from the fall, and he had trouble using the arm.

We were almost in Rivas. It was getting dark. We stopped at a busy restaurant near the main square of the old city, where several men were smoking lazily and some girls were preparing supper. It became an unforgettable evening, with lots of *mate* (an herb-tea), and reminiscences of our country, which the "Ford brothers" converted into songs, accompanying themselves on a guitar. Around seven o'clock we were served rice and fried chicken, hot from the fire. Guevara ate slowly, following his philosophy of "reserve" food. He and his companion had gone five days without a full meal, but now the air was charged with spontaneous optimism, stirred up by our unexpected reunion and the feeling that everything would turn out right in Guatemala.

Suddenly we realized what an unexpected and curious show we must be presenting, with our strange appearance and the Argentine folk music and songs. A silent ring grew around us as groups of children interrupted their games to take a closer look at us and listen to our singing.

"Do you know what I thought when I saw you?" Guevara asked, and answered himself immediately. "I thought: What lucky bastards these Yankees are. They have a car in this goddamn rain, and we have to walk."

True, the Ford had American license plates and a special insignia that said "Boston University."

It was in Rivas, a dot on the map where years later the dictator Anastasio (Tacho) Somoza was assassinated, that our friends with the Ford decided to give up their motor trip.

We saw in the new year. 1954, in San José de Costa Rica, the most Spanish and traditional of the Central American capitals. San José had become the general headquarters for an organization called the Caribbean Legion. Its role was that of a democratic Internationale, and it had drawn some of the most famous liberals of the Caribbean area and included the President of Costa Rica, José (Pepe) Figueres, among its members. It had been formed in Cuba when Carlos Prío Socarras was President and while Rómulo Betancourt and Juan Bosch were living in Havana. Later on it had proved strong enough to obtain the presidency of Costa Rica for Otilio Ulate Figueres candidate, and eventually for Figueres himself. In 1952, when Batista took power in Cuba, the leaders of the Legion had abandoned that country and sought refuge in San José.

Actually, the military effectiveness of the Caribbean Legion wasn't great. Nevertheless, the repeated expeditions of Cayo Confite and Luperón against Trujillo, the Dominican dictator, had inspired an embryonic military organization in the Caribbean and taught hundreds of young men how to handle modern weapons. More important, these adventures helped to arouse the romantic enthusiasm of students throughout Central America. The Legion had developed, as far as it could, a sense of brotherhood among its members, a sense that they were citizens of a nation larger than those bounded by narrow political limits. It was a concept based on Bolívar's idea of the great Latin American nation, although for the Legion it was really restricted to the Caribbean area, its own field of action. Cubans, Hondurans, and an equal number of Dominicans organized the expeditions against Trujillo; they were armed in Cuba with that government's blessing. Several of these expeditions operated out of Guatemala with the approval of the authorities. Nationalities had been overlooked in recruiting the Legion, as in the last century, when these countries had joined forces to fight Spanish domination.

The leaders of the Legion were living in a residential suburb of San José. There, in the same house, were the Venezuelans, Rómulo Betancourt and Raúl Leoni, and the Dominican, Juan Bosch. The fact that all three would become presidents of their countries in the following years indicates the intense movement of men and ideas through that house in San José.

Betancourt was not surprised one day when Ernesto Guevara and I came to his place and asked to discuss Latin American politics with him. Betancourt's dialectic facility betrayed a Marxist background, although his skill in debate also revealed a certain authoritarian streak. It was then impossible to determine the price he was willing to pay to satisfy his ambition. His store of information and his intelligent way of explaining points of view were impressive. We struck up a good relationship, encouraged by Betancourt's frequent invitations to lunch.

These meals were good news to us at the time, and what Betancourt treated us to in a small Italian restaurant nearby would have been good news to any gourmet, anywhere, in any age. The owner of the restaurant was an Italian woman, a little ripe but still attractive, who exchanged meaningful looks with Juan Bosch while she served.

Bosch, a mulatto with a profound look in his eyes and a natural, unpretentious elegance, wrote fiction and, occasionally, history. Guevara felt an immediate attraction for Bosch and an equal dislike for Betancourt. He used to talk about Latin American literature with Bosch, including the Dominican's writings; they also discussed Cuba, to which Bosch had just dedicated an enthusiastic book as yet unpublished. Guevara, who was an omnivorous reader, laid bare his deepest and most sensitive feelings during these lunches with Bosch.

But an invisible barrier stood between him and Betancourt. I believe they were divided initially by a spontaneous antagonism and then by a conflict of ideas. Betancourt talked about the United States having a double image: a friendly face that promised understanding and assistance, and a hateful, imperialist face he said he would fight. Guevara replied that this dichotomy set up a false choice and, like all false choices, benefitted only the powerful. The two could never make any headway on the subject of relations between the United States and Latin America, although Guevara was willing to listen respectfully to Betancourt's explanations.

Exchanging conversation from table to table, we established our relations with some other political exiles. They were also young, and hadn't been in the country very long either. They made up a disorderly and noisy group, discussing politics and women with great enthusiasm; and, like us, they were having a serious financial problem in a country where they knew few important people.

These were the Cubans of the 26th of July, 1953, Movement. In that small café in January 1954, they told us disturbing stories of the massacre following the failed attack on the Moncada barracks and the terrorism in the cities that was beginning to stain the streets with blood.

To both Guevara and myself, it seemed that these excited young men were living a fantasy. They talked of summary executions, dynamite attacks, military demonstrations in the universities, kidnappings, and machine-gun fire; and they talked in a way so natural that it made our heads spin. Then they would say goodbye and go calling from house to house, selling beach sandals they had made with their own hands; or else they went to cash the checks their families or friends had sent them from Cuba or the United States. It was from them that Guevara first heard about Fidel Castro.

There, in San José, they drew only a mocking incredulity from Guevara, and more than once he cut short some wild story with a sharp comment:

"Listen, why don't you tell us a cowboy movie now?"

We left Costa Rica for El Salvador by bus.

Our first stop was Santa Ana, the country's second largest city. I remembered that El Salvador's friendly ambassador to Guatemala had suggested a visit to a Colonel Vides, if I ever happened to be in Santa Ana. He turned out to be the most important man in the city and one of the most powerful in the country. We got in touch with him fast. When he learned who had sent us, he went out of his way to make our visit pleasant. We became his guests on an impressive coffee plantation called Dos Cruces (Two Crosses), intelligently cultivated with complex installations for processing the coffee. The Colonel had an exceptionally lovely daughter, who offered to show us the plantation.

As we strolled around, remarking on the efficient way the land was used, we noticed a few eye-opening details. The land was enclosed with a barbed-wire fence about six feet high and was patrolled by guards—uniformed, though not with the colors of the El Salvador army, and without insignia. They carried impressive .45 caliber revolvers, but at the time, they looked rather harmless.

The Colonel's daughter answered our curiosity. She told us the guards were the plantation's "internal" police, and their duty was to restore order at the first sign of rebellion from "those people," indicating some women and children waiting for their men outside a cluster of tumble-down shacks.

The girl's simple explanation left us dumbstruck. That night her father explained that the police were necessary because of the peasants' lack of obedience and affection for their work. As if to clarify this, he informed us that he hadn't earned his colonel's rank in military schools but in the suppression of a peasant movement twenty-five years before.

It was the last night we spent at Dos Cruces with the pleasant Colonel, who shot his workers, and his lovely daughter, who tried to convince us with the assurance "Papa is a good man."

When we reached Guatemala, the contrast struck us immediately. It was the middle of January, and the political temperature was climbing dangerously. By now our senses were well trained, and we smelled something in the air, ready to explode.

On January 29, President Arbenz charged that an invasion of his country was being plotted, that the forces were being readied in El Salvador, the Dominican Republic, Nicaragua, and Venezuela, and that the instigator of the conspiracy was a "government in the north." This declaration in itself implied a break between the governments of Guatemala and the United States—in Latin America anyone who mentions "a government in the north," even if the phrase comes from the southernmost country in the hemisphere, can be referring only to the government in Washington. The next day, with ominous speed, the State Department replied to the ministry in Guatemala that the charge was false and was part of a "Communist effort to disrupt the Tenth Inter-American Conference," to be convened in Caracas at the beginning of March.

Guevara and I stayed at the same boarding house where my friend, Chancellor Osequeda, had generously paid my bill the last time. One day the Argentine Ambassador, Nicasio Sánchez Toranzo, unexpectedly came to see us. Since I was a political refugee, he had been notified of my presence in the country by Guatemala's chancellery. But Sánchez Toranzo hadn't come to visit us as an enemy. On the contrary. He brought a token of friendship, some *yerba mate*, the best gift you could give two Argentines far from their homeland. Sánchez Toranzo was a Peronista diplomat and, moreover, had a brother who was known to be one of Peron's most devoted generals. Sánchez Toranzo's visits brought us our precious herb, which he received from Buenos Aires by air, and another priceless gift as well, newspapers from Argentina for Guevara and me to read not more than a week after publication. Sánchez Toranzo had followed the development of the revolution in Guatmelala with sympathetic eyes, but he could not hide his concern about America's reprisals. Our discussion of this led to an analysis of the relations between Peron and the government of

Guatemala. At this point, the anti-Peronista sentiments Guevara and I held became disconcerting. Peron had supported the Guatemalan government all the way, and he would continue this policy, as would shortly be seen at the Conference in Caracas. To see such a close affinity between Peron and Guatemala frankly shook us up.

On this same subject, the ex-President, Juan José Arévalo, told us something we hadn't known. A short time ago, a close relative of his had died. Arévalo was ambassador to Chile at the time, and he immediately returned home. He found out through Osegueda that we were in Guatemala and one day invited us to lunch near Amatitlán, a beautiful spot twelve miles from the capital. Guevara and I questioned him in a friendly way about why he had decorated Peron with the Order of the Quetzal, the highest distinction Guatemala could award a foreigner. Arévalo told us that shortly after his own government had passed the Labor Law in May 1947, the American steamship lines had announced that they would stop serving Guatemalan ports. The country had no fleet of its own, and this decision meant a full-scale blockade. Arévalo had started a secret negotiation with Peron. Their intermediary was the Honduran economist Juan Nuñez Aguilar, who had been with Peron at the Military Academy of Argentina. Aguilar visited his old schoolmate and explained Guatemala's problem. Immediately, Peron called the head of the merchant fleet and ordered that, from then on, ships flying the Argentine flag must call at Guatemalan ports. Arévalo admitted that Peron had done even more. The first ships to touch Guatemalan ports had brought arms from the munition plants in Buenos Aires. This explanation of why Guatemala had conferred diplomatic honors on Peron left two anti-Peron men completely confused.

The cafés in Guatemala in those days were alive with rumors and American CIA agents, many of whom operated openly. There was no mystery about their headquarters and hang-outs or where and how some interesting bits of information could be sold to them for U.S. dollars. The name of a U.S. Colonel. Carl Studder, always came up in our conversations, and while many people said they had seen him, it seemed more likely that this officer worked out of Managua through a large network of spies.

In one café we met some of the Cubans Guevara and I had known in Costa Rica. Just as we did, they watched with anguish the pressures on the Guatemalan revolution, even as they prepared their own. They said that the solution to Cuba's problem would begin as soon as Fidel

Castro, the leader of the 26th of July, left his prison on the Isle of Pines and joined them all in Mexico. From there they would go to work on their own country.

Our situation was different. One day Guevara suggested that we offer to work for the Guatemalan revolution in whatever capacity we could help most. As a doctor, Guevara assumed there would be no problem to his assignment.

But when we visited the Public Health Department, with a letter of introduction from Osegueda, we discovered that the matter was more complicated than we had thought. Guevara had come to offer his services as a physician and indicated that he was interested in working in the Petén region. An interesting program of aid to the Indian population was under way there; also, one of the most magnificent examples of Mayan culture is located there, the temple of Tikal, two hundred and thirty feet high. Guevara still had his archeological curiosity.

The conversation proceeded smoothly, and Guevara considered the job his until the minister said in passing:

"By the way, do you have your card?"

"What card?" Guevara answered.

"What do you mean, what card? The PGT membership card."

"No," Guevara said, unable to hide his surprise, "I'm a revolutionary and I don't believe affiliations of this kind mean anything . . ."

"I'm sorry," the minister said, getting to his feet to indicate that the interview was over, "but it's part of the usual procedure."

"Look, friend, the day I decide to affiliate myself, I'll do it from conviction, not through obligation, understand?"

Perhaps the minister did understand, but Guevara never got a chance to practice medicine in Petén only because he wouldn't fill out an identification card of the Guatemalan Labor Party (PGT), another name for the Communist Party. The leader of the Communists had carried his party's sectarianism to such extremes that, some years later, he couldn't put up with it himself and became an anti-Communist. With the same sectarianism, of course.

The colony of Latin American exiles in Guatemala included a dynamic and well-established group of Peruvian members of APRA. These Peruvians had been distributed among the organizations responsible for economic and agrarian planning, two areas in which many of them were experts. Our friendly sessions with them brought Guevara together with Hilda Gadea, a girl with an exotic face showing

traces of both Indian and Chinese blood in proportions difficult to figure out. Hilda Gadea was working for INFOP, an institute created by
the revolution to stimulate agrarian and industrial production. Eventually, she had a daughter by Guevara and married him in Mexico.
But at the beginning of 1954 she was only an unselfish companion of
the exiles, and Guevara soon fell in love with her.

In February the popular anti-American feeling rose even higher.
Two journalists from the United States were thrown out of the country in reprisal for a systematic campaign they had been conducting
against the government, which they accused of being a pawn of communism. The Catholic Church was also warned against interfering,
and one priest was forced to leave the country.

During those days we took part in an excursion organized by the
president's office. The idea of the trip was to show off the Public Health
Works that were being finished in Quetzaltenango, where the revolutionary government had already installed a potable water system and
a hospital.

Among others on the trip was an American couple, Robert Alexander and his wife. Alexander was a professor of economics at Rutgers
University. He and his wife asked questions and wrote down the
answers with the passion for order that makes American university professors a different breed from those in other parts of the world. This
careful recording of everything that was going on caught Ché's attention, and soon he couldn't take his eyes off Alexander and his notes.

Guevara and I, together with a high-ranking bureaucrat, got into
the front seat of a large station wagon and immediately discovered a
machine gun on the floor. Guevara asked what it was for and the
bureaucrat answered proudly: "So that we won't be caught like you
Argentines, without our weapons. Here they'll have to fight us to the
last man, you'll see . . ."

In the combat zone that the Caribbean seemed to be in those days,
this kind of bravado made us Argentines feel inhibited and inferior.
Some months later I was to ask Guevara what the bureaucrat had done
when the time for action came, but at that moment he gave the impression of being a fighter ready to sacrifice his life.

On our return from Quetzaltenango, Guevara might doubt everything he had seen, except one hing: the United States professor who
hadn't let a minute go by without writing something in his notebook,
he had to be a spy. I expressed my doubts.

"Too many *gringos*, too many *gringos*," was his answer. "What do you think they're doing here? What are they, private investigators, FBI agents?"

It was difficult to be reasonable about this, when every time we stepped into the street we could find agitators in the pay of the CIA. They gathered in the cafés, dropping their voices to ask for details about the political organization and, especially, how much confidence in the revolutionary government the army still had.

The problem of the army was the critical point in the whole process, although the revolutionaries didn't see it this way. Guevara was convinced that in this respect Guatemala's backwardness was much more dangerous than Bolivia's. There we had seen for ourselves a military organization of miners and peasants based, whatever its lack of consolidation, on the fact that the workers had defeated the professional army. The Guatemalan professional army had participated in the government for the past ten years, but would it allow the political revolution to continue now that the United States was officially opposed to it? Guevara didn't think so, and one day we went to question the staff of the revolutionary youth movement about this.

"You have tremendous confidence in the young officers, don't you?" Guevara asked.

"Yes," was the answer, "because they studied under Colonel Arbenz at the Military Academy . . ."

"But do you really believe that their way of life, their family upbringing, everything that sets this group apart socially will resist Yankee pressure, if it turns brutal?"

The young revolutionaries said yes. But Guevara advised them to arm peasant militias like the ones we had seen in Bolivia, but better ones, if possible — militias that not only could keep an eye on the army but, if necessary, could replace it and take over the country's defense.

Guevara's fears were dramatically realized a few months later, but I wasn't there to see it. I left Guatemala at the end of February 1954 for Mexico and the United States, where I was to spend almost a year.

We embraced.

"Wait for me in Mexico," he managed to yell at me as the bus pulled away.

In Guatemala the drama was nearing its final act.

# MUTUAL AFFECTION
## HILDA GADEA

from *ERNESTO: A MEMOIR OF CHE GUEVARA*

1972

O N FEBRUARY 18, ROJO and García came to my office, Guevara with them. They came to tell me that they were leaving the country. Rojo was going to the U.S.A.; García was returning to Argentina. Gualo was thinking of getting married and settling down. He said he was tired of traveling.

Guevara was suffering that day from an asthma attack. He tried to hide it but his breathing was difficult. To my question of "How are you?" he replied with a typical Argentine brusqueness that left me a little annoyed. Rojo noticed it and said: "We will leave you two alone to find some mutual sympathy." He and García left to go say good-by to the president of the institute. Months later Ernesto informed me that they used to tease him about me and my interest in him, although up to that time it was only intellectual and political. But it's true that I had a special consideration for Guevara because of his asthma. Rojo's comment had embarrassed me, and, to cover up, I asked Ernesto what he was doing. He said he was reading some books on Guatemala that the Venezuelan had lent him, and soon we were exchanging views on other works—on the *Popol Vuh*, which is the ancient, classic "creation account" of the Quiché Mayans; on Miguel Angel Asturias' *El Señor Presidente*, Landívar's poetry, José Milla's *Canasto del sastre*, and Luis Cardoza y Aragón's *Retorno al futuro* and *Pequeña sinfonía del Nuevo Mundo*.

Soon Rojo and García returned; they said good-by and asked me to help Ernesto since he was going to be alone and to introduce him to people in the Health Department, where he might get a job.

By this time almost all of the Peruvian and Venezuelan exiles had departed. One could see a coup in the offing, since at the end of January, President Arbenz had denounced an imminent armed invasion supported by "a government to the north." In spite of the denial on the part of the U. S. State Department, which claimed that the charge was aimed at undermining the Tenth International Conference to be held in March, everyone knew that a masquerade was being staged to condemn Guatemala and its efforts as being "communist." It had dared to expropriate large landholdings among which was property of the United Fruit Company.

Rojo had also realized this and left to avoid difficulties. Ernesto and I discussed the matter at length. We decided to stay to see if the U.S.A. really supported a direct attack and if the Guatemalan democracy could defend itself. We decided to be on the side of Guatemala.

Ernesto called February 21 and asked me to accompany him to a political rally in commemoration of the assassination of Augusto César Sandino, the Nicaraguan guerrilla leader. I accepted the invitation. When he called for me, I was surprised to see him dressed in a gray business suit. "I inherited it from Gualo," he explained. He looked very nice. It was the first time I had seen him in a suit; he usually wore sports clothes. He always did his own washing, and he told me that he wore nylon because it was much easier to care for, especially when traveling.

Up to that moment, I had not actually realized how simply he dressed and how unconcerned he was about clothes; moreover his personality lessened the importance of such details. Little by little it became clear that this was his way of deprecating mere form and material possessions.

On this occasion he made an observation that revealed another aspect of his personality. Present at the rally was a high Guatemalan official whom we had met. He was in the company of a very beautiful woman, a young starlet. We knew that he was married. Ernesto asked: "Why is he going around with another woman?" I answered: "Apparently he's having problems with his wife."

"Well," he said, "if they told me he was leaving his wife for somebody like you, a thinking woman, that would be all right, but to change one pretty face for another, for a man like him, a politician with other values, makes no sense."

I was surprised at his reference to me and I turned to look at him, but he had said it quite naturally: it was the way he thought.

Two days later, Ernesto called me at the office to tell me that he had not been able to come to see me the day before because he had been ill, and that the asthma attack would last several days. I promised to stop by to see him after work. Accordingly, around six o'clock in the afternoon I arrived at his boarding-house on Fifth Street. His room was upstairs, but in spite of his illness he was waiting for me in the downstairs hall. It was the first time I had seen him or anyone else suffering from an acute attack of asthma, and I was shocked by the tremendous difficulty with which he breathed and by the deep wheeze that came from his chest. I hid my concern but insisted that he lie down; he agreed that it would be better, but he couldn't climb the stairs and refused to accept my help. He told me where his room was and asked me to go up and bring him a syringe that was ready to use, and a bottle of liquid both of which were on his night table along with a bottle of alcohol and cotton swabs. I did as he said and watched him as he applied an injection of Adrenalin.

He rested a bit and began to breathe more easily. We went slowly up the stairs; we reached his room and he lay down. He told me that since the age of ten he had been able to give himself injections. It was in that moment that I came to a full realization of what his illness meant. I could not help admiring his strength of character and his self-discipline. His dinner was brought up—boiled rice and fruit. "That's all," he said: he had to eat simple fare in order to get rid of the toxins that he had accumulated going around with Rojo to the many farewell parties.

Trying to conceal how much I had been touched by all this, I conversed about everything and anything, all the while thinking what a shame it was that a man of such value who could do so much for society, so intelligent and so generous, had to suffer such an infliction; if I were in his place I would shoot myself. I decided right there to stick by him, without, of course, getting involved emotionally. I remember that at that time, as he talked to me about his mother, I came to the conclusion that his strength of character must have come from her. I was right; all his subsequent conversation about her confirmed it. For the next two or three days I visited him after work. His condition improved, thanks to the injections and the light diet. During these visits he explained what an allergy was, as I was vague about it. He told me of the recent experiments that were being carried out in Dr. Pisani's clinic with semidigested foods; and of how all of his family suffered from allergy. According to him the illness was passed along by heredity through his mother's family.

I discovered that he liked poetry. For something else to discuss I gave him a book of poems by César Vallejo and other poems published in Guatemala at that time. I remember a poem entitled "Tu Nombre," which had appeared in the newspaper. Two days after I gave it to him, he recited it for me. I do not imply that I took it personally, merely expressing my admiration for his ability to memorize. This was no novelty for Ernesto; he had a wide knowledge of Latin American poetry and could easily recall any poem of Pablo Neruda, whom he admired greatly. Among his favorite poets were Federico García Lorca, Miguel Hernández, Machado, Gabriela Mistral, César Vallejo; a few Argentines like José Hernández, whose "Martín Fierro" he could recite completely from memory; Jorge Luis Borges, Leopoldo Marechal, Alfonsina Stoni, and the Uruguayans Juana de Ibarorou and Sara de Ibáñez. In particular he loved the last mentioned, to whose work I introduced him. He considered her the best postmodernist woman and I agreed with him. He used to recite "Los Pálidos," "Pasión y Muerte de la Luz," and his favorite, "Tiempo III."

He was not familiar with Walt Whitman, and I gave him Whitman's "Song to Myself." Sometime later I also gave him León Felipe's work on Walt Whitman. This was the first time that Ernesto knew of this great Spaniard whom he would meet the following year in Mexico. Finally, I presented him with "Contracanto a Walt Whitman," by the Santo Dominican poet Pedro Mir.

It was a joyful surprise to discover that we shared philosophical points of view. Admiring the strength of character with which he endured his illness, I was reminded of Rudyard Kipling's famous poem "If." I had learned it as a little girl and it has never ceased to be a source of strength and life for me. I recited the first few verses and he continued to the end, disclosing that the poem was also an inspiration for him. Another book that we discovered had impressed both of us since our early youth was *Ariel*, the classic essay by José Enrique Rodó.

One day when we were reading he took my hand and placed it on his forehead, holding it there while he told me how good it felt. Afterward, when we said good-by, he kissed me, and I told myself that I was accepting the gesture just to cheer him up and not because there was anything serious between us.

Ernesto had given me Curzio Malaparte's *The Skin* and *Huasipungo* by the Ecuadorian writer Jorge Icaza, whom he had met in Guayaquil. These two books had led us to analyze Yankee penetration of Europe, especially in Italy, and also the life of the Indians not only in Ecuador but also in Peru, Bolivia, and Guatemala. Another book he gave me was *Mamita Yunai*, the author of which had given it to him when he went to Costa Rica. The reading of this book set us off into a discussion of the United Fruit monopoly throughout Central America.

To help him find work, I introduced him to Harold White, the North American whom I only knew through Benjamín de Yurre, a Cuban from the group affiliated with Prío. I had been offered the translation of his book on Marxism, and I thought that perhaps Ernesto could take the job instead of me. He needed the money more than I did. I offered to help him with it. He accepted and we undertook the job of translating the book together. Since I knew more English than he did and he more about Marxism than I, we had a very good basis for collaboration.

Ernesto and White became good friends, and through Ernesto I became better acquainted with White and actually grew to trust him. Once Ernesto told me: "This is a good gringo. He is tired of capitalism and wants to lead a new life."

Presently Ernesto, White, and I became a closer group, although we continued seeing the people in Myrna's group. The three of us began going on Sunday picnics, during which it became a custom to have long discussions between Ernesto, with his crude English, and White, on subjects that ranged from the international situation to Marxism, Lenin, Engels, Stalin, Freud, science in the Soviet Union, and Pavlov's conditioned reflexes.

Our friendship with White developed so well that at one point he, with his North American practicality, suggested that we should rent a house where the three of us could live, and very generously offered to pay all of the rent. This, he said, would be very convenient for him; he suffered from diabetes and was in need of special food. The food bill would be shared by him and me. Ernesto was also enthusiastic about the project; this would solve his lodging problem. I, on my part, did not share their enthusiasm because it would mean for me taking care of a house. Trying to convince me, Ernesto again promised that he would make no advances. I told him that this had nothing to do with my lack of interest but that, since I was working and involved in political activity, I needed the remaining time for study. A situation like the one proposed would entail numerous problems for me. Fortunately, White did not acquire the house he had been offered, which meant that I did not have to refuse.

I REMEMBER AN outing in San Juan Sacatepéquez. After walking around the countryside we sat down to a barbecue that Ernesto himself prepared. When later we wanted to return to the city, we discovered that a religious celebration was being held in the town and that consequently it would be rather difficult to find transportation to get back. White tried to convince us to stay in a hotel. I objected meekly: "What will they think in my boardinghouse?" Ernesto looked at me and decided that he would find a way to get me back no matter what. "We will find a way, even if it's only you who is able to return." Thanks to his efforts, the three of us were able to get back in a crowded bus.

This gesture on his part again heightened my opinion of him. I remember then how, at the beginning of our friendship, he had once warned me against "men who lie," having observed how some of my comrades were courting me. Above all, he had warned me in regard to one Peruvian who, although married, was constantly joking with me. I never took it seriously, but Ernesto had taken me aside and said: "Be careful, he is married; you know how men always lie."

There was mutual affection with us. He knew me and was aware of my reactions. One time, realizing how much I was missing my family, he said to me: "You should never have left your country." Another time, already aware of my point of view from our endless political discussions, he asked: "How can a woman who thinks like a Communist belong to APRA?" Like many student leaders I belonged to that party because I thought it was the radical party that would bring about the revolution. My belief was based on some of APRA's literature: "Anti-Imperialism in APRA," "Letters to the Prisoners," etc. We truly believed that the APRA leaders wanted to make a revolution, to transform our unjust society. Unfortunately every day brought closer the realization that this was not so.

# THE ARGENTINE

## MYRNA TORRES

from *ERNESTO: A MEMOIR OF CHE GUEVARA*

### 1972

**M**Y RELATIONSHIP WITH Ernesto Guevara was always more in the nature of true friendship than political comradeship. It was a friendship maintained through many years between Ernesto and my family: my father, my brother and me, and the rest. I regret that when I first knew him I lacked sufficient political development to discuss more things with him, and to profit from the long discussions I listened to, in which Hilda Gadea also took part. She was an exiled Peruvian Aprista, graduate in economic science, and she worked for the Institute of Production Development, an organization created by the Guatemalan Revolution to arrange credit for farmers. My father, the Nicaraguan politician Professor Edelberto Torres, had met her in political exile circles and introduced her to me when I began to work for the institute in August 1953.

At that time I was just back from the United States; I had been studying English for a year in Pasadena, California. I was keen to meet people from other countries and get into lots of activities; the political circles of my father and brother helped in that respect. At any rate I know that at that time I didn't have enough political sophistication, so my relationships developed more along social lines, although within the revolutionary set. I was one of a group, all offspring of political leaders or members of juvenile revolutionary organizations, which held convivial gatherings, trips to the country, or little parties. We all liked to meet people from other countries, and more so if they were revolutionaries. As a political exile Hilda knew many Latin Americans and was very social in addition. We got along well and for a time she was a part of my group; later when she dropped our gatherings, we still kept up our close friendship.

In those days I kept a diary, and I've used it now to help recall details of that memorable period of my life. From time to time I shall quote verbatim from it.

Through Hilda we met the Cuban exiles who took part in the Moncada Barracks assault: Antonio "Ñico" López, Armando Arencibia, Antonio "Bigotes" López (also called "Gallego"), and Mario Dalmau. Also two other Cubans, Benjamín de Yurre, the same one who later became secretary to President Urrutia when the Cuban Revolution won out, and José Manual Vega ("Cheché"). The first were really good revolutionaries, though not yet well prepared; the latter were sympathizers, and all of them became good friends. But the one I truly came to appreciate like a brother was Nico López, who always gave me good sound advice and indeed called me his "little sister."

Through Hilda I also met many exiled Venezuelans, Peruvians, and Hondurans. But the ones that impressed my friends and me most were the Argentines Ernesto Guevara and Eduardo García. They stood out from the other Argentines who arrived by their simplicity and naturalness, the others being very mannered and affected.

I remember it was the morning of December 27, 1953 (my diary confirms the details), that Hilda came to visit me with the two very attractive Argentines; Guevara was a doctor and García a lawyer. Shortly afterward the Cubans dropped in, Ñico, Armando, and Mario. We introduced everyone and I remember Ñico saying: "Ah, you're the Argentines; Hilda told me about you." Ernesto answered, laughing: "And you're the Cubans, of course. We knew about you from Hilda too."

A lively conversation started; Ernesto remembered that Hilda had invited them to a party on the twenty-fourth at my house, when we would have all met. But they hadn't been able to come because they had a date with the Venezuelans. Then we all went to the house of a Honduran exile family, the Velázquezes, to listen to Ramón, the older son, play the piano. He was a true artist and was studying the piano along with his last year of medical school. The Argentines and the Cubans hit it off very well. There was a lot of joking, everybody had a lot of fun, and we made plans to get together on the thirty-first.

For the 1953 year-end festivities my bunch and the Cubans had organized a *comparsa*, a masquerade group, to parade in a truck down Sixth Avenue, and then a dance at the home of Blanca Méndez, daughter of the engineer José Méndez Zobadúa, director of Petroleum Resources. I remember that Hilda didn't want to go. After lots of pleading she consented to go just to the party, but the Argentines weren't there. We had a good time: Alba de Rosario Díaz Rozzoto and Consuelo España sang, a Nicaraguan named Leonte did a whistling act, and we acted out "Jacinto Mico."

Alba de Rosario was the sister of the Communist leader Jaime Díaz Rozzoto and had been in the Guatemalan Embassy in Havana, where he had met Ñico and the other exiles. She and Consuelo frequently came to our gatherings and those of Hilda, who was a good friend of both of them and their families. As Ñico thought of me as a sister, he confided in me that he was in love with Alba, but they were on different social planes; he never said anything to her. "Her social position isn't mine," he said. "I can't offer her anything . . ." I think he felt that way because his goals were very different: he had an absolute faith that he would go back to Cuba and fight.

I got to know the Argentines better on Sunday, January 3, 1954. We and Hilda had organized an outing in the countryside at the ranch of a German-Jewish businessman, Señor Grifell.

My notes say: "Since Ñico and Armando couldn't remember if Hilda had given our addresses to Sr. Grifell so he could pick us up, we all decided to go to Hilda's house. We were Eduardo García, Ernesto Guevara and Oscar Valdovinos, Argentines, and the latter's wife, a Panamanian; Ñico and Armando, Cubans; Blanca Méndez, Mexican-Guatemalan; Consuelo España, Guatemalan; Hilda Gadea, Peruvian; Harold White, North American; and I, *'nica-chapina'* — Nicaraguan-Guatemalan.

"The ranch is at the end of Las Vacas Bridge, some 40 minutes from the capital. We rode horseback there. I got up on a very pretty mare, who promptly threw me but I got up again and rode off. Armando mounted and followed me. Both Armando and Guevara rode very well. Later we sprawled under a tree; for an hour or so I acted as interpreter between the gringo and Armando. We lunched late, and afterwards talked.

"It caught my attention that Eduardo and Ernesto liked to talk politics more than anything else. Ernesto seemed very happy that day, riding in the country."

Ernesto and Eduardo were different from other Argentines. These tended to be petulant, good dressers, well groomed, always talking about complicated things, full of formalisms—I didn't feel at ease with them. These two, on the other hand, appealed to me a lot; they were very casual in their dress, simple and happy-dispositioned; they liked sports, and although they were intelligent and preferred to talk politics, you could talk to them on any subject, in a simple way. They were anything but complicated.

Little by little I, and my friends too, came to realize that the Argentines, especially Ernesto, preferred to talk with Hilda because she could discuss politics. It became evident that Hilda wasn't inviting us to some of the gatherings. This bothered me some at first, but then I understood that they really wanted to know about the Guatemalan Revolution and were after Hilda to introduce them to the revolutionary leaders. They would come to our little parties, but they didn't dance: they preferred to converse with my father and my brother, who had just arrived from China and who also was secretary general of the communist Democratic Youth organization.

My friends and I kidded about the Argentines, and I remember that one of them was seriously interested in Ernesto, but she never let him know. I also remember very well a night after a party at my house, at which as usual the Argentines preferred to talk politics with my father and brother and Hilda. Blanca, who had no boy friend, had become quite aware of Ernesto's good looks. To tease her, I warned her that I'd met him first. She said: "Oh, come on; you've got this one and that one, and I haven't got anybody. Besides, you know I can't cook, and this Ernesto eats only tortillas, roast meat, and cooked vegetables. He's the man for me!" So we decided to toss a coin for him. Blanca won. Ernesto, of course, never knew anything about it.

A note in my diary: "Monday, January 11. These Argentine boys are the strangest persons: today they came through my office on their way to Hilda's, and all they said was, '*Buenos días*,' and when they came back, just, '*Adiós, Myrna* . . . ' It seemed odd to me because I'm so used to that effusiveness of the Cubans. Actually they were sociable enough; but they just preferred political connections."

I knew that with Hilda their talk was always on serious matters, although Ernesto needled Hilda a lot for being an Aprista. In spite of their serious interests, they shared a great sense of humor, with much joking and kidding. I remember that Armando Arencibia was courting me (it never came to anything because of his indecisiveness and also because he was always aware that first he had to go to Cuba to fight, an intention he repeated often and that Ñico corroborated), and one day, when they were all together, Ernesto said to him: "We were at the Torres' last night . . ."

"Oh? And Myrna . . . ?" Armando inquired.

"She was there," Ernesto replied, "and imagine our surprise to see her and Eduardo holding hands."

"Well . . ." Armando said, addressing Eduardo, "my warm felicitations. I congratulate you."

But apparently he must have looked so down in the mouth that Ernesto quickly explained it was a joke.

Ñico repaid Ernesto with the same coin, asking him slyly: "Is it true, Che, that you're engaged to marry Hilda?"

"No, it's *not* true," he answered. Nevertheless their mutual preference was obvious. They were always discussing, arguing, sometimes heatedly. Hilda got him interviews with Guatemalan leaders and officials; and one day she told me that henceforth he wouldn't be taking part in any more social gatherings, just political. This was January 16, 1954, my diary says.

Along about then I had a little party at my house for Armando's birthday with all these friends I've mentioned, and also Humberto Pineda, a comrade from the Youth Alliance whom I had just met and with whom I had hit it off immediately. Few of the group danced, but among those who did were Humberto and I — practically all night long. Ernesto didn't dance once, just conversed with my father. There's a note in my diary of a comment my father made when everyone had left: "*Caramba*, what a lad that Ernesto is! He's so young, but with so much talent and maturity!"

That week, the last in January, Ernesto came to ask for the phone number of Norma, a very nice friend of mine, whom I knew he dated just once. I don't know how it came out; doubtless just a passing interest with Ernesto.

I invited Hilda and Ernesto and the whole bunch to a Congress of the Youth Alliance, being held mainly to support the Guatemalan Revolution, because one could already detect various maneuvers of the imperialists, who couldn't pardon Guatemala for having instigated the agrarian reform and expropriated holdings of the United Fruit Company. For the congress, the Guatemalan Workers' Conference, the party, and the Youth Alliance organized meetings, assemblies, etc., to explain to the people what the imperialists were trying to do.

There was also a great campaign for peace, with a demonstration in front of the National Palace, in which the majority of the workers as well as my Cuban and Argentine friends signed a manifestation. It was a pledge by all the revolutionaries to defend the revolution in the event that Guatemala was invaded. Nothing was ever said, of course, about the exact form that defense would take. It was known that the government had bought arms from Belgium and that they were about due to arrive at Puerto Barrios (North American property). I well remember that there was much more fervor for collecting peace signatures than for talking of fighting. But it is also true on other occasions that the youth and other civilians flocked to headquarters to get arms when coups were imminent against both the Arévalo and the Arbenz governments; and not only did they ask for guns—they were given them and they used them.

My diary says: "Saturday, February 13. Unforgettable! . . . All morning working and organizing the Alliance affair . . . we left at 6.30 P.M. in trucks and two jeeps. Got to Amatitlán at 7, went right to the park, started an open air fire. Got the supper ready—hot dogs, tamales and bread. Present were Hilda Gadea, Ernesto Guevara, all my friends, the two Blancas, Norma, María Elena and most of the boys and girls of the Youth Alliance. Also Hilda had invited Wainahuer, the Honduran, who brought his accordion. Couples started to dance. The park is at the edge of a lake; sort of Greek-style, I would say, with a pool of lotus flowers. At the left side are several cooking areas, at the right an arbor with Ionic columns, several stone tables and seats in front of it. We put out plates, spoons and paper cups for coffee and around nine served the supper. Candles on the table because there was no light in the park. People sat wherever they wanted. My whole point with this was to get those not in the Alliance to become better acquainted with the members. I was making more coffee when a mariachi band and the 'Amatitlán Trio' showed up . . . At 11:30 we had to go back to the capital; we hated to leave. The only one disposed to stay was Ernesto, who had brought his traveling kit, a kind of zippered sleeping bag with which he could sleep wherever he wanted. We tried to get him to come back with us, but he stayed, with his bag, some books and his *bombilla* of maté . . ."

On the nineteenth, twentieth, and twenty-first was the first National Festival of the Alliance, in the Alameda of Chimaltenango. As I was responsible for Women's Affairs, I was in charge of lodgings for the girls who came from all over the republic. On Sunday Hilda arrived with Ernesto; then later Ñico, Armando, and Eduardo. They came as visitors and took part in the sports, the cultural activities, and the forums.

So February went, and the early part of March, with various little political doings. I had decided to go to Canada. My fiancé was there. I had promised to go up there and decide whether or not I was going to marry him. My sister Grazia and two other friends were also going; we would leave on the twenty-first. A round of farewell affairs started; I said good-by to all my friends, including Hilda and Ernesto.

Out of the country they were already talking about the invasion of Guatemala: I was sorry I had left. Early in June came a letter from our mother: ". . . one of these days, maybe when we least expect it, your papa and I are going to need one of you two." It was a dramatic note, bringing home to me the imminence of danger in Guatemala. I participated passionately in all the meetings in support of the revolution. In Vancouver at the end of June, there was a meeting organized by the Canadian Communist Party with the theme "Hands Off Guatemala," in which my sister and my friends and I took active part.

Thenceforth my diary recorded anxious moments: "Friday, July 18. The dentist where I work said: 'Did you hear the news about Guatemala?' We turned on the radio and just then they said: 'Castillo Armas and the Army of Liberation have bombarded the gas stores of Puerto Barrios.'

"Saturday, July 19. We tried to get a phone call through to our mother, but we couldn't as Guatemala has closed all the borders and there is no communication. The radio news was given every half hour, but only from Castillo Armas's side. They said that Arbenz's government was going to appeal to the United Nations, because it was an *invasion*. He accused the United States of financing it.

"August 11. So many things have happened. With the fall from power of Arbenz, thousands have been taken prisoner in Guatemala, among them my father. My brother is in hiding, and Humberto, my intended (I had accepted him after breaking off the engagement in Canada) has taken asylum in the Argentine Embassy . . . This Saturday I spoke with the ambassador and he says Humberto will soon leave Guatemala but doesn't know to which country he'll go. I'm not permitted to talk to Humberto, so I have to tell the ambassador what I want to say to him . . ."

In October 1954 we all went back to Mexico. My friends returned to Guatemala, but I couldn't. There was, however, a happy note among all the painful events: almost all the friends I had left just a few months earlier in Guatemala were now there in Mexico. Two days after I arrived I went to see Hilda Gadea. She lived on the ground floor—very cold as I remember it—of a new building on Pachuca Street in the Colonia Condesa. Lucila Velásquez lived with her. The day I came Hilda was preparing a Venezuelan specialty for a dinner. Among the invited guests was Ernesto. What a joy to see each other again!

Unlike Guatemala, life in Mexico for me was not parties and gatherings; I was alone there, without my bunch, and the first thing I did was look for work. My English helped me get a job right away.

As the days went by I caught up with my other friends from before. Ñico, Armando, and Antonio "Gallego" López were the first ones I saw. I remember that there was a big discussion in a room in the hotel where I worked, about what had happened in Guatemala and details on what each of them had done, complete with simulated machine-gun noises. Each time Ñico came to see me he brought along another Cuban for me to meet.

One day we met at the house of the aunt of Alfonso Guillén Zelaya (who later took part in the *Granma* expedition and attained the rank of captain). My father had just got out of the penitentiary and he was there, and Hilda, Ernesto, and Elena Leiva de Holst, who lived there. Hilda and my father and I went on to the Venezuelan exiles' house, but Ernesto stayed to talk to Elena, whom he liked very much. Thenceforth we all saw each other frequently, although not with the almost daily regularity of Guatemala.

The People's Kitchen, on Dr. Lucio Street, was a popular eating spot where the Guatemala exiles gathered, which my brother and a Guatemalan comrade, Conchita Mencos, had established to help out economically (although of course it didn't work out that way). One day Hilda and Ernesto showed up there for lunch and shared with us the news that they were married, and that as soon as they had vacation time together they were going to take a train trip to Yucatán. Ernesto was always intrigued by difficult travel, in which he could discover new things. He wasn't interested in comforts; he could adapt with amazing ease.

Shortly the newlyweds celebrated Ernesto's birthday in their new home on Rhin Street, near the Paseo de la Reforma. Lucila Velásquez still lived with them. They told me that lots of the Cubans came there often and they would have me over to meet Fidel Castro.

On my part, I was now married to Humberto Pineda, who had arrived in Mexico in April, crossing the river as so many exiles had. Ernesto invited us for a spaghetti dinner one time, but in those days I wasn't very fond of spaghetti and we decided not to go. We regretted it later; the next day Ernesto said Fidel had been there and he wanted us to meet him.

Later on, Ernesto and Hilda moved alone to Nápoles Street in Colonia Juárez, quite close to Hilda's work at the Pan American Health Office, a United Nations dependency. At that time Ernesto worked as a photographer and also at the General Hospital. One time at his house, when I was expecting, he said: "Have you had an Rh reaction test?" I had no idea what it was. I told him I hadn't, and asked what it was all about.

"Come around tomorrow morning to that department, and ask for me," he said. He explained how important the examination was.

So the following day I did as he had directed and Ernesto himself took the blood sample for analysis. A day or two later he told me the results: everything was all right.

On one of my visits to the Nápoles apartment he was full of questions. "The Guatemalans don't seem to be organizing anything; aren't they going back again . . . And Cruz Wer, what's he doing? Is he free yet . . . ? And Rosenberg . . . ?" The last two were among the few military loyal to Arbenz's government. Ernesto always evinced a great admiration for Cruz Wer, although he had never met him, because he was the only officer who had decided to stay and fight. I told him nothing was being organized.

Sometimes when I brought Humberto on these visits, the two of them reminisced and laughed a lot over their stint as exiles in the Argentine Embassy. They joked about the time Ernesto had to relay my amorous messages. Humberto couldn't talk to me, but Ernesto, being Argentine, could come into the room where the phone was, though he wasn't permitted to talk either. So when a call was announced from Canada for Humberto, Ernesto was summoned to stand by to carry my sweet talk from the ambassador. They also recalled how Humberto and his brother slipped away from the embassy in the trunk of a car. Humberto had not intended to take asylum, but he had no place to hide or to eat, and had to; this had been Ernesto's plight too. They both regarded the embassy as a temporary refuge.

"Patojo" Cáceres came to the Guevaras' house frequently. He had been a schoolmate of my brother and we became very good friends. One afternoon Ernesto said to me: "I don't know what's going to become of this kid; he won't study in spite of the fact that he's regis-tered in the School of Physics."

"I think instead of a scientist's he has the mind of an artist, of a poet," I reflected. "He's a dreamer."

Ernesto thought about it a bit. "I guess that's true," he said.

Their baby daughter, Hildita, was born February 15, 1996, in the English Hospital. Visiting hours were five to seven and I went to see Hilda one afternoon. Ernesto was at her side. I'll never forget the pres-ent I brought; it was a very small gift—a little bottle of Johnson's Baby Oil. "Forgive the present," I said, "but it's all a revolutionary exile can do." Ernesto joyfully thanked me; the value of the present was of no importance to him.

We had to leave at seven. He said good-by and kissed Hilda. The incident sticks in my mind because outwardly Ernesto was not of an affectionate nature, yet he was so tender then that I was struck by that facet of his character. Being a father had changed him. He seemed more human.

Several months went by in which we visited only rarely. Hilda occa-sionally came to my house, or I to theirs, but there were no gather-ings. When it became known that Ernesto had been arrested in the ranch in Chalco with Fidel and the other Cubans, I went to see Hilda. She told me how she had been taken to the jail with Hildita, only a few months old at the time. Hilda was preparing something to eat to take to Ernesto at the prison, so I went with her to the Miguel Schultz prison. This was before anyone could see him. We delivered the ham-per and waited for the employee to bring it back empty. I don't know what wiles Ernesto used, but along with the empty hamper came a little note saying that he was all right and "kisses for you and the baby." This small detail I also admired. Along with his outrage at injustice, Ernesto had this tender side—he was the kind who loves children and dogs—as these little incidents bespoke.

We had invited to dine with us on November 9, 1956, Hilda, Ernesto, Patojo Cáceres, and Che Moyano, another Argentine who frequently visited them. I planned a typical Guatemalan meal for this Day of the Dead (All Souls' Day), the classical *fiambre*.

Hilda arrived first with Cáceres and Moyano, and Hildita, then nine months. In a little while there was a knock at the door; it was Ñico López with Raúl Castro and several Cubans. I was delighted to see my good friend Ñico, and I invited them all to stay and dine; I had enough for the eight or ten of them. But they insisted they had no time; they only came by to ask Hilda where they could find Ernesto. The latter had had to call on someone first and she told them where he was. One of the Cubans whose name I never knew picked up my baby boy, Ivo, five months old. He looked at the child with great tenderness and said: "Mine must be just about this age." In many places it's unusual for a young man to bother with a small child, much less fondle him. But in Cuba it isn't.

About a half hour after the departure of the Cubans, Ernesto arrived and we had the *fiambre*, Hilda and Ernesto, Humberto and I, Patojo, Moyano and Nayo Lemus, a Guatemalan comrade who stayed with us and who had had a close relationship with Raúl Castro in Mexico. Like any good Argentine, Ernesto loved wine, and to go with the meal we had a decanter of Mexican *vino tinto*. Later Ernesto took photographs of Ivo, whom he'd only just met. "He's a boy," I remember telling him, as Ernesto played with the child.

In the middle of November, Hilda, Ernesto, and Hildita paid a visit to my parents. It was the first time the last mentioned had seen Ernesto since he got out of prison. They were there quite a while, Ernesto talking, seated in one of those famous huge armchairs from the Lagunilla, Mexico's cheapest market, while he petted our little dog, Ballerina. They talked a lot of politics. He agreed with my father in many viewpoints; always they stood together in disapproval of the resignation of Arbenz, maintaining that he should have fought: he had the example of Sandino in Nicaragua.

When it began to get late, my mother brought out a can of Spam and offered it. (I remember because it was a rather expensive food;

someone had given it to her.) Ernesto was delighted; he loved any kind of lean meat.

A few weeks later when we knew about the *Granma* we remembered this visit and realized that Ernesto had made it as a farewell to the family. And about a week after that visit, Ernesto had invited us and my brother and Nayo to lunch with them. It was a weekday and I couldn't reach them—they worked as salesmen and traveled around—so I went alone. Ernesto seemed excessively regretful that they weren't there. Again, some weeks later, this puzzle came clear: it was to have been his farewell to us who counted ourselves lucky to be his friends.

Early in December 1956 the story broke of the landing of the *Granma* and that all of them had been killed by the Batista air forces. Then subsequently, the news that the army had set fire to a canebrake where a few survivors were hiding, and that Ernesto Guevara had been given up for dead. We went to see Hilda immediately. That time and on the occasion of the news of his death in Bolivia were the only times I ever saw Hilda really sad, and crying. She rarely gave way; she had a very strong character.

She was staying with Doña Laura de Albizu Campos and was preparing to go to Peru. Che Moyano and Patojo were very helpful to her, packing up and selling things from her home. They and Doña Laura, Juan Juarbe, Rosita Albizu de O'Neill, Humberto and I and my parents, and Comandante Alberto Bayo and his whole family all stood by Hilda and Hildita during those hard moments, until they got on the plane to go south.

SHORTLY AFTER WE had returned from Cuernavaca, Ernesto had come home one night with Raúl Castro. Raúl's spontaneity and cheerful and easy manner opened the way into a strong friendship among us. The conversation with Raúl was very interesting. In spite of his youth, twenty-three or twenty-four years, and his even younger appearance, blond and beardless and looking like a university student, his ideas were very clear as to how the revolution was to be made and, more important, for what purpose and for whom. He had great faith in Fidel, not because he was his brother but as a political leader. It was his faith in Fidel that had led him to participate in the Moncada attack. He was convinced that in Cuba, as in most of Latin America, one could not expect to take power through elections: armed struggle was required. But this effort must be carried out in close union with the populace; power would come only with the support of the people. With this, one could go on to transform the capitalist society into a new society—socialist Raúl held communist ideas; he was a great admirer of the Soviet Union and had participated in the Youth Festival of Stockholm in 1952. He firmly believed that the power struggle must be in order to make a revolution for the people's benefit, and that this struggle was not only for Cuba but for all of Latin America against imperialism.

He promised to bring Fidel to our house as soon as the latter arrived in Mexico. From then on he came to our house at least once a week, and Ernesto saw him almost every day. He had already been introduced to some of our Latin American exile friends whom Ernesto had met through me. Raúl always gave us the latest news from Cuba; thus we learned that Fidel was on his way, that Ñico could not yet return to the capital and had to remain in Veracruz, that he was going to Cuba. He also told us how they had begun to organize the 26th of July Movement. Moreover it was spirit-lifting just to talk to him: joyful, communicative, sure of himself, and very clear in his ideas, he had an incredible capacity for analysis and synthesis. That is why he understood Ernesto so well.

Toward the beginning of July, Ernesto told me that Fidel was in Mexico City, and that he had met him at the house of María Antonia, a Cuban married to a Mexican, who lived at Number 49 Emparán. They had talked almost ten straight hours—from eight o'clock at night to the following morning. Fidel, he said, was a great political leader of a new type, modest, knowing where he wanted to go, with tenacity and firmness. They had spent the time exchanging ideas on the Latin American and international scenes. We knew that Fidel had a deep faith in Latin America. We had also learned from Ñico in Guatemala that Fidel had been in Colombia at the time Gaytán was murdered and that he wanted to fight alongside the Colombians. That is another quality that Ernesto discovered in Fidel, his being a true Latin American, a profound admirer of the ideas of José Martí, an inspiration for all Cubans. He also found in Fidel a deep conviction that in fighting against Batista he was fighting the imperialist monster that kept Batista in power.

He concluded: "Ñico was right in Guatemala when he told us that if Cuba had produced anything good since Martí it was Fidel Castro.

He will make the revolution. We are in complete accord . . . it's only someone like him I could go all out for."

Ernesto said that since that first day he had been meeting with Fidel three or four times a week. He had stopped making notes in his diary as a precaution. The Cubans were being harassed, and he would not be surprised if one day they were jailed; not only the Batista police were after them but also the FBI, the Yankee police whose activity is worldwide.

One night Ernesto announced: "Fidel is coming tomorrow. Let's have a dinner for him and invite Doña Laura and Juarbe."

We had the dinner. Lucila was of course also there. But Fidel was late and Lucila got tired of waiting and went up to her room. When Fidel finally arrived we talked with him for a while and then called Lucila to come down and meet him and perhaps read some of her poetry, which was about to be published. Lucila, however, couldn't be talked into coming down. "You'll see my poetry when it's published," she called down from her room. The following week when Fidel returned he got to meet Lucila.

It was certainly very impressive to meet personally this student leader who, on July 26, 1953, had led a group of workers and students in an attack on the Moncada Barracks. He was young, only thirty, light of complexion, and tall, about six feet two inches, and solidly built. His shiny wavy hair had a deep black tone; he had a mustache; his movements were quick, agile, sure. He did not look like the leader one knew him to be. He could very well have been a handsome bourgeois tourist. When he talked, however, his eyes shone with passion and revolutionary zeal, and one could see why he could command the attention of listeners. He had the charm and personality of a great leader, and at the same time an admirable simplicity and naturalness. I remember well how his insistence that Lucila should come down, and the deep respect he showed for Doña Laura, broke the ice that night. We had all been in awe of him, except Ernesto, who had already spoken at length with him.

Fidel had asked about the Puerto Rican situation, giving both Juarbe and Doña Laura a chance to explain it, and then showing his own knowledge and his conviction, shared by all Cubans from Martí on, that Puerto Rico should fight for complete sovereignty, without minimizing the difficulties in the fact that the territory was practically a Yankee colony.

Juarbe expounded on the cultural richness of Puerto Rico and its folklore, little known in the other Latin American countries. Later on, we talked about Peru and the rest of our continent.

Overcoming my awe, I dared to ask him: "All right, why are you here when your role is to be in Cuba?"

He answered: "Very good question. I'll explain."

His answer lasted four hours, during which he made an exhaustive analysis of the situation in his country and the weighty reasons that kept him from being there.

In the first place, he said, he could not remain in Cuba because he was being watched by the Batista police. He believed that the only alternative was to fight directly for power, that there was no hope in elections as some other political leaders maintained. They were merely a big masquerade. If nothing concrete was done, they'd have Batista for forty years. One must prepare for the struggle; no matter how long it might last it was the only solution. Cuba was being more and more corrupted each day. Yankee penetration was complete. The spirit of the Moncada attack had to be kept burning with an armed struggle that would little by little raise up the masses. Unfortunately Moncada had failed, but much had been learned from the defeat and the experience would be useful in the new strikes. He had come to Mexico to train a group of fighters to invade and openly confront the Batista army supported by the Yankees and call on the people to join with him. In order to do all this, he had to evade capture.

He went on to tell us of the methods that would be employed in this new venture. I can summarize them succinctly: training of men for combat; organization of the movement; setting up of support committees abroad as well as in the interior of the country; distribution of various tasks; establishment of security measures, ensuring the utmost secrecy, keeping in mind that there would always be infiltrators, but with proper security these could be detected in time. The security measures would apply to everything, men as well as arms and orders. In this they already had had positive experience, in planning and executing the Moncada attack, and they would intensify it.

Lastly, he explained that the struggle in Cuba was part of the continental fight against the Yankees, a fight that Bolívar and Martí had foreseen.

When Fidel ended his discourse, I was absolutely convinced and ready to accompany them. I did not say anything of course. I decided to leave it for a better opportunity. Later, I asked Ernesto if Fidel would take women. He looked at me and understood immediately what I meant: "Perhaps—women like you, but it would be very difficult. Why don't you talk with him?"

But I never had the chance.

I do remember very well that a few days later, as we were discussing the future, Ernesto asked me very seriously: "What do you think of this crazy idea of the Cubans, invading an island completely defended by coastal artillery?"

I realized perfectly well that he was asking my opinion as to whether or not he should participate in the expedition. I knew the risk that our separation would mean and the tremendous danger involved. Yet, aware of all this, honestly and out of conviction, I said: "There is no doubt. It is crazy, but one must go along."

Embracing me, he said: "I think the same, but I wanted to know what you'd say. I have decided to join the expeditionary force. We are only at the planning stage but we'll begin training soon. I will go in the position of doctor." Our destiny was thus sealed; pain and happiness at the same time. Pain because of the risks, happiness because we were contributing in a small way to the liberation of our continent.

ONE DAY SOMETHING happened that made me realize to what degree Ernesto was aware that the Cubans were being persecuted and how much he considered both of us to be one with them. We still lived in the apartment with Lucila. (We were waiting for the marriage permit and considering the large sum of money necessary as a bribe for speedy processing of our papers. Of course, this was impossible since it went contrary to our revolutionary principles, and besides, we could not have afforded it.) We were already looking for another apartment. One afternoon when I came back from work I found everything upside down in our room. I noticed that the typewriter, Ernesto's camera, some of his medical instruments, along with a few pieces of jewelry that I had, were missing. We had been robbed. There was no doubt about it. When Lucila arrived we agreed to wait until Ernesto came, and when he did, we showed him our room without saying anything. At first he did not realize what had happened. "Didn't you have time to straighten up the room?" he asked. "Did you get here very late after work?"

"No, this is the way I found it," I said. Later he said: "There's no doubt, this is the work of the FBI. We can't tell the police. Even if it were not a put-up robbery, we wouldn't have the things returned to us."

So we did not report the robbery; I too doubt very much whether we would have recovered anything, and besides, it would have been a great bother. We were especially sorry to see about some of our things. I had been helping him type his work on the doctors in Latin America. He would have to go for a long time without a camera; fortunately he was not using it anymore to take pictures in the street, since he had left the job entirely in the hands of Patojo, no longer having any free time. He had begun work in an allergy lab where he was preparing for the defense of his professor's dissertation in physiology, which he eventually passed.

We were forced to buy another typewriter on credit, although we were still paying for the previous one. Ernesto had written a paper on allergy to be presented at the congress to take place in Veracruz in September 1955, and I had to type it. Also, I helped him to compile the statistical data and figure out averages. According to him, I had helped a great deal, in lengthy discussions, to clarify his conclusions. His work was selected to appear in the *Journal of Allergy*. He gave me one copy and wrote at the top of the first page something like this: "With love, to Hilda, who has been my guide and stimulus, and without whose help I could not have reached my conclusions or finished this work."

Unfortunately I lost the copy of the magazine when I left Mexico, when many of the packages of books I sent to Lima never arrived. In September, by then legally married, Ernesto was invited to present his paper to the Congress on Allergy at Veracruz, but since I couldn't accompany him, he didn't go.

THE PROPOSAL AMONG the Cubans to organize a movement centered around Fidel Castro, to continue with the struggle that had begun with the abortive attack on the Moncada, was already generally accepted. The Cubans, with other Latin Americans, especially Venezuelans and Peruvians, organized a ceremony before the statue of Martí in Chapultepec Park, in commemoration of the first 26th of July that they were spending out of jail.

I could not attend because, if I remember correctly, the ceremony was to be held during working hours, but Ernesto took me later to the apartment of the Jiménez sisters in the Imperial Building, where Fidel offered dinner for all those who were present at the demonstration. The atmosphere was one of real joyous fiesta. In addition to the numerous Cubans, there were a few Peruvians, among whom I remember Jorge Raygada. Talking with a group of Latin Americans was Marco Antonio Villamar, ex-congressman from Guatemala.

Fidel had prepared *spaghetti alla vongole*, which he later ate with us. Ernesto, sitting at my side, was very silent. Fidel laughed and said: "Hey, Che! You're very quiet. Is it because your controller's here now?" Obviously, Fidel knew we were planning to get married; hence the joke. I then realized that they did a great deal of talking alone together. I knew very well that when Ernesto felt at ease he was talkative; he loved discussions. But when there were many people around he would remain withdrawn. Perhaps on this occasion he was a little more withdrawn than ordinarily, because he was at my side and concentrating on taking care of me. Perhaps it was that we were celebrating the forming of the 26th of July Movement, which aimed at taking political power in Cuba by means of armed struggle.

Ernesto told me that they had agreed to publish Fidel's Manifesto, that is, the defense speech he had made to the court in the Moncada trial, "History Will Absolve Me." This document would serve as the platform for the struggle, and so this meeting was historical. The 26th of July Movement was a brother movement to others already formed and fighting for the freedom and independence of their peoples, with a very important difference: Fidel Castro would dedicate himself to training a group of fighters that would sail to Cuba to fight against Batista's army, to defeat it and to make a true revolution for the people.

They told me how the ceremony had been, what a success. Several speeches followed, one by the Venezuelan Ildegar Pérez Segnini, whom I knew from Guatemala, followed by that of the Peruvian Raygada. The next was delivered by a Nicaraguan comrade, and lastly Fidel's. His speech was magnificent, a real example of fine oratory in which he committed himself publicly to go and fight in Cuba. On that occasion I met the Jiménez sisters, Eva and Graciela, both very good and charming women who helped Fidel a great deal, putting up several of the young men who were later to go on the expeditionary force. They became sponsors of several of these, which implied buying them arms and equipment. Graciela, in particular, became a real close friend of mine; from that time on she was always invited to our parties, where she used to sing revolutionary Mexican songs, accompanying herself on the guitar.

THE IMPRISONMENT HAD lasted about two months when one afternoon I rushed home from the office to pick up some things to take to the jail. I went hurriedly toward the baby's room to see how she was doing. Suddenly I saw a shadow behind the door. I went in, and there was Ernesto!

We hugged each other joyfully and stayed that way for several minutes, after looking down at the crib where Hildita slept peacefully. He was delighted by my surprise in seeing him: "I didn't want to call you at the office; I decided to surprise you here. Besides, I was dying to see 'love's petal most profound.' "

After explaining that he and Calixto were set free because of the large sum of money that Fidel gave the authorities to arrange all the immigration matters, he talked about how surprised he was with the baby: she had not cried all afternoon and she had grown so much. Hildita was four months old when he was first arrested, and now she had just completed her sixth month. I said she was a good baby because of her schedule: her tranquillity proved it was just right for her.

He told me he could spend only a short time home, then he would go finish his training. They had decided to split up into very small groups and live incognito in small towns until the time set for departure. He thought that the departure would be delayed since there were many details to take care of, but this time it was necessary that they remain underground in their activities.

He applied himself to arranging his papers, answering his mail, piled up by now, and writing his family in Buenos Aires. Hildita, who spent most of the time in her playpen observing everything while she held onto the bars of the crib with her chubby little hands, was beginning to mouth syllables. Ernesto felt badly about having forgotten what the baby's voice sounded like, and he would sit next to the crib talking to her or reciting poetry. Sometimes the two of them would burst out in laughter. He was home three days. On the fourth he got his things together and said good-by, promising to keep in touch with me. A week later he sent a note by Comrade Aldama, telling me to go with the baby to Cuautla, giving me the name of a hotel in that town and advising me that I should ask for Señor González. Friday was a holiday, so we could thus spend three days together, since I did not work on Saturdays.

The baby suffered from a slight cold, but I decided to take her because I knew what it would mean for Ernesto to see her. We arrived at the hotel, I asked for Señor González, and then came an unforeseen dilemma.

"Which Señor González?" the hotelkeeper asked. "There are two. . . ."

I didn't know what to say. I hesitated, finally deciding on Ernesto González. At that moment Ernesto appeared. This was, in fact, the name he had used. He was very happy to see us. He rocked the baby in his arms and fondled her. Then he became quite concerned about the cold—her first—and said that I should not have brought her, the first consideration should have been his daughter's health. I calmed him down: after all it wasn't that serious, and I hadn't wanted to deprive him of the pleasure of seeing her. The next day she was back to normal.

I told Ernesto that Aldama had delivered his money—everyone in training received a small sum for basic expenses—and that I had brought it to him. He asked me what money I had used to get to Cuautla. I laughed and assured him that it was money from my salary. He was so honest and conscientious—about the money that came from the movement. Collected through great effort, these sums must serve only for the most essential needs: transportation, housing, food, and the like—never for personal family matters.

Since May, when the preparations intensified, Ernesto had been gone from the hospital and had no income. My salary had to pay for all the expenses of the house. This was nothing remarkable of course; not only were we husband and wife, but also comrades, participants and supporters of the 26th of July Movement. It was a principle not to touch a penny of what he received, much less since I was working.

Field training in the small towns of Mexico lasted about two months. By November they had reason to believe that their precautions had made the police lose track of them and they became more confident. The traveling was not good for Ernesto because it often took him to tropical areas, sometimes close to the ocean, renewing his asthma attacks. That's why he began to come home weekends.

During the week someone always came with a note from Ernesto, asking for books or sending me letters to be mailed. I would send back his mail by these messengers. I still have one of the notes, brought by Guajíro. It reads:

> Hilda:
> The bearer is a dumb *guajiro*. Don't waste time on him. Just show him the baby so he'll appreciate the quality of the bull. A big hug and a little kiss, from—
> CHE.

The note included a message for Moyano, asking for a number of books on Marxism which Ernesto wanted him to get at the library. It ended with the following: "Get them as quickly as possible. Be sure they are there when I get there Saturday."

One note said that he couldn't come home that weekend, so I accepted an invitation from a fellow-worker to accompany her to the concert of a famous Soviet cellist. As I was getting ready that Sunday, Ernesto arrived. I explained about the date and said I would phone my friend and tell her that I wouldn't be going. He insisted that I go as I had planned. When I got back, he ragged me about abandoning him for music. Actually, he had enjoyed the three hours I was away playing with the baby, reading, and drinking maté. He decided to stay until Monday, explaining: "I have to make up for the hours you spent at the concert, leaving me alone."

At the ranch, before the prison period, Ernesto had developed a great admiration for Bayo, the Old Man, as he was affectionately called. He told me how the author of *Storm in the Caribbean*, wanting to go as an expeditionary, had gone on a crash diet to lose excess weight. He had lost twenty-two pounds in fifteen days and he wanted to lose ten more by following an even stricter diet, but there wasn't time. Ernesto ended by saying: "What a great old man!" I was surprised at this since few people impressed him so strongly. He added: "He's a great chess player. We had some memorable games when we finished working. At first the Old Man didn't want to admit that I could beat him. He plays very well—really the only good adversary I've had in a long time."

Ernesto used to be amused at the Cubans' mania for cleanliness. When the daily work was done, they all took baths and changed their clothes. "That's fine," he said, "but what will they do in the hills? I doubt we'll ever be able to take a bath or change clothes. The most we do is save enough soap to wash plates and eating utensils so we won't get sick."

During the underground period, when he came home, he used to like to take care of the child while I was busy cooking or busy with household chores. Our young girl helper went home on Sundays. Hildita was about eight months old at the time and she was no problem. She amused herself when she wasn't sleeping by playing by herself in her playpen or walking around it by holding onto the railing. When Ernesto tired of reading, he would take her in his arms and recite poetry to her, loud enough so that I could also hear. Sometimes when he stopped reciting, the baby would cry, and stop only when he started reciting again. Every recitation always included Machado's poem "To Lister."

Taking Hildita in his arms one day, he looked at her tenderly and said: "My dear daughter, my little Mao, you don't know what a difficult world you're going to have to live in. When you grow up this whole continent, and maybe the whole world, will be fighting against the great enemy, Yankee imperialism. You too will have to fight. I may not be here anymore, but the struggle will enflame the continent." He spoke very seriously. I was overwhelmed at his words and went to him and embraced him.

He called Hildita "my little Mao" because of her somewhat slanted eyes. In this she resembled me. He would say she was Chinese like her mother, although my slanted eyes come from an Indian grandmother. At the same time, however, he was implying his admiration of Mao Tse-tung.

During these weekends at home we continued to exchange ideas and discuss books on economics, particularly Keynes's work *The General Theory of Employment, Interest and Money*. He also practiced his touch-typing, which he could handle surprisingly well considering the lack of practicing time. In the countryside he had no typewriter, and the only chance he had to use one was when he came home on weekends. And I borrowed a typewriter for him.

On one of those weekend evenings he recited a poem that he had composed for Hildita: "To Hilda Beatriz in Adolescence." His mood surprised me because we usually didn't talk about the future. Sometimes when I got sad he would say: "Cheer up. Just keep working and don't think about it. . . ." That night, however, he was moved as seldom before, when he read the poem. Then he gave me the original.

It was a beautiful poem, in which he said in essence that he was wandering without direction through the paths of America, and had stopped in Guatemala to learn about a revolution, that there he found a comrade who had been the support and inspiration of his ideals. The two of them had defended a small country attacked by Yankee imperialism, and later, in Mexico, he had decided to go and fight for another small country, a piece of our continent, to defeat exploitation and poverty and help build a better world for Hildita, "love's petal most profound." At the end of the poem, he explained metaphorically the reasons why he was going to fight, and hoped that Hildita too would fight for justice, not only for her country but for the whole continent.

Unfortunately this poem too was lost in Lima during the time the terrible news of the landing came out, and my billfold was stolen along with the other poem from when he first proposed in Guatemala. In those later days his letters were few and far between; the news reports were vague, and I carried those poems as talismans that would keep him alive, not out of superstition but because of the great love that they bore and the fervor of hope that he would succeed in the hard revolutionary trial.

One weekend he brought some notes on emergency care of the wounded. He had made a summary of the first-aid medical data, and I typed up several copies. He explained that, although he would go as a doctor on the expedition, he would also be fighting, and that it was indispensable to teach others first-aid techniques and care of wounded who could not be brought to hospitals.

Every time he returned to the interior, it could have been farewell, since he couldn't tell me ahead of time when they were going to leave. This uncertainty, the repeated agony, brought us closer together. Trying to cheer me up once, he said that perhaps we would have a little free time to go to Acapulco. He would let me know at which hotel he was registered, and I could join him there with the baby for a farewell celebration.

One day, we were arranging books on the shelves, and almost casually Ernesto stopped and took me in his arms. He stroked my hair and looked at me with a tenderness that I had never seen before, while saying gravely: "It is possible that I might be killed, but the revolution will succeed. Don't ever doubt it. We are prepared for all eventualities."

I held him tightly while he kissed my hair.

I had begun to be hopeful about the Acapulco trip, if only for a weekend. Then came the news, from the newspapers as well as from some comrades, that the police had broken into the house of a Cuban woman in Lomas de Chapultepec, where Pedro Miret was staying, and that they had confiscated some weapons and arrested him. On Saturday, when Ernesto came, I told him about it. He reacted very calmly, saying only that precautions had to be doubled because the police might be watching. Early Sunday, Guajiro came. I knew right away he was nervous from the way in which he asked: "Where's Che?" I told him that Ernesto was taking a bath, whereupon he marched right into the bathroom. When Ernesto came out, still combing his hair, he said calmly: "It seems that the police are on the hunt, so we have to be cautious. We're going to the interior and I probably won't be back next weekend. Sorry, but we'll have to leave our Acapulco trip until later."

I became upset. I had the feeling something was going on. "Is something to happen?" I asked.

"No, just precautions . . ." he answered, gathering his things and not looking at me. When he finished, as he was always accustomed to doing before leaving, he went to the crib and caressed Hildita, then he turned, held me, and kissed me. Without knowing why, I trembled and drew closer to him. Afterward I would remember how he tried to remain natural at that time, and I knew how much he must have forced himself. He left that weekend and did not come back.

# CHE

## LETTERS

## ERNESTO CHE GUEVARA

From **BACK ON THE ROAD**

2001

Mexico,
*July 6, 1956*
Government Jail

DEAR FOLKS:

I received your letter (Dad's) here in my new and elegant Miguel Schulz mansion, together with the visit by Petit informing me of your fears.[1] I will give you a history of the case.

Some time ago—quite a while already—I met a young Cuban leader who invited me to join his movement, dedicated to the armed liberation of his country. I of course accepted. For the last few months, I have devoted my time to the physical training of the young men who would some day have to set foot in Cuba, keeping up the false impression that I was only an instructor. On June 21 (one month after I had

---

[1]Guevara was one of twenty-eight *Granma* expeditionaries and their supporters arrested by Mexican police; they were being held at the Miguel Schulz Jail in Mexico City. Guevara's parents, Ernesto Guevara Lynch and Celia de la Serna, were living in Buenos Aires, Argentina. Ulises Petit was a friend of the Guevara family.

left my house in Mexico City, since I was living on a ranch on the outskirts), Fidel was taken prisoner together with a group of comrades. In the house was a list of addresses where we were all staying, so everyone was caught in the roundup. My papers listed me as a student of Russian at the Mexican-Russian Institute for Cultural Exchange, which was sufficient for them to consider me an important link in the organization, and Dad's friendly news agencies began to make noise all over the world.

That is a summary of past events. The future ones are divided in two: medium-term and immediate. With regard to the medium term, I will state here that my future is linked to the liberation of Cuba. Either I will triumph with it, or I will die there. (This is the explanation for a rather enigmatic and romantic letter I sent to Mom a while back.) With regard to the immediate future, I can say little because I don't know what will become of me. I am at the mercy of the judge and it will be easy for them to deport me to Argentina, unless I obtain asylum in a third country, which I would consider beneficial to my political health.

In any case, whether I have to leave for a new destination, stay in this jail, or go free, Hilda[2] will return to Peru, which now has a new government that has announced a political amnesty.

For obvious reasons I will greatly reduce my correspondence. Besides, the Mexican police have the pleasant custom of censoring letters, to prevent all but the most banal, household things from being written. And no one is particularly eager to have some son of a bitch know about his intimate matters, regardless of how insignificant they may be. I ask you to give Beatriz[3] a kiss, and to explain why I am not writing, and tell her not to worry about sending newspapers for the time being.

We are just about to declare an indefinite hunger strike to protest the unjustified detentions and the tortures that some of my comrades were submitted to. The morale of the entire group is high.

For now, continue writing to the house.

If for any reason I am unable to write more—which I don't think likely—and later my number comes up, consider these lines as my farewell, not very grandiloquent but sincere. I have spent my life

[2]Hilda Gadea, Guevara's wife. Following the end of the revolutionary war they were divorced, and Che married Aleida March in June 1959.
[3]A reference to Guevara's aunt.

searching for my truth by fits and starts, and now that I'm on my way and have a baby daughter who will perpetuate me, the cycle is complete. From this time onward, I would not consider death a frustration. Rather, I would feel as Hikmet put it.[4] "I will bring to my grave only the sorrow of an unfinished song."

A kiss to everyone,

Ernesto

[4]Nazim Hikmet (1902–1963) was a Turkish poet and dramatist.

# PART
## three
# GUERRILLA

"With the help of his natural adaptability, [the guerrilla] becomes a part of the land itself where he fights."

**—ERNESTO CHE GUEVARA**

# from **GUERRILLA WARFARE**

## ERNESTO CHE GUEVARA

### 1961

"With the help of his natural adaptability, [the guerilla] becomes a part of the land itself where he fights."

**—ERNESTO CHE GUEVARA**

## essence of guerrilla warfare

THE ARMED VICTORY of the Cuban people over the Batista dictatorship was not only the triumph of heroism as reported by the newspapers of the world; it also forced a change in the old dogmas concerning the conduct of the popular masses of Latin America. It showed plainly the capacity of the people to free themselves by means of guerrilla warfare from a government that oppresses them.

We consider that the Cuban Revolution contributed three fundamental lessons to the conduct of revolutionary movements in America. They are:

(1) Popular forces can win a war against the army.

(2) It is not necessary to wait until all conditions for making revolution exist; the insurrection can create them.

(3) In underdeveloped America the countryside is the basic area for armed fighting.

Of these three propositions the first two contradict the defeatist attitude of revolutionaries or pseudo-revolutionaries who remain inactive and take refuge in the pretext that against a professional army nothing can be done, who sit down to wait until in some mechanical way all necessary objective and subjective conditions are given without working to accelerate them. As these problems were formerly a subject of discussion in Cuba, until facts settled the question, they are probably still much discussed in America.

Naturally, it is not to be thought that all conditions for revolution are going to be created through the impulse given to them by guerrilla activity. It must always be kept in mind that there is a necessary minimum without which the establishment and consolidation of the first center is not practicable. People must see clearly the futility of maintaining the fight for social goals within the framework of civil debate. When the forces of oppression come to maintain themselves in power against established law, peace is considered already broken.

In these conditions popular discontent expresses itself in more active forms. An attitude of resistance finally crystallizes in an outbreak of fighting, provoked initially by the conduct of the authorities.

Where a government has come into power through some form of popular vote, fraudulent or not, and maintains at least an appearance of constitutional legality, the guerrilla outbreak cannot be promoted, since the possibilities of peaceful struggle have not yet been exhausted.

The third proposition is a fundamental of strategy. It ought to be noted by those who maintain dogmatically that the struggle of the masses is centered in city movements, entirely forgetting the immense participation of the country people in the life of all the underdeveloped parts of America. Of course the struggles of the city masses of organized workers should not be underrated; but their real possibilities of engaging in armed struggle must be carefully analyzed where the guarantees which customarily adorn our constitutions are suspended or ignored. In these conditions the illegal workers' movements face enormous dangers. They must function secretly without arms. The situation in the open country is not so difficult. There, in places beyond the reach of the repressive forces, the inhabitants can be supported by the armed guerrillas.

We will later make a careful analysis of these three conclusions that stand out in the Cuban revolutionary experience. We emphasize them now at the beginning of this work as our fundamental contribution.

Guerrilla warfare, the basis of the struggle of a people to redeem itself, has diverse characteristics, different facets, even though the essential will for liberation remains the same. It is obvious—and writers on the theme have said it many times—that war responds to a certain series of scientific laws; whoever ignores them will go down to defeat. Guerrilla warfare as a phase of war must be ruled by all of these; but besides, because of its special aspects, a series of corollary laws must also be recognized in order to carry it forward. Though geographical and social conditions in each country determine the mode and particular forms that guerrilla warfare will take, there are general laws that hold for all fighting of this type.

Our task at the moment is to find the basic principles of this kind of fighting and the rules to be followed by peoples seeking liberation; to develop theory from facts; to generalize and give structure to our experience for the profit of others.

Let us first consider the question: who are the combatants in guerrilla warfare? On one side we have a group composed of the oppressor and his agents, the professional army, well armed and disciplined, in many cases receiving foreign help as well as the help of the bureaucracy in the employ of the oppressor. On the other side are the people of the nation or region involved. It is important to emphasize that guerrilla warfare is a war of the masses, a war of the people. The guerrilla band is an armed nucleus, the fighting vanguard of the people. It draws its great force from the mass of the people themselves. The guerrilla band is not to be considered inferior to the army against which it fights simply because it is inferior in fire power. Guerrilla warfare is used by the side which is supported by a majority but which possesses a much smaller number of arms for use in defense against oppression.

The guerrilla fighter needs full help from the people of the area. This is an indispensable condition. This is clearly seen by considering the case of bandit gangs that operate in a region. They have all the characteristics of a guerrilla army, homogeneity, respect for the leader, valor, knowledge of the ground, and, often, even good understanding of the tactics to be employed. The only thing missing is support of the people; and, inevitably, these gangs are captured and exterminated by the public force.

Analyzing the mode of operation of the guerrilla band, seeing its form of struggle and understanding its base in the masses, we can answer the question: why does the guerrilla fighter fight? We must come to the inevitable conclusion that the guerrilla fighter is a social reformer, that he takes up arms responding to the angry protest of the people against their oppressors, and that he fights in order to change the social system that keeps all his unarmed brothers in ignominy and misery. He launches himself against the conditions of the reigning institutions at a particular moment and dedicates himself with all the vigor that circumstances permit to breaking the mold of these institutions.

When we analyze more fully the tactic of guerrilla warfare, we will see that the guerrilla fighter needs to have a good knowledge of the surrounding countryside, the paths of entry and escape, the possibilities of speedy maneuver, good hiding places; naturally also, he must count on the support of the people. All this indicates that the guerrilla fighter will carry out his action in wild places of small population. Since in these places the struggle of the people for reforms is aimed primarily and almost exclusively at changing the social form of land ownership, the guerrilla fighter is above all an agrarian revolutionary. He interprets the desires of the great peasant mass to be owners of land, owners of their means of production, of their animals, of all that which they have long yearned to call their own, of that which constitutes their life and will also serve as their cemetery.

It should be noted that in current interpretations there are two different types of guerrilla warfare, one of which—a struggle complementing great regular armies such as was the case of the Ukrainian fighters in the Soviet Union—does not enter into this analysis. We are interested in the other type, the case of an armed group engaged in struggle against the constituted power, whether colonial or not, which establishes itself as the only base and which builds itself up in rural areas. In all such cases, whatever the ideological aims that may inspire the fight, the economic aim is determined by the aspiration toward ownership of land.

## the guerrilla fighter: social reformer

WE HAVE ALREADY described the guerrilla fighter as one who shares the longing of the people for liberation and who, once peaceful means are exhausted, initiates the fight and converts himself into an armed vanguard of the fighting people. From the very beginning of the struggle he has the intention of destroying an unjust order and therefore an intention, more or less hidden, to replace the old with something new.

We have also already said that in the conditions that prevail, at least in America and in almost all countries with deficient economic development, it is the countryside that offers ideal conditions for the fight. Therefore the foundation of the social structure that the guerrilla fighter will build begins with changes in the ownership of agrarian property.

The banner of the fight throughout this period will be agrarian reform. At first this goal may or may not be completely delineated in its extent and limits; it may simply refer to the age-old hunger of the peasant for the land on which he works or wishes to work.

The conditions in which the agrarian reform will be realized depend upon the conditions which existed before the struggle began, and on the social depth of the struggle. But the guerrilla fighter, as a person conscious of a role in the vanguard of the people, must have a moral conduct that shows him to be a true priest of the reform to which he aspires. To the stoicism imposed by the difficult conditions of warfare should be added an austerity born of rigid self-control that will prevent a single excess, a single slip, whatever the circumstances. The guerrilla soldier should be an ascetic.

As for social relations, these will vary with the development of the war. At the beginning it will not be possible to attempt any changes in the social order.

Merchandise that cannot be paid for in cash will be paid for with bonds; and these should be redeemed at the first opportunity.

The peasant must always be helped technically, economically, morally, and culturally. The guerrilla fighter will be a sort of guiding angel who has fallen into the zone, helping the poor always and bothering the rich as little as possible in the first phases of the war. But this war will continue on its course; contradictions will continuously become sharper; the moment will arive when many of those who regarded the revolution with a certain sympathy at the outset will place themselves in a position diametrically opposed; and they will take the first step into battle against the popular forces. At that moment the guerrilla fighter should act to make himself into the standard bearer of the cause of the people, punishing every betrayal with justice. Private property should acquire in the war zones its social function. For example, excess land and livestock not essential for the maintenance of a wealthy family should pass into the hands of the people and be distributed equitably and justly.

The right of the owners to receive payment for possessions used for the social good ought always to be respected; but this payment will be made in bonds ("bonds of hope," as they were called by our teacher, General Bayo,[1] referring to the common interest that is thereby established between debtor and creditor).

The land and property of notorious and active enemies of the revolution should pass immediately into the hands of the revolutionary forces. Furthermore, taking advantage of the heat of the war—those moments in which human fraternity reaches its highest intensity—all kinds of cooperative work, as much as the mentality of the inhabitants will permit, ought to be stimulated.

The guerrilla fighter as a social reformer should not only provide an example in his own life but he ought also constantly to give orientation in ideological problems, explaining what he knows and what he wishes to do at the right time. He will also make use of what he learns as the months or years of the war strengthen his revolutionary convictions, making him more radical as the potency of arms is demonstrated, as the outlook of the inhabitants becomes a part of his spirit and of his own life, and as he understands the justice and the vital necessity of a series of changes, of which the theoretical importance appeared to him before, but devoid of practical urgency.

This development occurs very often, because the initiators of guerrilla warfare, or rather the directors of guerrilla warfare, are not men who have bent their backs day after day over the furrow. They are men who understand the necessity for changes in the social treatment accorded peasants, without having suffered in the usual case this bitter treatment in their own persons. It happens then (I am drawing on the Cuban experience and enlarging it) that a genuine interaction is produced between these leaders, who with their acts teach the people the fundamental importance of the armed fight, and the people themselves who rise in rebellion and teach the leaders these practical necessities of which we speak. Thus, as a product of this interaction between the guerrilla fighter and his people, a progressive radicalization appears which further accentuates the revolutionary characteristics of the movement and gives it a national scope.

[1] Colonel Alberto Bayo, a Cuban veteran of guerrilla warfare in Spain, served as instructor of the forces assembled by Fidel Castro in Mexico for training prior to the invasion of Cuba in December 1956.

THE LIFE AND activities of the guerrilla fighter, sketched thus in their general lines, call for a series of physical, mental, and moral qualities needed for adapting oneself to prevailing conditions and for fulfilling completely any mission assigned.

To the question as to what the guerrilla soldier should be like, the first answer is that he should preferably be an inhabitant of the zone. If this is the case, he will have friends who will help him; if he belongs to the zone itself, he will know it (and this knowledge of the ground is one of the most important factors in guerrilla warfare); and since he will be habituated to local peculiarities he will be able to do better work, not to mention that he will add to all this the enthusiasm that arises from defending his own people and fighting to change a social regime that hurts his own world.

The guerrilla combatant is a night combatant; to say this is to say at the same time that he must have all the special qualities that such fighting requires. He must be cunning and able to march to the place of attack across plains or mountains without anybody's noticing him, and then to fall upon the enemy, taking advantage of the factor of surprise which deserves to be emphasized again as important in this type of fight. After causing panic by this surprise, he should launch himself into the fight implacably without permitting a single weakness in his companions and taking advantage of every sign of weakness on the part of the enemy. Striking like a tornado, destroying all, giving no quarter unless the tactical circumstances call for it, judging those who must be judged, sowing panic among the enemy combatants, he nevertheless treats defenseless prisoners benevolently and shows respect for the dead.

A wounded enemy should be treated with care and respect unless his former life has made him liable to a death penalty, in which case he will be treated in accordance with his deserts. What can never be done is to keep prisoners, unless a secure base of operations, invulnerable to the enemy, has been established. Otherwise, the prisoner will become a dangerous menace to the security of the inhabitants of the region or to the guerrilla band itself because of the information that he can give upon rejoining the enemy army. If he has not been a notorious criminal, he should be set free after receiving a lecture.

The guerrilla combatant ought to risk his life whenever necessary and be ready to die without the least sign of doubt; but, at the same time, he ought to be cautious and never expose himself unnecessarily. All possible precautions ought to be taken to avoid a defeat or an annihilation. For this reason it is extremely important in every fight to maintain vigilance over all the points from which enemy reinforcements may arrive and to take precautions against an encirclement, the consequences of which are usually not physically disastrous but which damages morale by causing a loss of faith in the prospects of the struggle.

However, he ought to be audacious, and, after carefully analyzing the dangers and possibilities in an action, always ready to take an optimistic attitude toward circumstances and to see reasons for a favorable decision even in moments when the analysis of the adverse and favorable conditions does not show an appreciable positive balance.

To be able to survive in the midst of these conditions of life and enemy action, the guerrilla fighter must have a degree of adaptability that will permit him to identify himself with the environment in which he lives, to become a part of it, and to take advantage of it as his ally to the maximum possible extent. He also needs a faculty of rapid comprehension and an instantaneous inventiveness that will permit him to change his tactics according to the dominant course of the action.

These faculties of adaptability and inventiveness in popular armies are what ruin the statistics of the warlords and cause them to waver.

The guerrilla fighter must never for any reason leave a wounded companion at the mercy of the enemy troops, because this would be leaving him to an almost certain death. At whatever cost he must be removed from the zone of combat to a secure place. The greatest exertions and the greatest risks must be taken in this task. The guerrilla soldier must be an extraordinary companion.

At the same time he ought to be close-mouthed. Everything that is said and done before him should be kept strictly in his own mind. He ought never to permit himself a single useless word, even with his own comrades in arms, since the enemy will always try to introduce spies into the ranks of the guerrilla band in order to discover its plans, location, and means of life.

Besides the moral qualities that we have mentioned, the guerrilla fighter should possess a series of very important physical qualities. He must be indefatigable. He must be able to produce another effort at the moment when weariness seems intolerable. Profound conviction, expressed in every line of his face, forces him to take another step, and this not the last one, since it will be followed by another and another and another until he arrives at the place designated by his chiefs.

He ought to be able to endure extremities, to withstand not only the privations of food, water, clothing, and shelter to which he is subjected frequently, but also the sickness and wounds that often must be cured by nature without much help from the surgeon. This is all the more necessary because usually the individual who leaves the guerrilla zone to recover from sickness or wounds will be assassinated by the enemy.

To meet these conditions he needs an iron constitution that will enable him to resist all these adversities without falling ill and to make of his hunted animal's life one more factor of strength. With the help of his natural adaptability, he becomes a part of the land itself where he fights.

All these considerations bring us to ask: what is the ideal age for the guerrilla fighter? These limits are always very difficult to state precisely, because individual and social peculiarities change the figure. A peasant, for example, will be much more resistant than a man from the city. A city dweller who is accustomed to physical exercise and a healthy life will be much more efficient than a man who has lived all his life behind a desk. But generally the maximum age of combatants in the completely nomadic stage of the guerrilla struggle ought not to exceed forty years, although there will be exceptional cases, above all among the peasants. One of the heroes of our struggle, Comandante Crescencio Perez, entered the Sierra at 65 years of age and was immediately one of the most useful men in the troop.

We might also ask if the members of the guerrilla band should be drawn from a certain social class. It has already been said that this social composition ought to be adjusted to that of the zone chosen for the center of operations, which is to say that the combatant nucleus of the guerrilla army ought to be made up of peasants. The peasant is evidently the best soldier; but the other strata of the population are not by any means to be excluded nor deprived of the opportunity to fight for a just cause. Individual exceptions are also very important in this respect.

We have not yet fixed the lower limit of age. We believe that minors less than sixteen years of age ought not to be accepted for the fight, except in very special circumstances. In general these young boys, nearly children, do not have sufficient development to bear up under the work, the weather, and the suffering to which they will be subjected.

The best age for a guerrilla fighter varies between 25 and 35 years, a stage in which the life of most persons has assumed definite shape. Whoever sets out at that age, abandoning his home, his children, and his entire world, must have thought well of his responsibility and reached a firm decision not to retreat a step. There are extraordinary cases of children who as combatants have reached the highest ranks of our rebel army, but this is not the usual case. For every one of them who displayed great fighting qualities, there were tens who ought to have been returned to their homes and who frequently constituted a dangerous burden for the guerrilla band.

The guerrilla fighter, as we have said, is a soldier who carries his house on his back like the snail; therefore, he must arrange his knapsack in such a way that the smallest quantity of utensils will render the greatest possible service. He will carry only the indispensable, but he will take care of it at all times as something fundamental and not to be lost except in extremely adverse situations.

His armament will also be only that which he can carry on his own. Reprovisioning is very difficult, above all with bullets. To keep them dry, always to keep them clean, to count them one by one so that none is lost: these are the watchwords. And the gun ought always to be kept clean, well greased, and with the barrel shining. It is advisable for the chief of each group to impose some penalty or punishment on those who do not maintain their armaments in these conditions.

People with such notable devotion and firmness must have an ideal that sustains them in the adverse conditions that we have described. This ideal is simple, without great pretensions, and in general does not go very far; but it is so firm, so clear that one will give his life for it without the least hesitation. With almost all peasants this ideal is the right to have and work a piece of land of their own and to enjoy just social treatment. Among workers it is to have work, to receive an adequate wage as well as just social treatment. Among students and professional people more abstract ideas such as liberty are found to be motives for the fight.

This brings us to the question: what is the life of the guerrilla fighter like? His normal life is the long hike. Let us take as an example a mountain guerrilla fighter located in wooded regions under constant harassment by the enemy. In these conditions the guerrilla band moves during daylight hours, without eating, in order to change its position; when night arrives, camp is set up in a clearing near a water supply according to a routine, each group assembling in order to eat in common; at dusk the fires are lighted with whatever is at hand.

The guerrilla fighter eats when he can and everything he can. Sometimes fabulous feasts disappear in the gullet of the combatant; at other times he fasts for two or three days without suffering any diminution in his capacity for work.

His house will be the open sky; between it and his hammock he places a sheet of waterproof nylon and beneath the cloth and hammock he places his knapsack, gun, and ammunition, which are the treasures of the guerrilla fighter. At times it is not wise for shoes to be removed, because of the possibility of a surprise attack by the enemy. Shoes are another of his precious treasures. Whoever has a pair of them has the security of a happy existence within the limits of the prevailing circumstances.

Thus, the guerrilla fighter will live for days without approaching any inhabited place, avoiding all contact that has not been previously arranged, staying in the wildest zones, knowing hunger, at times thirst, cold, heat; sweating during the continuous marches, letting the sweat dry on his body and adding to it new sweat without any possibility of regular cleanliness (although this also depends somewhat upon the individual disposition, as does everything else).

During the recent war, upon entering the village of El Uvero following a march of sixteen kilometers and a fight of two hours and forty-five minutes in a hot sun (all added to several days passed in very adverse conditions along the sea with intense heat from a boiling sun) our bodies gave off a peculiar and offensive odor that repelled anyone who came near. Our noses were completely habituated to this type of life; the hammocks of guerrilla fighters are known for their characteristic, individual odor.

In such conditions breaking camp ought to be done rapidly, leaving no traces behind; vigilance must be extreme. For every ten men sleeping there ought to be one or two on watch, with the sentinels being changed continually and a sharp vigil being maintained over all entrances to the camp.

Campaign life teaches several tricks for preparing meals, some to help speed their preparation; others to add seasoning with little things found in the forest; still others for inventing new dishes that give a more varied character to the guerrilla menu, which is composed mainly of roots, grains, salt, a little oil or lard, and, very sporadically, pieces of the meat of some animal that has been slain. This refers to the life of a group operating in tropical sectors.

Within the framework of the combatant life, the most interesting event, the one that carries all to a convulsion of joy and puts new vigor in everybody's steps, is the battle. The battle, climax of the guerrilla life, is sought at an opportune moment either when an enemy encampment sufficiently weak to be annihilated has been located and investigated; or when an enemy column is advancing directly toward the territory occupied by the liberating force. The two cases are different.

Against an encampment the action will be a thin encirclement and fundamentally will become a hunt for the members of the columns that come to break the encirclement. An entrenched enemy is never the favorite prey of the guerrilla fighter; he prefers his enemy to be on the move, nervous, not knowing the ground, fearful of everything and without natural protections for defense. Whoever is behind a parapet with powerful arms for repelling an offensive will never be in the plight, however bad his situation, of a long column that is attacked suddenly in two or three places and cut. If the attackers are not able to encircle the column and destroy it totally, they will retire prior to any counteraction.

If there is no possibility of defeating those entrenched in a camp by means of hunger or thirst or by a direct assault, the guerrilla ought to retire after the encirclement has yielded its fruits of destruction in the relieving columns. In cases where the guerrilla column is too weak and the invading column too strong, the action should be concentrated upon the vanguard. There should be a special preference for this tactic, whatever the hoped-for result, since after the leading ranks have been struck several times, thus diffusing among the soldiers the news that death is constantly occurring to those in the van, the reluctance to occupy those places will provoke nothing less than mutiny. Therefore, attacks ought to be made on that point even if they are also made at other points of the column.

The facility with which the guerrilla fighter can perform his function and adapt himself to the environment will depend upon his equipment. Even though joined with others in small groups, he has individual characteristics. He should have in his knapsack, besides his regular shelter, everything necessary to survival in case he finds himself alone for some time.

In giving the list of equipment we will refer essentially to that which should be carried by an individual located in rough country at the beginning of a war, with frequent rainfall, some cold weather, and harassment by the enemy; in other words, we place ourselves in the situation that existed at the beginning of the Cuban war of liberation.

The equipment of the guerrilla fighter is divided into the essential and the accessory. Among the first is a hammock. This provides adequate rest; it is easy to find two trees from which it can be strung; and, in cases where one sleeps on the ground, it can serve as a mattress. Whenever it is raining or the ground is wet, a frequent occurrence in tropical mountain zones, the hammock is indispensable for sleeping. A piece of waterproof nylon cloth is its complement. The nylon should be large enough to cover the hammock when tied from its four corners, and with a line strung through the center to the same trees from which the hammock hangs. This last line serves to make the nylon into a kind of tent by raising a center ridge and causing it to shed water.

A blanket is indispensable, because it is cold in the mountains at night. It is also necessary to carry a garment such as a jacket or coat which will enable one to bear the extreme changes of temperature. Clothing should consist of rough work trousers and shirt, which may or may not be of a uniform cloth. Shoes should be of the best possible construction and also, since without good shoes marches are very difficult, they should be one of the first articles laid up in reserve.

Since the guerrilla fighter carries his house in his knapsack, the latter is very important. The more primitive types may be made from any kind of sack carried by two ropes; but those of canvas found in the market or made by a harness maker are preferable. The guerrilla fighter ought always to carry some personal food besides that which the troop carries or consumes in its camps. Indispensable articles are: lard or oil, which is necessary for fat consumption; canned goods, which should not be consumed except in circumstances where food for cooking cannot be found or when there are too many cans and their weight impedes the march; preserved fish, which has great nutritional value; condensed milk, which is also nourishing, particularly on account of the large quantity of sugar that it contains; some sweet for its good taste. Powdered milk can also be carried. Sugar is another essential part of the supplies, as is salt, without which life becomes sheer martyrdom, and something that serves to season the meals, such as onion, garlic, etc., according to the characteristics of the country. This completes the category of the essentials.

The guerrilla fighter should carry a plate, knife, and fork, camping style, which will serve all the various necessary functions. The plate can be camping or military type or a pan that is usable for cooking anything from a piece of meat to a "malanga" or a potato, or for brewing tea or coffee.

To care for the rifle, special greases are necessary; and these must be carefully administered—sewing machine oil is very good if there is no special oil available. Also needed are cloths that will serve for cleaning the arms frequently and a rod for cleaning the gun inside, something that ought to be done often. The ammunition belt can be of commercial type or homemade, according to the circumstances, but it ought to be so made that not a single bullet will be lost. Ammunition is the basis of the fight without which everything else would be in vain; it must be cared for like gold.

A canteen or a bottle for water is essential, since it will frequently be necessary to drink in a situation where water is not available. Among medicines, those of general use should be carried: for example, penicillin or some other type of antibiotic, preferably the types taken orally, carefully closed; medicines for lowering fever, such as aspirin; and others adapted to treating the endemic diseases of the area. These may be tablets against malaria, sulfas for diarrhea, medicines against parasites of all types; in other words, fit the medicine to the characteristics of the region. It is advisable in places where there are poisonous animals to carry appropriate injections. Surgical instruments will complete the medical equipment. Small personal items for taking care of less important injuries should also be included.

A customary and extremely important comfort in the life of the guerrilla fighter is a smoke, whether cigars, cigarettes, or pipe tobacco; a smoke in moments of rest is a great friend to the solitary soldier. Pipes are useful, because they permit using to the extreme all tobacco that remains in the butts of cigars and cigarettes at time of scarcity. Matches are extremely important, not only for lighting a smoke, but also for starting fires; this is one of the great problems in the forest in rainy periods. It is preferable to carry both matches and a lighter, so that if the lighter runs out of fuel, matches remain as a substitute.

Soap should be carried, not only for personal cleanliness, but for washing eating utensils, because intestinal infections or irritations are frequent and can be caused by spoiled food left on dirty cooking ware. With this set of equipment, the guerrilla fighter can be assured that he will be able to live in the forest under adverse conditions, no matter how bad, for as long as is necessary to dominate the situation.

There are accessories that at times are useful and others that constitute a bother but are very useful. The compass is one of these; at the outset this will be used a great deal in gaining orientation, but little by little knowledge of the country will make it unnecessary. In mountainous regions a compass is not of much use, since the route it indicates will usually be cut off by impassable obstacles. Another useful article is an extra nylon cloth for covering all equipment when it rains. Remember that rain in tropical countries is continuous during certain months and that water is the enemy of all the things that the guerrilla fighter must carry: food, ammunition, medicine, paper, and clothing.

A change of clothing can be carried, but this is usually a mark of inexperience. The usual custom is to carry no more than an extra pair of pants, eliminating extra underwear and other articles, such as towels. The life of the guerrilla fighter teaches him to conserve his energy in carrying his knapsack from one place to another, and he will, little by little, get rid of everything that does not have essential value.

In addition to a piece of soap, useful for washing utensils as well as for personal cleanliness, a toothbrush and paste should be carried. It is worthwhile also to carry a book, which will be exchanged with other members of the band. These books can be good biographies of past heroes, histories, or economic geographies, preferably of the country, and works of general character that will serve to raise the cultural level of the soldiers and discourage the tendency toward gambling or other undesirable forms of passing the time. There are periods of boredom in the life of the guerrilla fighter.

Whenever there is extra space in the knapsack, it ought to be used for food, except in those zones where the food supply is easy and sure. Sweets or food of lesser importance complementing the basic items can be carried. Crackers can be one of these, although they occupy a large space and break up into crumbs. In thick forests a machete is useful; in very wet places a small bottle of gasoline or light resinous wood, such as pine, for kindling will make firebuilding easier when the wood is wet.

A small notebook and pen or pencil for taking notes and for letters to the outside or communication with other guerrilla bands ought always to be a part of the guerrilla fighter's equipment. Pieces of string or rope should be kept available; these have many uses. Also needles, thread, and buttons for clothing. The guerrilla fighter who carries this equipment will have a solid house on his back, rather heavy but furnished to assure a comfortable life during the hardships of the campaign.

## civil organization

THE CIVIL ORGANIZATION of the insurrectional movement is very important on both fronts, the external and the internal. Naturally, these two have characteristics that are as different as their functions, though they both perform tasks that fall under the same name. The collections that can be carried out on the external front, for example, are not the same as those which can take place on the internal front; neither are the propaganda and the supply. Let us describe first the tasks on the internal front. Here we are dealing with a place dominated, relatively speaking, by the forces of liberation.

Also, it is to be supposed that the zone is adapted to guerrilla warfare, because when these conditions do not exist, when the guerrilla fighting is taking place in poorly adapted terrain, the guerrilla organization increases in extension but not in depth; it embraces new places, but it cannot arrive at an internal organization, since the whole zone is penetrated by the enemy. On the internal front we can have a series of organizations which perform specific functions for more efficiency in administration. In general, propaganda belongs directly to the army, but it also can be separated from the army if kept under its control. (This point is so important that we will treat it separately.) Collections are a function of the civil organization, as are the general tasks of organizing the peasants and workers, if these are present. Both of these classes should be governed by one council.

Raising supplies, as we explained in a previous chapter, can be carried out in various ways: through direct or indirect taxes, through direct or indirect donations, and through confiscations; all this goes to make up the large chapter on supplies for the guerrilla army.

Keep in mind that the zone ought by no means to be impoverished by the direct action of the rebel army, even though the latter will be responsible indirectly for the impoverishment that results from enemy encirclement, a fact that the adversary's propaganda will repeatedly point out. Precisely for this reason conflicts ought not to be created by direct causes. There ought not be, for example, any regulations that prevent the farmers of a zone in liberated territory from selling their products outside that territory, save in extreme and transitory circumstances and with a full explanation of these interruptions to the peasantry. Every act of the guerrilla army ought always to be accompanied by the propaganda necessary to explain the reasons for it. These reasons will generally be well understood by a peasantry that has sons, fathers, brothers, or relations within this army, which is, therefore, something of their own.

In view of the importance of relations with the peasants, it is necessary to create organizations that make regulations for them, organizations that exist not only within the liberated area, but also have connections in the adjacent areas. Precisely through these connections it is possible to penetrate a zone for a future enlargement of the guerrilla front. The peasants will sow the seed with oral and written propaganda, with accounts of life in the other zone, of the laws that have already been issued for the protection of the small peasant, of the spirit of sacrifice of the rebel army; in a word, they are creating the necessary atmosphere for helping the rebel troops.

The peasant organizations should also have connections of some type that will permit the channeling and sale of crops by the rebel army agencies in enemy territory through intermediaries more or less benevolent, more or less friendly to the peasant class. Joined with a devotion to the cause which brings the merchant to defy dangers in such cases, there also exists the devotion to money that leads him to take advantage of the opportunity to gain profits.

We have already spoken, in connection with supply problems, of the importance of the department of road construction. When the guerrilla band has achieved a certain level of development, it no longer wanders about through diverse regions without an encampment; it has centers that are more or less fixed. Routes should be established varying from small paths permitting the passage of a mule to good roads for trucks. In all this, the capacity of the organization of the rebel army must be kept in mind, as well as the offensive capacity of the enemy, who may destroy these constructions and even make use of roads built by his opponent to reach the encampments more easily. The fundamental rule should be that roads are for assisting supply in places where any other solution would be impossible; they should not be constructed except in circumstances where there is a virtual certainty that the position can be maintained against an attack by the adversary. Another exception would be roads built without great risk to facilitate communication between points that are not of vital importance.

Furthermore, other means of communication may be established. One of these that is extremely important is the telephone. This can be strung in the forest with the convenience that arises from using trees for posts. There is the advantage that they are not visible to the enemy from above. The telephone also presupposes a zone that the enemy cannot penetrate.

The council — or central department of justice, revolutionary laws, and administration — is one of the vital features of a guerrilla army fully constituted and with territory of its own. The council should be under the charge of an individual who knows the laws of the country; if he understands the necessities of the zone from a juridical point of view, this is better yet; he can proceed to prepare a series of decrees and regulations that help the peasant to normalize and institutionalize his life within the rebel zone.

For example, during our experience in the Cuban war we issued a penal code, a civil code, rules for supplying the peasantry and rules of the agrarian reform. Subsequently, the laws fixing qualifications of candidates in the elections that were to be held later throughout the country were established; also the Agrarian Reform Law of the Sierra Maestra. The council is likewise in charge of accounting operations for the guerrilla column or columns; it is responsible for handling money problems and at times intervenes directly in supply.

All these recommendations are flexible; they are based upon an experience in a certain place and are conditioned by its geography and history; they will be modified in different geographical, historical, and social situations.

In addition to the council, it is necessary to keep the general health of the zone in mind. This can be done by means of central military hospitals that should give the most complete assistance possible to the whole peasantry. Whether adequate medical treatment can be given will depend upon the stage reached by the revolution. Civil hospitals and civil health administration are united directly with the guerrilla army, and their functions are performed by officers and men of the army, who have the dual function of caring for the people and orienting them toward better health. The big health problems among people in these conditions are rooted in their total ignorance of elementary principles of hygiene. This aggravates their already precarious situation.

## the role of the woman

THE PART THAT the woman can play in the development of a revolutionary process is of extraordinary importance. It is well to emphasize this, since in all our countries, with their colonial mentality, there is a certain underestimation of the woman which becomes a real discrimination against her.

The woman is capable of performing the most difficult tasks, of fighting beside the men; and despite current belief, she does not create conflicts of a sexual type in the troops.

In the rigorous combatant life the woman is a companion who brings the qualities appropriate to her sex, but she can work the same as a man and she can fight; she is weaker, but no less resistant than he. She can perform every class of combat task that a man can at a given moment, and on certain occasions in the Cuban struggle she performed a relief role.

Naturally the combatant women are a minority. When the internal front is being consolidated and it is desirable to remove as many combatants as possible who do not possess indispensable physical characteristics, the women can be assigned a considerable number of specific occupations, of which one of the most important, perhaps the most important, is communication between different combatant forces, above all between those that are in enemy territory. The transport of objects, messages, or money, of small size and great importance, should be confided to women in whom the guerrilla army has absolute confidence; women can transport them using a thousand tricks; it is a fact that however brutal the repression, however thorough the searching, the woman receives a less harsh treatment than the man and can carry her message or other object of an important or confidential character to its destination.

As a simple messenger, either by word of mouth or of writing, the woman can always perform her task with more freedom than the man, attracting less attention and at the same time inspiring less fear of danger in the enemy soldier. He who commits brutalities acts frequently under the impulse of fear or apprehension that he himself will be attacked, since this is one form of action in guerrilla warfare.

Contacts between separated forces, messages to the exterior of the lines, even to the exterior of the country; also objects of considerable size, such as bullets, are transported by women in special belts worn beneath their skirts. But also in this stage a woman can perform her habitual tasks of peacetime; it is very pleasing to a soldier subjected to the extremely hard conditions of this life to be able to look forward to a seasoned meal which tastes like something. (One of the great tortures of the war was eating a cold, sticky, tasteless mess.) The woman as cook can greatly improve the diet and, furthermore, it is easier to keep her in these domestic tasks; one of the problems in guerrilla bands is that all works of a civilian character are scorned by those who perform them; they are constantly trying to get out of these tasks in order to enter into forces that are actively in combat.

A task of great importance for women is to teach beginning reading, including revolutionary theory, primarily to the peasants of the zone, but also to the revolutionary soldiers. The organization of schools, which is a part of the civil organization, should be done principally through women, who arouse more enthusiasm among children and enjoy more affection from the school community. Likewise, when the fronts have been consolidated and a rear exists, the functions of the social worker also fall to women who investigate the various economic and social evils of the zone with a view to changing them as far as possible.

The woman plays an important part in medical matters as nurse, and even as doctor, with a gentleness infinitely superior to that of her rude companion in arms, a gentleness that is so much appreciated at moments when a man is helpless, without comforts, perhaps suffering severe pain and exposed to the many dangers of all classes that are a part of this type of war.

Once the stage of creating small war industries has begun, the woman can also contribute here, especially in the manufacture of uniforms, a traditional employment of women in Latin American countries. With a simple sewing machine and a few patterns she can perform marvels. Women can take part in all lines of civil organization. They can replace men perfectly well and ought to do so, even where persons are needed for carrying weapons, though this is a rare accident in guerrilla life.

It is important to give adequate indoctrination to men and women, in order to avoid all kinds of misbehavior that can operate to hurt the morale of the troops; but persons who are otherwise free and who love each other should be permitted to marry in the Sierra and live as man and wife after complying with the simple requirements of the guerrilla band.

# from GUEVARA: ALSO KNOWN AS CHE
## PACO IGNACIO TAIBO II

### 1997

### 21. the mau mau in santa clara

AS THE REBELS headed for Santa Clara, their reputation preceded them. That they were called the Man Mau meant that they were men of honor, who magnanimously released their prisoners after explaining to them the reason for the revolution. They treated both their own wounded and the enemy's, they never abandoned comrades in battle, they gave warning of their attacks, they avoided useless bloodshed, they avenged offenses against the people, and they were never defeated.

Captain Rogelio Acevedo followed in the celebrities' wake, with an enormous responsibility weighing on his seventeen-year-old shoulders. He had been sent ahead with his squad on reconnaissance missions. The suicide squad followed him, and then came the rest of the column, headed by its commander, Ernesto Guevara, known as Che, of whom it was said that he could be in all places at once while also fighting where he stood. Next to him, in a red Toyota jeep, rode a woman called Aleida March, who knew the city like the back of her hand and would open the doors to popular support for Che. She would also clear a path for him along the roads, on the rooftops, and in the alleyways.

The city was calm; police sirens had not been heard for twenty-four hours. The soldiers were holed up in their barracks or in the defensive positions detailed by their commanding officers. Acevedo's advance guard approached Santa Clara in two jeeps at two in the morning. He arrived at the university and first encountered a couple of streetwalkers from the neighborhood; he asked them for information, but obtained no useful intelligence about the army. Batista's forces did not appear; the rebels found only milk trucks on their way into the city.

The second contingent of rebels arrived at the university at daybreak. Che Guevara came two hours later, at around six A.M., while Acevedo, who had gone ahead with his column, was taking the CMQ radio station, two kilometers down the highway.

Lolita Russell, an M26 sympathizer living on the road into Santa Clara, saw Acevedo's skinny, dirty men arriving. Her mother greeted them from the door with shouts of "¡Viva Cuba libre! Long live free Cuba!" Her father asked, "Are these Che's men, the ones who are coming to take the Leoncio Vidal barracks?" She harangued him: it was morale that counted. . . . Her father told his wife, "Lola, start packing, because when they come back this way, we'll have to go up with them to the hills."

A very young rebel asked Lolita, "How many soldiers has Batista got in the city?" She told him five thousand, and seeing the look on his face, asked, "Is that a lot?"

"I don't know if it's a lot—but with the chief we've got, it won't be. That much I do know."

Acevedo sent Pacho Fernández's platoon ahead, and they managed to further penetrate the outskirts of the city and set up an ambush in a side street. Fernández saw a milk delivery truck and let it go by, thinking, Who knows when the townspeople will be able to get milk again in the next few days? A truck carrying army forces drew up some minutes later and gunfire broke out, killing a soldier. The first enemy column appeared shortly afterward. After a brief clash, Fernández's squad withdrew to regroup with the column.

The greater part of No. 8 Column began to advance from the university toward eight in the morning. They went in two long lines, Indian file, along the ditches. Che was in the middle with a small escort. Harry Villegas: "When we entered Santa Clara, people were saying that Che was coming with three women: one blond, who was Aleída, one dark, who was me, and a frail one, who was Parrita. They were confused by Parrita and me, because we had haystacks of hair and no beards."

When the advance guard got to the CMQ radio station, they found two students holding a soldier, whom they wanted to hand over to the rebels. While they were interrogating him, a Jeep turned up on the highway; they shot at it and it backed away, tires screeching. Acevedo gave the order to advance, because the men in the jeep were bound to give their presence away. Guile Pardo said,

> We had advanced about 300 meters when all of a sudden a light tank appeared at a bend in the highway, and opened fire while on the move. We immediately stood and returned fire. I remember going over a wire fence with my rucksack and rifle, and my hat didn't even fall off.

The guerrillas took up positions in doorways and fired back. The light tank withdrew, but not before killing five rebels and leaving several wounded and bleeding on the highway. Just then, shots began to be fired on the advancing column's left flank. They came from soldiers from the armored train, who had taken up positions on the Capiro hill.

An improvised blood transfusion center was set up in the university's Faculty of Pedagogy. Dr. Adolfo Rodríguez de la Vega recalled:

> Fernández Mell and I bedded down in a corner of one of the university lecture halls. We stayed asleep even though the planes were strafing. At times broken glass fell on us from above, but we didn't feel a thing. The wounded began to arrive at about one o'clock. . . . We had arranged for only the most serious cases to be treated there. The rest could be taken to Camajuaní, which was close by.

The rebels reached the railroad tracks and set up a first line of defense there, to cut off the soldiers on the hill and hold up any reinforcements appearing on the highway. Meanwhile, the air force had been bombing since 8:35 A.M. Ten B-26s and F-47s flew over the city and strafed the outlying neighborhoods. A bomb that fell opposite the maternity hospital destroyed eight houses. The rebels approaching the Capiro hill and the Directory forces approaching the Los Caballitos barracks were strafed with particular intensity. Unlike the people of the Escambray, the population of Santa Clara had not previously been under bombardment, and they were terrified. The city was left shaken by the bomb blasts.

The Directorio troops had entered Santa Clara along the Manicaragua highway toward ten A.M. There were about a hundred men in a convoy of trucks preceded by two cars. Their progress had been slow because of obstacles placed along the way by the rebels themselves, but there had been no clashes with the army. Their objectives were the Los Caballitos highway patrol barracks and the Rural Guards' No. 31 Squadron headquarters, where 400 soldiers were waiting, backed up by four tanks. After the first clashes with army squads, the column split into two and advanced under the bombing.

By eleven A.M., the Directorio's troops were 600 yards away from the barracks. Nieves and Dreke's groups took up positions in the Coca-Cola building and the Cabrera maternity clinic. Abrantes began the attack on Los Caballitos and was repulsed, but Lieutenant López's forces managed to scurry over to the enemy's rear. Dreke reported:

> At about eleven in the morning or noon, the situation became very critical, as some soldiers had left the squadron headquarters in light tanks and were firing on our positions and on the comrades posted around the houses. The guards were firing and then retreating to the barracks, while others were advancing in the light tanks.

In the Leoncio Vidal barracks, Colonel Casillas was in despair; he had no clear idea of what was happening to him, except that he had the Mau Mau on the streets, harassing the military posts, and that he was on the defensive. He called the high command at the Columbia base in Havana to ask for reinforcements to be airlifted from Cienfuegos and for more bombing raids. The Columbia base responded by ordering a new wave of bombing; the B-26s and Sea Furies attacked Santa Clara neighborhoods again. The actions lasted from 10:42 A.M. until 4:54 P.M.

A harsh voice with an Argentine accent, somewhat blurred by

exhaustion, was heard from CMQ: Che, calling the population to col-laborate with the rebels. *The régime's military situation is getting worse by the day, as its soldiers do not wish to fight.* The message was rebroad-cast at two A.M. from Sancti-Spiritus and relayed from there by Radio Tiempo, Unión Radio, and Radio Nacional. A mysterious network passed on a message: Che asked that streets be blocked off to prevent armored cars from moving, and ordered the city's water and electric-ity supplies cut in order to increase pressure on the garrisoned forces. Another (and even more powerful) network in Santa Clara began to carry out Che's orders, blocking streets with cars that had flat tires, and with mattresses and furniture thrown out of windows.

A girl asked Che to pose for a photograph as he was leaving Sta-tion CMQ, and he agreed.

Che was perplexed; the situation was far from clear. True, his forces were making their way into the city, but they were far outnumbered and the light tanks made a great difference. A counterattack could have been fatal. Che told Fernández Mell that at least a month's fighting would be needed to take Santa Clara. The pressure had to be stepped up.

Che ordered the actual infiltration into the center of the city to begin. While Ramón Pardo's platoon, supported by the suicide squad, engaged the soldiers from the armored train who had been firing from the Capiro hill, the rest of the rebels advanced on the center of Santa Clara. They found, to their surprise, that people opened their doors to offer them glasses of water or cups of coffee.

On the southern front, the Directorio troops took advantage of the waning light after the bombing to launch a counterattack, which forced the Los Caballitos troops back into their barracks. On the Santo Domingo front, west of Santa Clara, Victor Bordón's troops had engaged, and managed to hold up, an enemy convoy with reinforce-ments for the city. In the approaches to Jatibonico, Olo Pantoja, and San Luis Reyes's platoons tried to ambush and check the advance of reinforcements headed for the garrison.

At nightfall, the rebels had come out ahead, despite their casual-ties and their very slow progress. They had managed to block rein-forcements coming from the east and west of Santa Clara, and they had practically taken Trinidad. With great difficulty, they were begin-ning to put pressure on the central districts of the city. The army, despite its enormous superiority in matériel and numbers, had not been able to launch a counterattack or even to mobilize its huge reserves in the Leoncio Vidal barracks. Civilians were barricading the streets to prevent tanks from coming into action.

That morning, as Captain Acevedo was setting up a machine gun in a house near the university, the owner, Professor Luis García, had asked if he would be allowed to retreat with the rebels if there was a withdrawal. Acevedo answered: "There'll be no retreat here, Doctor." It seemed he was about to be proven right.

On the night of December 28, Che regrouped his forces and tried to learn some sad lessons, to identify the most important things that the day had to teach them. He sent a message to Cubela: *We could barely advance. We lost four dead and several wounded. We will try our luck tonight. Give me your exact position so I can act more precisely. Che.*

Che did not sleep that night, but ran up and down the railroad tracks with an escort looking for a weak point in the armored train, and for the best place to pull up the rails. Shortly before dawn, using a yellow D-6 Caterpillar from the Santa Clara Agronomy Department, the rebels did destroy the rails, at a spot two and a half miles from the train. Now the army would not be able to pull the train back to the Leoncio Vidal barracks. Captain Acevedo recalled that Che "would at times do or order things whose immediate purpose escaped us, but which were the product of his great intuition as a fighter."

Once the train and the Capiro hill were cut off, Che ordered the advance into Santa Clara to proceed. The suicide squad was sent to attack the police station, Acevedo's men to fight in the area of the courthouse and prison, and Alberto Fernández's small platoon to the Grand Hotel. Captain Zayas's squad was ordered to fight the troops on the Capiro hill and Captain Alvarez to reinforce the Directory troops, who were contending with forces from the No. 31 Squadron headquarters and the Los Caballitos barracks. The reserve squad, led by Lieutenant Pablo Rivalta, was ordered to enter the Del Condado district and attack the Raúl Sánchez Building and the Martí Building and to undertake a holding operation against the forces from the Leoncio Vidal barracks. Cut the central forces off and attack the weaker positions — those had been Che's principles over the previous month.

Che's forces entered Santa Clara. Rivalta had been born in the neighborhood, so his men may have known where they were headed. But that was not the case with Acevedo's forces, who were advancing along the opposite sidewalk — or with the suicide squad, which was totally lost in Santa Clara. Che himself, who knew no more of Cuba than the Sierra Maestra, the Sierra Escambray, and the route he covered between them during the Invasion, had had to use the underground leadership to find his way in the blacked-out city, and particularly needed Aleida March's help. Santa Clara was now cut in half.

By dawn on December 29, the rebels were dispersed throughout Santa Clara. Years later Che was to comment, maybe in recalling that night, that the guerrilla fighter is a nighttime fighter; to say that is also to say that he has all the features of a nocturnal animal.

December 29 was to mark a turning point in the fighting in Santa Clara. Batista's army had managed to recover from the initial surprise, to mobilize and deploy its troops, and to counterattack against the guerrillas, whom they vastly outnumbered and outgunned. But Che's front was invisible — a nonexistent firing line that kept moving forward, cutting off enemy strongholds, immobilizing soldiers, and obtaining support from the population. Several years later, Che wrote a line in his book *Guerrade Guerrillas, Guerrilla Warfare*, that was to drive military theorists mad, being imbued with Che's particular humor: There are no definite firing lines. A firing line is more or less theoretical. Back then, on December 29, no mapmaker could have drawn the dividing line between soldiers and rebels; it did not exist. The rebels had infiltrated and blended into the urban landscape, broken through Colonel Casillas's defensive cordon, and hit straight home.

The Directorio's troops, which were attacking the Los Caballitos barracks, began a new approach at dawn. Rolando Cubela was injured in a burst of machine-gun fire, so Gustavo Machín Hoed, who had come to Che's forces from the Directorio, took charge of the attack.

Santa Clara, meanwhile, again lay helpless beneath an air raid: two B-26s were strafing the city. The journalist José Lorenzo Fuentes reported:

> Those living in the most fought-over zones fled their houses, horrified. Old people, women, and children were wandering the streets with small bundles of clothes under their arms, looking for the safest place to shelter and save their lives. Hunger, suffering, and terror were written on their faces. The air force was strafing the rooftops, and groups of civilians were wounded or killed. Many bodies had to buried in backyards without so much

as a coffin. A twelve-year-old boy was hit in the chest by machine-gun fire, and his parents could not even come close to him.

Acevedo's platoon attacked the barracks and the courthouse. Rivalta's entered the Del Condado district—where he was well known—amid popular acclamation. People came out into the street and gave the rebels food and coffee. Molotov cocktails began to be made, and citizens' militias were set up in the neighborhood. Pressure was brought to bear on the vicinity of the Leoncio Vidal barracks. The military made a couple of attempts to break through using tanks, but were driven back by gunfire and did not persist. Che brought the combat zone command headquarters closer, from the university to the Public Works Department offices and buildings on the Central Highway, less than a mile away, at the point where the railroad tracks had been pulled up.

Despite the initial successes, the fighting was not easy. *Our men were fighting against soldiers supported by armored units; we put them to flight, but many paid with their lives, and the improvised hospitals and cemeteries began to fill up with the dead and wounded.*

The Cowboy Kid's squad had taken over the railroad station. First Lieutenant Hugo del Río took a remarkable phone call there:

> The phone rang and I picked it up. It was a military chief asking me what the situation in the zone was like. I replied that the rebel army was on the city streets. He then told me not to worry, as the police would soon restore order. I answered that that would be difficult, since the rebel army dominated the situation. He asked who was talking. I answered First Lieutenant Hugo del Río. He asked whether I was with the Guards or the police. I answered neither, but the rebel army instead. . . . He became somewhat nastily annoyed and said it would take courage to come and see him at the Esperanza barracks. I informed Che, and he told me to go.

Toward one A.M., Che spoke with two of his captains, Guile Pardo and the Cowboy Kid, in a house belonging to Dr. Pablo Díaz. He had been directing military operations on the run, turning up suddenly at one point or another wherever in the city fighting was under way. He had a chaotic—but at least broad—view thanks to his contact with all the combat zones and his constant control of the action. A little later, the fighting for the police headquarters began, as did the attack on the Capiro hill, led by Guile's and Alfonso Zayas's platoons.

The rebels split into three groups and climbed the hill, lobbing grenades to flush out the soldiers. They were fired on with mortars. The rebels used the hill itself as cover from the train and managed to dislodge the soldiers in a frontal attack, with hand-to-hand fighting. The troops went down the other side of the hill and took refuge in the train cars. Toward three P.M., the train retreated to escape fire from the rebels, who were now taking advantage of being able to shoot downhill. The two locomotives pushed the train swiftly backward, but after about four kilometers the engineers suddenly realized that some twenty meters of track had been pulled up a short way ahead. The train buckled and ran off the rails. The locomotive crashed into a garage and destroyed some cars there. The noise was incredible — not just the crash, but the screech of metal from the derailed cars. The novelist Edmundo Desnoes observed:

> The train was lying immobile, all askew. Green Coca-Cola bottles, dark Hatuey beer bottles and colorless ones of Cawy; cans of Libby's tomato juice, of Bartlett pears, Campbell's soup, of asparagus and peas, were thrown all over the cars, overturned and twisted from end to end in the smoke and dust that enveloped the convoy.

Lieutenant Roberto Espinosa, with part of Guile's squad (Guile was with Che in the city center just then) advanced on the railroad cars at the junction of Independencia Street and the Camajuaní highway and captured forty-one soldiers without giving them a chance to react. Espinosa recalled: "The guards didn't dare to leave the train, so they didn't know how many of us there really were. We never stopped firing at them, and if anybody stuck his head out, that was that. Besides, they were confused by the crash and the derailing."

Eighteen rebels now controlled the 350 soldiers left on the train. A .30-caliber machine gun was set up on a rooftop thirty-five or forty yards away and riddled the cars' unarmored roofs. The first Molotov cocktails began to rain down on the train. Having taken three of the twenty-two cars, Espinosa kept up the pressure on the rest.

Che and Captain Pardo were in the town center engaging a tank when they were told of these events. Che got to the scene as fast as he could, then could not resist the temptation to throw himself into the middle of the fighting. He climbed onto the roof of one of the derailed cars, where there was a 20-millimeter cannon.

A very interesting fight then got under way, in which men were driven out of the armored train with Molotov cocktails. They were incredibly well armed, but willing to fight only at a distance, from comfortable positions and against a practically defenseless enemy, like the colonizers with the Indians in the American West. They were harassed by men who threw bottles of lighted gasoline at them from nearby points and adjacent cars. Thanks to its armor plating, the train became a real oven for the soldiers.

While he was fighting, a messenger came running to report that reinforcements for Batista's men were coming along the Camajuaní highway. Che left Pardo in command of the assault forces and headed off to organize the defense.

The shooting and Molotov-throwing continued. An hour later, Pardo proposed a truce. After talking to a sergeant, who threatened him with a Thompson submachine gun and refused to surrender, and then with the train's chief medic, he managed to speak to Commander Gómez Calderón, who agreed to parley with Che, but only on board the train. Pardo sent a messenger to find him. Che reappeared shortly; the news of the army's advance from Camajuaní had proved false, and he had not gone far. With him was Leovaldo Carranza from the Red Cross, who climbed up a lamppost and waved the white flag with the red cross in the middle of it to clear Che's way to the train. He heard a voice behind him saying, "Are you scared?" Aleida was there, smiling.

Leaving his gun behind, Che went halfway to meet Commander Gómez, who was carrying his. When Che pointed this out, he handed his pistol over to Carranza.

"I want to speak out of earshot of the troops," Gómez said, and Che agreed. They walked over to a railroad car together.

"Commander, I give you my word of honor that if you let us return to Havana, we won't fire another shot," Gómez said.

Che smiled. *I believe in your word of honor, but I cannot allow those bullets to kill more Cubans, either here or there.*

Che gave the troops a quarter of an hour to surrender and made the commander personally responsible for any subsequent bloodshed. But Gómez did not last the fifteen minutes. Seconds later the soldiers began to get down, unarmed.

The rebels gazed in amazement at the booty they had captured, like Ali Baba in the cave, like Pizarro finding the Incas' treasure: six bazookas, five 60-millimeter mortars, four .30-caliber machine guns, a 20-millimeter cannon, thirty-eight Browning light machine guns, grenades, 600 automatic rifles, a .50-caliber machine gun and almost a million rounds of ammunition: their anti-aircraft guns and machine guns; their fabulous quantities of ammunition . . . It was more weaponry than all the rebel forces put together had in Santa Clara.

The arms were taken to different parts of the city. By Che's order a bazooka quickly found its way to Camilo Cienfuegos in Yaguajay. As agreed, Che ordered three of his men — Dr. Adolfo Rodríquez de la Vega, Antonio Núñez Jiménez, and Serafín Ruiz de Zárate — to take the disarmed prisoners (almost 400 of them) to Caibarién, to be handed over to the commander of a navy frigate tied up there and be transported to Havana. Guevara had to get prisoners off his hands: he could not spare the men to guard them while the battle was in full swing. Besides, he was thinking about how demoralizing it would be when the defeated soldiers from the train turned up in Havana. Meanwhile the situation remained rather absurd: three revolutionaries transporting 400 men.

The air force began to bomb the wreckage of the train shortly afterward. Che asked an M26 activist to take a message to be broadcast from the radio station asking that reinforcements be sent down from Caballete de Casas, now that there were weapons to arm them with.

In Santa Clara, meanwhile, the rebel advance continued. Alberto Fernández's platoon was advancing on the Vidal barracks, after some heavy fighting on the way. The Cowboy Kid's squad, guided by a teenager, was approaching the police station. The Directorio forces were closing in on the No. 31 Squadron barracks. Hugo del Río's platoon joined forces with the Cowboy Kid's after a dramatic confrontation in which they collided with a light tank and an armored car and exchanged fire.

Although there was no electricity, a large number of townspeople continued to follow the fighting into the night; they found out about the armored train by listening to CMQ, which had been made operational by a group of underground M26 members under Che's orders. The station was using an auxiliary power plant and could be heard on battery-powered radios. The airwaves carried the following message:

> Attention; this is the Ciro Redondo Column, No. 8 Column of the July 26 Movement Rebel Army speaking. In a few moments we shall broadcast a message to the people of Cuba and especially Las Villas, about the advance of the rebel forces storming Santa Clara. Over three hundred officers and men belong to the Army Engineering Corps have just surrendered.

The next morning, December 30, Radio Rebelde denied in international news agency wire reports that Che was dead:

> For the peace of mind of relatives in South America and of the Cuban people, we wish to assure you that not only is Ernesto "Che" Guevara alive and in the line of fire, but he has occupied the armored train that we referred to some moments ago and will soon take the city of Santa Clara, which has been under attack for some days now.

The weaponry on the train had been used to mobilize the rest of the reserves in the camps at Caballete de Casas, El Pedrero, Gavilanes, and Manacas to reinforce the troops in the combat zone. Thanks to these new forces, the momentum from the day before, and the full support of the population, the various rebel squads were able to chalk up more victories.

The air force launched thirty sorties against the city that day. Shortly after the bombing, the Los Caballitos barracks fell into rebel hands. Some soldiers desperately tried to break out and make it to No. 31 Squadron headquarters, but were caught in the crossfire between the rebels and the Guards. Several were killed or wounded, and the Directory took the rest prisoner.

The fiercest fighting that day was at the police station, defended by almost 400 policemen supported by light tanks and commanded by Colonel Cornelio Rojas. Rojas had good reason not to want to surrender: he was known for his recent torture and murder of civilians. The Cowboy Kid's squad had engaged the station, but the rebels were having great difficulty in approaching it. Even with five other squads and some of Che's platoon helping them out, they had no more then seventy men among them. They could not move freely in the narrow streets around the station, and several had already been wounded. To make matters worse, the police station, facing the Del Carmen park, was just 500 yards away from the Leoncio Vidal barracks: a counter-attack might be launched at any time. Emérido Meriño had been drawing his squad closer to the police station, fighting house by house, picking off the guards one by one; by now his hat looked like a sieve. The Cowboy Kid ordered him to use a new tactic to find a better position from which to launch an attack: now they would advance *through* the houses. They began to knock down walls, with cooperation from the neighbors, and thus advance toward the church opposite the police station. A series of invisible avenues began to crisscross the neighborhood.

They advanced over the rooftops, too. The Cowboy Kid was taking too many risks, and his comrades chided him for it. As usual, he answered: "You never hear the bullet that's going to get you." He took up a position on a rooftop in Carofalo Street, some fifty meters from the police station, along with Orlando Beltrán and Leonardo Tamayo, who had recovered from his wounds at the Cabaiguán hospital. Orlando had this to report: "We had barely taken cover, and then we saw a group of six guards running across the park. We attacked them, but two tanks that were nearby began to fire at us with their thirty-caliber guns."

Tamayo provided the rest:

> I shouted, "Kid, hit the deck, or they'll kill you!" but he didn't. Just after that, I shouted, "Hey, what's up, why aren't you firing?" He didn't answer. I looked and saw he was covered in blood. We picked him up immediately and took him to the medic. But the wound was fatal, a shot in the head from an M1.

Che was advancing through the houses toward the positions from which the police station was being attacked when he saw the men carrying the Cowboy Kid's body. His grief-stricken words when he found that his most aggressive, flamboyant, and fearless captain had died were these: *They've killed a hundred of my men.*

After ordering that the Kid's body be taken to the hospital, Che went to the cordon surrounding the police station and named Tamayo and

Hugo del Río joint commanders of the platoon. Some soldiers wept while they fought. The pressure on the station was stepped up:

> We had managed to take the power station and the entire northwest of the city, broadcasting the news that Santa Clara was almost in rebel hands. In that announcement, which I made as commander-in-chief of the armed forces in Las Villas, I remember I had the sad duty of informing the people of Cuba that Roberto Rodriguez, the Cowboy Kid, was dead. He was short in stature and in years, the chief of the suicide squad, who took his life in his hands a thousand and one times in the fight for freedom.

Shortly afterward, Orestes Colina encountered Che, who had an enemy prisoner, a lieutenant, with him. In a fit of anger, Colima said, "What we have to do is kill this one." Che calmly replied: *Do you think we're like them?*

Zayas's squad was fighting to take the provincial government headquarters, which was protected by snipers on the roof of the Grand Hotel. There was fighting in the prison, in the courthouse. The soldiers fighting in the Carmelite church surrendered.

Night fell.

The day had also favored the rebels fighting on the other fronts in the city. In spite of air raids, Bordón's column liberated Santo Domingo for a second time and took the bridge over the Sagua River. To the east, in Jatibonico, San Luis and Olo Pantoja's platoons had been meeting with fierce resistance from enemy columns supported by armored cars, and had had a great day ambushing them. In Trinidad, the Directorio forces commanded by Faure Chomón had taken the last Batista stronghold there, the jail.

Ramiro Valdés, No. 8 Column deputy commander, had been in command of troops fighting on the eastern front since December 29. Now he took charge of getting the new "subcolumn" into shape, using Olo's and Acosta's platoons. This move allowed Che not only to bolster the holding operation and widen his range of options, but also to create a strategic reserve in case things did not turn out as planned in Santa Clara. Although he was placing all his bets on one single action, Che did retain the option of saving an important force from a possible defeat and thereby keeping the ability to rebuild the front should that prove necessary.

On December 31, a young journalist met Commander Guevara in the Public Works Building, where the Rebel Army's operations room was located. The bomb blasts from Batista's B-26s, still raiding the city, could be heard in the distance.

> Someone by my side pointed out Che to me, and indeed there he was, skinny, with his háir all matted, his arm in a sling, his uniform in shreds. Anyone would have taken him for the most ordinary soldier, were it not for the penetrating and unusually bright stare emanating from that tired face.

Che, on the verge of exhaustion, still had to handle the police station, which had cost him one of his best captains, and the Leoncio Vidal barracks, which, with its 1,300 men, still had firepower superior to all the revolutionary forces in the city. He also had to dislodge the snipers posted in the Grand Hotel and the courthouse, and take the Rural Guards barracks confronting the Directory column.

Che planned one last blow, which he based on an accurate assessment of the attitude prevailing among Batista's soldiers: their tendency not to take the offensive. He had the responsibility of throwing into combat, for the fourth day in a row, troops who had barely slept and were worn down by several weeks of continuous fighting, who had sustained major casualties among their commanding officers, and who had often fought against superior enemy forces that enjoyed tank support.

> I remember an episode that summed up the spirit of our forces in those final days. I had admonished a soldier for falling asleep during combat and he told me he had been disarmed for having missed a shot. With my usual terseness, I answered him, "Win yourself another rifle by going unarmed to the front line . . . if you're capable." Later, in Santa Clara, when I was encouraging the wounded at the blood transfusion center, a dying man touched my hand and said, "Remember, Commander? You asked me to go after a rifle in Remedios . . . well, I won it here." It was the fighter who'd missed the shot. He died a few minutes later, and he looked happy to have demonstrated his bravery to me.

The dead teenager was called Miguel Arguín.

There was fighting everywhere in Santa Clara that morning. Opposite the police station, the suicide squad, supported by reinforcements and wishing to avenge the death of the Cowboy Kid, was preparing the final attack. Inside the station, Colonel Rojas had murdered one of his men, a Captain Olivera, because he wanted to surrender. From the Carmelite church, which had been taken the day before by a group of rebels who had made a hole at the back, fighters were harassing the headquarters. A tank driver trying to leave the headquarters was hit in the head by a rebel bullet and his body stayed where it was. The dead inside the station were beginning to decompose, and the wounded could not be treated. The police were hungry, demoralized, and constantly under fire. Towards four P.M., Colonel Rojas asked for a truce to remove the wounded. Tamayo granted two hours and hinted that Rojas might consider surrender. They negotiated in the middle of the street, but did not reach an agreement. When the firing was about to get under way again, the colonel spoke once more to Tamayo, who walked off toward the station followed by some rebels, whom he had to stop. Once inside, he spoke directly to the policemen, telling them that if they no longer wished to fight, they should just throw down their guns and line up outside. The policemen began to leave the station as if Colonel Rojas himself had given the order. There were 396 of them, and just 130 rebels surrounding them. Rojas escaped in the confusion. The townspeople who entered the station found instruments of torture in the cellars.

The police station was not the only place to fall. The provincial government building, with its hundred soldiers, was attacked by Alfonso Zayas's forces in the front, and in the rear by Alberto Fernández's platoon, which managed to enter the building by knocking some walls down. There, Captain Pachungo Fernández, grenade in hand, took some soldiers by surprise and forced them to surrender.

Captain Acevedo's forces took the courthouse despite the tanks defending it. Five aircraft raided the city with 500-pound bombs, which destroyed houses as if they had been made of paper. The bombers struck particularly hard at the recently taken courthouse, but the anti-aircraft guns captured from the armored train were brought into action and the planes vanished from the skies over Santa Clara. The jail then fell to the rebels; the political prisoners were released, while the common criminals took advantage of the turmoil to escape through a hole in a wall. Rebel platoons coming from the city center began to put the Leoncio Vidal barracks under pressure, as did Rivalta's forces from the Del Condado district, who managed to dig themselves in a hundred yards from the base.

Fighting was under way at the Grand Hotel, where there were a dozen snipers on the tenth floor, as well as policemen and torturers — members of the hated SIM, the Military Intelligence Service. They were fired on from the park and the buildings opposite. Alberto Fernández led a group assigned to set fire to the second floor using Molotov cocktails. The soldiers were trapped in the hotel; their water had been cut off and they had no food. But they had wounded many civilians and militiamen crossing the park by sniping at them from the roof, and they still had ammunition. The squad led by the youngster Acevedo took part in a "window-breaking contest" with Batista's snipers. They were getting closer and closer.

In midafternoon, Che heard on the radio that the Yaguajay garrison had surrendered to Camilo's forces, which were now free for the final attack on the Leoncio Vidal barracks.

Colonel Casillas Lumpuy spoke to Batista at ten P.M., telling him that the city was about to fall to the rebels and that he urgently needed reinforcements. He did not get so much as a false promise from the dictator. After haranguing his officers and men and demanding heroic resistance from them, Casillas Lumpuy disguised himself in a straw hat and mufti and, claiming he had to make a tour of inspection in the province, escaped from the barracks together with his operations chief, Fernández Suero.

Batista's forces had just three armed enclaves left: the Grand Hotel, No. 31 Squadron headquarters, and the Leoncio Vidal barracks. Che knew that the final offensive on Santiago de Cuba was about to begin and that he urgently needed to mop up those three pockets of resistance. The year 1958 was about to end.

## 22. day one of the revolution

IN THE EARLY hours of January 1, 1958 — at 3:15 A.M., to be precise — four Aerovías Q civilian aircraft took off from the Columbia military base on the outskirts of Havana. Before climbing into the first one, Fulgencio Batista told General Eulogio Cantillo he was putting him in charge of the country, the business, the whole kit and caboodle.

Then he vanished into the skies. Batista was off to exile in Miami, although his entourage changed its flight plan on the wing and instead landed in Santo Domingo, home to that other bloodthirsty dictator Leónidas Trujillo. The Havana newspapers carried an Associated Press wire report that "government troops, with tank and air support, have routed rebel troops in the outskirts of Santa Clara and thrown them back toward the east of Las Villas Province."

Day had yet to break in Santa Clara; the guards in No. 31 Squadron headquarters had stopped shooting. Victor Dreke cautiously drew near. A white flag was waving from a window. Rolando Cubela, back with the troops after a lightning visit to the hospital, had just received a brief note from Che: *Rolando. Demand unconditional surrender. I will support you with the necessary forces. Greetings. Che.* No. 31 Squadron now surrendered. A rumor that Batista had fled made the rounds of the soldiers who had given themselves up. The rebels looked at each other in amazement. Was it all over? Captain Millán, in charge of the troops who had surrendered, was granted permission by the Directorio to use a microwave relay to contact the Leoncio Vidal barracks; the officer in charge there answered him with insults. The civilians came out onto the streets and, overjoyed, looked at the defeated soldiers in front of the barracks, which was pockmarked by hundreds of bullet holes. The prisoners were taken to Che at the rebel command headquarters.

The Grand Hotel was also about to fall. The snipers cut off on the tenth floor had had to drink coffee from ashtrays and had looted the bar. Captain Alfonso Zayas posted a tank in front of the hotel and shot the windows to pieces. Lieutenant Alberto Fernández's troops attacked and the snipers surrendered. The dozen policemen, stool pigeons, and torturers came out with their hands up and were showered with insults.

Only the Leoncio Vidal barracks was left. Colonel Cándido Hernández had taken charge there, replacing the runaways Casillas Lumpuy and Fernández Suero. Lieutenant Hugo del Río contacted the regiment from a radio in a patrol car captured from the police headquarters, and the officer who answered requested a truce. Del Río answered that only Che could grant the request but agreed to look for him to inform him of it. He found Che in the command headquarters in a meeting with the geographer, Antonio Núñez Jiménez, and Dr. Adolfo Rodríguez de la Vega. He and Che went to the patrol car and contacted the regiment by radio again. Che agreed to send Núñez

Jiménez and Rodríquez de la Vega to talk with Colonel Hernández. Shortly afterward the latter requested an indefinite truce, to which the emissaries replied that the only available option was unconditional surrender. Colonel Hernández, arguing that his brother and his son had already lost their lives in the fighting, that he had done more than enough to serve his country, handed over the command and the decision to his next in line, a Commander Fernández and his superior officers. Fernández then insisted on speaking with Che.

Just as the negotiations were about to begin, a broadcast by General Cantillo, speaking from the high command headquarters in Havana, was received at the Leoncio Vidal barracks.

> The news was very contradictory and extraordinary. Batista had fled the country that day, and the armed forces command came tumbling down. Our two delegates established radio contact with Cantillo, advising him of the offer to surrender, but he reckoned it was not possible to accept as it constituted an ultimatum and that he had occupied the army command under the strict orders of its leader Fidel Castro.

> Hernández asked Núñez and Rodrígnez to talk to Cantillo, who offered them a truce. They repeated that there could be only unconditional surrender. Cantillo tried to trick them, saying he had nominated a provisional government under Fidel Castro's orders and that under such conditions he could not hand over the barracks. The conversation ended amid insults.

A few hours earlier at 7:30 A.M. at the main quarters in the America sugar mill, Fidel Castro went to the door to drink a cup of coffee, cursing the irresponsible rebels for wasting ammunition by shooting into the air to celebrate the new year. The surprising news Batista's flight, picked up by Radio Rebelde, made Fidel angry: the dictator had escaped and the event smelled like a coup d'état. He began to gather his captains together to march on Santiago.

The news was confirmed. Supreme Court judge Carlos Piedra was now president. Cantillo, who had been conspiring with the aid of the U.S. embassy to find an easy way out of the revolution, was army chief.

Fidel set a piece of paper on a wardrobe and wrote: "Revolution, yes, military coup, no." Then he wrote a call for a general strike. He took a jeep to the Radio Rebelde station to record the message. It was on the air by ten A.M. and was later relayed by dozens of radio stations across the country and in Latin America.

Che heard Fidel's message at about the same time as he received the latest information from the besieged barracks.

> We got in touch with Fidel immediately, giving him the news but telling him our opinion of Cantillo's attitude, which was just what he thought, too. To create a military junta would just waste the revolution by forcing it to negotiate with the remains of the dictatorship.

Commander Hernández insisted on speaking to Che. Núñez and Rodríguez went with him. Che was very sharp with the regiment's new commander. He reportedly said:

> Look, Commander, my men have already discussed this matter with the high command. It's either unconditional surrender or fire, but real fire, and with no quarter. The city is already in our hands. At 12:30 I will give the order to resume the attack using all our forces. We will take the barracks at all costs. You will be responsible for the bloodshed. Furthermore, you must be aware of the possibility that the U.S. government will intervene militarily in Cuba; if that happens, it will be even more of a crime as you will be supporting a foreign invader. In that event, the only option will be to give you a pistol to commit suicide, as you'll be guilty of treason to Cuba.

Commander Hernández went back to talk matters over with his officers. Soldiers were already deserting their posts and fraternizing with the rebels. The military hesitated. With a few minutes left before the appointed time and with the rebel rifles primed and ready to fire, they agreed to a negotiated surrender: they could leave the barracks unarmed and be sent to Havana via Caibarién. Those who had committed violence against the population would be excluded from the agreement.

As the negotiations proceeded outside the barracks, and with ten minutes left before firing would resume, the soldiers began to throw their weapons down of their own accord and walk unarmed over to the rebel lines. It was 12:20 P.M. on January 1, 1959. With the fall of the Leoncio Vidal barracks, the battle for Santa Clara was over. The rebel forces took the airfield without firing a shot.

Photographs show the townspeople of Santa Clara looking in amazement at the smashed-up boxcars and the mass of twisted iron that are the wreckage of the armored train: the victorious rebels in front of immobile tanks; the bearded young rebels, the *barbudos*, in front of the pockmarked barracks, now in silence; groups of Batista's disarmed soldiers around a young rebel who is lecturing them; Che giving instructions beside a tank, holding his injured left arm up with his right. Below the beret with the metal crossed-swords badge on it, his eyes are glassy with fatigue; a cigar hangs loosely from his lips, and he's cracking a smile.

Fidel urged the final attack in a quick succession of communiqués over Radio Rebelde that demanded the surrender of the Santiago garrison and ordered Che and Camilo Cienfuegos to advance on Havana. Che was to take the La Cabaña fortress and Camilo Batista's stronghold at Columbia. Víctor Mora's column was ordered to take the cities of Guantánamo, Holguín, and Victoria de las Tunas. The general strike in Santiago was called for three P.M.

Enrique Oltuski, the July 26 Movement regional coordinator, who had been frantically traveling, with one mishap after another, as to bring a message to Che from Fidel, arrived at Santa Clara in the midst of street parties. He found Che in the operations room at the Public Works Building:

Che was standing behind a large bureau, opposite me. He had one arm in a cast and a sling made from a black rag. We briefly exchanged greetings. He waved at me to wait while he gave instructions to a rebel who, too young for a beard, had let his hair grow.

The room was small and completely closed in. I began to feel hot. Then I could smell the clinging odor of Che's body. The time went by very slowly. I took Fidel's message out of the lining of my pants; it was the order to advance on Havana. Finally, the rebel left and I handed the paper over to Che.

When he'd finished reading it, he turned to the window and looked outside:

Yes, I already knew. We'll set off in a few hours.

"But how?"

We managed to establish radio contact with Fidel.

I felt enormously frustrated. . . .
He has already designated a civil governor of the province. He was referring to a man from his column (Captain Calixto Morales), but at the heart of the matter was the political mistrust in which Che held us, the representatives from the Plains.

In Havana, meanwhile, as soon as the news broke that Batista had fled the country, students began to gather at the university, and M26 banners were unfurled on the university hill. The population crowded the streets. There was looting in the Biltmore and the Sevilla Plaza hotels and the casinos. M26 militias took over newspapers sympathetic to Batista. The police machine-gunned the boroughs; political prisoners in the Príncipe prison were freed. The Resistencia Cívica group took over the CMQ radio station. In the midst of the turmoil, urban M26 and Front II cadres began to fill a very precarious power vacuum, as there were still thousands of Batista's soldiers in the barracks who might rush in to set up a military dictatorship. The police abandoned various stations, and only a few precincts fired in response to the growing crowds on the streets.

At two P.M. U.S. ambassador Earl T. Smith, accompanied by the rest of the diplomatic corps, met with Cantillo (not with President Piedra; they were under no illusions about where power really lay). The United States was looking for a way, with the departure of the dictatorship, that would avoid backing Fidel and the M26 but would also exclude forces loyal to Batista and keep up the appearance of neutrality. The takeover sector was the "good military" group, headed by Colonel Ramón Barquín and Borbonet, who had conspired to overthrow Batista. They were in jail, but Cantillo gave way to U.S. pressure and at seven P.M., released the officers from Pinos Island, along with M26 leader Armando Hart.

The people were out on the streets. Street parties were engulfing Santa Clara with cheering and shouts, and the rebels were the crowds' booty. Singing and dancing were the order of the day in the liberated city, but there were also demands that captured torturers be sent to the firing squad.

Oltuski also recalled:

The news that the dictatorship's army had surrendered spread throughout the city and thousands closed in upon the building where we were. They knew that Che was there and no one wanted to miss the opportunity to meet him. We had to put guards at the entrance to keep from being overwhelmed by the mass of humanity.

On the floor above was an improvised prison for war criminals from the forces of repression who, one by one, were being uncovered and caught by the people.

The sources contradict each other concerning names and numbers, but there is no doubt that in the hours following the liberation of Santa Clara, Che signed death warrants for several of Batista's policemen whom the people accused of being torturers and rapists, beginning with detainees who had acted as snipers in the Grand Hotel, including Casillas Lumpuy, who was captured by Víctor Bordón's men while attempting to leave town. *I did no more and no less than the situation demanded—i.e., the death sentence for those twelve murderers, because they had committed crimes against the people, not against us.* As it happened, Casillas was not executed but died in a struggle with one of the guards taking him to the firing squad. The photo of Casillas in a short-sleeved checked shirt, trying to take a rifle from the soldier guarding him, was to go around the world. Police chief Cornelio Rojas, who had been arrested in Caibarién while attempting to escape, was shot a couple of days later.

Whereas Che's and the Directory's fighters kept a tight grip on weapons and the situation on the street in Santa Clara, the crowds in Havana were exacting a long-delayed justice. A sort of reasoned and selective vandalism took hold of the crowds, who attacked the gas stations belonging to Shell, which was said to have collaborated with Batista by giving him tanks. They also destroyed the casinos belonging to the American Mafia and the Batista underworld, trashed parking meters—one of the régime's scams—and attacked houses belonging to leading figures in the dictatorship. (They threw Mujal's air-conditioning unit out the window.) There was no control by the repressive apparatus of the dictatorship, which was falling apart by the second with the massive exodus of Batista's cadres; neither Cantillo nor Barquín could fill the resulting power vacuum, because the revolutionary forces refused to enter into negotiations. Television studios were taken over and witnesses gave spontaneous testimony to the horrors of the now-ended Batista régime.

The surrender of Santiago was agreed to at nine P.M. Fidel entered the capital of Oriente Province; Judge Manuel Urrutia swore him in as president; and he announced his march on Havana and reiterated his call for a revolutionary strike. Radio Rebelde declared a liquor ban in the occupied cities.

Che began to regroup the separate platoons in his column in Santa Clara. Víctor Bordón's and Ramiro Valdés's forces were called up. Cars with loudspeakers cruised the streets, calling the rebels to rejoin the column. Che found out that some fighters were taking cars abandoned in the streets by escaped Batista supporters; he angrily ordered the keys to be handed over. *They were not going to ruin in one second what the Rebel Army had maintained as a standard: respect for others. They were going to Havana—by truck, bus, on foot, but it was the same for everyone.* He really chewed out Rogelio Acevedo, who was still a teenager and had requisitioned a '58 Chrysler.

During this time, Che received a communiqué from Eloy Cutiérrez Menoyo, placing the Front II forces at his disposal. There was no problem. We then gave them instructions to wait as we had to settle civilian affairs in the first major city to be conquered. A fighter named Mustelier asked Che to grant him leave to go and see his family in Oriente Province; the commander tersely told him no.

"But, Che, we've already won the revolution."

*No, we've won the war. The revolution begins now.*

Camilo arrived at the head of his column that night, and the two friends met up in the Public Works Building while Camilo's column prepared 600 sandwiches and twenty-four crates of Hatuey malt beer. They were to be the first to set off for Havana. By order of Fidel Castro, Che marched without the Directorio forces that had accompanied him during the previous days of fighting in Santa Clara. Why? Was Fidel's decision due to a burst of sectarianism, or to political mistrust, in those moments of uncertainty, of a force composed in large part of the radical student wing? Was it due to a desire that the July 26 Movement alone capitalize on victory? The reason behind this unfortunate decision will never be clear. A little earlier, Che had met with Faure Chomón from the Directorio, who had just arrived from Trinidad. He had to explain to Faure that his orders were to march alone to the capital. After a month of complete cooperation between the two revolutionary forces, it was no easy task to explain why Fidel had excluded Chomón's troops (or at least kept them on the sidelines) from the final offensive.

Oltuski remembered:

> There were few of us left in the Public Works Building. The fatigue accumulated over many days had taken its toll, and some went home; others lay down on the ground or on the sandbags in the ramparts.
>
> Everybody was asleep in the hall, except for Camilo—who had just arrived—Che, and I. Camilo was pouring out his endless witticisms relating the funny aspects of his latest adventures. We were stretched out on the floor, leaning on some sacks, in the faint lamplight coming in through the windows.
>
> Somebody came and brought a basket full of apples and then we realized it was the new year—and, despite the differences that had arisen between us, I felt good among those men. The noise was building up outside, and then some rebels came in and said they were ready. We stood up and went out. The night was cool. The air was filled with the sound of engines and light from motor headlamps. There were few bystanders around at that time. Relatives of some of the murderers were lying against the walls, asleep.

Camilo's column set off toward Havana at 5:50 A.M. on January 2.

## 23. the long january of 1959

THROUGHOUT THE MORNING of January 2. cars with loudspeakers drove around the streets relaying a message that was also broadcast on Radio Rebelde and repeated over and over: "Members of Number 8 Column are hereby advised that by order of Commander Ernesto Che Guevara, they are to regroup immediately at the camp, to get organized and march on."

Toward three P.M., some 400 men lined up outside the Leoncio Vidal barracks and left Las Villas in jeeps, trucks, and tank transports. Che traveled in a decommissioned olive-colored Chevrolet, with Aleida March and his entourage: Harry Villegas, Hermes Peña, Mendoza Argudín, and, at the wheel, Alberto Castellanos. It was not very comfortable with six in the car. Che, who was not too confident of the countryfolk's driving abilities, threatened with a smile that: *I'll shoot anyone who hits a pedestrian or crashes.*

A second contingent from No. 8 Column, headed by Ramiro Valdés, who had to gather some soldiers, would follow later.

Meanwhile in Havana, with the remains of Bastista's dictatorship either fleeing or collapsing, sporadic gunfights were breaking out between urban militias and the police or paramilitary forces such as Senator Mansferrer's "Tigers." The Príncipe prison was raided and the inmates freed. Cars cruised the streets with their hoods up. In the early afternoon, workers gathered in the Central Park in support of the revolution. The July 26 Movement flag was flown from surrounding buildings, and posters supporting Fidel appeared.

The 150-strong Angel Amejeiras column—militiamen who had been operating in the city's outskirts and were led by Che's old friend Victor Paneque—was the first to enter the city. They billeted themselves in the Sports Palace. Eloy Gutiérrez Menoyo arrived at the head of the Escambray Front II column, which was quartered in the Vedado Institute. He had "heroically" entered Havana. We thought it might be a maneuver to try to build their strength up, to take power or stir something up. We already knew them, but were getting to know them better by the day.

The advance guard from Camilo Cienfuegos's column entered the Columbia base at 5:15 P.M. with no opposition from the "good" military officers who had replaced Batista's men in command at the country's most important military base. Camilo received a call there from Che, who was halfway to Havana with a column whose ranks had been swelled by militiamen.

Che beheld Havana, the country's capital city, for the first time in the middle of the night. He had heard a thousand tales of Havana, but had never seen it. He went up the Boyeros road to the La Cabaña camp in a three-car convoy. Che did not hesitate; he walked straight in. Just as Camilo had done some hours before. He was received by Varela, a "true military" officer, who immediately handed over command to him. Varela had spent the previous hours refusing to eat or drink, terrified that the garrison, loyal to Batista, might have poisoned him.

Is that what victory was like? A lackluster entry into a barracks in the dead of night whose commanding officer surrendered before being asked?

Che assigned guard duty and ordered that accounts be drawn up and weapons be strictly accounted for. He then deployed the 600 men who were now in his column. At dawn he went to CMQ, the most important radio and TV station in Havana, where he was held up at the door by militiamen in the July 26 Movement urban network who did not recognize him. But he was allowed through without having to make too many explanations, and managed to establish radio contact with Fidel, who was in Bayamo with Camilo, who had flown east to report on the bloodless occupation of the garrisons in Havana.

Che was worn out, but as Antonio Sánchez Díaz — "Pinares" — one of Camilo's officers, put it: "You couldn't rest in Havana, either on your laurels or in bed; the place was buzzing."

The eighteenth-century fortress of La Cabaña dominates Havana, looking out over a deep bay, a complex of barracks, moats and forts, casemates, and office buildings. The ramparts are covered in ivy and colonial-era cannons can still be seen on the old patios. In the early hours of January 3, Che assembled the 3,000 soldiers from Batista's army who were in the fortress and made a conciliatory speech; The rebels still did not know what to expect from them. The guerrillas will have to learn about discipline from you, and you will have to learn from the guerrillas how to win a war. He had not slept.

In one of the barracks offices, Che found a sergeant behind a typewriter. He stared at him.

Did you take part in the fighting?

"No, I'm an office worker."

Have you tortured anyone?

The man shook his head. Che asked him if he could type. He nodded.

Go, take off your uniform and come back here.

He thus struck up a friendship with José Manuel Manresa that was to last for the next five years.

There were celebrations in the streets, and the general strike began. In those first three days, 800 exiles flew back from all over the Americans. Fidel slowly and surely buttressed his political conquest rather than consolidating the military victory as he advanced toward Havana. He later said: "I had some trouble getting the column on the move and calling it to order with machines here, there, and everywhere, and I'll say it was just as well we didn't have to fight. The way things were, an order for mortar fire would have led to a journalist shooting pictures."

The news of a new government, first broadcast by Radio Rebelde, had now made the newspapers: Manuel Urrutia was president, Dr. José Miró Cardona prime minister; the cabinet was dominated by the moderate bourgeois opposition, with a sprinkling of July 26 Movement members, but minus the other two allied forces in the rebellion, the Communist People's Socialist Party and the Directory. The rebels were in almost complete control of the army (they had taken over the post of commander-in-chief and named regional commanders, although they did relinquish command in Santiago for several days to Rego Rubido, a Batista supporter who had been minister of war) and the police (whose new head was Efigenio Ameijeiras). They were also in charge of the recently created Ministry of Embezzled Goods (Faustino Pérez) which would investigate corruption in Batista's administration; the Ministry of Education (Armando Hart); the Health Ministry (Julio Martínez Páez, a medic from the Sierra); the Interior Ministry (Luis Orlando Rodríguez); the Labor Ministry (Marcelo Fernández); and the Communications Ministry (Enrique Oltuski). The liberal opposition was a bland group. All in all, an odd government.

Some of those excluded showed little readiness to accept the fact. To show that they occupied some space in the revolutionary process, the Directorio column entered Havana at four P.M. and occupied the National Palace.

After Carlos Franqui arrived in Havana, the July 26 Movement's *Revolución* became a widely circulated newspaper. The movement took over the plant and offices of a pro-Batista paper. An advertisement ran on an inside page showing, in plain fifties style, a bearded rebel (grenade in belt) and a painter finishing a slogan declaring "All our trust" between the two figures. The ad also praised the DuPont Interamerican Chemical Company; that love affair was to be short-lived.

On the night of January 4, the Directorio announced that it would expect to set forth three conditions at meetings with President Urrutia in the National Palace. On January 5, while Fidel was still marching toward Havana, Che met Camilo in the Columbia base. Carlos Franqui was present:

Then Che turned up in his Bohemian suit, calmly smoking a pipe and looking like a revolutionary prophet. There was trouble in the Presidential Palace. The Revolutionary Directorio had moved in there. Che hadn't been to see Faure Chomón, and

Rolando Cubela hadn't wanted to receive him. . . . The Directorio never took to Urrutia. . . . There was no lack of mistrust, intrigues, and so on, on one side or the other. . . . Camilo half-jokingly said we should fire a couple of cannonades to warn Cubelas that he'd better hand over the Palace. As I had no liking for the Palace, I said it sounded like a good idea to me, but Che, with his responsible attitude, said it wasn't the time for cannonades of that sort; he patiently went back to the Palace, met Faure Chomón, and worked things out.

A confrontation had been avoided, but dissension had not. The Directorio agreed to leave the palace, and its troops then occupied the University of Havana, but Faure Chomón issued a statement to the press saying: "We understand that what is happening in Santiago de Cuba is not correct; we believe that if our sacrifices are not to have been in vain, the entire revolutionary movement should be organized in one single revolutionary party." Naming Santiago the provisional capital was a tactical measure by Fidel to prevent the emergence of a conciliatory government in Havana. The designation would not last a week, and that annoyed the unfairly sidelined members of the Directorio.

That night Che took a light plane to the Camagüey airport in the middle of the island to report to Fidel on the situation in Havana. Fidel was slowly approaching Havana in a triumphal convoy. The two commanders had not seen each other for almost six months, since Che left the Sierra Maestra at the head of No. 8 Column. They were later to be joined by President Urrutia, who flew in from Santiago. The World Wide Press photo taken of them shows Fidel and Che sharing knowing smiles.

U.S. Ambassador Earl Smith was far from all smiles when he left the Columbia base after meeting with Camilo to ask the rebels not to execute General Cantillo. Smith, frankly hostile to the winners, would later say that the bearded revolutionaries reminded him of characters from a movie he had just seen about John Dillinger.

On January 5, after constant delays and several false starts, President Urrutia landed at Boyeros airport on the outskirts of Havana. Camilo had decreed martial law and deployed men from his column. The Directorio handed the palace over to Urrutia at seven P.M. Strife among the revolutionaries had been held in check. Martial law was lifted during a first cabinet session. Earl Smith turned up toward the end of the meeting; accused of having been Batista's most important prop, he was not popular, and his presence and pretensions of dictating conditions angered the armed revolutionaries. *Bohemia* magazine reported: "The fighters' anger was checked only out of respect for our northern neighbor."

Che gave his first interviews in his office in La Cabaña, in a narrow room with a desk at one end, whose best attribute was four small windows looking out over Havana Bay. The Capitol dome could be seen in the distance. He spoke first to the Argentina newspaper *La Tarde*, then to *Revolución* and *El Mundo*, and over the following days to *Prensa Libre*, *Bohemia*, and a host of international correspondents. For a whole week he was waylaid by the press. First he offered a counterattack: *To label "Communists" all those who refuse to bow down is an old dictator's trick; the July 26 Movement is a democratic movement.*

The interviewee answered phone calls, each of which hurt his injured wrist. He was not quite comfortable with the press, not used to the flood of journalists: *what we are doing for the freedom of the people is not for publication, and even less so are aspects of our personal lives.* In one of those interviews from the first week of the revolution, someone told him the anecdote about how Batista's army's broadcasts used to call him the "rebel on a donkey." *Praise indeed,* Che replied.

He did not quite feel as if he fitted in, maybe because he did not understand what his place and position were at that stage of the revolutionary process. Even his opinions on agrarian reform were cautious: *One of the basic measures will be to give campesinos the treatment they deserve,* he said, as if a radical agrarian reform were not essential for him, as if he did not know what rights the countryfolk had after contributing to the victory. He offered commonplaces, such as *Unity is an essential factor* or truisms, such as *The lie has been given to the assertion that you cannot rebel against the army in Cuba.* He seemed unsettled ideologically, lacking in clarity, inclined to self-censor his comments to the press. He obviously had not found a place for himself in the victory.

The journalists found Aleida March among the rebel army officers in Che's entourage. They were not in Las Villas, and Aleida was an unknown quantity. She also granted an interview, one of the few she ever gave:

I can't say I'm Che's secretary, because I'm a fighter. I fought beside him in the Las Villas campaign and took part in all the engagements there. That makes me his orderly. . . . When it became practically impossible for me to continue living in Santa Clara, due to my revolutionary activities, I decided to join the ranks of those fighting the dictatorship by taking up arms. . . . I confess that I found life there difficult at first, but then got used to it, especially after our first clashes with the enemy were over.

They could get no more out of her.

On January 8, Che heard the popular acclaim that greeted the arrival of Fidel's column from the La Cabaña fortress. Through binoculars, he watched the jeep at the head of the column, in which Fidel stood beside Camilo. The crowd made it physically impossible for vehicles to move.

# FRIENDS AND COMRADES
## HILDA GADEA

from *ERNESTO: A MEMOIR OF CHE GUEVARA*

### 1972

A t Lima's airport one of my sisters greeted me joyfully: "Ernesto wrote to you!"

"How do you know?"

"Because we opened it," she said.

I protested: "But it was a letter for me."

"But we were just as anxious as you," she went on; "the envelope had Cuban stamps and we were sure that it was from him. We opened it but the handwriting was illegible, but it does say something like 'Ernesto . . .'"

As soon as I arrived at the house I read the letter. At last I was hearing from him. He was alive, he was thinking of me and the baby. He expressed his deep trust in the campaign that had been begun and in the future of our struggle. I remembered his words of farewell in Mexico: "Anything can happen to us, but the revolution will triumph."

Knowing what it would mean to them, I wrote his parents and forwarded Ernesto's letter, asking them to please return it. From then on, although always with a certain anxiety, we looked forward to his letters. This is what the first one said:

January 28, 1957

*Querida vieja:*

Here in the Cuban jungle, alive and bloodthirsty, I'm writing these inflamed, Martí-inspired lines. As if I really were a soldier (I'm dirty and ragged, at least), I am writing this letter over a tin plate with a gun at my side and something new, a cigar in my mouth. It was rough. As you probably know, after seven days of being packed like sardines in the now famous *Granma*, we landed at a dense, rotting mango jungle through the pilots' error. Our misfortunes continued until finally we were surprised in the also now famous Alegría, and scattered like pigeons. I was wounded in the neck, and I'm still alive only due to my cat's lives—a machine-gun bullet hit a cartridge case in my chest pocket and the bullet ricocheted and nicked my neck. For a few days I walked through those hills thinking I was seriously wounded because the bullet had banged my chest so hard. Of the boys you met there in Mexico, only Jimmy Hirtzel was killed, executed after surrendering. Our group, including Almeida and Ramirito, whom you know, spent seven days of hunger and terrible thirst until we were able to slip through the cordon and, with help from the peasants, get back to rejoin Fidel. (One of those reported possibly dead is poor Ñico.) After lots of difficulties we got reorganized and rearmed, and attacked a troop barracks, killing five soldiers, wounding others, and taking some prisoners. It was a major surprise to the army, who thought we were completely dispersed. They increased the martial law rules throughout the country and extended them for 45 days more, and sent picked troops after us. We fought these off and this time it cost them three dead and two wounded. They left the dead on the mountain. Soon after we caught three guards and took their guns. Add to all this the fact that we had no losses and the mountain is ours and you'll get an idea of the demoralization of the army. We slip through their hands like soap just when they think they have us trapped. Naturally the fight isn't all won, there'll be many more battles. But so far it's going our way, and each time it will do so more.

Now, to you. Are you still at the address I'm writing to? And how are you all, specially "love's petal most profound"? Give her the biggest hug and kiss she can take. To the rest, an *abrazo* and my best. With my rushed departure I left my things at Pancho's. Your pictures and the baby's are among them. Please send them when you write. You can write to my uncle's house, using Patojo's name. The letters will be delayed a while, but I think I'll get them. A big *abrazo* for you.

CHANCHO.

Along with everything else, during those days, I had the misfortune of losing my mother. The emotional load broke me down physically and I had to see a doctor. He recommended that I try to keep my mind occupied, busying myself with a variety of tasks. I began to work as an auditor in a school, and I kept the accounting books for several small businesses. In addition, with the idea of carrying on propaganda for the 26th of July Movement—or M-26, as it was now abbreviated—I rejoined the Aprista Party. Soon I was elected to the post of secretary of statistics on the National Executive Committee.

From the moment I got Ernesto's first letter, I searched for some way to help the M-26. The struggle was very difficult and the odds great. But Ernesto still had enthusiasm and faith in the success of the venture, if each worked in whatever area he could. I couldn't fight in Cuba because I had to take care of my daughter, but I could carry out tasks outside.

I asked General Bayo, with whom I regularly corresponded, to put me in touch with the Committee for Activities Abroad. He did so, sending the address of José Garcerán, who was in charge of the Mexican committee. Later he would be smuggled into Cuba and would take part in the action against the Goycuría Barracks, where he died. Garcerán put me in touch with the New York committee, headed at the time by Mario Llerena, and he, in turn, sent me a credential so that I could represent the 26th of July Movement in Peru. Afterward the committee would be headed by Antonio Buch, Haydée Santamaría, and José Llanuse, the last mentioned in office when final victory came.

I worked, complying with instructions sent me by the committee, on propaganda and money collection. The committee would send me the newspaper *Sierra Maestra*, Fidel's speeches, and the news bulletins that were issued in *Sierra*. These I would have reprinted, distributed, or published in certain newspapers and magazines in Peru. I founded a movement for the liberation of Cuba, with the support of the members of the leftist wing within APRA, and we were able to help several Cuban exiles who took refuge in Peru.

Letters came from time to time from Ernesto. Only a few of mine managed to reach him, however, although I followed his instructions. He never got the pictures of the baby and me he had asked for. Later, when I had set up formal communications with the committee in New York, he began getting my letters. When Hildita was two years old, February 15, 1958, I wrote Ernesto and asked him to authorize my coming to the mountains of Cuba, to be with him and help; the child was then old enough to be cared for by either my family or his. His reply took about four or five months to arrive. He said I couldn't come yet; the fight was at a dangerous stage, and an offensive would begin in which he himself would not remain in any one place. The coup of March 13 by the Directorio against Batista had failed, as had the strike of April 8 sponsored by the 26th of July Movement, and the opposition was intense. But in the mountains Fidel and his comrades grew daily stronger. Not only had they turned back the June–July offensive of Batista's army, but they had opened a second front, commanded by Raúl Castro. They planned to come down from the mountains onto the plains in August.

Several more times there were announcements of Ernesto's death in combat, each a time of anguish for me. I particularly remember toward the end of December 1958, the news that Ernesto had died in the battle for Santa Clara, heading the column Ciro Redondo. This was the battle that had been fought by the people of Las Villas Province against the Batista puppets, in which the people derailed the bulletproof train carrying government reinforcements. With this action government resistance was practically wiped out. On January 1, 1959, the bloody ex-sergeant Batista fled the country with his closest collaborators.

The well-known events subsequent to that date now belong to history.

It was also on January 1, 1959, that I arrived in Havana with my little daughter. With the candor that always characterized him Ernesto forthrightly told me that he had another woman, whom he had met in the campaign of Santa Clara. The pain was deep in me, but, following our convictions, we agreed on a divorce.

I am still affected by the memory of the moment when, realizing my hurt, he said: "Better I had died in combat."

For an instant I looked at him without saying anything.

Though I was losing so much at that time, I thought of the fact that there were so many more important tasks to be done, for which he was so vital: he *had* to have remained alive. He had to build a new society. He had to work hard to help Cuba avoid the errors of Guatemala; he had to give his whole effort to the struggle for the liberation of America. No, I was happy that he had not died in combat, sincerely happy, and I tried to explain it to him this way, ending with: "Because of all this, I want you always."

Moved, he said: "If that's how it is, then it's all right . . . friends, and comrades?"

"Yes," I said.

The divorce was granted on the twenty-second of May 1959. Ernesto remarried on the second of June.

# PART four
# CASTRO'S BRAIN

"Our economic war will be fought against the big power to the north. . . .
Our road to liberation will be opened up with a victory of the monopolies,
and concretely over the U.S. monopolies."

*—ERNESTO CHE GUEVARA, 1960*

# THE SUPREME PROSECUTOR
## JON LEE ANDERSON

from *CHE GUEVARA: A REVOLUTIONARY LIFE*

1997

It is impossible for revolutionary laws to be executed unless
the government itself is truly revolutionary.

**—LOUIS ANTOINE LEON DE SAINT-JUST, *1789*,**
**DURING THE FRENCH REVOLUTIONARY "TERROR"**

■

The executions by firing squads are not only a necessity for the people of Cuba,
but also an imposition by the people.

**—CHE GUEVARA, FEBRUARY 5, 1959,**
**IN A LETTER TO LUIS PAREDES LÓPEZ OF BUENOS AIRES**

I

IN BUENOS AIRES, the Guevara family was celebrating the New Year
when they heard the news flash of Batista's flight. Exactly two years
since a mysterious hand had delivered "Teté's" letter with confirma-
tion that he was still alive, now the Guevaras once again had a reason to rejoice for Ernesto: The international wires were reporting that

the rebel columns led by Che Guevara and Camilo Cienfuegos were advancing on Havana.

Their jubiliation was short-lived. As his father recalled, "In our house we had not yet put down the drinks toasting the fall of Batista when some terrible news came. Ernesto had been fatally wounded in the taking of the Cuban capital." Once again, Guevara Lynch made desperate inquiries to find out if the news was true, and two agonizing hours went by before the July 26 representative in Buenos Aires called to say the report was false. "We celebrated the New Year that night with the happiness that Ernesto lived and that he was in charge of the La Cabaña garrison in Havana," wrote his father.

Che's entourage arrived at the huge old Spanish colonial fortress in the predawn darkness of January 3. Its regiment of three thousand troops, which had already surrendered to July 26 militiamen, stood in formation as Che arrived. He addressed them patronizingly as a "neocolonial army" who could teach his rebel troops "how to march," while the guerrillas could teach them "how to fight." Then he and Aleida installed themselves in the *comandante*'s house, built against the stone buttresses overlooking Havana.

The day before, Camilo had shown up at the military headquarters of Camp Columbia across the city and taken over its command from Colonel Ramón Barquín; General Cantillo had been arrested. Fidel had also made his triumphal entry into Santiago. Speaking before cheering crowds, he declared the city Cuba's provisional "capital," and proclaimed Manuel Urrutia, who had flown in from Venezuela, as the new president.

Carlos Franqui, who was with Fidel, couldn't understand why Che had been relegated to La Cabaña. "I remember pondering at length the reasons for this order of Fidel's: Camp Columbia was the heart and soul of the tyranny and of military power. . . . Che had taken the armored train and the city of Santa Clara, he was the second most important figure of the Revolution. What reasons did Fidel have for sending him to La Cabaña, a secondary position?"

Fidel had undoubtedly chosen the less visible position for Che because he wanted him out of the limelight. To the defeated regime, its adherents, and Washington, Che was the dreaded "international Communist," and it was only asking for trouble to give him a preeminent role so early on. By contrast the handsome, Stetson-wearing, baseball-playing, womanizing, humorous Camilo was Cuban, not known to be a Communist, and had already become a popular folk hero. *He* could take center stage.

Fidel needed Che for the indispensable job of purging the old army, to consolidate victory by exacting revolutionary justice against traitors, *chivatos*, and Batista's war criminals. Just as his brother Raúl, the other radical, was to be in Oriente—where Fidel had left him behind as military governor—Che was essential to the success of this task in Havana.

**II**

FROM THE GREEN rolling head of land where La Cabaña and its adjacent fortress El Morro sprawled, guarding Havana harbor, Che's view in January 1959 would have been much like that evoked in Graham Greene's latest novel, *Our Man in Havana*, published just months earlier.

"The long city lay spread along the open Atlantic; waves broke over the Avenida de Maceo and minted the windscreens of cars. The pink, grey, yellow pillars of what had once been the aristocratic quarter were eroded like rocks; an ancient coats of arms, smudged and featureless, was set over the doorway of a shabby hotel, and the shutters of a night-club were varnished in bright crude colours to protect them from the wet and salt of the sea. In the west the steel skyscrapers of the new town rose higher than lighthouses."

Closer up, Havana was a seamy, exciting city, booming with casinos, nightclubs, and whorehouses. There were even porno movie-houses, and the live sex show in Chinatown's Shanghai theater featured a performing stud called "Superman." Drugs such as marijuana and cocaine were available to those who wanted them. Havana's very seaminess had attracted Greene, who had made several recent visits to Cuba. "In Batista's day I liked the idea that one could obtain anything at will, whether drugs, women or goats." Through Greene's eyes, his fictional British vacuum cleaner salesman, Worm-old, walked the streets of Old Havana, taking it all in. "At every corner there were men who called 'Taxi' at him as though he were a stranger, and all down the Paseo, at intervals of a few yards, the pimps accosted him automatically without any real hope. 'Can I be of service, sir?' 'I know all the pretty girls.' 'You desire a beautiful woman?' 'Postcards?' 'You want to see a dirty movie?' "

This was the raucous milieu into which Che and his men plunged after two largely abstinent years in the mountains, with fairly predictable results. Che kept his *escolta* (bodyguards) under strict control, but for Alberto Castellanos, the temptation was too much. "I was in wonderment. . . . I had never been in the capital before and I was in shock. . . . Because he kept me working with him until dawn, I didn't have time to see anything. [So], some nights I escaped to see the city, especially the cabarets. It fascinated me to see so many beautiful women."

Sex was heavy in the air. The guerrillas slipped out of La Cabaña's walls for trysts with girls in the bushes under the huge white statue of Christ that looms over the harbor. Aleida March raised her eyebrows in a suggestive expression of mock-scandal when recalling this period. It was a chaotic situation and had to be taken in hand. With an eye to the rebel army's public image and its own internal discipline, Che soon organized a mass wedding for all those fighters with lovers whose unions had not been made "official," inviting a judge to come and take their vows, and a priest for those wanting a religious ceremony. The wayward Castellanos, for instance, who had a fiancée back in Oriente, was one of those whose wings were clipped, in a La Cabaña ceremony presided over by Che himself.

Around the hemisphere, the celebratory mood brought about by Cuba's revolutionary triumph was less libidinous, but still widely shared. The war had captivated public interest, and hordes of foreign journalists descended on Havana to cover the installment of the new regime. "In Buenos Aires it was the only thing people talked about," wrote Che's father. "I felt as though I was suspended in the air. Our relatives and friends barraged us with questions and we responded with everything we knew. But the truth is that the greatest interest of our family was the life of Ernesto. And Ernesto was alive and the war had ended."

But even in Cuba, few people understood what it all meant. While still in Santiago, Fidel had taken pains to give the new regime a moderate front, but he had also set the pattern for his future relationship with "President" Urrutia by allowing him to name but one appointee, the justice minister, while *he* named the rest. Evidently feeling grateful to Fidel for making him president, Urrutia did not put up a fight. Even so, only a few July 26 men, mostly from the llano, were included in the initial cabinet roster.

From Santiago, Fidel began making his way slowly overland toward

Havana, savoring his victory before adoring crowds. Reporters caught up with his caravan and followed its progress, filing dispatches to the outside world. To their interrogations, he repeated again and again that he had no political ambitions. He was at the orders of "President Urrutia," he said, and, as for its future policies, the revolution would obey the "will of the people." He had, however, "accepted" Urrutia's request that he serve as "Commander in Chief of the armed forces."

Wherever they appeared, throngs of civilians cheered the ragged guerrillas. A young rebel from Holguín, Reinaldo Arenas, recalled the atmosphere. "We came down from the hills and received a heroes' welcome. In my neighborhood in Holguín I was given a flag of the 26th of July Movement and for a whole block I walked holding that flag. I felt a little ridiculous, but there was a great euphoria, with hymns and anthems ringing out, and the whole town in the streets. The rebels kept coming, with crucifixes hanging from chains made of seeds; these were the heroes. Some, in fact, had joined the rebels only four or five months earlier, but most of the women, and also many of the men in the city, went wild over these hairy fellows; everybody wanted to take one of the bearded men home. I did not yet have a beard because I was only fifteen."*

In Havana, the atmosphere was a mix of festive anarchy and uncertainty. Hundreds of armed rebels were camped out in hotel lobbies, treating them as they would a guerrilla bivouac in the countryside. Most government troops had surrendered after Batista's flight and had remained in their barracks, but here and there a few snipers still held out, and manhunts were on for fugitive police agents, corrupt politicians, and war criminals. In a few places, mobs had attacked casinos, parking meters, and other symbols of Batista corruption, but quickly had been brought under control as the July 26 militias came out onto the streets. Even Boy Scouts were acting as ad hoc policemen. Meanwhile, the embassies were filling up with those military officers, police, and government officials left in the lurch by Batista's sudden flight.

On January 4, Carlos Franqui left Fidel's rolling caravan in Camagüey and flew ahead to Havana. He found the capital transformed. "The gloomy Camp Columbia, mother of the tyranny and of crime, which I had known as a prisoner, was now almost a picturesque the-

*This quotation appears in Arenas's *Before Night Falls*. Arenas went on to become a well-known author, but suffered because of his homosexuality. Years later, he fled Cuba and settled in New York until his death.

ater, impossible to imagine. On the one hand, the bearded rebels with Camilo, no more than five hundred of them, and on the other hand, twenty thousand army soldiers intact—generals, colonels, majors, captains, corporals, sergeants, and privates. When they saw us walk by, they stood at attention. It was enough to make you burst out laughing. In the comandant's office was Camilo, with his romantic beard, looking like Christ on a spree, his boots thrown on the floor and his feet up on the table, as he received his excellency the ambassador of the United States."

Afterward, Che arrived. There were difficulties at the Presidential Palace. The Revolutionary Directory had installed themselves there and appeared to have no plans to give it up. Che had tried to talk with the leaders, but they had refused to see him. Wrote Franqui: "Camilo, half joking and half serious, said a couple of cannonballs should be fired off as a warning. . . . As I was not an admirer of the palace, I said it seemed like a good idea, but Che, with his sense of responsibility, told us it wasn't the right time to waste cannonballs, and he patiently returned to the palace, met Faure Chomón, and matters were straightened out. Camilo aways listened to Che."

By the time Fidel arrived on January 8, Urrutia was installed in the palace, and a semblance of governmental authority had been restored. The rebels had taken over public buildings, police stations, newspaper and trade union offices, while the Communist party had come out of the woodwork to call for mass demonstrations in support of the victorious rebels. Its exiled leaders began returning from exile, and its banned newspaper, *Hoy*, began publishing again. Even Carlos Prío, the former president, arrived back from Miami. Abroad, the major Cuban embassies had been occupied by July 26 representatives. Venezuela had recognized the new government, and so had the United States. The Soviet Union followed suit on January 10.

Cuba's civic and business institutions declared their support for the revolution with hyperbolic expressions of gratitude and fealty. The "nightmare" of Batista was over, the Fidelista honeymoon had begun. The business community bent over backward to pay tribute, volunteering to pay back taxes, and some major corporations announced new investments while declaring their optimism about Cuba's brave new future.

The media lionized Fidel and his heroic *barbudos*. The weekly magazine *Bohemia* became an unabashed revolutionary fanzine, printing obsequious homages to Fidel: One artist's depiction went so far as to render him with a Christlike countenance, complete with halo. Its pages were full of commercial advertisements tailored to suit the moment: The Polar beer brewery emblazoned a page with a graphic of a sturdy peasant cutting cane and the words, "Yes! IT IS TIME TO GET TO WORK. With the happiness of being free once more and feeling ourselves prouder than ever to be Cubans, we must blaze a trail of work: constructive and intense work to meet the demands of the Fatherland. . . . And after working, IT IS TIME FOR POLAR! There is nothing like a really cold Polar to complete the satisfaction of a duty fulfilled." The Cancha clothiers came out with a new men's shirt, the "Libertad," its ads showing a model sporting an appropriate revolutionary beard.

Carlos Franqui, who began bringing out the once-clandestine July 26 newspaper, *Revolución*, added to the flood of tributes by lauding Fidel as Cuba's "Hero-Guide." A theater debuted a play called *The General Fled at Dawn*, with a bearded, uniformed actor playing the role of Fidel Castro. After being hastily commissioned by some grateful citizens, a bronze bust of Fidel was erected on a marble plinth at an intersection near Havana's military complex, with an engraved inscription honoring the man who had "broken the chains of the dictatorship with the flame of liberty."

Che too came in for his share of lyrical tributes. Cuba's foremost living poet, the Communist Nicolás Guillén, was in exile in Buenos Aires when the triumph came, and at the request of a weekly newspaper editor there wrote a poem in honor of Guevara.

CHE GUEVARA

*As if San Martín's pure hand,*
*Were extended to his brother, Martí,*
*And the plant-banked Plata streamed through the sea,*
*To join the Cauto's love-swept overture.*

*Thus, Guevara, strong-voiced gaucho, moved to assure*
*His guerrilla blood to Fidel*
*And his broad hand was most comradely*
*When our night was blackest, most obscure.*

*Death retreated. Of its shadows impure,*

*Of the dagger, poison, and of beasts,*
*Only savage memories endure.*

*Fused from two, a single soul shines,*
*As if San Martin's pure hand,*
*Were extended to his brother, Martí.*

If Che was already a well-known figure to readers abroad, his literary consecration by Guillén—a peer of Federico García Lorca, Pablo Neruda, and Rafael Alberti—launched him into the pantheon of Latin America's most venerated historical heroes. Here he was, at the age of thirty, being compared with "The Liberator" José de San Martín.

The hyperbole had a resounding effect on Cuba's hero-hungry public. When, a few days after his arrival, Che sent for Juan Borroto, the sugar expert who had smuggled him economic intelligence reports while he was in the Escambray, Borroto felt overawed. "He was already a legend," Borroto recalled. "To actually see him for many Cubans was like a vision; you rubbed your eyes. He was physically imposing, too, with very white skin, chestnut-colored hair, and he was very attractive."

To the American embassy officials in Havana, however, Che was already being eyed as the fearsome Rasputin of the new regime. His ideological influence with Fidel and his uncertain new role behind the forbidding walls of La Cabaña was a topic of much worried speculation.

### III

WHEN HE ARRIVED, Fidel enacted his triumphal entry to Havana like a grand showman, riding into the city at the head of a noisy calvacade on top of a captured tank. After paying his respects to Urrutia in the palace, he hopped aboard the *Granma*, which had been brought to Havana and was now moored in the harbor. Then, accompanied by Camilo and Raúl—while Che stayed discreetly out of sight in La Cabaña—he proceeded to Camp Columbia through streets lined with thousands of ecstatic, flag-waving *habaneros*.

That night, Fidel gave a long speech broadcast live on television stressing the need for law and order and revolutionary unity. In the "new Cuba," there was only room for one revolutionary force; there could be no "private armies." His words were a warning to the Directorio, whose fighters had vacated the palace but still occupied the university's grounds, and were reported to be stockpiling arms. Adding to the ominous signs that a confrontation was in the offing, Directorio leader Chomón had publicly voiced the group's concerns about being shut out of power. But Fidel's speech and its implied threat of force brought about the appropriate response: Before Fidel had finished speaking, the Directorio relayed word that it would hand over its weapons. It was the end of the threat posed by the Directorio as a rival armed organization; Fidel's display of force majeure had won out.

Fidel also used his presence to reinforce the nationalistic nature of the new regime. Asked by a reporter what he thought of the rumored offer by the U.S. government to withdraw its military mission, he replied quickly:

"It *has* to withdraw it. In the first place, the Government of the United States has no right to have a permanent mission here. In other words, it's not a prerogative of the Department of State, but of the Revolutionary Government of Cuba." If Washington wanted good relations, Fidel was saying, it had some fence-mending to do, and the first step was to deal with Cuba as an equal.

Meanwhile, he told the nation, the army would be reorganized, made up of men "loyal to the Revolution," who would defend it if the occasion arose. He warned that the victory was not yet secure. With his stolen millions, Batista had fled to the Dominican Republic and sought the protection of that other reviled dictator, General Trujillo, and it was always possible the two of them might launch a counterattack.

Fidel had deftly prepared Cubans for things to come, but what most people remembered from that night was the moment when several white doves flew out of the audience to alight on his shoulder. To many, it was a mystical epiphany that validated Fidel's standing as the charismatic *maximo lider* of the revolution; to others it was a masterful example of Fidel's ability to put forward an awe-inspiring public image at exactly the right moment.

In the blur of rapid-fire events that followed, contradictory signals about the direction of the revolution kept observers off balance and Cubans in a constant state of flux. By quickly recognizing the new regime, Washington had tried to appear conciliatory. In a second diplomatic gesture of appeasement, the Batista-tainted Earl Smith resigned as ambassador and left the country, leaving a chargé d'affaires in his place.

The Eisenhower administration could hardly complain about the makeup of the new regime. Urrutia's cabinet was stacked with politically "safe" Cuban political veterans and aspirants, virtually all solidly middle-class, probusiness anti-Communists, including many of Fidel's former rivals. By giving them posts with apparent authority in the new government, Fidel had swiftly placated the conservative political and business community and co-opted potential sources of opposition.

The biggest surprise was his appointment of Dr. José Miró Cardona, an eminent lawyer and secretary of the Civic Opposition Front, as the new prime minister. "Miró Cardona's designation was a bombshell," wrote Franqui later. "He was president of the Havana Bar Association, the representative of great capitalistic enterprises, and one of Cuba's most pro-North American politicians. Years before, he had defended the biggest thief among Cuban presidents, in the celebrated case of Grau San Martín, who had stolen 84 million pesos. He had defended Captain Casilla, the murderer of the black sugar workers' leader, Jesús Menéndez. We did not understand Fidel's choice but it was understood by those whom Fidel wanted to understand. It was actually an intelligent move, which confused the Americans, the bourgeoisie, and the politicians."

Bouncing back from the ill-fated Miami Pact, the redoubtable Felipe Pazos was made president of the National Bank; Justo Carrillo became president of the Development Bank; and Harvard-educated economist Regino Boti returned from the United States to become minister of the economy. Rufo López Fresquet, an economist and analyst for the influential conservative newspaper, *Diario de la Marina*, was named minister of finance, while foreign affairs went to the Ortodoxo politician Roberto Agramonte.

Others, such as Faustino Pérez, appointed to head the newly created "Ministry for the Recovery of Illegally Acquired Property," came from the July 26 Movement's right wing. The Education Ministry went to Armando Hart; while Che's wartime nemesis Enrique Oltuski ("Sierra") became minister of communications. Fidel's old publisher friend, Luis Orlando Rodríguez, who had helped set up Radio Rebelde and *El Cubano Libre*, was made interior minister. Another new post, "minister for revolutionary laws," was given to Osvaldo Dorticós Torrado, a Cienfuegos lawyer with discreet PSP links. His appointment seemed innocuous enough at the time, but Torrado was to play a key role in Fidel's future plans.

The cabinet got to work, holding marathon sessions to reform the country's constitution, rebuild the country's damaged infrastructure, and clean up Cuba's debauched society; at the top of Urrutia's agenda was a bill to ban gambling and prostitution. At the same time, the new ministers began housecleaning, firing employees who had been receiving secret sinecures, or *botellas*, from the Batista regime. Their initial decrees were of a similar "purging" nature: All political parties were temporarily banned, while Batista's properties, as well as those of his ministers and of all politicians who had participated in the last two Batista-era elections, were confiscated.

Simultaneously, Fidel began speaking before large crowds in an ingenious exercise he dubbed "direct democracy." These were spontaneous referendums on revolutionary policy in which he took soundings of the crowd, similar to his first speech at Camp Columbia. Using his popular authority as the undisputed caudillo of the revolution, Fidel employed these forums to test, mold, and radicalize the public mood and, ultimately, to pressure the government. He repeated over and over that it was the duty of the new government to obey "the will of the people," because the revolution had been fought "by the people."

Fidel also began to reform the army, his true power base. The ranks of the "old" army and police forces were weeded out, their officers either sidelined or purged. Colonel Ramón Barquín was made chief of the military academies, while Major Quevedo, one of several career officers who had defected to the rebels after the failed summer offensive, became head of army logistics. Others were shipped off to "gilded exile" as military attachés in foreign countries. The new military elite was made up of loyal rebels. Camilo, already the military governor of Havana province, became the army chief of staff. Augusto Martinéz Sánchez, a lawyer who had served as auditor with Raúl's Second Front, was named minister of defense. Efigertio Almeijeras, the head of Raúl's elite "Mau-Mau" guerrilla strike force, became chief of police. The pilot Pedro Díaz Lanz, Fidel's rebel "air force" commander in recent months, was now given that title officially. Perhaps most telling, loyal July 26 men had been installed as military governors in all of Cuba's provinces.

It was soon evident that the real seat of revolutionary power lay not in the ornate Presidential Palace in Old Havana, but wherever Fidel happened to be at the time—and for now, Fidel seemed to be everywhere. His base camp was a penthouse suite on the twenty-third floor of the new Havana Hilton in downtown Vedado, but he also slept and worked out of Celia Sánchez's apartment nearby—and in a villa in the fishing village of Cojímar, about thirty minutes east of Havana. It was in this villa, rather than at the Presidential Palace, where the future of Cuba was truly being decided. Over the coming months it became the setting for nightly meetings among Fidel, his closest comrades, and the Communist party leaders, aimed at forging a secret alliance to meld the PSP and the July 26 Movement into a single revolutionary party. Fidel, Che, Raúl, Ramiro, and Camilo represented the guerrillas, while Carlos Rafael Rodríguez, Aníbal Escalante, and Blas Roca, the party's secretary-general, led discussions for the Communists.

## IV

ON THE SURFACE, Che and Raúl were the odd men out in the distribution of plum appointments. Raúl was military governor of Oriente, while Che had the minor title of "commander of La Cabaña." But such job descriptions were misleading. As Fidel concentrated on presenting a moderate front for his revolution, hopefully avoiding a premature of confrontation with the United States—vociferously denying accusations of "Communist influence"—Raúl and Che worked secretly to cement ties with the PSP and to shore up Fidel's power base in the armed forces.

Che kept up a formidable pace of activity. On January 13, he inaugurated the "Academia Militar-Cultural" in La Cabaña, to "raise the cultural level of the army." In addition to basic literacy and education, the academy was designed to impart "political awareness" to the troops. It included courses in civics, history, geography, the Cuban economy, "the economic and social characteristics of the Latin American republics," and current affairs. It also sought to reform his charges. After discovering that cockfighting had become popular among the troops, he banned it. As substitutes, he organized chess classes, an equestrian team, and sports events, and arranged for art exhibits, concerts, and theater productions to be held at La Cabaña. Movies were shown nightly in the fortresses' several cinemas. He founded a regimental newspaper, *La Cabaña Libre*, and soon helped kick off *Verde Olivo*, a newspaper for the Revolutionary Armed Forces.

Amid all this activity, Che quietly placed the school under the supervision of PSP men. Armando Acosta, his commissar in the Escambray,

was already close by, commanding the small fortress of La Punta immediately across the harbor from La Cabaña, and before long Che named
him the academy administrator.

By the end of January, Che had an additional title—"Chief of the
Department of Training of the Revolutionary Armed Forces"—but it
did not give a full picture of his activities, either. On Fidel's instructions, he was secretly meeting with Raúl—who shuttled back and forth
between Havana and his Santiago post—and Camilo, Ramiro Valdés,
and PSP man Victor Pina to create a new state security and intelligence apparatus. The resulting agency, Seguridad del Estado, or G-
2, was placed in the able hands of Ramiro Valdés, Che's wartime
deputy. Osvaldo Sánchez, a PSP Politburo member and head of its
"Military Committee," was his second in command.

Meanwhile, Cuban exiles were arriving home from all over the
hemisphere. An airplane was sent to Buenos Aires to bring back the
exiles living there, and the Guevara family was invited to board it.
Che's parents, his sister Celia, her husband Luis Argañaraz, and Juan
Martín, now a teenager of fourteen, accepted the offer. (Family and
work obligations kept Roberto and Ana María at home, and it would
be another two and a half years before they saw their famous brother.)
They arrived in Havana on January 9, and an emotional Guevara
Lynch kissed the tarmac at Havana's Rancho Boyeros airport. "We were
immediately surrounded by bearded soldiers," Guevara Lynch wrote,
"wearing really dirty uniforms and armed with rifles or machine guns.
Then came the obligatory salutes and in a rush, they led us into the
interior of terminal, where Ernesto awaited us. I understand that they
had wanted to surprise him and he only knew of our arrival minutes
before. My wife ran to his arms and could not contain her tears. A
mountain of photographers and television cameras recorded the scene.
Soon afterward I hugged my son. It had been six years since I had last
seen him."

One of the photographs taken that day shows Che, in fatigues and
beret and sparse beard, flanked by his mother and father, pressed in
amid a tumult of curious onlookers. A submachine gun pokes up into
view behind Che's back. What is truly memorable, though, is the look
of deep, passionate pride on Celia's face, and on Che's. His con-
servatively dressed father stands to one side like a bystander, smiling
bemusedly.

The Guevara family was installed as guests of the revolution in a suite of the Havana Hilton, just a few floors below Fidel's own rooms. As the de facto seat of government, the hotel's swank lobby had become a rowdy pandemonium of disheveled armed guerrillas, thrusting journalists, favorseekers, and perplexed-looking American tourists whose holidays had been interrupted by the revolution. Finally alone with his son, Guevara Lynch produced some bottles of Argentine wine that had been his son's favorite brands back home.

"His eyes shone upon seeing those bottles. . . . Their sight surely brought back to him pleasant memories of other happy times, when the whole family lived together in Buenos Aires." As they celebrated, Guevara Lynch observed his son and thought he saw ". . . in his physique, in his expressions, in his happiness . . . the same boy who had left Buenos Aires one cold July afternoon more than six years before."

Guevara Lynch's estimation contained a fair degree of wishful thinking. His son Ernesto had become "Che," the man he wanted to be. And if "Ernesto" was pleased to see his family, the truth was they couldn't have arrived at a more inconvenient time. Even as his family settled into the Hilton, Che had to rush back to La Cabaña; there were revolutionary tribunals to be carried out, and he was the man in charge.

Throughout January, suspected war criminals were being captured and brought to La Cabaña daily. For the most part, these were not the top henchmen of the ancien régime; most had escaped before the rebels assumed control of the city and halted outgoing air and sea traffic, or remained holed up in embassies. Most of those left behind were deputies, or rank-and-file *chivatos* and police torturers. Still, Che, as supreme prosecutor, took to his task with a singular determination, and the old walls of the fort rang out nightly with the fusillades of the firing squads.

"There were over a thousand prisoners of war," explained Miguel Angel Duque de Estrada, whom Che had placed in charge of the Comisión de Depuración, or "Cleansing Commission," "with more arriving all the time, and many didn't have dossiers. We didn't even know all of their names. But we had a job to do, which was to cleanse the defeated army. Che always had a clear idea about the need to cleanse the army and exact justice on those found to be war criminals."

The trials began at eight or nine in the evening, and, more often than not, a verdict was reached by two or three in the morning. Duque de Estrada, whose job was to gather evidence, take testimonies, and prepare the trials, also sat with Che, the "supreme prosecutor," on the appellate bench, where Che made the final decision on men's fates.

"Che consulted with me," said Duque, "but he was in charge, and as military commander his word was final. We were in agreement on almost one hundred percent of the decisions. In about one hundred days we carried out about fifty-five executions by firing squad, and we got a lot of flak for it, but we gave each case due and fair consideration and we didn't come to our decisions lightly."

On top of his new job administering La Cabaña's finances, Che also made his twenty-one-year-old accountant Orlando Borrego a tribunal president. "It was very difficult because [most of us] had no judicial training," recalled Borrego. [Our] paramount concerns were [to ensure] that the sense of revolutionary morality and of justice prevailed, that no injustice was committed. In that, Che was very careful. Nobody was shot for hitting a prisoner, but if there was extreme torture and killings and deaths, then yes—they were condemned to death. . . . The whole case was analyzed, all the witnesses seen, and the relatives of the dead or tortured person came, or the tortured person himself, and in the tribunal, displaying his body, he would reveal all the tortures that he had received."

Each night, Che would go over the cases with his judges, but, detailing his role in the trials to some hostile Cuban television interviewers, he said that he never attended the trials or met with defendants himself. Instead, he explained, he examined their cases based on the evidence alone so as to reach his final verdicts coldly and neutrally. According to Borrego, Che also took great care in selecting judges and prosecutors; rebels who had been mistreated were not allowed to pass judgment on their former torturers, for instance. "The trial strategy was elaborated with great care," Borrego said, "because there were sometimes prosecutors who were on the extreme left, and . . . one had to moderate those who always asked for the death sentence."

When it came to the executions themselves, however, Che evidently overcame his earlier reservations about the American volunteer Herman Marks whom he had cashiered in Camagüey, because Marks reappeared at La Cabaña, where he took an active role in Che's firing squads.*

Over the next several months, several hundred people were offi-

---

*Borrego, who got to know Marks at La Cabaña, described him as a strange, aloof man, who was "sadistic" and who liked to participate in the firing squads. He was about forty years old, spoke little Spanish, and was rumored to be on the run from U.S. justice. After several months, he disappeared from Cuba.

cially tried and executed by firing squads across Cuba. Most were sentenced in conditions like those described by Borrego: above board, if summary affairs, with defense lawers, witnesses, prosecutors, and an attending public. On a lesser scale, there were also a number of arbitrary executions. The most notorious incident occurred when, soon after occupying Santiago, Raúl Castro directed a mass execution of over 70 captured soldiers by bulldozing a trench, standing the condemned men in front of it, and mowing them down with machine guns. The action crystallized Raúl's reputation for ruthlessness and a proneness to violence, one that the years since have not mitigated.

In truth, though, there was little overt public opposition to the wave of revolutionary justice at the time. On the contrary: Batista's thugs had committed some sickening crimes, the Cuban public was in a lynching mood, and the media gloatingly chronicled the trials and executions of the condemned while dredging up the most sordid details of their crimes. In between exposés of Batista-era graft and corruption, Cuban papers were full of morbid revelations and gruesome photographs of the horrors and brutalities that had been committed by Batista's *esbirros*, or henchmen. *Bohemia* took its boosterism to unseemly lengths, publishing snide interviews with suspects awaiting trial, attending their executions with a ready camera, and providing sanctimonious captions.

An interview with a former Batista propaganda broadcaster appeared in its February 8 issue under the title "A Rat of the Tyranny Is Trapped." Under his photograph, the caption reads:

> This is the effigy of one of the most notorious henchmen of the dictatorship—Otto Meruelo—the mere mention of whose name besmirches the national atmosphere, one of the most repulsive spokesmen of the *batistato*. . . . The physical integrity of Meruelo—who never had moral integrity—is intact. What will the Revolution do about "this"? The question is on the lips of all Cubans.

Meruelo was, in the end, sentenced to a thirty-year prison sentence. In the same issue, *Bohemia* covered the trial of two of Rolando Masferrer's "Tigre" gunmen responsible for several murders in Manzanillo, the Nicolardes Rojas brothers, in an article entitled "The Accursed Brothers." Its author transcribed the culminating moment of the trial:

The Prosecutor, Dr. Fernando Aragoneses Cruz: "Do the Nicolardes brothers deserve freedom?"

Noooo! was the thundering shout of the enormous multitude.

"Do they deserve prison with the hope that one day they can be useful to Society?"

Noooo!

"Should they be shot, as exemplary punishment to all future generations?"

Yeeees!

The Prosecutor . . . glanced over the infuriated multitude. And, in the face of their unanimous opinion, he expressed himself calmly, while directing a look that was part anger and part pity, to those who had been condemned by the People.

"That is, ladies and gentlemen, the petition of the citizenry, whom I represent in this session."

The Nicolardes brothers were immediately taken out and shot.

The *Bohemia* account seems to have been a fairly accurate depiction of the atmosphere prevailing in Cuba's revolutionary courtrooms. According to Orlando Borrego, he often felt under great pressure from his civilian audiences to be severe in his verdicts. "They [often] thought the sentencing was too benign. . . . Sometimes one asked for [a sentence of] ten years and the people wanted it to be twenty." Making Borrego's job doubly uncomfortable was the mounting criticism of the tribunals from abroad, with American congressmen decrying them as a bloodbath. Indignant over the accusations, in late January Fidel decided to hold some high-profile public trials—of Major Sosa Blanca and several other ranking officers accused of multiple acts of murder and torture—in Havana's sports stadium. Attending foreign reporters were repulsed, however, at the spectacle of jeering crowds and hysterical cries for blood, and Fidel's gambit backfired. A sympathetic Herbert Matthews tried to rationalize the trials from the "Cuban's perspective" in an editorial that the *New York Times* editor in chief refused to print.

Che was undeterred and pushed on. He warned his judges to be scrupulous about weighing the evidence in each case so as not to give the revolution's enemies any additional ammunition, but the trials had to continue if Cuba's revolution was to be secure. He never tired of telling his Cuban comrades that in Guatemala Arbenz had fallen because he had not purged his armed forces of disloyal elements, a mistake that permitted the CIA to penetrate and overthrow his regime. Cuba could not afford to repeat it.

In his memoirs, Guevara Lynch avoided the issue of Che's leading role in the tribunals, but did allude to his shock at discovering his son's transformation into a hard man. As he told it, one night he decided to go and visit his son at La Cabaña. Che wasn't there when he arrived, so he decided to wait. Before long, a jeep pulled up at the entrance and he saw a figure jump out. It was Che. "He confronted an armed youth who was on guard duty, grabbed his rifle away, and in a firm, dry voice, ordered his arrest. I saw the desperation on the boy's face, and I asked [Che] why he was arresting him. He answered me: 'Old man, nobody here can sleep on guard duty, because it puts the whole barracks in danger.' "

Until that moment, Guevara Lynch wrote, he had thought of his son as "the same boy who had said good-bye to us in 1953 in Buenos Aires." He now knew he was mistaken and began to see him in a new light.

Another day, Guevara Lynch asked Che what he planned to do about "his medicine." Smiling, Che replied that, since they both had the same name, his father could substitute for him if he wanted, hang up a doctor's shingle, "and begin killing people without any risk." Che laughed at his own joke, but his father insisted, until his son gave a more serious reply: "As for my medical career, I can tell you that I deserted it a long time ago. Now I am a fighter who is working in the consolidation of a government. What will become of me? I don't even know in which land I will leave my bones."

Guevara Lynch was baffled and didn't understand the significance of Che's last remark until much later. "It was hard for me to recognize the Ernesto of my home, the normal Ernesto. An enormous responsibility seemed to float above his figure. . . . Upon arriving in Havana, Ernesto already knew what his destiny was. He was aware of his personality and he was transforming into a man whose faith in the triumph of his ideals reached mystical proportions."

His father's befuddlement was shared by some of Che's old friends and acquaintances. Initially thrilled over his guerrilla war exploits, their delight had turned to horror with the news of his role in the summary executions, and they could not fathom what had happened to their friend to make him merciless.

Tatiana Quiroga and Chichina's cousin Jimmy Roca, Che's old Miami roommate, were now married and living in Los Angeles, and in early January they sent him a telegram offering their congratulations for the revolution's victory. "I sent a telegram to La Cabaña and it cost me five dollars," Tatiana recalled. "I still remember because, as a student, it was a lot of money for me, but I spent the five dollars to congratulate him. Then came the killings of La Cabaña, and I'll tell you I have never felt so horrible as to have spent five dollars on that telegram. I wanted to die."

Dr. David Mitrani, Che's old colleague at the General Hospital in Mexico City, was similarly revolted—and, when he arrived in Havana at Che's invitation eighteen months later, he told him so. Che gave an explanation that was as straightforward as it was unsatisfactory to Mitrani. "Look, in this thing either you kill first, or else you get killed."

# INDIVIDUALISM MUST DISAPPEAR

## JON LEE ANDERSON

from *CHE GUEVARA: A REVOLUTIONARY LIFE*

1997

## VI

THE FACE OF Havana was changing dramatically. The days of privilege for Cuba's upper and middle classes were coming to an end, and
increasing numbers of them were leaving on the ferries and shuttle
flights to Miami. As many as sixty thousand had already fled by the
late spring of 1960. The city that a year before had still been an American playground of exclusive yacht clubs, private beaches, casinos, and
brothels—and whites-only neighborhoods—was disappearing. The
roulette wheels were still spinning in the big hotels, but most of the
prostitutes were off the streets. Instead, uniformed and armed blacks
and *guajiros* chanting revolutionary slogans roamed the city.

A very different type of visitor was taking their place. Trade and cultural delegations were arriving from socialist-bloc nations, along with
a growing stream of current and future Third World leaders; delegates
to an international Communist youth congress filled hotels now emp-
tied of weekending American tourists and businessmen. Left-wing European and Latin American intellectuals flocked to Havana to attend

cultural congresses laid on by the revolution. Among the visitors were Jean-Paul Sartre and Simone de Beauvoir, who had been invited by Carlos Franqui.

Che's mystique had grown, and when the famous French couple went to see him, they talked for hours. For Che, it must have been a very gratifying experience, playing host to the renowned French philosopher whose works he had grown up reading. For his part, Sartre came away extremely impressed and after Guevara's death, gave him the highest possible tribute; to the Frenchman, Che was "not only an intellectual but also the most complete human being of our age."

Their visit had coincided with the *La Coubre* tragedy, and Sartre and de Beauvoir witnessed the funerals and Fidel's two-hour speech the next day. Afterward, they walked through the streets of Old Havana, where they saw the public fund-raising campaign already under way for a new consignment of arms. De Beauvoir was bewitched by the sensual, fervent mood.

"Young women stood selling fruit juice and snacks to raise money for the State," she wrote in her memoir. "Well-known performers danced or sang in the squares to swell the fund; pretty girls in their carnival fancy dresses, led by a band, went through the streets making collections. 'It's the honeymoon of the Revolution,' Sartre said to me. No machinery, no bureaucracy, but a direct contact between leaders and people, and a mass of seething and slightly confused hopes. It wouldn't last forever, but it was a comforting sight. For the first time in our lives, we were witnessing happiness that had been attained by violence."

On March 23, Che gave a televised speech called "Political Sovereignty and Economic Independence." Through the revolutionary seizure of power, he said, Cuba had attained its political independence but had not yet won its economic independence, without which it was not a truly *politically* sovereign nation. This was the revolution's current "strategic objective."

There had been some inroads made against the foreign, mostly U.S.-owned monopolies that had previously held sway over Cuba's economic freedom. The electricity and telephone rates had been cut, rents had been lowered, the large landholdings had been turned over to the people, but the island's oil, mineral, and chemical wealth were still in the Americans' hands.

It is good to speak clearly. . . . In order to conquer something

**JON LEE ANDERSON**
216

we have to take it away from somebody. . . . That something we must conquer—the country's sovereignty—has to be taken away from that somebody called monopoly. . . . It means that our road to liberation will be opened up with a victory over the monopolies, and concretely over the U.S. monopolies.

The revolution had to be "radical," and had to "destroy the roots of evil that afflicted Cuba" in order to "eliminate injustice." Those who opposed the revolution's measures, those who resisted losing their privileges, were counterrevolutionaries. The workers of the reigned-in CTC were contributing 4 percent of their wages to the "industrialization" program; it was time the rest of society shouldered its fair share of the revolutionary sacrifice.

Lately Che had been driving home the point that Cuba no longer was just Cuba but was the revolution, and the revolution was the people; going one step further, the people, Cuba, and the revolution were Fidel. It was time to get on board the new ship of state, or get off. Just as the men of the *Granma* had put aside their individual lives, ready to die if necessary in the war against Batista, so now did all Cubans have to sacrifice for the common aim of *total* independence. The enemy might well retaliate, he warned. And when the counterrevolutionary soldiers came—paid for perhaps by those same "monopolies" whose interests were being affected—Cuba's defense would be fought for not by a handful of men but by millions. All of Cuba was now "a Sierra Maestra," and together, Che said, quoting Fidel, "we will all be saved or we will sink."

The "individualistic" university students with their "middle class" mentalities seemed to especially provoke Che; perhaps in the students he saw his self-absorbed former self, and it rankled him. He had given up his self, his "vocation" for the revolution; why couldn't they? In early March he had gone back to Havana University to remind the students that they had a duty to perform in the economic development of Cuba, and there could be no duality of principles, with the students separated from the revolution. An individual's sense of "vocation" alone wasn't justification for deciding a career; a sense of revolutionary duty should and would take its place. He used himself as an example:

I don't think that an individual example, statistically speaking, has any importance, but I began my career studying engineering, I finished as a doctor, later I have been a comandante and now you see me here as a speaker. . . . That is to say, within one's individual characteristics, vocation doesn't play a determinant role. . . . I think one has to constantly think on behalf of masses and not on behalf of individuals. . . . It's criminal to think of individuals because the needs of the individual become completely weakened in the face of the needs of the human conglomeration.

In practical terms, this meant certain faculties would be expanded, others would be collapsed. Humanities, for instance, was a field that would be reduced to the "minimum necessary for the cultural development of the country."

In April, Che's guerrilla warfare manual, *Guerra de Guerrillas*, was published by INRA's Department of Military Training. He had dedicated the book to Camilo Cienfuegos, and a photograph of Camilo graced the cover; his old comrade was seen astride a horse, holding aloft a rifle, his face beaming under a straw hat. "Camilo," wrote Che, "is the image of the people." Excerpts were widely published in the Cuban media and, before long, not only Cubans but U.S. and Latin American counterinsurgency specialists would be studying the manual with acute interest.

In his prologue, "Essence of the Guerrilla Struggle," Che outlined what he believed to be the cardinal lessons for other revolutionary movements seeking to emulate Cuba's successful guerrilla struggle:

1. Popular forces can win a war against the army.
2. It is not necessary to await for the conditions to be right to begin the revolution; the insurrectional *foco* (guerrilla group) can create them.
3. In underdeveloped Latin America, the armed struggle should be fought mostly in the countryside.

Within Cuba itself, opposition was hardening. An underground movement had begun forming under Manuel Ray, teaching at Havana University since his ouster from government, while another openly dissident quarter was the militant Juventud Católica, ever more vociferous since [Soviet First Deputy Premier Anastas I.] Mikoyan's visit. In the radicalized countryside, inflamed by uncompensated land seizures and general chaos, violence had broken out. Small counter-revolutionary groups were becoming active, many of them composed of former rebel army men. In Oriente, one of Che's old comrades, Manuel Beatón, had taken up arms against the state, having murdered another of Che's former fighters, evidently for personal reasons, and fled to the Sierra Maestra with twenty armed followers. In Raúl's old turf in the Sierra Cristal, one of *his* former fighters, Higinio Díaz, had gone back to war as well, allying himself with the disaffected July 26 veteran Jorge Sotús, who had led the first rebel reinforcements from Santiago into the mountains in March 1957. They had formed the MRR (Movimiento de Rescate de la Revolución), organizing them-selves around Manuel Artime, a former naval academy professor liv-ing in exile in Miami. With Artime in Miami, Díaz in the sierra, and a network of underground supporters in Havana, the MRR had quickly come under the benevolent eye of the CIA.

It was not long before Fidel's "listeners" among Cuba's swollen exile community in Miami picked up rumors of the CIA's recruitment drive. In late April Fidel went to the podium to accuse the United States of trying to create an "international front" against him, and warned Wash-ington that Cuba "was not another Guatemala." Guatemalan Presi-dent Ydigoras Fuentes countered with a public accusation that Che was trying to organize a guerrilla invasion force against his country. On April 25, the two countries broke off relations.

Undeterred by the public fuss, the CIA program continued expand-ing, including broadcasting anti-Castro propaganda to Cuba from a radio transmitter installed on tiny Swan Island, near the Cayman Islands. The man running the station was David Atlee Phillips, who six years earlier in Guatemala had first brought the agency's attention to Ernesto Guevara.

One of the Cuban exiles to join the CIA's recruitment drive that summer was Felix Rodríguez. He was now nineteen years old and, in the aftermath of the Trinidad invasion fiasco of the year before, had returned to his military academy in Pennsylvania. After graduating in June 1960, he returned to his parents' home in Miami, then ran away to hire on with the CIA program. By September, he would join sev-eral hundred other Cuban exiles in Guatemala and begin receiving guerrilla training from a Filipino West Point graduate who had fought both the Japanese and the Communists in his country. Their force would eventually be called Brigade 2506.

On May Day, Fidel spoke to a Plaza de la Revolución packed with armed Cubans marching past his podium. He praised the new militias and, like Che, invoked the threat of an impending invasion; Cubans, like the Spartans, would stand, fight, and die without fear. He also took the opportunity to make two important points clear: If *he* died, Raúl would take his place as prime minister. What's more, there were not going to be any elections; since "the people" ruled Cuba already, there was no need to cast votes. The crowd cheered, repeating the catchphrase "*Revolución Sí, Elecciones No!*" and a new slogan, "*Cuba Sí, Yanqui No!*"

By that May Day, the United States estimated that Cuba's armed forces had doubled to fifty thousand since January 1959, with another fifty thousand civilians already incorporated into the new people's militias—and there was no end in sight. If the training and arming continued unchecked, Cuba would soon have the largest army in Latin America. Washington's private fears that Fidel may have already obtained Soviet military support gained credence on May 3, when the U.S. Senate heard testimony from two Batista-era officers, former Chief of Staff Tabernilla and Colonel Ugalde Carrillo; the latter accused Fidel of building Soviet missile bases in the Ciénaga de Zapata. Cuban Foreign Minister Roa quickly denounced the charge, and few gave it credit at the time, but, within a year, the fantastic notion would become a reality.

Fidel's militaristic May Day rally, and his decision to renew diplomatic relations with the Soviets a week later, sparked the final round between his government and Cuba's last surviving independent media. *Diario de la Marina*'s right-wing editorials compared Castro to "the Antichrist"; within days, its offices were attacked and occupied by "workers," and its presses closed down permanently. It's editor sought asylum and fled the country. By the end of the month, the two main remaining independent dailies, *Prensa Libre* and *El Crisol*, were also put out of circulation, soon to be followed by the English-language *Havana Post* and *La Calle*.

The first Soviet tankers were already crossing the Atlantic with oil for Cuba, fulfilling part of the barter agreement signed with Mikoyan. The U.S.-owned Esso and Texaco, and British-owned Shell, each of which had refineries in Cuba, had until now been supplying the island with oil from Venezuela. But Cuba had not paid for some time, and the outstanding bill amounted to some fifty million dollars. Che Guevara, as president of the National Bank, was the man to see about getting bills paid. But Esso's American manager got a cold reception and no clear answers when he asked Che about the debt.

Che now felt confident enough to take on the U.S. petroleum companies, and he told Alexiev his plan to offer them a deal he knew they would *have* to refuse, giving him the pretext he needed to seize their installations. Alexiev counseled caution, but Che went ahead anyway. On May 17, he informed the American oil firms that in order for him to pay off the debt owed them, they each had to buy three hundred thousand barrels of the Soviet oil that was arriving, and process it in their refineries. The companies did not reply right away but sought counsel in Washington, where the government advised them to reject Che's offer.

The opposition activities continued to grow, and so did the government's crackdown. The members of a rebel group in the Escambray, made up mostly of students from the University of Las Villas, were captured and shot. Former CTC leader David Salvador went underground and soon joined forces with Manuel Ray's creation, the MRP (Movimiento Revolucionario del Pueblo). The archbishop of Santiago, Enrique Pérez Serantes, a former Fidel supporter, issued a pastoral letter that both denounced Fidel's new Communist ties and seemed to bless the spreading antigovernment violence with the words: "Shedding blood is preferable to losing liberty." Still wishing to avoid a showdown with the church, Fidel remained mute. In Miami, the CIA hammered together "unity" among the anti-Castro exiles, merging Artime's and Justo Carrillo's MRR with a group led by Prío's former prime minister, Tony Varona. The result was the Frente Democratico Revolucionario (FDR), intended to provide a political front to the military force being trained in Guatemala.

But while the dissidents formed separate groups with different agendas to oppose him, Fidel's revolution had acquired an unstoppable momentum. In June he ordered the seizure of three of Havana's luxury hotels, justifying the action on the same grounds as Che's earlier "interventions" of factories: Their owners were intentionally underfinancing them, making them unprofitable, and therefore state takeover was necessary. Fidel also took up the gauntlet Che had thrown to the American oil companies. They would do as Cuba requested and process the Soviet oil, he declared, or face the confiscation of their properties. Days later, Cuba expelled two U.S. diplomats, accusing them of spying; in response, the Americans expelled three Cuban diplomats.

The war of wills quickly escalated. Fidel warned the United States that it ran the risk of losing all its property in Cuba; he would seize one sugar mill for every pound of sugar cut from Cuba's quota if Washington took that threatened step. On June 29, the same day that two Soviet oil tankers docked in Cuba, he ordered Texaco's Cuban installations seized; they waited for twenty-four hours before seizing Esso's and Shell's as well. In one fell swoop, Cuba had freed itself of a fifty-million-dollar debt and gained an oil-refining industry.

On July 3, the U.S. Congress authorized President Eisenhower to cut Cuba's sugar quota; Fidel responded with a legal amendment permitting the nationalization of all American properties in Cuba. On July 6, Eisenhower canceled the Cuban sugar quota for the rest of the year, some seven hundred thousand tons. Calling it an act of "economic aggression," Fidel now dropped broad hints of his Soviet arms deal, saying he would "soon" have the weapons he needed to arm his militias; ominously, he also ordered six hundred U.S.-owned companies to register all their assets in Cuba.

Khrushchev now entered the game openly. On July 9, he warned the United States, stressing that he was speaking "figuratively," that, "should the need arise, Soviet artillerymen can support the Cuban people by missile fire," pointing out that the United States was now within range of the Soviets' new generation of intercontinental ballistic missiles. Eisenhower denounced Khrushchev's threats and warned that the United States would not permit a regime "dominated by international communism" in the Western Hemisphere, something, he said, Khrushchev was obviously attempting in Cuba. The very next day, Khrushchev announced that the Soviet Union would buy the seven hundred thousand tons of sugar cut from the American sugar quota.

In Havana, Che shook a happy fist at Washington, saying that Cuba was now protected by "the greatest military power on earth; nuclear weapons now stand in the face of imperialism." Nikita Khrushchev insisted that he had been only speaking "figuratively," but before long, the world would discover that the threat was very real. And, as always, Che had been the first to say so.

# CHE

## ERNESTO (CHÉ) GUEVARA:
# THE "RED DICTATOR"
# BACK OF CASTRO

### U.S. NEWS AND WORLD REPORT

### JULY 18, 1960

Look behind Fidel Castro and his brother Raúl for the real "Red dictator" of Cuba.

Ernesto (Ché) Guevara is the "brains" of Castro's Cuban Government. Guevara is not Cuban, but Argentine; not an emotional Latin by temperament, but a cool, calculating Communist.

To Guevara, Castro's Cuba is only a steppingstone to a Red conquest of all Latin America.

## havana

ERNESTO (CHÉ) GUEVARA, an Argentine and not a Cuban, is turning out to be the real "Red dictator" of Cuba.

Guevara, not Fidel or Raúl Castro, is at the controls in this fast-moving period when vast U.S. investments are being seized.

It is Guevara—described as an agent of international Communism—who must find the means to finance the economy of Cuba. Guevara, among other things, is president of the National Bank of Cuba. His hand is on every bank account, corporate and private, in the island. His are the decisions that determine the direction and the use of Cuban resources.

Guevara is surrounded and advised by a team of highly trained Communists drawn from Chile, Ecuador, Mexico and other Latin-American countries. These men, for the most part, have been trained in the national banks and Government offices of these Latin-American countries, waiting for just such an opportunity as Guevara is now affording them in Cuba.

Also advising Guevara has been Alexander Alekseyev, head of the Latin-American division of the Soviet Foreign Ministry. Alekseyev, however, now is moving on to Uruguay, headquarters of Soviet activity in Latin America, and thence into Argentina. This move ties in with Guevara's plans for Cuba.

**Plan for a take-over.** To Guevara, Cuba is only an incident in what he and his Communist aides regard as their real mission. This mission, according to those who work closely with Guevara, is to develop Cuba as a base for a Communist take-over of much of Latin America. What is taking place in Cuba is regarded as only a warm-up operation.

Guevara is described as the real "pro" among Latin-American Communists, a man who is the intellectual superior of Fidel Castro, Fidel's brother Raúl, and all the other leaders of the revolutionary "26th of July Movement."

Guevara's aides find him hard, ruthless, fast to act and little given to pointless talking. He is not, they say, a man of Latin temperament, but he understands and uses such emotional men as Fidel Castro, who loves the spotlight and the cheers of a crowd.

For himself, the "Red dictator" of Cuba avoids the spotlight. Guevara seldom makes a public address. He can and does delegate authority, but he expects and gets complete obedience from his subordinates. Guevara's work day starts at noon and runs until 5 the next morning. It is in the early hours of the morning that he often can be found in the company of Fidel and Raúl Castro and their cronies, planning the next move for the revolution.

*From doctor to Red agent.* Guevara, trained as a physician but active through his adult life as a Communist agent, is credited with supplying the brain power to the guerrilla forces led by the Castro brothers. The Argentine, it is said, used Castro's guerrilla forces to needle Batista into desperate measures of repression, then used Batista's enemies to arouse world opinion.

Now, as head of Cuba's central bank, Guevara holds the purse strings of the whole Government and, particularly, of the vast operations of INRA—the National Institute of Agrarian Reform.

It is INRA that is taking over the industry, the farm land and the essential services of Cuba. On the day of "intervention"—the term used by Castro's men to describe Government seizure of private property—an employe of INRA, who can be fired at Guevara's will, turns up as the new boss.

*Communist aides.* Guevara has built up a strong organization of Communists who stay out of the limelight. Some of these Red experts are Cubans, but many are Communists from other Latin-American countries.

At Guevara's side in the National Bank there is Jaime Barrios, a Chilean Communist who once was employed as an economist in the Banco Central de Chile. An official of that bank in Santiago, Chile's capital, reported that six of the bank's economists, all known in Chile as members of the Communist Party, quit their jobs and went to Cuba to work for Guevara.

Also under Guevara's control is the Banco Cubano de Comercio Exterior, which directs the financing of Cuba's foreign trade. In key posts at this institution are two other Guevara men—Raul Maldonado, described as a member of Ecuador's Communist Party, and Jacinto Torres, a Cuban Communist who once directed the economic page of "Hoy," the party's organ in Havana.

Although Guevara concentrates on running Cuba through the Bank and INRA, he has carefully retained certain jobs given to him early in the revolution. One of these is the task of directing the indoctrination of Cuba's armed forces—both the regular armed forces and the "Peoples' Militia" of civilian volunteers.

In addition, military instructors of the Cuban Army now rely on a recently published book entitled, "Guerrilla Warfare." The author: Ché Guevara.

*The story of Soviet oil.* An indication of how Cuba's "Red dictator" works is provided by the experience of U. S. oil companies. Last January, when Soviet First Deputy Premier Anastas I. Mikoyan visted Cuba, Guevara arranged—among other things—for the importation of Soviet oil. To process the oil, Guevara seized a small Cuban-owned refinery. The first Soviet oil reached Cuba this spring. By mid-June, imports from Russia were more than the single refinery could handle.

At this point, Guevara "requested" U.S. and British-owned oil companies to refine Soviet oil. If the companies agreed, Guevara hinted, he might approve payment to the companies of 60 million dollars owed them by the Cuban Government. The companies rejected this deal. Their refineries in Cuba were seized.

It is Guevara who has supervised INRA's operations in "land reform" in Cuba. Fidel Castro barnstormed the countryside, promising Cuba's landless farm workers that they would get land. A few did. But, gradually, Guevara persuaded Fidel Castro that the huge estates owned by rich Cubans and by U. S. sugar interests could be better operated as "cooperatives" under INRA's direction. Now Cuban workers, still landless, find Guevara's INRA agents merely taking over the direction of big estates, while the peasants remain wage earners, not land-owners.

*After Cuba?* Sooner or later, those who know Guevara agree, the Argentine Communist expects Cuba's workers and peasants to turn against the Castros and their Communist backstage manager. By that time, however, Guevara hopes to be reaching into Mexico, Argentina, Guatemala, Panama and other Latin-American countries on the mainland where his Cuban-based Communists are already an influence.

For Guevara, Cuba is but a stepping-stone to the conquest of all of Latin America by Communists who, Guevara is said to believe, will one day rule the whole world.

# FIVE YEARS OF CASTRO'S CUBA
## THEODORE DRAPER

*COMMENTARY*

JANUARY 1964

O N THE FIFTH anniversary of Fidel Castro's regime, it is clearer than ever before that his crucial problem is and has been economic. For about half of these five years, he seemed to enjoy a charmed life. Every crisis worked to his advantage, every enemy made him stronger. After his total, dizzying triumph at the Bay of Pigs in April 1961, nothing seemed impossible to him any longer.

The turning point, at least visibly, came early in 1962. Ever since the purge of the old-time Communist leader, Aníbal Escalante, in March of that year, nothing has turned out quite right for Castro. We now know that the Escalante purge was part of an internal crisis far more serious than had previously been realized. The gravest aspect of this crisis was hidden deep in the Cuban countryside. It amounted to nothing less than a rebellious Cuban peasantry. I would not use these terms, "serious crisis" and "rebellious," if two of the foremost Cuban leaders—in the first case Minister of Industries Ernesto Che Guevara and in the second President (now Minister) Carlos Rafael

Rodríguez of INRA, the agrarian reform organization—had not used them already.[1]

Both Guevara and Rodríguez agree that the crisis was generated in 1961. According to Rodríguez, who has given the most detailed account, "serious errors" were committed in the last half of 1961 and the first two months of 1962. In 1961, food production was still largely in private hands, and the crisis hinged on the right of the private peasants to sell their products. As Rodríguez put it, "the great mass of *campesinos*—even the poor ones—showed the class tendency with respect to profit." They wanted, in other words, to sell at the highest price instead of handing over their wares to INRA for much lower fixed prices.

It was a classical confrontation. Faced with this traditional peasant desire to take advantage of a sellers' market, the Cuban authorities cracked down. Rodríguez specifically blamed INRA officials, local political leaders, and even the armed forces. The peasants' goods were seized and in some cases their land confiscated. This was not a war against *latifundistas* or large landowners, for there were no more. It was a fierce struggle against small and middle peasants, predominantly the former. The severity of the methods may be gathered from Rodríguez's observation that they violated "revolutionary legality" and made no discrimination between rich and poor. The strength of the resistance may be inferred from his allusion to the peasants' "disagreement and rebelliousness" [*inconformidad y rebeldia*].

In effect, the peasants sold on the black market or they went on strike. They sowed less and grew less. In 1962, especially in the months of March and November, the peasants had their revenge in the country-wide shortages that developed. Rodríguez, another old-time Communist, was brought in as the new President of INRA in February. Castro reversed INRA policy and temporarily gave way to the peasants by lifting all restrictions, but the damage had been done. The regime was so acutely worried that in June it ordered a parade of tanks and machine-guns in the city of Cárdenas as a warning to housewives who had come out in the streets beating pots and pans to protest food

[1]Che Guevara, *Siempre* (Mexico City), interview with Victor Rico Galán, June 19, 1963; Carlos Rafael Rodríguez, *Revolución*, May 18, 1963. (In the following notes, I have cited the source, mainly newspapers, that I happened to obtain. Most of the information cited, however, appeared in all the Cuban papers but not always of exactly the same date.)

shortages.[2] Rodríguez implies that it was a rather close shave: "Only faith in the revolution, only faith in Fidel, prevented the peasantry from losing confidence in the revolution."[3]

But the private peasants were not the only ones in trouble. The "cooperatives" were also caught up in the crisis. The essential reason was that they were cooperatives in name only. In practice, as Rodríguez later admitted, they had been transformed into *granjas del pueblo* or state farms. INRA administered them from above without in the least taking their members' wishes into account, giving them any voice in their affairs, or even holding *pro forma* meetings. From the point of view of their members, the cooperatives had all the disadvantages of state farms and none of the advantages, the most important of the latter being a guaranteed wage. Here again the crisis built up in the last half of 1961 and burst out in the first half of 1962. In November 1961, Castro himself remarked that the peasants had become so "allergic" to the cooperatives that they "feared" the very word.[4] In June 1962, Rodríguez reported that the cooperatives had become "dead organisms" and their members had been fleeing to the *granjas* and private farms.[5] And in August, they were officially transformed into *granjas*.

Not that the *granjas* had been doing too well. They were so badly run at the time, their chief administrator has revealed, that 80 per cent of the local administrators had to be removed.[6] In 1962, then, the Castro regime ran into trouble on all three of its agricultural fronts—privately-owned lands, "cooperatives," and *granjas*. One of the more durable myths about Castro's Cuba is the idea that the "agrarian reform" has been the most successful aspect of the revolution. If this were true, the past two or three years would have been very different.

---

[2]A pro-Castro writer, Maurice Zeitlin, who visited Cuba after the Cárdenas demonstration, has confirmed the essential facts: "*Organized* dissent is prohibited, if one can judge by the government's response to a recent demonstration of a group of housewives in Cárdenas who went marching through the streets banging pots to protest food shortages. The next day the government put on an impressive military display which included helmeted soldiers (a sight one rarely sees in Cuba) and tanks" (*The Nation*, New York, November 3, 1962, p. 287). I described the incident at some length in *The Reporter*, January 17, 1963.

[3]Carlos Rafael Rodríguez, *Revolución*, May 18, 1963. His fullest analysis of the crisis appeared in *Cuba Socialista*, May 1963, pp. 12–14.

[4]*Revolución*, November 11, 1961.

[5]*Ibid.*, June 19, 1962. More details are given in *Cuba Socialista*, May 1963, p. 12.

[6]Interview with Crostóbal Díaz, Vallina, Administrador General de Granjas del Pueblo, *Hoy*, July 6, 1963.

Gradually, the agricultural miasma settled over the entire economic landscape. It made rationing necessary, which in turn brought on inflation, because the urban population had more to spend but less to buy. The inflationary spiral infected the workers who no longer had the incentive to exert themselves for what they could not get anyway. Workers' absenteeism began to reach alarming proportions because workers found they could earn enough in two or three days to buy the little that was available. The quality of work also suffered with declining morale and reduced effective purchasing power. From the viewpoint of the regime, the chief culprits were the skilled workers, formerly the hard core of the organized Cuban proletariat. Castro had complained bitterly about the attitude of the electrical workers as long ago as December 1960, but his wrath with what he called "worker-aristocrats"—whom he grouped with the big and little bourgeoisie and imperialist monopolies—came out most forcefully in a speech addressed to party members in the construction industry in July 1963. He assailed the drop in productivity in the construction industry and accused the workers of doing more under the capitalists than under his regime.[7] Guevara recently ascribed the "terrible loss of conscience for quality" to the "initial scarcity of raw materials, and the suppression of private property."[8]

Yet one of the most significant aspects of this crisis was the fact that the Cuban leaders were not prepared for it. Nothing that had happened in 1961 had forewarned them because 1961 had been a relatively good year, so good that the former President of the Cuban National Bank, the late Dr. Raúl Cepero Bonilla, called it "the year of the highest agricultural production."[9] This was especially true of Cuba's key crop, sugar, which still provided over three-quarters of its export earnings. The 1961 sugar crop was an exceptionally large one of 6.8 million tons, the second largest in its history. But the 1962 crop was only 4.8 million tons and the 1963 crop was still less, only 3.8 million.[10] Between 1961 and 1963, the only negative factor beyond human control was the drought, which could not, however, by itself have accounted for such a drastic drop. All the other fac-

[7]*Obra Revolucionaria*, December 15, 1960; *Revolución*, July 2, 1963.
[8]*La Tarde*, November 11, 1963.
[9]*Cuba Socialista*, January 1963, p. 89.
[10]Gerardo Bernardo, *Hoy Domingo*, August 11, 1963.

tors were man-made, and the results should have made the Cuban leaders happy.

But they did not. Why they did not is the economic key to Castro's first five years in power.

## II

IN THE FIRST year, 1959, Guevara had been put in charge of INRA's Department of Industrialization. His group worked on the "first simple and tentative lines" for the future Cuban economy. As Guevara himself later told the story, they made lists of products that had for many years been imported chiefly from the United States, and then began a "search for offers" of longterm foreign aid for the development of Cuba's own "basic industry." The "search" ended with the arrival of Soviet First Deputy Premier Anastas I. Mikoyan in Havana on February 4, 1960, and the signing of the first Soviet-Cuban trade agreement on February 13 of that year. Then Guevara went on a junket of Eastern Europe, lining up Soviet bloc commitments of large-scale credits "to build a good number of basic industries." The Soviets promised $100,000,000 for a steel industry, electric plants, an oil refinery, and a geological survey; Czechoslovakia, an automobile factory; China, $60,000,000 for twenty-four different factories; Rumania, fifteen; Bulgaria, five; Poland, twelve; East Germany, ten. The offers were snapped up.[11]

Soon after Mikoyan's departure, Guevara and other top Cuban leaders began a campaign to prepare Cuban public opinion for a rupture of the traditional economic ties with the United States, especially the preferential sugar quota. Guevara initiated the drive on March 2, 1960, in a speech which referred to the "quantity of slavery represented for our country by the three million tons which we sell at supposedly preferential prices." The leading Cuban Communist, Blas Roca, went to Moscow in May for his first meeting with Nikita Khrushchev and, unable to restrain himself until his return, wrote a letter published in the official Communist organ: "Cuba cannot be blockaded economically by the U.S. imperialists. Our factories will not be paralyzed from lack of oil, neither will our homes run short of bread in case the U.S. monopolies decide to reduce the sugar quota and refuse to send what

[11]Guevara, *Cuba Socialista*, March 1962, p. 30.

we need for our normal life." Fidel Castro boasted that Cuba could produce more sugar and get more for it if there were no U.S. sugar quota.[12]

At this point, the Eisenhower administration, against the better judgment of the U.S. Ambassador, Philip W. Bonsal, played into the Cubans' hands. In June, 1960, three U.S.-and British-owned oil refineries in Cuba, in consultation with Washington, refused a Cuban request to process two barge-loads of Soviet crude oil. The Cubans promptly took over the oil refineries; the Eisenhower administration suspended the remainder of the 1960 sugar quota; the Cubans expropriated all U.S.-owned properties; the United States retaliated with a trade embargo. In retrospect, it appears clear that only a Cuban government which was already inwardly committed to, and had prepared the way for, a break would have pushed the matter of the oil to such an extremity; and only a U.S. government which had grossly miscalculated the forces at work or did not care any longer for other reasons would have made the break so easy.[13]

The Cubans welcomed the U.S. embargo. "Now," exulted Blas Roca, "Cuba has freed her foreign commerce from the monopoly of an imperalist power. Now Cuba has won freedom of trade with every country in the world." Fidel Castro scoffed at the idea that the United States could hurt Cuba, since the Cubans could obtain all they needed and wanted from the "socialist countries" and "neutrals." Guevara assured the Cuban people that the U.S. embargo would have few serious consequences, that it would not imperil the revolution, and that the U.S. would be hurt even more than Cuba by its own action.[14]

THERE WAS AN important internal political side to Cuban-Soviet relations. Cuban-Soviet economic ties were closely coordinated with Cuban Communist-*Fidelista* political ties. The process of Communist-*Fidelista* fusion was lengthy and complex from 1958 to the end of 1960, and the whole story cannot yet be told. But we know—to cite a single example—that, as late as May 1959, Fidel Castro personally

[12]Guevara, *Revolución*, March 3, 1960; Blas Roca, *Hoy*, May 24, 1960; Fidel Castro, *Hoy*, May 29, 1960.

[13]We now know that President Eisenhower authorized the training of a stand-by Cuban exile force in March 1960.

[14]Blas Roca, *Hoy*, October 13, 1960; Fidel Castro, *ibid.*, October 16, 1960; Guevara, *ibid.*, October 21, 1960.

engaged in an acrimonious public controversy with the Communists.[15] By the end of the year, however, it was impermissible in Cuba to say about the Communists what Castro had said earlier; and with the arrest of Major Hubert Matos in October 1959, anti-Communism was made a counter-revolutionary crime. Castro intervened to save the Communists from rout at the trade union congress in November. This transition to anti-anti-Communism in public policy preceded the Cuban-Soviet economic agreement of February 1960. After the agreement, the active process of fusion speeded up. It all took place behind the scenes, of course, but we can now situate it in the context of Cuba's economic changeover.

Immediately after the suspension of the U.S. sugar quota, Guevara told a youth congress in Havana in July that the Cuban revolution was "Marxist." The following month, as U.S. businesses in Cuba were being expropriated, Blas Roca called for the perspective of "complete union" or "fusion" of all the revolutionary forces "in a single movement."[16] We have more recently been told that this was not the beginning but rather near the end of the process of fusion. On December 2, 1960, Castro presided at a meeting to set up schools, *Escuelas de Instrucción Revolucionaria*, to train cadres for the "united party." The director of these schools, Lionel Soto, a pre-1959 Communist, has disclosed that this meeting was the first formal manifestation of "the integration of the revolutionary forces."[17]

These dates are extraordinarily revealing. For Guevara did not discover that the Cuban revolution was "Marxist" in July 1960 and Blas Roca did not call for fusion in August because the ideas had suddenly popped into their heads; the first *formal* manifestation of fusion did not take place in December without a considerable period of gesta-

[15]In a television interview on May 21, 1959, Castro discussed unrest in the village of San Luis and remarked that there were "many coincidences" between the Communists and the "counter-revolutionaries" responsible for the unrest. The Executive Bureau of the Communist *Partido Socialista Popular* immediately issued a statement protesting against "such an unjust and unjustifiable attack" (*Hoy*, May 23, 1959), This incident, together with simultaneous attacks on the Communists at the *Fidelista*-controlled sugar workers congress, was taken so seriously that the P.S.P. Central Committee was hastily called together on May 25 to deal with the situation (*Hoy*, May 26, 1959). In his "I am a Marxist-Leninist" speech on December 2, 1961, Castro alluded to his past anti-Communist "prejudices" and said that he had been a victim of imperialist propaganda.

[16]Partido Socialista Popular, *VIII Asamblea Nacional*, August 16–21, 1960, p. 209.
[17]*Cuba Socialista*, February 1963, p. 30.

tion. The "search for offers" in 1959, the Soviet-Cuban trade agreement of February 1960, and the Communist-*Fidelista* fusion later that year were parts of a single, continuous process, not isolated incidents.

Another major decision came up at the end of 1960. This one grew out of the suspension of the Cuban sugar quota by the Eisenhower administration in July. The Soviet Union had committed itself to purchasing 1,000,000 tons annually for five years or one-third of the former U.S. quota. The Cubans could see no way, in the depressed world sugar market of 1960–61, to dispose of the remainder. Moreover, they were then obsessed by two main objectives—rapid industrialization and agricultural diversification. Sugar represented all that had stood in the way of industrialization and diversification in the past. Instead of facing the loss of the U.S. market with a certain trepidation, the Cuban leaders could barely repress their joy. They viewed more industrialization and less sugar production as opposite sides of the same coin, and embraced both causes with equal enthusiasm. When the U.S. quota was suppressed, therefore, they considered it to be a positive good and, as Castro later put it, "took the decision to cut down on all that sugar-cane and reduce sugar production."[18]

Drought or no drought, then, there would have been a much smaller Cuban sugar crop in 1962 and 1963 (not in 1961 because the preparations had been made the year before). The sugar acreage was deliberately reduced, replanting neglected, and weeding pursued half-heartedly: in general, the entire industry was given a very low order of priority. The drought hurt other crops but, in the all-important case of sugar, it might have been part of the plan. Between the drought and government policy, there was in the period 1961 to 1963 a reduction of 14 per cent in sugar area cut, of 42 per cent in ground cane, and 33 per cent in unit yield.[19]

Nevertheless, as 1961 opened, Castro's mastery of events, helped along perhaps by more than a bit of luck, seemed infallible. He had freed himself from all economic and diplomatic ties to the United States in a manner that made him seem to many the aggrieved and innocent party. The Eisenhower administration's decision to suspend the sugar quota had fallen in with his own desire not only to get rid of the quota but to cut sugar production. The Soviet bloc had appar-

---

[18]*Revolución*, June 28, 1963.
[19]Gerardo Bernardo, *Hoy Domingo*, August 11, 1963.

ently agreed to underwrite what Guevara had called "a process of accelerated industrialization."[20] A new Ministry of Industries was created in February of that year with Guevara in charge. And after the April invasion fiasco, the Cuban cup ran over.

## III

WHAT WENT WRONG?

The private peasantry, the cooperatives, and the *granjas* were not the only things that went wrong. When a Latin American sympathizer asked Guevara to name some of the errors which had been made in Cuba, his answer, only half in jest, was: "It will have to be only some, because we would need ten days to recount all the errors."[21]

Guevara's own program of "accelerated industrialization" was the source of some of the worst disenchantment. The original conception was almost childishly simple. Its aim was the substitution of homemade goods for those previously imported from the United States. Its method was the physical transplantation across half the globe of dozens of factories in the shortest possible time. Its financial basis was long-term credits or outright gifts from the Communist world.

By early 1962, Guevara knew that there was something radically wrong with the scheme. At that time, he analyzed the trouble as follows: "We failed to put the proper emphasis on the utilization of our own resources; we worked with the fixed purpose of producing substitutes for finished imported articles, without clearly seeing that these articles are made with raw materials which must be had in order to manufacture them."[22]

In short, the Cuban industrializers thought solely in terms of factories, not in terms of raw materials for the factories. They were stunned to learn that, in many cases, the raw materials cost almost as much as the imported finished articles. In order to free themselves from dependence on the importation of finished articles, they had made themselves even more dependent on the importation of raw materials which they could not afford. Guevara subsequently explained: "We began to

[20]*Hoy*, June 21, 1960.
[21]*Revolución*, August 21, 1963.
[22]*Cuba Socialista*, March 1962, p. 33.

acquire factories, but we did not think of the raw materials for them that we would have to import." In this way, he said, two years had been lost "installing factories for a series of articles which could be bought at almost the same price as the raw materials that we needed to produce them."[23]

This unforeseen, though hardly unforeseeable, relationship between finished products and raw materials led to a Cuban balance-of-payments crisis. In 1960, when the Soviet bloc was anxious to displace the United States in the Cuban economy, it had been lavish in promises and credits. Two years later, however, it was less interested in what the Cubans wanted than in what the Cubans could afford. Either the credits had run out or they had been used so badly that the bloc had balked at throwing good money after bad.

At some point toward the end of 1961 or beginning of 1962, it is clear, the Soviets called a halt and demanded an accounting. We know from Carlos Rafael Rodríguez that, by March 1962, Soviet bloc "advisers," who had become ubiquitous in the Cuban administrative apparatus, had become highly critical of Cuban methods, especially in the Ministry of Foreign Trade. In the same month, Guevara published an article in which he warned that Cuba would have to pay for its raw materials through its own foreign trade and not with Soviet credits or handouts. To be sure, the Cubans did receive further credits from the Soviet Union, but as Guevara later explained, they were to cover the existing unfavorable balance of payments, not to build industries.[24]

The indications are that it took some time and not a little anguish for the Cubans to give up the view of industrialization as a simple, rather naïve, two-way process of factories-finished products and to think in terms of the far more complex, critical triangle of factories-raw materials-exports.

In a sense, the Cuban problem had come to resemble the Chinese problem — how far would the Soviets go to pay for their speedy industrialization? In both cases, the Soviets started to go part of the way, but then, for reasons of their own, not necessarily the same in both cases, they demanded a slow-down of the pace and payment for services rendered. Consciously or unconsciously, the Cubans had gone ahead after 1960 as if the Soviets had given them not a $100,000,000

[23]*Revolución*, August 21, 1963.
[24]Rodríguez, *El Mundo*, March 25, 1962; Guevara, *Cuba Socialista*, March 1962, p. 33; Guevara, *Hoy*, February 12, 1963.

five-year credit but an unlimited account. There would have been no balance-of-payments crisis if the Soviets had not called for payments.

As of the middle of 1963 at least, the Cubans still had few of the factories that the Soviet bloc had promised to install. It appears that only eight new factories had come from the bloc (Czechoslovakia three, East Germany three, USSR one, Poland one).[25]

ONCE THE CUBANS had to face the realities of production costs, profit margins, and balance of payments, all their other problems came down on them too. If they had to pay for imports with exports, they were driven back to the key economic fact of Cuban life from which they had fled — that sugar made up over three-fourths of Cuban exports. But for about two years, the Cuban leaders had been denigrating the importance of sugar production and had deliberately cut it down. The resistance of the private peasantry, the "disagreement and rebelliousness" in the sugar-growing "cooperatives," and the mismanagement of the *granjas* were not merely symptoms of an agricultural crisis; they were not merely contributing factors in the vicious cycle of rationing, inflation, absenteeism, high costs, and low quality; they were directly linked to the neuralgic points of Cuban-Soviet economic relations — the trade agreements, the negotiation of credits, the balance of payments.

Thus what Guevara called the "two fundamental errors" — the "declaration of war on sugar cane" and the desire for factories without "thinking of the raw materials for them"[26] — intersected and interacted, exacerbating each other.

Guevara recently gave some examples of the blundering that brought the industrialization program to a standstill. Two of the factories from Czechoslovakia were to make picks and shovels. Cuba could just as well have bought the finished products from East Europe. Instead, the factories had to import raw materials which depleted the already extremely scarce monetary reserves. Another Cuban factory made sacks; it required imports of jute, which cost more than the finished sacks. The Cubans have now decided to buy another factory which will use a native fiber. Guevara also lamented the fact that Cuba had factories to make metal containers — but no tin-plate.[27] Judging from the fre-

---

[25]*Hoy*, June 2, 1963, p. 6.

[26]*Revolución*, August 21, 1963.

[27]*La Tarde*, November 11, 1963.

quency and pain with which the Cuban leaders have mentioned their expensive education in the economics of raw materials, these miscalculations must have been the rule rather than the exception.

In effect, Castro's first year in power, 1959, was one in which there was no "socialist" planning; in the second year, the "old order" was completely shattered but only the rudiments of a new order could be established; in the third year, the Castro regime was for the first time able to impose its basic ideas on the economy, and it thereby generated the subsequent crisis; in the fourth year, ironically called the "Year of Planning," the crisis erupted and caused a preliminary reconsideration of the policy; and in the fifth year, the crisis deepened in the first months and brought about a change of line in the second half.

The new line is, in theory, not so much a clear-cut choice between agriculture and industry as a reversal of their previously allotted roles. The old line had encouraged industry at the expense of agriculture. The new one is based on the development of agriculture as the precondition of industrialization. In practice, however, agriculture will get such a high priority that not much is expected to be left over, at least in the foreseeable future, for industry.

Above all, the Cubans have been rudely awakened from the dream of industrialization by courtesy of the Soviet Union. Henceforth, Cuba's industrialization will depend primarily on the classical method of "primitive accumulation" — squeezing its own peasantry to extract the savings necessary for industrial investment. In a sense, the Cuban leaders have had to go all the way back in order to start over again.


## IV


THE CUBAN LEADERS have tried to account for the crisis in characteristically different ways. The three who have done the most talking — Castro, Guevara, and Rodríguez — have revealed not only a great deal about the crisis but also about themselves. Their main problem has not been to tell the people how bad the situation was, for this was common knowledge in Cuba, but to explain why it happened and who was to blame.

Castro spoke frequently and at great length in the last half of 1963 on what had been wrong in Cuba, and his emphasis was overwhelmingly on what the Cuban people had done that was wrong.

**THEODORE DRAPER**
238

Sometimes, as on June 4, he seemed to hold his own "Cuban revolutionaries" mainly responsible for the economic mess. He accused them of "agitating" and "mobilizing" too much, of building "in the air," blissfully oblivious to "the economic basis for everything." He was, he said, even "a little ashamed" of them. Sometimes, as on July 1, he complained bitterly that the workers did not work long and hard enough. "And we have to carry on this struggle," he said, "implacably, in all places, in all parts of the country, without a truce, without vacillation, one day demanding that the sugar workers, the agricultural workers, the shoe workers should produce more, should improve their quality." Or, on August 10, he turned on the "socialist administrators" whose waste, he said, was comparable to what the capitalists used to steal, who "consolidated" everything from garages to bars into nation-wide bureaucratic monstrosities, who could not manage the former U.S.-owned lands as well as the "Yankee monopolies" had managed them. He made the broad generalization, on October 2, that "our weakness is principally in the lack of experience and ability of the people who have been in many places in agriculture." On October 21, he lit into the trade unions for accumulating funds by means of compulsory deductions and fund-raising parties, both of which were to be forbidden, and for their grievance committees, which he called an example of "illusionism" and "revolutionary infantilism." On October 30, he turned on most of his cabinet ministers for spending too much money. On October 31, he incited a crowd, not for the first time, against "the bum [*vago*], the parasite, the *lumpen*" (the latter has become one of Castro's favorite expressions since he officially adopted Marxism-Leninism).

The notable thing about almost all this criticism, scolding, and abuse is that they were directed at the people rather than at his own policies. The people were rarely in positions of any real power and most often totally without power. And by avoiding policies and power, Fidel Castro did not have to criticize, scold, or abuse Fidel Castro.

Guevara's emphasis, on the other hand, has been refreshingly different. He has made several attempts to analyze what went wrong, two of which are worth noting at some length. The first was his reply to a question from the French correspondent, Jean Daniel, on whether the U.S. "blockade" had endangered Cuba:

We have serious difficulties in Cuba. But not from the fact

of what you call the blockade. First, there has never been a complete blockade. We have not ceased increasing our trade with Great Britain and France, for example. . . .

Our difficulties come principally from our errors. The greatest, that which did us the most harm, is, as you know, the under-exploitation of sugar cane. The others involve all the inevitable gropings which the adaptation of collectivism to a local situation implies.[28]

But a speech by Guevara in Algiers on July 13, perhaps the most revealing confession of Cuba's misplanning on record, does not make the other errors seem so "inevitable." The fundamental trouble, said Guevara, came about because the Cubans tried to do two things that were contradictory. On the one hand, they "copied in detail the planning techniques of a fraternal country whose specialists came to help us," and on the other hand, they insisted on making their own decisions with "spontaneity and lack of analysis." He gave as an example of this planless planning the way they had arrived at their annual rate of economic growth. Instead of attempting to find out "what we had, what we should spend, and what we had left over for development," the Cuban planners simply assumed a 15 per cent rate of growth and made everything else in the plan conform to it. Cuba had never made more than 10,000,000 pairs of shoes but the plan called for 22,000,000, and cattle and technical facilities were already inadequate. The chief of the forestry department sent up such a fantastic estimate of lumber production that Cuba, traditionally an importer of lumber, planned to export it. "Result: we continued to import lumber," said Guevara, "but we imported it late, badly, desperately looking around where to get it."

One may imagine the frustrations of the "fraternal specialists" in Cuba in this period. If the full story ever comes out, we may be sure that neither side will be lacking in tales of woe. But even if the planning had been less "ridiculous," which is how Guevara characterized it, the major policy decisions, as Guevara described them, would have been near-disastrous anyway. "In industry," he said, "we made a plan of development based fundamentally on the idea of being self-sufficient in a series of durable consumption goods or intermediate

[28]*L'Express* (Paris), July 25, 1963.

industrial articles, which, however, could be obtained with relative facility from friendly countries. In this way we committed our investment capacity without completely developing our own resources of raw materials, including some intermediate products that we now make." And "in agriculture, we committed the fundamental error of scorning the importance of sugar cane, our fundamental product, trying to achieve quick diversification, as a consequence of which the cane stocks were neglected, and this, added to an extra-ordinarily intense drought that afflicted us for two years, led to a serious drop in our sugar production."

IN SOME WAYS, then, Guevara has been far more candid than Castro, but he has not been any more self-critical. The "errors" of high policy, which he has expressed more clearly than anyone else, obviously strike at the very top, including Guevara himself. Yet like the others, he always speaks of them as if they had been committed by some anonymous force and not by the top leadership itself. In fact, the reversal of Cuban policy has been in large part a defeat for some of Guevara's favorite ideas. It was he who first put forward the slogan of "accelerated industrialization." It was he who played the leading role in negotiating the trade agreements with the Soviet bloc. It was he who broached the theory that "Cuban socialism," unlike the other varieties, should be based predominantly on "moral" rather than on "material" incentives.

This last point is typical of what might be called "Guevara-ism." As late as March 1963, Guevara still insisted publicly that the "moral stimulus" should take precedence over the "material stimulus," which he scornfully described as a "residue of the past" to be removed from the popular consciousness with every advance of the revolution. He told Jean Daniel in July: "For me, it is a question of doctrine. Economic socialism without Communist morality does not interest me."[29] Yet by

[29]A further point he made in this interview raises an interesting question about his Marxism. Guevara continued: "We are struggling against poverty, but at the same time against alienation. One of the fundamental objectives of Marxism is to eliminate interest—the factor of 'individual interest'—and profit from psychological motivations." But Marx located "alienation" in the capitalist system of production, in capitalist exploitation. The concept had nothing to do with counterposing "material" and "moral" stimuli in a *socialist* economy, which is itself supposed to do away with alienation. For Marx, the solution for "alienation" was a material one, in the economic order though its consequences would be moral or psychological. The very dissociation of

August, even he had to recognize that the "moral stimulus" had not been very stimulating, and he grudgingly admitted that it was necessary "for the moment to give the material stimulus the importance which it has."[30] One can almost hear the debates in Cuba over relaxing or tightening the economic pressure on the peasants and workers in the guise of offering them more material or more moral "stimulus."

In a sense, Guevara has represented both the most distinctive and the most dubious sides of this Cuban revolution. In the name of Marxism, he has identified himself with theories—the peasantry as the leading revolutionary class, the countryside as the main revolutionary battleground, the primacy of the "moral stimulus"—that are far closer to the tradition of pre-Marxist Russian Populism and homologous movements elsewhere than to orthodox Marxism. He has embodied a peculiar doctrinairism of will and force to overcome all obstacles and enemies. His undoubtedly keen mind has invariably gravitated to the more extreme positions, which, sooner or later, and more often than not, have turned out to be Fidel Castro's positions.

Carlos Rafael Rodríguez has apparently represented a somewhat different tendency. He took over INRA with the slogan "technique, discipline, responsibility." While Guevara was stressing the "moral" over the "material," Rodríguez cautiously advocated both types of incentive. He has complained against what he once called "a certain Jacobin attitude" of underestimating the importance of the scientific approach. "The man of the Revolution," he said pointedly, "formed in the hard school of combat, caught in the clamor of battle, does not always understand the utility and the necessity for the intellectual, for long and patient work, hoped-for results and failures sooner or later overcome."[31] Early in 1963, Guevara and Rodríguez seemed to be engaged in a struggle over control of the sugar industry. The question

---

"socialist economy" and "Communist morality" would be alien to Marx's thought. From a Marxist viewpoint, a "socialist economy" should have a "socialist morality," and a "Communist economy" should have a "Communist morality" (assuming that Guevara is making the traditional distinction between socialism and Communism). Guevara's viewpoint actually implies that "alienation" can exist in a socialist as well as in a capitalist society, which may be true, but not in a Marxist sense. I am not suggesting that Guevara has no right to mix his categories; I merely question that it should be done in the name of poor, dead Marx.

[30]*Revolución*, March 25, 1963; *L'Express*, July 25, 1963; *Revolución*, August 21, 1963.
[31]Rodríguez, *Hoy*, March 12 and 24, 1963.

had arisen in the top leadership whether, in view of the sad state of the agricultural side of the industry under Rodríguez's jurisdiction, it might not be better to transfer control of the whole operation to the industrial side under Guevara's jurisdiction. The decision went in favor of leaving the agricultural sector of the industry in Rodríguez's INRA. But Guevara, evidently not satisfied, soon denounced the lack of coordination in the industry and demanded "only one road, only one view, only one voice." Rodríguez came back with a reminder that the decision had been made to leave the production of the sugar cane to INRA, but agreed that there was a problem and added that he intended to discuss it further with Che. Nothing more of this little squabble was heard publicly, and Rodríguez still has charge of the growing of sugar cane in the field.[32]

A WELL-KNOWN FRENCH agronomist and Castro sympathizer, Professor René Dumont, who was given unusual opportunities to study Cuban agricultural policy and practice, has told revealing stories of his experiences. Dumont came to Cuba for the first time on his own initiative in May 1960. At that time he was struck by the dangerously excessive tendency to centralize and socialize (a better term would be the French *étatisé*). He foresaw that the centralization would lead to a top-heavy, deadening bureaucracy and the "socialization" to macrocephalic, inefficient production units. Significantly, he confided his doubts to Carlos Rafael Rodríguez, then editor of the official Communist organ, *Hoy*, who asked him to repeat them to Fidel Castro in person. Castro seemed most grateful to hear Dumont's criticisms, and a press interview was arranged for Dumont. Encouraged by Castro's seemingly favorable reception, Dumont publicly voiced his misgivings, but great was his astonishment when the entire Havana press failed to carry a word about the interview the next day.

He returned, however, three months later, in August 1960, at Castro's personal invitation. As he put it, "my disquiet increased." He was taken by Castro on a personal tour of the Ciénaga de Zapata, a large swampland into which Castro had sunk millions of dollars in an extravagant reclamation project. His disquiet increased because Castro told him privately during this tour that he intended to set up the large-scale state-owned *granjas*. Dumont tried unsuccessfully to dissuade him.

[32]Guevara, *Hoy*, February 12, 1963; Rodríguez, speech of February 24, 1963.

Not only did Castro go ahead with the *granjas* in 1961 but, as we have seen, they swallowed up the "cooperatives" the following year.[33]

In September 1963, Dumont returned to Cuba for the third time. Most of his fears about the *granjas* had been realized. He encountered on a large scale what he has called "bureaucratized anarchy." Again he recommended smaller and more controllable units of production with a view toward trying to do less and to achieve more. Whatever may be the merits of Dumont's views, his insight into the different tendencies within the Castro regime is particularly important:

> The most realistic Cuban leaders, headed by President of the Republic Osvaldo Dorticós and president of INRA Carlos Rafael Rodríguez, have well understood these problems. The dogmatists in the Planning Board and the Ministry of Industries, on the contrary, continue to defend the dangerous thesis of *ultra-centralized leadership of the economy, managed by means of budgetary credits*. The latter scorn the experience accumulated by the other socialist countries. Their justification is that Cuba is a small island endowed with good commercial media, where centralization will be easier than in the U.S.S.R.! Even more serious is the fact that they present the results of their system to the government with an over-optimistic slant and continue to make unrealistic, unattainable forecasts of production, even when the experience of the past years proves them to be wrong (*italics in original*).

The Planning Board (*Junta Central de Planificación*) is headed, it should be noted, by Prime Minister Castro, and the Ministry of Industries, of course, by Guevara. But Dumont still saw one source of hope:

> But to fall into the other extreme of pessimism, to speak of the economic defeat of Cuba, would be an even more serious error. Fidel's intellectual grasp of the economic necessities becomes daily more concrete, more realistic. I would tend to believe that he would make even more rapid progress if he did not fear being treated as a "Bukharinist" or a "Titoist" by the Chinese.[34]

[33]Dumont wrote about his first trip in *L'Express*, July 28, September 8 and 22, 1960, and in Chapter VII of his book *Terres Vivantes* (Plon, 1961).
[34]*France Observateur* (Paris), October 3, 1963.

At least one highly qualified observer, then, had reason to believe that Guevara and Rodríguez belong to somewhat different tendencies within Castro's regime. My own experience with Rodríguez in March 1960 may be worth recalling. After he had patiently answered my questions for about two hours, he suddenly turned the tables and said: "Now I would like to ask you some questions. An outsider sometimes sees things that we are too close to see. What are your impressions of Cuba?" I replied: "My chief impression is that you are declaring war on your entire middle class. If that is what you want, you will get it, but if that is not what you want, you are heading for trouble." Rodríguez thought a moment and then said quietly: "I have tried to tell the same thing to my colleagues but they will not listen."

Nevertheless, one can easily get the wrong impression about a man like Rodríguez. He joined the Communist party of Cuba at the age of twenty in 1933. He went through all the twists and turns of the entire Stalinist period without any record of protest or embarrassment. When the party told him to become a minister in Batista's cabinet in 1944, he became a minister. He has had thirty years of Communist molding, discipline, and loyalty—to the Soviet Union. He has the mentality and training of an intelligent intellectual functionary, not an independent political thinker or leader. He has, whatever his private convictions, faithfully accepted the party line under Castro as he did under Stalin. And he is likely to continue doing so as long as Soviet Russia considers it to be in its interest to support Castro.

There is reason to believe, then, that a struggle of policies and personalities took place in the Cuban top leadership for perhaps a year or more. Out of this struggle has emerged a new stage of Castro's revolution as it enters its sixth year.

**v**

THE NEW STAGE is being called the Second Agrarian Reform. Its repercussions and implications are quite as drastic and far-reaching as those of the first "reform" in May 1959.

The timing of the new order suggests that it came out of the agreements reached by Castro and Khrushchev in Moscow in May 1963. In his report on his Soviet tour on June 4, Castro made known that an "international division of labor" was necessary, according to which

Cuba would specialize in what she was best fitted by nature — namely agriculture. On June 27, he intimated that the "medium farmers," whom he accused of "sabotaging sugar production," were in for a bad time. On July 27, he announced that compulsory military service was coming. On August 10, he touched on a new "agrarian reform," but said that the final details had not yet been decided. On October 2, he publicly proclaimed the Second Agrarian Reform. And on November 12, his brother, Minister of the Armed Forces Raúl Castro, made the official pronouncement on compulsory military service.

This sequence of events in the last six months of 1963 was interconnected because the new "agrarian reform" is but part of a much larger, sweeping changeover in the aims and methods of the regime.

Formally, the Second Agrarian Reform differs from the first in the proportion of privately-owned to state-owned land it establishes. By 1961, the first one had established a balance of 29.16 per cent state-owned *granjas*, 11.83 per cent "cooperatives," and 59.01 per cent privately-owned.[35] After the first two were merged, the balance became more simply about 40 per cent state-owned and about 60 per cent privately-owned. This relationship was, in effect, the ultimate result of the first Agrarian Reform.

The privately-owned 60 per cent was divided into three categories: 140,000 landowners with less than two *caballerías* of land (one *caballeria* equals 33 acres); 60,000 with two to five *caballerias*; and 10,000 with between five and thirty *caballerías*. The first two were classified as small farmers and the third as medium farmers.[36] The *latifundistas* or large landowners had been liquidated in 1959.

In its most elementary sense, the Second Agrarian Reform has shifted the balance from 40–60 in favor of the private sector to 70–30 in favor of the state sector. The shift has been accomplished by another great wave of expropriation, this time of the 10,000 "medium farmers." The remaining 30 per cent of small farmers, however, will also decline because those who drop out will not be replaced. In any case, the small peasants are totally dependent on the state and tightly controlled by an association closely linked to INRA. Gradually the state sector in agriculture will edge up to the 95 per cent of industry already owned by the Cuban state.

[35]Report of Antonio Núñez Jiménez, *Bohemia*, May 28, 1961.
[36]Raúl Cepero Bonilla, *Cuba Socialista*, January 1963, for the division of the privately-owned lands; Fidel Castro, *Hoy*, August 11, 1963, on the classification of small farmers.

Technically, the Second Agrarian Reform has another important side to it. It will attempt to combine more state ownership with more decentralized operation. The plan calls for more regional control and smaller productive units, with greater responsibility for local farm administrators. The regime is counting heavily on youngsters sent to agricultural schools for periods of a few months to as much as two years to staff the new state farms. In effect, if anything, a larger and more efficient bureaucracy will be needed than ever before.

Whether the new system will work out any better than the old remains to be seen. The "bureaucratic anarchy" may get worse rather than better. I do not mean to suggest that there cannot be any fluctuations in Cuba's economic fortunes. The spectacular rise in the world sugar price will prove to be an enormous windfall if the shortage should continue and the Cuban sugar crop can be substantially increased in the next year or two. Castro has indicated that he expects to benefit from high sugar prices in 1965 and 1966, but that the price will plunge again toward 1970. But whatever the short-term factors, the agricultural crisis has had its roots in long-term, basic policies. The errors and misdeeds which Castro has been denouncing—exorbitant costs of production, lax or non-existent methods of accounting, administrative ignorance and bungling—have been symptoms rather than causes.

The underlying cause has been the determination to build "Cuban socialism" on agriculture if it could not be done on industry, and to "socialize" the peasants after socializing the workers had done little good. In large part, the new system is merely the old one writ large. The extension of state ownership in agriculture has become an immediate reality; the institution of efficient decentralization is only a goal. INRA will have to incorporate hundreds of thousands of acres more at the same time as it attempts to exercise less direct control over each unit. There will be more *granjas* than ever before, despite Professor Dumont's touching faith in Fidel Castro; and the only question is whether they will be more efficiently run.

IF THE ECONOMIC side of the Second Agrarian Reform is still questionable, the political side is only too clear. The stage has been set for an unprecedented, government-induced paroxysm of "class warfare" in the countryside. Castro himself used the expression in a speech to agricultural students on October 2 in which he told them to expect a "harder class battle" than had taken place after the first agrarian reform. He did his utmost to whip the boys into a frenzy against the new "class enemy," the "rural bourgeoisie" of medium farmers, who were even more dangerous than the large landowners, he said, because the former had "a certain training, a certain education, many friend-ships."

Oddly enough, in all the criticisms of Cuban agriculture by Cas-tro, Guevara, and especially Rodríguez for many months before the Second Agrarian Reform, the medium farmers had hardly been men-tioned. After all that had been said about the misplanning at the top, the perversion of the cooperatives and the maladministration of the *granjas*, the political ax came down on the medium farmers.

The background of the compulsory military service law is equally curious. The Cuban military buildup was so great by the middle of 1963 that Castro saw fit to boast on June 4 that Cuba enjoyed a "situation of security," as far as any direct invasion by the United States was con-cerned. On June 27, he claimed that the last "counter-revolutionary infiltrators" were being wiped out and had been abandoned by those who had sent them. Thus, his first explanation on July 27 for com-pulsory military service was purely internal in character. He said that it was one of two measures—the other was compulsory junior high school [*Secundaria Básica*] attendance—to prevent "the parasitical ele-ment, the potential *lumpen* of tomorrow" from developing. He linked the military service law solely with adolescents who dropped out of sec-ondary school and became "uneducated, ignorant, parasitical."

It was apparently realized that it might be considered peculiar for "Socialist Cuba" to solve social problems by military means. By the time Raúl Castro officially presented the compulsory military service law on November 12, he found it necessary to make a special point of deny-ing that it had been conceived "to do away with *los vagos*." He pointed out that the new law would mean a substantial saving in soldiers' salaries, because the recruits would get only seven pesos a month and not what they had earned as civilians, as in the former system; he argued that it would enable the armed forces more easily to discharge troops who had served their terms of enlistment.[37] But he did not succeed altogether

[37]In connection with this argument, Raúl Castro made an unexpectedly revealing ref-erence to the arrival of Soviet troops in Cuba in August 1962. He recalled that one unit on the Isle of Pines was supposed to be demobilized that month, and then gave this explanation for the delay: "At those very moments, the Soviet troops were arriv-ing in our country. It was logical to think that, for one reason or another, difficult days might be approaching." Raúl used the expression "*la tropa soviética*," or "Soviet troops,"

in disposing of the suspicion that the new law may be far more important for economic and social than for strictly military reasons.

The unusually low age limit of seventeen will put many youths in the armed forces. Most of the new recruits, Raúl said, will actually come from the 17–20 age group. They will spend three to four months a year cutting sugar cane or picking coffee beans. Raúl justified a three-year service period on the ground that it would enable the armed forces to cut more cane and pick more coffee. In fact, the future Cuban army will be curiously divided into two classes: those who will and those who will not be permitted to bear arms. The latter category will be made up of "the *vagos*, the *lumpen*, the *gusanos*" and other undesirables.[38]

Whether it is the main reason or a most important by-product, the compulsory military service law will give the Castro regime a cheap, militarized labor corps. This corps will take the place of the "volunteer" system on which the regime had previously depended in emergencies. For some time, it had become clear that the "volunteers" were less and less voluntary; they were, in fact, groups of workers hauled off in trucks from government offices and state-owned factories to perform agricultural tasks for which they were ill-fitted and ill-disposed. They were also highly inefficient; they cut the cane too high or picked unripe coffee beans. Worst of all, they were exorbitantly expensive. Fidel Castro admitted that the volunteer system had resulted in an economic loss because, as he put it, "we pulled out a worker with a productivity of $10 and we probably set him picking coffee with a productivity of $1.50." Raúl Castro cited the case of fourteen electrical workers who cost $5,800 in salaries and other expenses and picked $304 worth of coffee.[39]

There is little reason to wonder at a law which is designed to solve labor and social problems through militarization. It is but part of a trend that is reflected in Cuba's penal system. There is, for example, Law No. 1098 which was enacted early in 1963. It provides for twenty to thirty years imprisonment for robbery or larceny of as little as $100 if minors

not technicians or instructors or some other circumlocution. Fidel Castro had previously made known that the Soviet-Cuban negotiations, which had resulted in "the strengthening of our Armed Forces and the dispatch of strategic missiles to our country" had taken place in June 1962 (*Revolución*, April 20, 1963).

[38]"*Gusano*" (worm) is the generic term of abuse in Cuba for "counter-revolutionaries." Thus, after the death of Dag Hammarskjöld, Guevara called him "*un servil gusano imperialista*"—a servile, imperialist worm (*Revolución*, October 30, 1961).

[39]Fidel Castro, *Revolución*, October 22, 1963; Raúl Castro, *ibid.*, November 13, 1963.

are involved and the death penalty if committed in uniform. The accused must be brought to trial in twenty-four hours and sentenced within seventy-two hours.[40] This law can only mean that militiamen in uniform went on a rampage of housebreaking and robbery, and that the regime could not regain control without resorting to methods no longer considered tolerable in civilized countries. And precisely such a rampage had taken place in Cuba, as the Cuban press has admitted in congratulatory articles and editorials on the efficaciousness of Law No. 1098.

There is also the revival in Cuba of labor camps, of which the world probably expected to hear the last when Stalin died. Since the Cuban government has refused to permit the International Red Cross or any other disinterested body to investigate these camps and other penal institutions, most of the information about them has had to come from Cuban exiles. At least one of these camps, however, has been mentioned in the Cuban press. It is located on the forsaken peninsula of Guanahacabibes at the westernmost tip of the island and seems to be chiefly populated by administrators or officials charged with infraction of rules. In a recent interview with Guevara in a Havana newspaper, it was suggested that this camp might have been responsible for producing "inhibitions" in the bureaucracy. Guevara was not impressed.[41]

It should not be impossible, especially for self-professed Marxists, to see the connection between the increasingly repressive and retrogressive penal system, the deepening economic crisis, and deteriorating social conditions. What is harder to understand is the lack of protest or even interest among those who would be shocked by such methods in any other country in the world.

## VI

"WE WILL NOT establish Military Service because it is not right to force a man to put on a uniform and a helmet, to give him a rifle and force him to march."[42]

---

[40]This law was explained and defended by the Public Prosecutor, Dr. Santiago Cuba, in *Hoy,* March 29, 1963.

[41]*La Tarde,* November 11, 1963. An excellent study, *Cuba and the Rule of Law,* was published by the International Commission of Jurists in Geneva in 1962, but it does not report the worst excesses, such as Law No. 1098 and the labor camps, which had not yet appeared.

[42]Fidel Castro, speech of January 13, 1959 (*Revolución,* January 14, 1959).

These words of the Fidel Castro of January 1959 are so far from the Fidel Castro of January 1964 that there is no point in belaboring the difference. What is more significant and less well known is Castro's own attitude toward his past, both the more distant past of his struggle for power and the more recent past of his exercise of power.

Toward the period before 1959, the Cuban leaders have adopted an attitude of worldly-wise political estrangement. They speak of it as if they were blasé grownups looking back at their innocent and somewhat brainless childhood. Guevara, for example, told the Algerians on July 13 that the leaders of the Cuban revolution "were only a group of fighters with high ideals and little preparation." On October 30, after holding forth on the necessity of avoiding "tedium, uniformity, and monotony" under socialism, Castro thought of saying: "It is possible that we ourselves could not have expressed these things to the people years ago, because we did not know; but we knew that we did not know." And he went on with even greater modesty to say that they did not know any more than they had known when they had landed in the "Granma," the yacht that had brought them from Mexico to Cuba, in December 1956. All he could claim seven years later was that they were far more aware than they had been of the "extraordinary possibilities."

Of the period between 1959 and 1963, Castro has been equally disparaging. In October 1963, the month of the Second Agrarian Reform, he referred to these years as "the era of spoiled children, of being tolerant around here, of mistakes, of infantilisms." A few days later, he said that "we cannot go into the sixth year of the Revolution with short kindergarten pants," and he asserted that it was necessary "to leave behind the stage of economic cretinism."[43]

This harsh judgment of the revolution's immediate past, which is, after all, his own, does not prevent Castro from assuring the same audience that he has at last found the right road and that the agricultural future is just as bright as the industrial past was to have been. But the admission of ingenuous blundering is not without political purpose.

It serves, above all, to emphasize the sharpness of the coming break with the recent past, as if, in its sixth year, the Cuban revolution is going to enter not merely another stage but its first real stage and begin to take itself seriously. The Cuban leaders have felt a need to tear down and poke fun at most of their first five years in power in order to free

[43]*Revolución*, October 22 and 31, 1963.

themselves of all past commitments. This revolution has been peculiar in that it has periodically required a *tabula rasa*. Ironically, therefore, the very things about it that charmed and won over foreign sympathizers like Jean-Paul Sartre, C. Wright Mills, Waldo Frank, and others are busily being repudiated and denounced in Cuba. After "a few conversations and a quick look round" on the island in 1961, Mrs. Joan Robinson reported enthusiastically: "This free-hand style of administration, which astonishes visitors from East and West alike, can work (and somehow it does work, errors and omissions excepted) because the country is small and the administrators know each other, having been under fire together in the mountains."[44] That "free-hand style of administration" is exactly what the Cuban leaders are determined to wipe out because it could not work. Those little concrete houses for peasants that went up in the first year or two of Castro's regime are now regretted as having been "unproductive." In the long list of errors that Guevara recited in Algiers, one was "too much emphasis at the beginning to the satisfaction of social needs."

If any democratic leader confessed to the kind of errors made in Cuba, he would risk becoming a laughingstock. But the Cubans are not judged by ordinary democratic standards. They enjoy, in some circles, a special dispensation given to them by the old magic word, "Revolution," and in Latin America, the new magic word, "Marxism." The first one has virtually lost all meaning, and the same thing seems to be happening to the second. As it is widely used in Latin America, however, it might better be called "magic Marxism," because it has little in common with the original. Socialism, after all, was not invented by Marx. He spent a lifetime trying to put the earlier utopian thought on a "scientific" foundation, that is, to determine the social and economic conditions necessary for its realization. There have been many "socialisms," but in our time, the old varieties tend to reappear in new guises under the single brand name of "Marxism." Thus, we now have Cuban "Marxists" who were capable of ordering factories and overlooking the little detail of raw materials; and who, when they could not make a success of 40 per cent nationalized agriculture, nationalized 30 per cent more.

As ONE LOOKS back at Castro's five years in power, the main thread of continuity seems to be Castro's power itself. This power has rested

[44]*The Listener* (London), August 24, 1961, p. 265.

primarily on those—in the leadership as well as among the masses—
who have supported him unconditionally rather than on those who
have supported what he has stood for. His personal cadre has been loyal
to him for about ten years through his different public manifestations,
as a constitutional democrat, an anti-Communist and anti-capitalist
"humanist," a "Socialist," a "Marxist-Leninist," and a Communist. It
is spread throughout the government and the party, but its chief stronghold is the armed forces which have become the virtually private preserve of the unconditional *Fidelistas* of longest standing. In his early
period, Leon Trotsky once observed that the party organization substitutes itself for the party, the Central Committee substitutes itself for
the party organization, and finally "a single 'dictator' substitutes himself for the Central Committee." Castro has reversed the process. He
started as the Leader and only afterward felt a need for a Central Committee, a party organization and a party. But at all times, he has retained
an inner group and an outer mass loyal to himself alone, and they have
given him a margin of maneuverability vis-à-vis the old-time Cuban
Communists and the other Communist states and parties that he would
not have had with control of the government and party alone.

Without an original, creative, and indigenous doctrine of his own,
he filled the void in himself—the void expressed in his *"No sabiamos,"*
we did not know—with Communism, as he had previously filled it with
other movements. But the challenging and difficult problem of his
Communism is that he has filled it partly with his personal idiosyn-
cracies and partly with hang-overs of the Latin-American revolutionary tradition. The result is a peculiar variant from any Communism
we have known, and variants by their nature tend to be the same and
different, depending on what one chooses to emphasize. Those who
think of him as Khrushchev's puppet or Mao's secret agent have
grotesquely underestimated Fidel Castro's stake in Fidel Castro.

Hence, Castro has worked out a system of governing which he is
both within and above. He does everything but cannot be blamed for
anything. When Carlos Rafael Rodríguez told of the mistreatment of
the peasantry in the last half of 1961 and first months of 1962, he found
it necessary to add: "Many times the peasant showed his disagreement
and rebelliousness against situations that were not just with these
words: 'If Fidel knew about it.' "[45] But how could Fidel have failed to

[45]*Revolución*, May 18, 1963.

know? After all, he had in that very period been President of INRA, and the former Executive Director, Antonio Núñez Jiménez, had been directly responsible to him. If the peasants, including the poorest ones, had for at least eight months been provoked to rebelliousness by INRA officials, local political leaders, and even "comrades of the Revolutionary Armed Forces," as Rodríguez said, what was the Maximum Leader, the Prime Minister, the head of the Party, and the President of INRA doing all that time? At the end of 1963, the same actors played out the same little drama. This time Rodríguez was on the receiving end of one of Castro's tantrums. On October 30, 1963, as a result of another agricultural shakeup, Castro cried out: "Enough of revolutionary theoreticians, enough of purely theoretical Marxists! The purely theoretical Marxist-Leninist is really an unproductive expense to society." Whom did he mean? Forty-eight hours later, Rodríguez and the entire staff of INRA signed a long, self-debasing letter, addressed to Castro, confessing to all the errors and misdeeds that Castro had inveighed against.

The internal perspective for Castro's Cuba is a somber one. "Magic Marxism" has lost its spell, and all that remains is to exhort and drive the peasants to grow more sugar cane and the workers to put in longer hours for the state. The only thing that could conceivably enable Castro to regain his old bravado would be a *Fidelista* seizure of power in another Latin American country, for which reason he has been willing to gamble so heavily in Venezuela.[46] But in the event of an even more extreme crisis at home, Castro is prepared to take even more extreme measures to remain in power. In the first year, he glorified the uniqueness of the Cuban revolution which, he said, enjoyed the support of 90 to 95 per cent of the people and sought "the unity of all sectors of all conditions of society" (May 21, 1959). In the fifth year, as the percentage of popular support had dropped sharply, and ways of disuniting more and more of Cuban society had been found, he came forth with a theory of revolution which will make it impossible

[46]It should be added: against the precepts in Guevara's little manual, *Guerrilla Warfare*. Guevara wrote: "Where a government has come into power through some form of popular vote, fraudulent or not, and maintains at least an appearance of constitutional legality, the guerrilla outbreak cannot be promoted, since the possibilities of peaceful struggle have not yet been exhausted." But the Venezuelan government came into power through an undeniable popular vote. Guevara also wrote that "it is the countryside that offers ideal conditions for the fight." But President Betancourt was strongest precisely in the Venezuelan countryside.

for him to run out of enemies. "The Revolution," he said, "needs the enemy; the proletariat does not flee from the enemy; it needs the enemy. The Revolution needs for its development its antithesis which is the counterrevolution."[47] In different circumstances, Stalin developed a related theory that the class struggle sharpens as socialism advances. If he did not have enough enemies, he invented them. Castro's enemies are also more and more of his own making, and more and more among the peasants and workers who must be "disciplined."

The ultimate tragedy of Cuba may well be that there was no country in Latin America in 1959 where the social and psychological conditions were more favorable for a truly progressive democracy, and that there is one country in Latin America in 1964 where all that socialism once stood for is being discredited.

[47]*Hoy*, February 24, 1963.

# PART
## five
# AMERICAN
# REVOLUTIONARY

"Many will call me an adventurer, and I am, but of a different kind—
one who risks his skin in order to prove his convictions."

—ERNESTO CHE GUEVARA,

LETTER TO HIS PARENTS, 1965.

# WITH FIDEL, NEITHER MARRIAGE NOR DIVORCE

## JORGE G. CASTANEDA

from *COMPAÑERO*

1997

W HEN ON JULY 3, 1964, Che lost his direct tutelage of the sugar industry, which would now have its own ministry—albeit headed by Orlando Borego, one of his closest advisers—he could hear one shoe falling.* At the same time, President Osvaldo Dorticós replaced Regino Boti at the Ministry of the Economy, and was also named head of the Central Planning Council. This amounted to a second attack on Che, not because he had a poor relationship with Dorticós but because a second power center was being established in Cuban economic policy—as important as his own. Che pursued the debate throughout 1964, publishing three essays on his major areas of disagreement with the Soviets, the old Cuban Communists, and the new Cuban technicians: centralization, the budgetary system, and material incentives. Charles Bettelheim would note thirty years later that there was always a bureaucratic bias in Che's analysis. He regarded

---

*At first, Che did not give much importance to the emergence of the new ministry: "There are to be two new ministries . . . One of them, naturally, is that of Sugar under Borego, which is nothing more than an offshoot of the existing Ministry. . . ." Ernesto Che Guevara, Meeting of July 11, 1964, *Ministry of Industries Minutes*, p. 508.

the Cuban economy from the perspective of the large companies within the Ministry of Industries, where there could indeed be appropriate forms of oversight and control. But for the countless small firms that had been nationalized in 1963 no centralized direction was feasible; there was not enough administrative capacity, nor enough cadres or resources. Che saw the forest, but not the trees; he did not acknowledge that the changes wrought in the Cuban economy and society worked against his system.

He continued to develop his views during this period, within the Marxist discourse of the time but also with undeniable sincerity:

> The consciousness of men in the vanguard . . . may perceive the right path to carry a socialist revolution to victory . . . even if . . . the contradictions between the development of the forces of production and the relations of production which would make a revolution necessary or possible are lacking.

In this reply to Bettelheim, Che concluded that even if Cuba was not "ready" for the precise and comprehensive planning he would have wished, or the moral incentives and extreme industrial centralization he advocated, it made no difference. What counted was the prevalence of an advanced consciousness among the Cuban leadership and the most enlightened sectors of the people, for the process to be forced through. This stance permeated all his views: about sugar and industry, the budget and centralization, moral and material incentives. His positions were not strictly economic; they were essentially political, and stemmed from a central premise: consciousness (which for Che meant will power) is the driving force behind change. Administration comes later, and is entirely secondary.

Che was right, to a certain extent. If the degree of political awareness and mobilization he called for had existed, it would perhaps have been possible to run an economy as simple as Cuba's like clockwork: centralize everything in a few hands, and structure prices, salaries, and investment in light of moral criteria. Indeed, that level of activism seemed ready to dawn at certain moments of the Revolution: the Bay of Pigs, the missile crisis, the literacy campaign. It was Che's misfortune that this higher consciousness always faded, and that his own passion and dedication were not shared by all — nor could they be, as he all too often failed to understand.

The debate went back and forth from centralization to the budgetary system to the central management of investment, salaries, and banks; then it would shift back to moral versus material incentives, its original starting point. Carlos Rafael Rodriguez stated over twenty years later that he and Che "had small differences in our conception of incentives." From a distance, the discrepancy between Che and the other economic policy-makers was more a matter of degree than substance, though this did not prevent furious arguments. Che once stalked out of an INRA meeting so abruptly that even his bodyguards were left behind, according to a Soviet technician. A man so hotheaded could hardly debate matters of historical importance with any degree of calm.

The Cuban government mounted a retroactive whitewashing campaign to minimize its differences with Che, insisting that they were only a matter of emphasis. Thus, Rodriguez notes that Che never sought to eliminate material incentives—which is true. Nor did the old Communists demand that moral incentives simply be eliminated. But the dispute—whether a matter of substance or degree—was very real. For Che, moral incentives were the key: for the others, it was material incentives.* The cycle ended with Fidel Castro's second trip to Moscow in January 1964. Cuba's alignment with the USSR was now virtually complete and in a sense beneficial to the island, as its depleted economy was able to accumulate foreign-currency reserves, take advantage of high international sugar prices, and ensure a long-term market for its produce.

And so Che Guevara began his final year in Cuba relatively marginalized from the daily running of the economy. But he continued laboring in other areas of government and in his private activities. In early 1963, he turned again to volunteer work. During the sugar harvest of that year, he broke records in cane-cutting and consecutive hours of labor, providing a twofold example. First, he strengthened the government's revolutionary resolve and proved that Cuba's leaders could still sustain the effort and sacrifice they demanded of the

---

*The following passage makes the point very succinctly: "The discussion of 'moral incentives' is being made the center of all issues, and moral incentives in themselves are not the center. . . . Moral incentives are the predominant . . . form which incentives must take in this phase of the construction of socialism . . . but they are not the only form. . . . Material incentives are also valid." Ernesto Che Guevara. *Minutes*, p. 345.

people; secondly, he showed that volunteer work helped solve the daunting problem of scarce manpower. After 1963, the sugar harvest fell precipitously; when the government decided, in 1964, to reemphasize sugar production, it came up against a shortage of labor. The countryside was not entirely deserted, but the rural population had fallen and the machinery promised by the Soviets (and eagerly awaited by Che, who even experimented with several designs) never arrived. By that time Guevara's conception of volunteer work was gradually changing; he acknowledged that it could not be sustained without adequate planning:

> Last Sunday I went and lost my time at volunteer work, and something happened that had never happened to me during volunteer work, except for cane-cutting, which was that I kept looking at my watch every fifteen minutes to see when my hours would be up so I could leave, because it didn't make any sense.

Volunteer work was a partial solution. Others were mandatory military service, instituted in December 1963 (the first recruits were called up in March 1964), and legislation on labor norms and salary classifications, promulgated in the first half of 1964. The consolidation of the armed forces and reorganization of the militias served the same purpose, and strengthened the leadership as a whole. But they also undermined Che's influence. Indeed, neither the exiles in Miami nor the Mafia in the United States considered him as important as they once had; the price on his head fell to $20,000, while Fidel Castro's was worth $100,000.

Che continued to write essays and grant interviews to the international media: along with Fidel Castro, he remained the most effective spokesman for the Cuban Revolution—and perhaps the most credible. But the revolutionary process was foundering in Latin America, despite efforts in Venezuela, Guatemala, and Peru. He felt alone caught in a dead end. As he wrote to the director of a primary school in the provinces, "Sometimes we revolutionaries are alone: even our children see us as strangers." With each passing day, there was less for him to do in Cuba. Increasingly, he yearned for movement, for a radically different situation less fraught with ambivalence. Fully aware of his predicament, at the end of March and before leaving on a new trip to Africa and Europe, he spoke with Tamara Bunke in his office for several hours. She had by now completed her training as a Cuban intelligence agent, and Guevara gave her the following instructions: "Go and live in Bolivia, where you will establish relations within the armed forces and the governing bourgeoisie, travel around the country . . . and wait for a contact who will signal the moment for definitive action." The contact would be Che himself, two and a half years later.

Aside from his defeat in economic policy and Cuba's alignment with the U.S.S.R., other, more personal factors were pushing him to leave. On March 19, 1964, a woman named Lilia Rosa Pérez gave birth to a son of his in Havana. He was the only child conceived out of wedlock that Che would ever acknowledge though there is partial evidence of others. Lilia Rosa was an attractive Havana woman about thirty years old who had met Che in Santa Clara in 1958 and then again at La Cabaña in 1959; in 1996 she still attended the annual commemoration of the occupation of the fortress on January 2. Faithful to his heritage, Omar Pérez (named after Omar Khayyam, author of the *Rubaiyat*, an edition of which Che gave to Lilia Rosa) is a dissident poet and translator who has, for opposing the regime and refusing military service, done time in one of the labor camps his father founded.* He has the eyes, eyebrows, and smile of his father, on the few occasions he has a reason to be glad, his face lights up just as Che's did. He does not speak of his lineage, though he has Guevara's long, straight black hair, prominent brow, and sad, mysterious expression. His gestures, look, and reticence also betray his antecedents.

Toward the end of the eighties, Lilia Rosa appeared one day at the home of the companion of Che's daughter, Hilda Guevara Gadea, with a pile of books by Guevara and others full of handwritten inscriptions. Lilia thus confessed her past relationship with the *comandante*, and introduced Omar, who became a close friend of Che's firstborn. Hildita, as she was known in Cuba, was already beset by cancer, alcoholism, and depression, the latter partly brought on by the ostracism she had always suffered from Che's official widow and children. Until her death in August 1995, she and Omar would share an especially dear part of their father's inheritance: his rebelliousness, individualism, and lack of favor with official circles. Hilda Guevara never had any doubt that Omar was her brother, she treated him accordingly,

*Lilia Rosa Pérez kindly indicated the origins of her son's name, as well as the circumstances under which she met Che, in a letter to the author dated November 2, 1996.

and asked her children to consider him as such. Omar's story is well known in Cuba, as is that of Che's other presumed illegitimate offspring.† Omar's case is different, however, for a simple reason: Che's Mexican grandson, Canek Sánchez Guevara, told this author (in both Havana and Mexico, in a private conversation and a taped interview) that his mother, Hilda, introduced Omar to him in those terms, and loved him as a sibling. The many reports about Omar, his physical likeness to Che, and the account by Che's daughter, all confirm his birthright.‡

It is not known if Che was aware of his son's birth in 1964, but in any case, this situation must not have been an easy one for him. He had always opposed his colleagues' frequent affairs as a matter of principle, and had succeeded in avoiding the erotic temptations of power in the tropics. But something happened in mid-1963, if not before, that can only have exacerbated his growing restlessness in Cuba.

Hence his more moderate and flexible attitude in the Ministry of Industries as was evident in the case of an official named Mesa, a director of the Toy Company in the Ministry. A married man with children. Mesa fell in love with his secretary and was spotted with her in dubious circumstances. The case was presented to Che on July 11, 1964, four months after the birth of Omar. His response was revealing:

> No one has yet established in human relations that a man must live with one woman all the time. . . . I said I didn't know why all the discussion was necessary, because I consider this a logical case that can happen to anybody, and we should perhaps analyze whether the sanction . . . is not extreme. . . . Obviously, if something happens, it is because the woman is willing; otherwise, it would be a serious crime, but this doesn't happen without the woman's consent. . . . We have tried not to be extreme in these matters. There is also a degree of Socialist saintliness in this area, and the real truth is that if one could enter into everybody's conscience we would have to see who would cast the first stone. . . . We have always advocated not going to extremes, and especially not making of this a capital matter, or making it pub-

†One in particular, Mirko, was even under investigation for a time during the eighties.
‡Lilia Rosa, in the cited letter to the author, confirmed the story while noting that she had not taken the initiative to reveal it. Lilia Rosa Lopez, letter to the author, November 2, 1996.

lic; this could go so far as to destroy homes which could have survived, as these are quite natural, normal things that happen.

So Che was restive: his predicament and his eternal wanderlust led him, as always, to travel. On March 17, he left for Geneva as head of the Cuban delegation to the first United Nations Conference on Trade and Development (UNCTAD), whose Secretary-General was his compatriot Raúl Prebisch. Che spent most of his month abroad in Switzerland, with brief stopovers in Prague and Paris, and a couple of days in Algiers to see his friend Ben Bella. His speech at the United Nations was substantive and historic, presenting several of the concerns that would dominate his thinking and public statements in the following year.

The hall at the Palais des Nations erupted into applause as Guevara made his way to the podium: he was already a legendary figure. He began by castigating the conference for excluding several delegations—China, North Vietnam, and North Korea—and for inviting others with dubious credentials, like South Africa. Then he staked out his position, in ideological and political terms:

> We understand clearly—and express frankly—that the only correct solution to the problems of humanity at this time is the complete elimination of the exploitation of dependent countries by developed, capitalist countries, with all the consequences implicit in that fact.

Che's speech was short, ironic, and rhetorical ("the imperialists will insist that underdevelopment is caused by underdeveloped countries"), but lacking in vision and proposals. It was respectful of the Socialist countries, but no more. Guevara repeatedly emphasized the plight of poor nations, the peoples "struggling for their liberation," "the needy of the world," with hardly any mention of the Soviet Union. In contrast, he subtly presented the problem that was beginning to obsess him, and which would set him increasingly at odds with the Cuban regime.

He noted the worsening terms of trade, whereby the price of raw materials exported by developing countries tended to fall, while that of goods and services exported by industrialized countries tended to rise. This meant that poor nations were forced to export more and more in order to maintain the same volume of imports. He observed that "many underdeveloped countries reach an apparently logical conclusion": in their trade relations with Socialist countries, the latter "benefit from the current state of affairs." He then explained that this reality must be acknowledged "honestly and bravely," granting that it was not entirely the fault of the Socialist bloc. And the situation changed when countries reached long-term agreements, as Cuba had with the Soviet Union. Yet his term for Cuba's sugar pact with the USSR— "relations of a new type"—while reflecting his conviction that it was not the same to do business with Socialists as with capitalists, was hardly enthusiastic. He resented the way he was mistreated by the other Socialist delegations: he simply was no longer part of the family, if he ever had been:

> Guevara complained of the poor impression he brought back of the contacts with Soviet comrades and the other Socialist countries in Geneva, who did not trust him. The Cuban delegation was isolated; the delegations of Eastern Europe would meet and talk things over and only afterwards, for appearances' sake, notify the Cubans of their decisions. The Cuban delegation was isolated.

Guevara's days in the Calvinist city of Jean Jacques Rousseau had an element of mystery. Very few heads of delegation stayed for the entire month of the UNCTAD meeting. Che had a tense relationship with many of his fellow Latin Americans; according to a member of the Mexican mission, he was not even invited to meetings of the regional group. He stayed at a modest hotel near the lake, with a large security detail, and sometimes visited with the Mexican delegates to drink tequila and sing tangos and boleros. He expressed a certain nostalgia for Mexico, asking about people and events there and recalling his time with an affection he acquired only after he left for Cuba. One day, a Mexican delegate saw him walking alone on the banks of Lake Geneva, pausing for a long time on a rock at the water's edge and contemplating the Salève in the distance; perhaps he was reflecting upon the hard decisions that awaited him in Cuba.

A lightning trip to Algeria—officially to attend the first Congress of the National Liberation Front—allowed him to review events in Africa with Ben Bella. By now, the African struggle for liberation had become a leitmotif in Guevara's speeches: in Geneva, he evoked Congolese independence martyr Patrice Lumumba several times. Renewed combat in the Congo and the growing weakness of the central government were the issues of the day. He met in Algiers with some of the Congolese exile leaders, and became convinced that the 1961 rebellion, crushed since the assassination of Lumumba, was about to erupt again.*

Che's interest was not merely academic. In January he had Pablo Ribalta, a close aide of African-Cuban origins from his Sierra Maestra days, appointed the Cuban ambassador to Tanzania. The newly formed republic included the island of Zanzibar, where Cuba had had relations with the Nationalist Party: it had been training combatants and militants from the island.

On his way back to Cuba, Che stopped in Paris, where he had lunch with Charles Bettelheim on the Boulevard Saint-Michel. He finally admitted that he had been wrong in his appraisal of the Soviet Union and in trusting its promises on aid and development. He returned to Havana at the end of April—back to the economic controversy and his administrative duties at the Ministry. Though he continued to discharge them diligently, he seemed bored and listless. His interest in economic matters was fading, and he had less influence in government deliberations. In the meantime, the team of Soviet advisers at the National Bank was gaining the upper hand. According to a British Embassy cable,

> Some observers see the recent strengthening of the Soviet team of advisers at the Cuban National Bank and other evidence of assumption by the Russians of more detailed responsibility for getting the Cuban economy to work, as a sign that both the Soviet and Cuban Governments have committed themselves reluctantly to a greater degree of Russian control.†

*Che's evaluation was similar to that of a CIA national intelligence estimate dated August 5, 1964 (drafted in the spring of that year), which began by saying: "In recent months, regional dissidence and violence have assumed serious proportions even by Congolese standards, and produced the threat of a total breakdown in governmental authority. The difficulties confronting Prime Minister Tshombe are enormous." Director of Central Intelligence. "Special National Intelligence Estimate: Short-Term Prospects for the Tshombe Government in the Congo," August 5, 1964 (Secret). *Declassified Documents Catalog.* Research Publication (Woodbridge. Conn.). vol. 16, #5. Sept.–Oct. 1990, file series no. 2439.

†Havana Telegram No. 48 to Foreign Office Cuban Political Situation, November 23, 1964 (Restricted). Foreign Office Archive FO371/174006, Public Record Office, London. Che was already on bad terms with Bank officials, especially its Soviet advisers: "You know that we have always had rather strained relations with the Bank, prac-

By November, Che was ready to ship off again, now as Cuba's representative to the anniversary of the Russian Revolution. The visit was particularly important as Khrushchev had just been ousted, and replaced by the troika of Leonid Brezhnev, Alexei Kosygin, and Nikolai Podgorny. Though there had been no love lost between Khrushchev and the Cubans since the missile crisis, the new Moscow leaders were completely unknown to them. Che's trip was a success in terms of protocol, but devoid of substance. Several witnesses remember him on the flight from Murmansk to Havana: he was euphoric, tipsy, and unusually chatty about his private life. It was during this trip that he confessed to Oleg Daroussenkov that he had agreed to marry Hilda Gadea after a few too many drinks. It was also then, while sitting between the secretary-general of the Mexican Communist Party, Arnoldo Martinez Verdugo, and that of the Bolivian Party, Mario Monje, that he made his marvelous comment to Salvador Cayctano Carpio, leader of El Salvador's Communist Party: "Here you have me, Carpio, sitting between a monk [*monje*] and an executioner [*verdugo*]."

On his return to Havana, Che convened one of his last official meetings with aides at the Ministry. After recounting with brutal frankness his impressions of the Socialist countries, he explained why he was against the so-called "economic reforms" underway in Eastern Europe and the USSR. His comments are worth quoting, both because they have not been published and because they reflect the dilemmas Guevara faced on the eve of his new odyssey:

> In Moscow I had a meeting with all the [Cuban] students who wanted to talk. So I invited them to the Embassy. I found myself face to face with about 50 of them. I was prepared to wage a huge battle against the self-management system. Well, I have never, during a mission of this sort, had a public as attentive, concerned, and able to understand me. Do you know why? Because they lived there, and many of the things I have told you, and tell you here in theoretical terms because I don't know any better, they know very well. They know because they are there, they go to the doctor, they go to the restaurant or to stores to buy something, and incredible things happen in the Soviet Union today. . . . Paul

tically since I left the Bank. It has always been, through its Czech and Soviet advisers, the champion of financial self-management." Ernesto Che Guevara, Meeting of July 11, 1964, *Minutes*, p. 530.

Sweezy says in an article that Yugoslavia is a country headed toward capitalism. Why? Because in Yugoslavia the Law of Value reigns supreme, and more so every day. Khrushchev said that [what was happening in Yugoslavia] was interesting, he even sent people to study there. . . . Well, what he saw in Yugoslavia that seemed so interesting to him is far more developed in the United States because it is a capitalist [country]. . . . In Yugoslavia they have the Law of Value: in Yugoslavia they close factories because they aren't profitable: in Yugoslavia there are delegates from Switzerland and Holland looking for unemployed workers so they can take them back to their own countries . . . as foreign labor in an imperialist country. . . . This is what is happening in Yugoslavia. Poland is now following the Yugoslav path, of course, collectivization is being reversed, they are going back to private land ownership, establishing a whole series of special exchange systems, cultivating relations with the United States . . . In Czechoslovakia and Germany they are also beginning to study the Yugoslav system in order to apply it. So we have a whole series of countries changing course, in the face of what? In the face of a reality which we can no longer ignore—which is, though nobody says it, that the Western bloc is advancing faster than the people's democracies. Why? That is where, instead of getting to the bottom of it, which would solve the problem, a superficial answer has been sought, which is to reinforce the market, introduce the Law of Value, reinforce material incentives.

By this time, Che had an uninhibited and definitive opinion of the Socialist countries. They were losing the race with the West not because they had followed the axioms of Marxism-Leninism, but because they had betrayed them. As they realized they were falling behind in the battle with capitalism, they shifted to a diametrically different course—mistakenly, in Che's view. His position, especially when viewed against the backdrop of the simmering Sino-Soviet conflict, was coming dangerously close to the edge. The Communists he met on the plane from Moscow and Murmansk had just sojourned in Beijing. They had joined Carlos Rafael Rodriguez on a Latin American mission to China hoping to mediate between the two Socialist powers, following a proposal by Martinez Verdugo at the meeting of Latin American Communist parties in Havana. The Cubans were pivotal in the Latin American

Communists' decision to go to China and mediate; they organized the trip and may even have instigated the Mexican proposal while ensuring that Rodriguez would figure as spokesman. According to Martinez Verdugo, Mao received them hospitably but exclaimed, "You are here because the revisionists sent you; we do not agree with you, but we welcome you all the same." The effort at mediation floundered, as would that undertaken by Che two months later.

One of the reasons for these attempts was that Che, Cuba, and the Socialist powers were about to be sucked into the African maelstrom. In the summer of 1964, Pierre Mulele, Lumumba's minister of education and his spiritual and political heir, had rekindled the Congolese rebellion in the central-western region of Kwilu. A National Liberation Committee had accomplished the same in the east and north, near Stanleyville. They all rose up in arms against the regime imposed three years earlier by the United Nations, Belgium, and the CIA. The Congolese government was on the verge of collapse, and Washington and Brussels stood ready to help it. When the rebels captured Stanleyville in August, Belgium and the United States became seriously alarmed. Two months later, they flew in several battalions of paratroopers to crush the uprising, retake the city, and regain control over the eastern part of the country. Another ostensible goal was to prevent a repeat of the bloodbath that had occurred when the rebels entered Stanleyville, taking hostage the U.S. consul, dozens of U.S. missionaries, and three hundred Belgian citizens and, according to some reports, executing 20,000 Congolese from the urban middle class.

This new rebellion in the Congo had a twofold effect on Che and the Cubans. First, it persuaded them that Lumumba's anticolonialist struggle had finally revived. Second, the intervention of Washington and the colonial powers seemed to confirm the anti-imperialist nature of the reborn rebellion in Africa. Thus Guevara's wholehearted commitment to the Congolese cause; he immediately stepped into the breach to uphold what he saw as a just and ongoing struggle for freedom.

Che's African campaign began in New York, where the travel arrangements were made. It would continue in Africa at the end of 1964 and throughout all of 1965. On December 9, just three weeks after his return from the USSR, he packed his bags again, this time on his way to the United Nations. His designation as head of the Cuban delegation to the Nineteenth General Assembly, at its very end, made no great impression in Havana. Along with his UNCTAD mission several months earlier, it was seen by some as a sign of his fading authority:

> Che Guevara's appointment to lead the Cuban delegation at the United Nations seems less important. Guevara similarly represented Cuba at the UNCTAD conference at Geneva; and in any case his political advice seems to carry less weight than ever.

As he embarked upon the path that would lead him to glory elsewhere, Che also entered his twilight phase in Cuba.

GUEVARA'S EIGHT DAYS in the United States—the first since visiting Miami fifteen years earlier—afforded him little respite. His activities were varied and somewhat eccentric. An old friend, Laura Berquist of *Look* magazine, organized a meeting with New York intellectuals and journalists. Berquist was a childhood friend of Bobo Rockefeller, the widow of Winthrop, former governor of Arkansas: she owned a splendid townhouse across the street from the Cuban mission to the UN. The location was ideal for a security detail overwhelmed by anti-Castro demonstrations and for a gathering of New York leftists eager to meet with Che. His interpreter was Magda Moyano, the sister of Dolores, Guevara's neighbor in Córdoba and a cousin of Chichina Ferreyra. She and Che shared memories of their now faraway youth.

He also appeared on the Sunday television program *Face the Nation*. His performance was so skillful and convincing that several Latin American governments protested to the White House over the CBS invitation.* Guevara met secretly with Democratic senator Eugene McCarthy, and talked at length with Arab and African delegates in the UN corridors and delegates lounge. He was already preparing for his next trip which, beginning on December 18, would take him to nine countries in three months and impel him to leave Cuba forever.

---

*"Numerous LA delegations have protested what they feel to be unnecessarily helpful US publicity to Fidel Castro result of CBS TV interview of Guevara. . . . LAs also miffed no US press coverage LA replies to Che Guevara in GA." Department of State, Incoming Telegram, Cuba: Che Guevara CBS Interview, December 14, 1964 (Confidential). NSF, Country File Cuba, Activities of Leading Personalities, Cuba, no. 62 cable, LBJ Library.

Che's UN speech was fiery in both its tone and its content. He reiterated Cuba's traditional stance toward the United States—including the five points of October 1962—and Cuba's denunciation of the OAS and its Latin American "puppets." The new element, however, was his emphasis on Africa. Like his Geneva address, it would be recalled as a sign of his drift away from the USSR and Socialist countries. But this time he was more explicit. Though still somewhat elliptical, he skipped the euphemisms of his Geneva speech:

> We must also clarify that concepts of peaceful coexistence must be well-defined, and not only in relations involving sovereign States. As Marxists, we have maintained that peaceful coexistence among nations does not include coexistence between exploiters and the exploited, between oppressors and the oppressed.

But Che's most forceful passages were those about the Congo, and especially the airlift operation of Stanleyville:

> Perhaps the children of Belgian patriots who died defending their country's freedom are the same ones who freely murdered millions of Congolese on behalf of the white race, just as they suffered under the German boot because their Aryan blood count was not high enough. . . . Our free eyes now look toward new horizons, and are able to see what our condition as colonial slaves kept us from seeing only yesterday: that "Western civilization" conceals under its lovely façade a gang of hyenas and jackals. That is the only possible name for those who have gone on a "humanitarian" mission to the Congo. Carnivorous animals, feeding on defenseless peoples: that is what imperialism does to man, that is what distinguishes the imperial "white" . . . All the free men in the world must stand ready to avenge the crime of the Congo.

In his conversations with Americans, he staunchly defended the Cuban Revolution and refused to acknowledge any split with Fidel Castro. On television, he refrained from taking sides in the conflict between China and the USSR, highlighting instead the need for unity. He let slip some of his reservations regarding the Soviets but with such discretion that observers were forced to read between the lines.* Tad Szulc, who participated in the *Face the Nation* program and then chatted with Guevara at length, noted "Che's gradual withdrawal from economic policy-making, and his growing concentration on contacts with the Third World, evidently in concurrence with Castro. Guevara seemed to enjoy this mission."

There was a curious element in Che's conversation with Eugene McCarthy, the liberal senator from Minnesota who three years later would become the principal opponent of the Vietnam War in the United States, forcing Lyndon Johnson to renounce any attempt at reelection in 1968. They met at the insistence of Lisa Howard, the journalist who had previously interviewed Che and Fidel in Havana and had undertaken to mediate between Cuba and the United States. She had attempted to persuade her contacts in the Johnson administration to meet with Che during his trip to the United Nations, while doubtless making the same proposal to him. Washington was less than receptive to her ploy:

> The Che Guevara matter has gone up to George Ball. The idea for now is to use a British delegate at the United Nations to make the contact. (Ball and everybody else agree that we should stay away from Lisa Howard.) The Englishman would say to Che tomorrow: "An American colleague informs me that a press source has told him that you have something to say to an American official. My American colleague is not at all sure of the accuracy of this report. Is it true?" If Che answers "yes," the British contact would say something like, "I got the distinct impression that my American colleague is willing to listen to what you say, but I would have to check back with him to make sure." Ball and others in State agree fully that we should not appear to be taking the initiative. In this regard, if the modalities of setting up this operation can be done only by indicating eagerness, the talk isn't worth it. . . . I doubt whether Che has

*The first foreign official Che met with in New York, Enrique Bernstein of Chile, later reported to the U.S. Embassy in Santiago that Che had completely embraced "the position of Beijing." WTDentzer/AmEmbassy Santiago to ARA/DOS Washington, December 21, 1964 (Confidential), NSF, Country File, Cuba, Activities of Leading Personalities. Document no. 57, LBJ Library.

anything to say that we do not already know, but a chance to listen to him might be worthwhile.

As the encounter with Washington officials did not materialize, Che agreed to Howard's plea for him to meet briefly with McCarthy at the journalist's apartment. According to the senator's report to George Ball the next day, the Cuban *comandante* was bursting with self-confidence. He assured McCarthy that the Alliance for Progress would fail, and that Central America and Venezuela were on the brink of revolution. He then reviewed the most sensitive items on the bilateral agenda—U.S. overflights, the sale of medicines. Guantánamo, the CIA's involvement in Cuba, and so on. The most striking thing about the memorandum of this conversation, declassified just recently—indeed, the identity of Che's interlocutor was revealed only in 1994—is the candor, if not impudence, with which Che boasted of Cuban support for revolution in Latin America. According to McCarthy's notes,

> Guevara did not attempt to conceal the subversive activities which Cuba was undertaking. He explicitly admitted that they were training revolutionaries and would continue to do so. He felt that this was a necessary mission for the Cuban Government since revolution offered the only hope of progress for Latin America.

This happened just as Fidel Castro was trying to trade his support for Latin American revolution in exchange for peaceful coexistence with Washington,* and when the new Soviet leadership appeared willing to ease tensions with the United States. At that precise moment, Che used the highest-level contact Cuba had had with the United States in years to boast of Havana's international ventures. The episode can only evoke his behavior fifteen years earlier, at the immigration bureau in Mexico City, when the brash young Argentine doctor proclaimed himself a Communist, damning the consequences.

His animosity toward the United States had by now reached new

---

*In a long interview with Richard Eder of the *New York Times*, Castro "proposed an agreement to cease helping the guerillas in Latin America" if Washington suspended its own assistance to the Cuban exiles in Miami, *New York Times*, July 6, 1964, front page.

heights. Che openly expressed his feelings during a speech in Santiago, Cuba, before leaving for New York:

> We must learn this lesson, learn the lesson about the absolutely necessary abhorrence of it [imperialism], because against that class of hyena there is no other help than abhorrence, there is no other medium than extermination.

This growing anger at the U.S. was perhaps a symptom of how the world was closing in on him. Throughout 1964, especially in the final weeks of the year. Che had displayed a growing restlessness and need for change. Many friends and acquaintances sensed that he was on the brink of a threshold in his life. Though none predicted a tragic outcome, many had political and personal glimpses into the change ahead. An official at the British Embassy had been cabling premonitory reports to London since 1964: "It would not surprise me if Guevara himself were soon to receive a more appropriate post—or a sinecure designed to free him for his important duties as liaison with other Latin Americans." Another observer who predicted a shift in Guevara's existence was Gianni Corbi, an Italian journalist for *L'Espresso* who visited Cuba during the summer of 1964 and spent countless hours in conversation with Che: "I should not be at all surprised to see Che Guevara and his buddies, those traveling salesmen of the permanent revolution in Latin America, shake the dust of Castro's Cuba off their feet and head for the hills. When next heard of, they'll be heading partisan bands in the barren peaks of the Andes." For the moment, his destination was Africa.

Che's time in Cuba was drawing to a close. Though he would return for several months in 1966, in convalescence and in training for Bolivia, his Cuban saga came to an end, for all practical purposes, after his trip to New York in December 1964. The African and Algerian chapters of his history remained to be written. But the die was cast, particularly in that small space where two of the great epics of our age had intersected: his own, and that of Fidel Castro.

During that long year of 1964, when he lost both friends and battles, undertaking endless struggles over topics crucial to the fate of the Revolution, Che discovered two indisputable facts about his role in Cuba. One was that Castro held him very dear, indeed; he would back him in all his projects for Argentina, Algeria, Venezuela, and now

Africa. Fidel never disputed the place Guevara had carved out for himself, or reproached him for his errors or outbursts. Che could nurture no grudges on that account. But Guevara also understood that Fidel, consummate politician that he was, did not really commit himself to Che's stances. He had to wage his own battles, and suffer his own defeats. Without ever disputing his sporadic victories, Castro never extended Che Guevara his full consent. At times, he even sided with his opponents, either because *révolution oblige*, or because he simply did not agree with Che's ideas.

Moment by moment, battle by battle, Che gradually realized he was alone: neither with nor against Fidel. But Castro was everywhere; lacking his support, Che had nothing, no ground to stand on. His situation was untenable: the slogan of neither marriage nor divorce with Fidel became unsustainable for Che. Nothing could have affected Che more than this tangle of ambiguities and contradictions—the half-tones of his twilight in Cuba. Once again, it was time to leave.

# from THE AFRICAN DREAM: THE DIARIES OF THE REVOLUTIONARY WAR IN THE CONGO

## ERNESTO CHE GUEVARA

### 2000

We are grateful for the effort and application that our Commander in Chief gave in carefully checking this document.

**—CHE'S PERSONAL ARCHIVE**

### first impressions

UPON ARRIVAL, AFTER a brief nap on the floor of the hut among backpacks and assorted tackle, we began to strike up an acquaintance with Congolese reality. We immediately noticed a clear distinction: alongside people with very little training (mostly peasants), there were others with greater culture, different clothes and a better knowledge of French. The distance between the two groups could hardly have been greater.

The first people I got to know were Emmanuel Kasabuvabu and Kiwe, who presented themselves as officers on the general staff: the former in charge of supplies and munitions, the latter of intelligence. Both were talkative and expressive young men, and what they said and what they held back soon gave you an idea of the divisions inside the Congo. Later, Tremendo Punto invited me along to a small meeting, which was attended not by those comrades but by another group comprising the Base Commander and several brigade leaders: there was the head of the First Brigade, Colonel Bidalila, who commanded the Uvira front;[1] the Second Brigade, under the command of Major-General Moulane, was represented by Lieutenant-Colonel Lambert; and André Ngoja, who was fighting in the Kabambare area, represented what seemed likely, from people's remarks, to become another brigade in the future. Tremendo Punto excitedly proposed that Moja, the official head of our forces, should take part in all meetings and decisions of the general staff, together with another Cuban chosen by himself. I watched the others' faces and did not notice any approval of the suggestion; Tremendo Punto did not seem all that popular among the brigade leaders.

The reason for the hostility among the groups was that, one way or another, some men did spend a certain amount of time at the front, whereas others merely travelled back and forth between the Congo base and Kigoma, always looking for something not at hand. The case of Tremendo Punto was graver in the fighters' eyes, because, being the representative in Dar es Salaam, he came only occasionally to the Congo.

We chatted on amicably without mentioning the proposal, and I found out a number of things that I had not known before. Lieutenant-Colonel Lambert explained with a friendly, festive air that aeroplanes had no importance for them, because they had the *dawa* medicine that makes you invulnerable to gunfire.

"They've hit me a number of times, but the bullets fell limply to the ground."

He said this with a smile on his face, and I felt obliged to salute the joke as a sign of the little importance they attached to enemy weapons. Gradually I realized that it was more serious, that the magical protector was supposed to be one of the great weapons with which they would triumph over the Congolese Army.

This *dawa*, which did quite a lot of damage to military preparations, operates according to the following principle. A liquid in which herb juices and other magical substances have been dissolved is thrown over the fighter, and certain occult signs—nearly always including a coal mark on the forehead—are administered to him. This protects him against all kinds of weapons (although the enemy too relies upon magic), but he must not lay hands on anything that does not belong

---

[1]According to the latest information, he has been promoted general.

to him, or touch a woman, or feel fear, on pain of losing the protection. The answer to any transgression is very simple: a man dead = a man who took fright, stole or slept with a woman; a man wounded = a man who was afraid. Since fear accompanies wartime operations, fighters found it quite natural to attribute wounds to faintheartedness — that is, to lack of belief. And the dead do not speak; all three faults can be ascribed to them.

The belief is so strong that no one goes into battle without having the *dawa* performed. I was constantly afraid that this superstition would rebound against us, that we would be blamed for any military disaster involving many deaths. I tried several times to have a talk about the *dawa* with someone in a position of responsibility, so that an effort could be started to win people away from it — but it was impossible. The *dawa* is treated as an article of faith. The most politically advanced say that it is a natural, material force, and that they, as dialectical materialists, recognize its power and the secrets held by the medicine men of the jungle.

After the talk with the brigade leaders, I met Tremendo Punto alone and explained who I was. He was devastated. He kept talking of an "international scandal" and insisting that "no one must find out, please, no one must find out". It had come as a bolt from the blue and I was fearful of the consequences, but my identity could not be hushed up any longer if we wanted to make use of the influence I was able to exert.

That same night, Tremendo Punto set off to inform Kabila of my presence in the Congo; the Cuban officials who had been with us on the crossing and the naval technician left together with him. The technician had the task of sending two fitters — by return mail, as it were — since one of the weak points we had spotted was the complete lack of maintenance of the various engines and boats assigned to the crossing of the lake.

The next day, I asked for us to be sent to the permanent camp, a base five kilometres from the general staff, at the top of the mountains that rose (as I said before) from the shore of the lake. That is when the delays began. The Commander had gone to Kigoma to sort out some business, and we had to wait for him to return. Meanwhile, a rather arbitrary training programme was being discussed, and I came up with an alternative position: namely, to divide 100 men into groups no larger than 20, and to give them all some notion of infantry activity, with some specialization in weapons, engineering (mainly trench-digging), communications and reconnaissance, in accordance with our capacities and the means at our disposal. The programme would last four to five weeks, and the group would be sent to carry out operations under the command of Mbili; it would then return to base, where a selection would be made of those who had proved their worth. In the meantime, the second company would be in training, so that it in turn could go to the front when the first one returned. This, I thought, would allow the necessary selection to be made, at the same time as the men were being trained. I explained once more that, given the form of recruitment, only 20 would be left as possible soldiers out of the original 100, and only two or three of them as future cadre commanders (in the sense of being capable of leading an armed unit into combat).

As usual, we received an evasive response: they asked me to put my proposal in writing. This was done, but I never found out what became of the paper. We kept insisting that we should move up and start work at the Upper Base. We had counted on losing a week there to get things in shape for us to work at a certain rhythm, and now we were waiting just for the simple problem of our transfer to be resolved. We could not go up to the base, because the Commander had not arrived; or we had to wait because they were "having a meeting". One day after another passed like this. When I raised the matter again (as I did with truly irritating tenacity), a new pretext always arose. Even today, I do not know what to make of this. Perhaps it was true that they did not want to start preparatory work out of regard for the relevant authority, in this case the Base Commander.

One day I ordered Moja to go with some men to the Upper Base, on the pretext of training them for a march. He did this and the group returned at night, weary, soaked and chilled to the bone. It was a very cold and wet place, with constant mist and persistent rain; the people there said they were making a hut for us, which would take another few days. With patience on both sides, I set forth the various arguments why we should go up to the base: we could help build the shelter in a spirit of sacrifice, so that we would not be a burden, etc. etc.; and they sought new excuses to delay matters.

This enforced break saw the beginning of delightful talks with Comrade Kiwe, the head of intelligence. He is a tireless conversationalist, who speaks French at almost supersonic speed. In our various conversations, he made a daily analysis for me of important figures in the

Congolese revolution. One of the first to be lashed by his tongue was Olenga, a general in the Stanleyville area and in Sudan. According to Kiwe, Olenga was little more than an ordinary soldier, perhaps a lieutenant, who had been charged by Bidalila to make some incursions in the direction of Stanleyville and then return. But instead of doing this, Olenga started his own operations during those easy moments of revolutionary flux, and raised himself by one rank whenever he captured a village. By the time he reached Stanleyville he was a general. The conquests of the Liberation Army stopped there— which was something of a solution, because if they had continued, all the grades known to the military world would not have sufficed to reward Comrade Olenga.

For Kiwe, the true military leader was Colonel Pascasa (who later died in a fight among the Congolese in Cairo); he was the man with real military knowledge and revolutionary attitude, and the representative of Mulele.

On another day, Kiwe very subtly broached his criticisms of Gbenye, remarking, as if in passing, that his attitude had been unclear at the beginning that now, sure, he was president and a revolutionary, but there were more revolutionary ones, and so on. As the days went by and we got to know each other better, Kiwe's picture of Gbenye became that of a man more suited to lead a gang of robbers than a revolutionary movement. I do not have a record of all of Kiwe's assertions, but some are very well known: for example, what he said about the history of his involvement in the arrest of Gizenga, when he was interior minister in the Adoula government. Others are less well known, but if they are true, they cast a murky light on such matters as the attempts on Mitoudidi's life and connections with the Yankee embassy in Kenya.

On another occasion, the victim of Kiwe's tongue was Gizenga— characterized as a revolutionary, but a left-wing opportunist—who wanted to do everything by the political road, who thought a revolution could be made with the Army, and who, when given money to organize the revolutionary forces in Leopoldville, had even used it to form a political party.

The chats with Kiwe gave me an idea of what certain figures were like, but mainly highlighted the lack of solidity in this group of revolutionaries, or malcontents, who constituted the general staff of the Congolese revolution.

And the days passed. The lake was crossed by messengers with a fabulous capacity to distort any news, or by holidaymakers going off to Kigoma on some leave or other.

In my capacity as a doctor (actually an epidemiologist—which, if this illustrious branch of the Aesculapian tree will forgive me for saying so, gave me the right to know nothing about medicine), I worked for a few days with Kumi at the clinic and noticed various alarming facts. The first of these was the high number of cases of venereal disease, often caused by infection in Kigoma. What concerned me at that moment was not the state of health of the population or of the Kigoma prostitutes, but the fact that the opportunities for crossing the lake meant that so many fighters could be infected. Other questions also occurred to us. Who paid those women? With what money? How were the revolution's funds being spent?

From the first few days of our stay, we also had a chance to see some cases of alcohol poisoning caused by the famous *pombe*. This is a spirit distilled from the juice of maize and manioc flour, which is not high in alcohol yet has terrible effects. Presumably these arise not so much from the alcoholization *per se*, as from the amount of impurities, given the rudimentary methods of production. There were days when *pombe* washed over the camp, leaving behind a trail of brawling, poisoning, indiscipline, and so on.

The clinic began to be visited by peasants from the surrounding area, who had heard on Radio Bemba that some doctors were nearby. Our supply of medicines was poor, but a Soviet medical consignment came to our rescue. It had been chosen, however, not with the civilian population in mind, as was natural, but to meet the needs of an army in the field—and even then, it did not contain a complete range of requirements. Such imbalances were to be a constant feature of our time in the Congo. Highly valuable shipments of weapons and equipment always turned out to be incomplete; supplies from Kigoma inevitably featured guns and machine-guns without ammunition or essential components; rifles might arrive with the wrong ammunition, or mines without detonators.

In my view, although I have not been able to find an actual explanation, all these failures were due to the disorganized state of the Congolese Liberation Army, and to the shortage of cadres capable of minimally assessing equipment as it arrived.

The same happened with medical supplies, with the additional factor that they were stored in one big jumble in La Playa, where the reserves of food and weaponry also jostled one another in fraternal chaos. I tried several times to gain permission for us to organize the stores, and I suggested that some types of ammunition—such as bazooka or mortar shells—should be moved away from there. But nothing happened until much later.

Every day, contradictory news reached us from Kigoma. Occasionally, by dint of being repeated, some item eventually proved true: for example, that there was a group of Cubans waiting for a boat, an engine or something to get through; that Mitoudidi would cross over tomorrow or the day after, and then—when the day after tomorrow arrived—that he would be crossing in another day's time.

During this time, news also arrived from the Conference in Cairo, via Emmanuel on one of his frequent trips to Kigoma and back. The outcome had been a complete triumph for the revolutionary line. Kabila would stay for a while to make sure that the agreement was implemented, then he would go somewhere else to have an operation on a cyst (not very serious but a nuisance), and this would delay him a little.

We had to do something to avoid complete idleness. We organized lessons in French and Swahili, as well as classes in general culture, which were quite badly needed by our troops. Given the nature of the classes (and of the teachers), this could not add a lot to the comrades' cultural heritage, but it did have the important function of using up time. Our morale remained high, even though the comrades were starting to murmur that they watched the days pass to no useful purpose. Also hovering over us was the spectre of malaria and the other tropical fevers that struck nearly everyone in one form or another; these often responded to special drugs, but left behind most troublesome after-effects, such as general debility or lack of appetite, which added to the pessimism creeping into the men's view of things.

As the days went by, the picture of organizational chaos became more evident. I myself took part in the distribution of Soviet medical supplies, and it resembled a Gypsy fair; each representative of the armed groups produced figures, and cited facts and reasons why he should have access to a greater quantity of medicine. There were several clashes as I tried to stop some medicine or special equipment being pointlessly carted off to the front lines, but everyone wanted to have something of everything. They started to bandy fantastic totals for the number of men in their group: one declared 4,000, another 2,000, and so on. These were inventions, which hardly had an objective basis even in the number of peasants living close to the Army and potentially recruitable to it. The real number of soldiers or armed men in the base camps was greatly inferior to such figures.

During these days, the various fronts were almost completely passive, and if people with gunshot wounds were nevertheless expected, it would be as a result of accidents. Since scarcely anyone had the faintest idea about guns, they tended to go off when they were played with or treated without care.

On 8 May, 18 Cubans headed by Aly finally reached us. Mitoudidi, the head of the general staff, arrived at the same time, but he had to return at once to Kigoma to search for guns and ammunition. We had a friendly conversation, and he left me with an agreeable impression of reliability, seriousness and organizational spirit. Kabila sent word that he had many reservations about my identity, and so I remained incognito as I went about my apparent tasks as doctor and translator.

We agreed with Mitoudidi that the transfer to Upper Base would take place the next day. This was done, but we left below Moja, Nane and Tano, who had gone down with fever, and the doctor Kumi in attendance at the infirmary. I was sent to the base as doctor and translator. There were barely 20 Congolese there, looking bored, lonely and ill at ease. I began the fight to break down this sluggishness; we began classes in Swahili (given by the political commissar at the base) and in French (assigned to another comrade there). In addition, we started building shelters against the intense cold. We were at 1,700 metres above sea level and 1,000 metres above the level of the lake, in an area where trade winds from the Indian Ocean condense and give rise to continual rainfall. We quickly set about the task of putting up some constructions, and fires were soon blazing to keep the nocturnal cold at bay.

The basic feature of the People's Liberation Army was that it was a parasitic army; it did not work, did not train, did not fight, and demanded provisions and labour from the population, sometimes with extreme harshness. The peasants were at the mercy of groups who came on leave from the camps to demand extra food, and who repeatedly ate their poultry and little luxury items they kept in reserve.

The soldier's staple food is *bukali*, which is made as follows. Manioc root is peeled and left to dry in the sun for a few days; then it is ground in a mortar exactly like those used for grinding coffee in our mountain regions; the resulting flour is sifted, boiled in water until it forms a paste, and then eaten. If the will is there, *bukali* provides you with the necessary carbohydrates, but what was eaten there was semi-raw, unsalted cassava; this was sometimes complemented with *zombe*, cassava leaves pounded and boiled, and seasoned with a little palm oil or the meat of some hunted animal. (There was quite a lot of game in that region, but the meat was eaten only on occasion, not regularly.) It cannot be said that the fighters were well fed; very little was caught in the lake. But one of their bad habits was that they were incapable of marching to the base to look for food. On their shoulders were only a rifle, a cartridge-belt and their personal effects, which generally did not go beyond a blanket.

After a while, when we had begun living communally with this original army, we learnt some exclamations typical of the way they saw the world. If someone was given something to carry, he said: *"Mimi hapana motocari"* — that is, "I'm not a truck." In some cases, when he was with Cubans, this would become: *"Mimi hapana cuban"* — "I'm not a Cuban." The food, as well as the weapons and ammunition for the front, had to be carried by the peasants. Clearly, an army of this kind can have a justification only if, like its enemy counterpart, it actually fights now and again. As we shall see, this requirement was not met either. As it did not change the existing order of things, the Congolese revolution was doomed to defeat by its own internal weaknesses.

## winds from the west, breezes from the east

IT WAS CLEAR to me that I had to do something to stop the rot—a process which, paradoxically, had begun with the only offensive operation we had seen the revolutionary movement undertake since our arrival. One thing followed another after the first Cubans proposed to withdraw from the struggle. Two more comrades followed suit— Achiri and Hanzini, one of them a Party member—and shortly afterwards two doctors who had only recently arrived, both Party members, made the same request. I was less stormy and much more cutting with the two doctors than with the ordinary soldiers, who had reacted to events in a more or less primal manner.

The selection in Cuba was obviously not good enough, but it is difficult to get it right in the present conditions of the Cuban Revolution. You cannot base yourself only on the great precedent of a man's record under arms, for later years of easier living have also changed people—and the revolution turned the huge majority into revolutionaries. Nevertheless, it is a mystery to me how such a selection can be made before the test of fire, and I think that every measure must take account of the fact that no one can be given the final approval until he has undergone selection in the theatre of battle. The reality was that, at the first serious setback (accompanied, it must be said in their defence, by the visible disarray of the forces in action), a number of comrades lost heart and decided to withdraw from a struggle for which they had come to die if necessary—as volunteers, moreover—surrounded by a halo of bravery, self-sacrifice, enthusiasm, in short, invincibility.

What meaning there is in the soldier's response: "Until death, if necessary!" It carries the solution to serious problems involved in creating our men of tomorrow.

Incredible things have been happening among the Rwandans. Mundandi's second-in-command has been shot, they say, but in reality brutally murdered. Thousands of conjectures are being spun around this event. The least favourable—which is not to say they are untrue—suggest it had something to do with women. The result is that Commander Mitchel, a soldier and a peasant have all gone to a better life. The formal charge against him was that he supplied a bad *dawa* which was responsible for the death of 20 of his comrades, but it did not specify whether the *dawa* directly caused their deaths or gave them inadequate protection, or whether operations outside the camp to find the *dawa* were the pretext on which he was denounced.

The incident had links to others taking place at the same time, which it would have been good to get to the bottom of. It came after a serious defeat for which Mundandi was the main person responsible, but another man was shot. And the whole thing happened at a time of virtual rebellion against Kabila and the high command of the Liberation Army, when the Rwandans, flatly refusing to carry out any military action, were either deserting or (in the case of those who remained at the camp) saying that they would go to fight only when they saw the Congolese doing the same. Even if Kabila were to go and see them, they would give him food without salt and tea without sugar, as they themselves took them, so that he would understand what it was to make sacrifices. (This was hardly a real threat, of course, because Kabila did not have the slightest intention of going there.)

A Congolese commissar, who was at the front on the day of the events, tried to intervene but was simply blocked and forced to leave the camp. This commissar was the same Alfred about whom I have already spoken, and his reaction was expressed in the following alternative: either Mundandi is shot for murder, or I withdraw from the struggle.

Some Rwandans who had grown close to us, and whom we had accepted as troops under Cuban discipline, were demoted and treated with hostility by their compatriots. This portended a cooling of relations, or something worse.

I talked these problems over with Masengo and stressed what, in my view, was the key point: that if we were to succeed in the struggle, we would have to integrate ourselves more and more into the Liberation Movement and come to be seen by the Congolese as other people who were just like them. Instead, we had limited ourselves to the circle of Rwandans, who were foreigners in the country and very eager to remain such, so that in their company we were condemned to the situation of perpetual outsiders. In reply, Masengo gave permission for some of our men to go and help Calixte in his work—and we quickly acted upon this.

Moja received instructions to organize fresh operations with any volunteers he could obtain, but on condition that it should be a mixed force, with the same number of Cubans and Rwandans. We had discussed with Mbili how to lay the ambush; my aim was for him to learn the basics of this type of warfare, and so he was ordered to attack only one vehicle in the first action.

This was set to take place on the road from Front de Force to Albertville, in an area scouted by Azi that had the right conditions for groups to harry the enemy or for a sizeable column to operate. There was thick forest on the mountainside, although it would be necessary to organize a supply system.

Aly arrived with news from the Kabimba front. On a reconnaissance trip, he had come across four enemy policemen on a mission to improve visibility by burning the nearby hills; three of them had been captured, while the fourth had been killed. Of the 20 Congolese who set off with Aly, 16 took to their heels; the only armed policemen had been the one who was killed. The soldiers' morale and combat readiness on this front gave no reason for envy among their colleagues at Front de Force or Calixte's front.

The base commander at Front de Force was now Captain Zakarias, and the idea was that he would come down with Mbili to carry out the action. Mundandi took quite a large force with him to the lakeside base: he looked threatening, but in fact he was afraid and wanted to make sure he would be safe when he went to Kigoma to talk with Kabila. Soon he fell ill (it was a real illness) and took the familiar month off together with some men loyal to him.

He visited me and behaved with solicitude, almost with humility. First we talked about general problems of the offensive, then moved on to the matter of the killing.

He explained the death of those comrades as follows. Commander Mitchel, trusting in the friendship of some local inhabitants, had confided the secret of the attack to them; one of them, however, was a spy who passed on the information to the enemy. When his comrades found out, it was necessary to shoot them; he, Mundandi, had disagreed, but he was in a minority at the meeting and had to carry out the wishes of the majority, given that the fighters were threatening to withdraw from the struggle.

I went over some aspects of the incident with him. First of all, the defeat could not be attributed to an act of betrayal, even if there had been one; it was due to the way in which the military action was carried out, to defects in the conception and execution of the attack — which was not to deny that we might also carry some blame as a result of Inne's attitude. Citing numerous examples from our own revolutionary war, I explained that it was highly negative to depend on soldiers' assemblies in cases such as this, that in the end revolutionary democracy had never been applied in the running of armies anywhere in the world, and that any attempt to implement it had ended in disaster. Finally, the shooting of a field commander who belonged to the Congo Liberation Army, without even informing the general staff and still less asking its views, was a sign of great indiscipline and complete lack of central authority; we all had to do what we could to ensure that such things never happened again.

When I commented to Masengo on the weakness of Mundandi's arguments, he replied that Mundandi had told him a different story but had been reluctant to speak frankly to me, because in reality it was superstition that lay behind the drama.

Mundandi was called to a meeting with leaders from various areas to try to improve relations between their groups. Apart from Mundandi himself, it was attended by Captain Salumu, Calixte's second-in-command, and Comrade Lambert, the head of operations in the Fizi zone, and a bevy of assistants.

Masengo, trapped by his lack of authority, could not get out of the crisis in the only way possible, by starting all over again and saying: "I'm in charge here!" He did not say that. Instead, he proposed to maintain the independence of action of the different fronts but to urge that no incident such as these should occur again—which left the problem unsolved and went right against my recommendation that a unified front should be formed under firm leadership.

Measures were taken with only a display of firmness, which then resulted in a multitude of weaknesses. Masengo had a list of weapons supplied to the various fronts, and not one figure coincided with the one given by the leader in question. No one doubted that the weapons really had been delivered, but assertions to the contrary were accepted and more military equipment was sent to the guzzling morass of the fronts. A commission had been set up to recover weapons from the large number of deserters all over the region, who were now lording it over others with the persuasive power of rifles they had taken with them from the front. There was even talk of capturing the parents of each man in question, if he could not be taken himself. But in the end they did not capture any deserters, nor recover any weapons, nor—as far as I know—imprison any lax parent among the peasantry.

When I suggested leaving for the front in a few days, Masengo refused and repeatedly invoked the excuse of my personal safety. I attacked him head-on by asking if he distrusted me in some way, since the reasons he gave were not valid. I demanded that he should treat me with greater frankness and say if he had any misgivings about me. The blow was too direct and he gave way; so we left it that we would make the trip together in five or six days' time, when a report would arrive from some men he had sent to carry out an inspection there.

There were misgivings, however, for the simple reason that neither Kabila nor Masengo had set foot at the various fronts for a very long time and the fighters were bitterly critical of them for this; the fact that the head of the Cuban expeditionary force could go and take part in life at the front, when those in charge of the war did not do the same, might give them fresh reason to feel censorious. Masengo was aware of this, but—apart from my concern to make a direct assessment of the situation—he also calculated that the Congolese leaders might feel obliged to make a journey around the fronts, and thus get to know and try to solve problems relating to the supply of food, clothing, medicine and ammunition.

To make ourselves more familiar with every aspect of the area in preparation for our planned trip, we went with the chief of staff to Kasima, 27 kilometres north of Kibamba. There too we found the scenes of indiscipline that have been a recurrent feature of this report, although Masengo was able to take some correct measures such as the replacement of a commander who spent the day sheltering in nearby mountains (afraid of aircraft) with the lieutenant who had been deputizing for him. Our own men, four machine-gunners, were laid low with malaria, and we took them to Kibamba for treatment.

We had advanced deep into the political territory of General Moulane, and the coldness toward Masengo was reflected in the attitude of the local population and the fighters, who were reluctant to accept what he wanted to be a central authority.

We pressed on and came to another place called Karamba. There we found one of the most original "barriers", manned by a group of Rwandans who were independent of Mundandi and had political-ideological differences with him that I would not know how to define. They had set up a recoilless 75mm gun on a hillock—the craziest place they could have found, because it had no strategic importance and all the gun could do was sink a boat that might pass nearby. It had, of course, already let loose some volleys without hitting the target, because the artillerymen did not know how to handle it and, in any case, the boats kept sufficient distance to remain out of range. It was another unit that was wasting its time. I recommended their immediate transfer to Kibamba, where there were no artillery pieces or training in how to use them, but this advice, as so often, fell on deaf ears. It was not that Masengo did not understand such matters, but simply that he did not have the authority. He did not feel that he had the power to impose decisions that went against the customary grain. A weapon that landed in a group of fighters was held sacred, and the only ones who could snatch it away (rather easily, in fact) were the enemy.

Masengo, wanting to changing the course of events through some offensive operations, suggested to me an attack on Uvira. I had to object to this, because inspections of that area had revealed the same general conditions, the same basic unfamiliarity with military methods, and a total lack of combat readiness. The scouts in that area had instructions to cross enemy lines and investigate the possibility of laying ambushes on the other side of the little town of Uvira, at the tip of Lake Tanganyika where the roads from Bukavu, and from Bujumbura in Burundi, come to an end. The idea, then, was to cross to the other side of Uvira and break the enemy's communications. Given the vast expanse of the Congo, it is quite easy to carry out such incursions. But not only had there been no one to take our men across the lines; they were even refused permission to go themselves, on the grounds that an attack was under preparation and they might alert the enemy.

During the days when all these diverse events were being recounted, we received news from Dar es Salaam—some of it good. A ship had arrived from Cuba with a cargo of weapons, provisions and 17,000 rounds of ammunition for our fighters; it would be sent by road very soon. I learnt that news of the Cubans killed in the Congo had appeared in all the newspapers, and that the ambassador had persuaded the Congolese formally to deny our presence there. This did not seem to me a wise course, because such things cannot be kept hidden and the only correct thing to do was to remain silent. I let Pablo Rivalta know this.

Along with the letter for the ambassador and the other reports, two comrades set off: Otto, who had been ill for some time, and Sitaini, whose bilateral hernia had become a medical case. I now had the opportunity to release him and to end the annoying situation that his reluctance to be there with us had brought about; I found it painful to do, but it was the best solution. Those who "cracked" and were forced to remain against their will tried to justify themselves by making negative propaganda, which found a ready echo among other comrades. In this case there was the justification of an illness, and that is why I allowed the escape.

My Swahili teacher, Ernest Ilunga, whom I already treated as a younger brother, was also due to leave in a few days' time. He had had some seizures of an epileptic kind, and the doctors suspected that a tumour was developing in his upper nervous centres. Masengo disagreed and explained to me that it was a fairly simple matter of evil spirits; the local doctors would cure him in Kigoma—and that is where he went, instead of to Dar es Salaam, where he had been advised to go for a cure, or at least for a diagnosis.

Following instructions, Moja visited Calixte's front and sent me a note which I have copied because it casts light on a number of questions I have already raised here.

Tatu:

*I am writing to you from the Kazolelo-Makungo front, where the group of ten men were sent. I reached them yesterday, having learnt that a Congolese patrol had arrested a civilian with a Tshombe identity card in a settlement on the plain.*

*Today, the 19th, I met Commander Calixte, who personally interrogated the prisoner; he is kept locked up in a house far from the front, and has not seen any of the Cubans.*

*According to Calixte, the prisoner told him that he had been under arrest in Force at the time of the attack; that four officers had been killed there, with another two in Katenga, as well as a number of soldiers; that he did not know the dead officers by name, but had been able to see their rankings; that the prisoner's identity card was not an army card but of the kind issued to everyone going to Albertville; that in Nyangi there were 25 guardsmen, a mortar and an artillery piece, these weapons being located on the road to Makungo; that the prison where they had gathered the attacking revolutionaries was a kilometre from Force in the direction of Albertville, that the guardsmen had taken some of their watches and shoes, and that they had had to be buried by civilians.*

*Commander Calixte agrees that some men should be trained to go there with a mortar, a gun and anti-aircraft weapons, although he has none of these, and so we are awaiting the return of Captain Zakarias (Mundandi's replacement) to take these men to the Force front.[3] Today, the comrades at the Makungo front began to give classes to the rest of Commander Calixte's force. About Faume, I cannot yet tell you anything.[4] In a few days I'll send you more details about the situation—with a Cuban, as is natural for such details, and in a sealed envelope.*

*Moja*

---

[3]Captain Zakarias refused to accept the Congolese at his front, on the grounds that they went to his camp to steal.

[4]From what we knew, Commander Faume had split off from Calixte—apparently because of friction between them—and was on the plain with a lot of weapons. At that time, we were groping around in search of someone among the Congolese leaders.

Shortly afterwards, the best news of these days arrived: the light breeze. The ambush had gone off quite successfully: 25 Rwandans and 25 Cubans, led respectively by Captain Zakarias and Mbili, but in reality under the latter's leadership, had carried out the engagement, if it deserves that name.

Azi's inspection had shown that the lorries passed there in single file, without protection. The 50 men attacked a lorry with five soldiers. A bazooka round from Sultán opened the proceedings, and for a few minutes the vehicle and the mercenaries (all of them black) were riddled with bullets. Only one was carrying a weapon, since the lorry was transporting food, cigarettes and drinks. From the point of view of gradually preparing for large-scale actions, the prize could hardly have been better—but a number of accidents were a blot on the record.

When the shooting began, the Rwandans ran backwards firing their weapons. This put our men in danger, and in fact Comrade Arobaini lost a finger when a bullet crushed the metacarpus of one hand.

Two examples will give some idea of the primitive mentality that still holds sway in the Congo. When Captain Zakarias learnt of the wound caused by the FM burst, he examined, it and decreed that the guilty man should lose two of his fingers, in accordance with the principle of an eye for an eye; he took out his knife there and then and would have cut off the poor devil's extremities if Mbili had not very tactfully persuaded him to exercise pardon. The other example is of a Rwandan soldier who took to his heels almost as soon as he heard gunfire (our own fire, as there was no fighting); since each Rwandan was accompanied by a Cuban, our man in question caught him by the arm to hold him back, and the terrified boy, in order to shake off an attacker who was stopping him from protecting himself, gave the Cuban a huge bite on the hand.

These are two indications of the long road we will have to travel to make an army out of this shapeless mass of men. Unfortunately, the tragicomedy of this ambush did not end there. After the first moments of stupor, the brilliant victors realized that the greatest prize was on top of the lorry: namely, bottles of beer and whisky. Mbili tried to get the food loaded and to destroy the drink, but it was impossible. In a few hours all the fighters were drunk, under the astonished and reproving gaze of our men who were not allowed a drop. Then they held a meeting and decided they would not return to the plain for the other planned actions, but would return to base—they had done enough already. Mbili, diplomatically trying to avoid being left only with the Cubans, accepted the decision. On the way back, a drunken Captain Zakarias ran into a peasant and finished him off with a few shots, claiming that he had been a spy.

Strangest of all, when I explained to Masengo how dangerous it was to behave in this way with the peasants, he to some extent vindicated Zakarias, on the grounds that the tribe living in this region was hostile to the revolution. This meant that people were not to be catalogued according to their personal qualities, but to be incorporated in a tribal concept from which it was very difficult to escape; when a tribe was friendly; all its components were friendly; and likewise when it was unfriendly. Such schemas did not help the revolution to develop, but they were also clearly dangerous, because—as we saw later—some members of the friendly tribes were enemy informers, and in the end nearly all of them turned into our enemies.

We had had our first victory, and it was as if it had rid us of some of the bad taste left from before. But the problems posed by the things I have described were mounting up in such a way that I was beginning to change my time scale. If everything depended on the development of these armed groups into a fully fledged Liberation Army, then five years was a very optimistic target for the Congolese revolution to reach a victorious conclusion—unless something changed in the way the war was conducted. But that possibility seemed more remote with every day that passed.

## various escapes

DESPITE ALL THE fears, we kept trying to incorporate Congolese into our little army and to give them the rudiments of military training, so that this nucleus might save the most important thing: the soul, the presence of the revolution. But the Cubans charged with imparting the divine breath had an ever weaker grip on it themselves. The effects of the climate were still being felt, as gastro-enteritis was added to the endemic malaria. Until the rigours of the job got the better of my scientific spirit, I noted in my field diary the statistics of my own case: I had the runs more than 30 times in 24 hours. Only the scrub knows how many more there were after that. Many comrades suffered from the same malady; it did not last long or fail to respond to strong antibiotics, but it did serve to undermine a morale that was already ailing. Nor did anything happening outside our camp help to raise our spirits; not one high-minded gesture, not one intelligent action.

The few Congolese we had managed to recruit went to a get a *dawa* in a nearby camp, or to be examined by a Congolese doctor (sorcerer), and then simply deserted. This made me feel the impotence that comes from a lack of direct communication. I wanted to instil into them everything I felt, to convince them that I really did feel it, but the translation transformer — my skin as well, perhaps — undid everything. After one of the frequent transgressions (they had refused to work — another of their characteristics), I spoke furiously to them in French; I rattled out the worst things I could find with my poor vocabulary and, at the height of my rage, said that they should be made to wear skirts and carry manioc in a basket (a female job), because they were good for nothing and worse than women; I preferred to have an army of women than people of this kind. But while the translator turned the "volley" into Swahili, all the men looked at one another and guffawed with a disconcerting simplicity.

Perhaps the most constant enemy was *dawa* and the various things it required. I called in a *muganga*, probably one of those considered second-rate, but he immediately sized up the situation; he settled into the camp and happily idled away the time in a way appropriate to a first-rate *muganga*. He was certainly intelligent. The day after he arrived, I told him that he ought to go off with a group of men who were to spend several days at an ambush, because *dawa* lost its effect with time and people did not remain at their position. But he answered with a flat refusal; he would prepare a stronger *dawa* for them that would last a fortnight. Such a forceful argument had to be accepted from someone with his authority, and the men left with the stronger *dawa* which, combined with the speed and smoothness of the road, gave excellent results.

Several days before, I had spoken with Masengo about practical training in the Kalonda-Kibuye area, so I started making preparations to send a team of Cubans who, operating in two groups, would select the best Congolese fighters on the basis of their actions in an ambush. We would use the same system as in the area closest to Katenga, where we had by now lifted all the ambushes because the number of Congolese had kept dwindling until only one or two were left. We left the ailing Azi behind with a couple of comrades and concentrated the rest together with ourselves. Despite our efforts, disease and dispersal at the various fronts left few men available, so that it was 13 who set off with Mbili for Kalonda-Kibuye. Ishirini was the second-in-command.

Ishirini was an ordinary soldier in Cuba. But his qualities were such that we decided to try him out on assignments of responsibility, as part of a plan of training leaders in case we built our army up into an operational group with enough Congolese soldiers. The comrades were scheduled to spend roughly 20 days at the ambush—not longer, because the rigours of the climate did not agree with the men, especially the Cubans. After that time had passed, another group would transfer the operation to a different region, so as not to saturate the same area with ambushes, while the first group rested and cleaned up. Mbili had already left to cross the Kimbi and begin operations when, with just a few hours' difference, an affecting little note arrived from Siki and another from Masengo. The one from Siki said:

> Moja:
> The guardsmen are advancing on Fizi, and there's nothing to stop them; nor do they want to stop them. We are going from Fizi to Lubondja. I'll try to knock out the bridges. Tell Tatu my trip was a failure.
> Siki 10-10-65

The note from Masengo gave the news that Fizi had fallen and gave instructions that the whole of the Kalonda-Kibuye group should place itself under my orders.[5]

Meanwhile, some of the previous work was starting to bear fruit; a consignment of food and some medicine was brought up from the lake by a number of peasants, and we shared some of our things with them. It was not a lot, but we could give them some salt and sugar, and our men were able to have sweetened tea. A quite unnecessary letter arrived from Aly with the story of an ambush they had tried to set in the Kabimba area. Upon finding a packet of cigarettes on a trail, they turned back and finally reached the main path with their numbers

[5] This group was never incorporated in fact. A few isolated elements did come, under the orders of a political commissar who seemed a good type, but I couldn't do anything with that rabble. The rest had remained in the peasants' houses. I sent them all away, including the political commissar; I didn't want any more disorder there.

much reduced; of the 60 Congolese soldiers, only 25 were left; they took prisoner some peasants who were passing down the road (they had been instructed to clear it), and who said that a lorry would be passing in a few hours from the cement factory in Kabimba. When the commander of the Congolese detachment heard this, he decided to lift the ambush an hour before the lorry passed, since guardsmen might be coming; that brought the week-long operation to an end. Shortly afterwards came the promotions—from captain to major or field commander, and so on; rewards were rained on them for the bravery of their action.

Siki arrived from Fizi, having travelled with forced marches because of the situation. He recounted the vicissitudes of the trip. The conversations with General Moulane passed through too many mouths (Siki speaks neither French nor Swahili, and the general no French) to have any guarantee of authenticity, but—to cut a long story short— Siki presented our ultimatum and argued that it was necessary to dig trenches immediately. The existing defences were a "barrier" consisting of three men, a bazooka man with his assistant and another with a *pepechá*,[6] plus the usual bit of wire in the middle of the road to stop anyone passing; they had not dug a trench or done any reconnaissance. After I had spoken with Siki, General Moulane had his say and launched into an extremely sharp attack on Comrade Masengo, blaming him for everything because he had not asked for arms or ammunition and had not requested Cubans to come and fight. Under these conditions, he would not defend Fizi: he was not a corpse to be digging holes (fortunately he was still alive), and Masengo should take all the blame. Masengo did not even react. We don't know if this was due to his lack of character or to his being on enemy territory (which is how this area might be described)—anyway, he weathered the storm in silence. That night they no longer slept in Fizi.

Some comrades were of the view that the general could not be so stupid, that he must be colluding with the mercenaries. I have no evidence of this, and he did proudly remain in his Fizi area when we withdrew. I think that the time lag may explain this attitude of his, but in practice he played into the enemy's hands.

The fact is that internal dissensions were resulting in a number of extreme cases such as these. The 37 kilometres by road from Baraka

[6]An old-model Soviet machine-gun, named after the letters PPCH indicating its factory of origin.

to Fizi cross hills where there are many possibilities to lay an ambush, as well as a river that forms a defensive barrier quite hard for vehicles to negotiate. The bridge there is already a semi-wreck and had only to be destroyed completely to create good defensive possibilities; at least this would have slowed down the enemy advance. But none of this was done.

On 12 October the enemy took Lubondja in a triumphal procession. Colonel Lambert had learnt of the capture of Fizi and set off there with 40 men, leaving some heavy weapons behind in Lubondja that were then lost in the scrub. He was not open to argument, and Masengo did not have the presence of mind to order him to stay and defend the last point preventing a link-up of the forces from Lulimba with those landing in Baraka: namely, the barrier in the mountains.

When Masengo arrived in our camp, I lost patience and told him that, with the men I had, I could not take responsibility for defending it from a two-pronged attack. Mbili had strengthened the eastern end by crossing with his 13 men on forced marches, but all we could count on were 13 Cubans on one flank and ten on the other; to go to extremes of defence would mean getting 23 men killed, since the rest were not willing to lift a finger. At the barrier they had an arsenal with 150 boxes of the most varied ammunition, especially for heavy weapons, mortars, artillery pieces and 12.7 machine-guns, and the previous night every means had been tried to get the people to save it. We had to threaten to throw water over them, to remove the blankets from on top of them, in short, to exert extreme physical pressure, while Masengo, who was spending the night there, was powerless to force them to work and Lambert's deputies ran off with his followers.

Masengo's response was to send Lambert a letter ordering him to return and take charge of the defence with his men. I don't know if this letter reached its destination, but it certainly had no effect. Soon news arrived that the position, under threat from both the Lulimba and the Lubondja end, had fallen without a fight, and that the retreat had turned into a rout. The attitude of our men was bad, to say the least. They let the Congolese have weapons such as mortars for which they were responsible, and which were then lost; they showed no fighting spirit and, like the Congolese, thought only of saving themselves; and the retreat was so disorderly that we lost a man without knowing how, since his own comrades could not tell whether he had simply got lost or been wounded or killed by enemy soldiers who were firing on a hill over which they were retreating. We thought he might have headed towards the lake base or be somewhere else, until his failure to appear convinced us that he was either dead or a prisoner—in any case, we heard no more of him. At the end of the day, a huge number of weapons were lost. I gave instructions that any Congolese who unexpectedly turned up without being ordered for some reason to do so should be disarmed forthwith. The next day, I had a considerable war booty, as if we had laid the most productive of ambushes: the 75mm gun, with a good amount of ammunition; one anti-aircraft machine-gun intact, and remnants of another; mortar parts, five submachine-guns, ammunition, hand grenades and 100 or so rifles. The man responsible for the gun, Comrade Bahaza, had remained alone at the position, but when the guardsmen advanced and he received an alarmist report from another Cuban, he had pulled back and abandoned it. The mercenaries did not advance so quickly, and Moja gave orders in time for the gun to be saved, but I sharply criticized that comrade (a Party member), as well as a number of others.

I agreed with Masengo that all runaway soldiers should be disarmed and stripped of their rank; we would build a new force with those that remained, and I hoped in my heart of hearts there would be very few of them; I said I would accept only those who showed they were serious and had a fighting spirit.

A meeting was organized with the Congolese comrades, at which I told them very sharply what I thought of them. I explained that we were going to form a new army, that no one was obliged to come with us and anyone who wanted to leave could do so; but he must leave his weapons there, and the arsenal we had saved with so much effort would also remain with us. I asked those present to raise their hand if they wanted to leave; no one did. This seemed strange, as I had previously asked two or three Congolese (who had agreed to stay). Then, keeping an eye on one of those I had selected, I asked everyone who wanted to stay to take one step forward; two stepped forward, and immediately the whole column did the same—which meant that they would all remain part of the force. I was not convinced by the way this had worked out, so I asked them to think it over and discuss among themselves before we decided. The result of this was that some 15 men felt they would like to leave. But it did bring some gains; one commander decided to remain as a soldier (as I was not accepting former ranks), and the number of volunteers was larger than anticipated.

It was agreed that Masengo should return to the base together with Tembo, Siki and the doctor-translator, Kasulu. Paradoxically, the political situation could not have been better, since Tshombe had fallen and Kimba was making vain attempts to form a government. Things were ideal for us to mount further operations and take advantage of the disintegration in Leopoldville. The efficiently led enemy troops struck out on their own, however, far from events in the capital and with no serious opposition to face.

Comrade Rafael, who was in charge of our affairs in Dar es Salaam, came to do a tour and to have a talk with me. We found ourselves agreeing on the basic issues: the head of signals would be at the site of operations and would have a transmitter capable of reaching Havana; a weekly batch of food would be sent to the new army's base, which would be supplied as well as possible; and a comrade from Dar es Salaam would go to Kigoma to replace Changa, who did not speak Swahili and was having a number of difficulties; Changa would come over here and be in charge of the boats.

With regard to provisions, my previous attitude had proved wrong and I now changed it. I had come with the idea of forming an exemplary nucleus, of enduring all hardships alongside the Congolese and, with our spirit of self-sacrifice, displaying the true path of a revolutionary soldier. The result, however, had been that our men went hungry and had to make do with worn shoes and clothes, while the Congolese divided among themselves the shoes and clothes that reached them by another route; all we had achieved was that discontent became rife among the Cubans themselves. It was therefore decided to form the nucleus of an army that with which we had already made contact with Kigoma from the Upper Base; at least we received and got through well, despite the fact that the equipment was designed for 20 kilometres rather than the 70 or so to the Tanzanian port.

In the meantime, a number of telegrams explaining the situation had been sent by radio; this one went on the 18th:

*Rafael:*
*Things are falling apart: whole units and peasants are going over to the enemy. None of the Congolese troops can be relied on. From today we may not be able to go on the air with the main apparatus. We will maintain contact with Kigoma by auxiliary*

*apparatus. Changa here because of mechanical difficulties. Crew and boats in good condition urgently needed.*

In the end, it was possible to get Changa across, with a huge load of women and children, which caused a row with the Kigoma commissioner; he said that we were only bringing him idlers and parasites, and that we should take them back to where they came from—which we did not do, of course.

On the same day, Rafael sent me the following telegram.

*Tatu:*

    *Second conversation with Kabila; we forcefully presented the situation to him and asked for immediate supply of materials; he promised to resolve this before leaving for Korea. We saw on the road to Kigoma a lorry with very few things for there. We spoke with Cambona yesterday; he promised to look into it and give us reply today from conversation with president. It was a direct and definitive discussion that made them responsible for consequences. We spoke with Soviets and Chinese and informed them of absurd situation with delivery of material they have sent. We propose telling ambassadors of UAR, Ghana and Mali that, under Accra agreement, Tanzania is not delivering material to nationalists resisting white mercenaries, that responsibility for annihilation will lie with African leaders and Tanzanian government. Kabila in coordination with ourselves met government figures and made the same points, also to Chinese and Soviets.*

I sent him the following reply:

*Rafael:*

    *We want to know result of last report to Cuba about commission to discuss with Tanzanian government. On discussions with governments of Ghana, Mali and UAR, put it in form of question: what was actual agreement, and was it to leave us in present plight? We think measures you are taking will come too late. That will take around a month. We are thinking of evacuating here and then evacuating most Cubans in second stage. A small group of us will remain as symbol of Cuba's prestige. Inform Cuba.*

I was intending to send back the sick, the frail and everyone "weak in the legs" and to fight on with a small group of men. With this in mind, I carried out a little "decisive test" among the comrades that yielded discouraging results; if it was up to them, almost no one was disposed to keep on fighting.

One of the problems of an evacuation was that Mafu had sent a couple of his men to reconnoitre Kasima and they had not returned. It was decided that another comrade would go to find them and come back as soon as possible. They should leave the heavy weapons that they could not transport and move off with the rest; some comrades such as Mbili and his group would have to complete a very long march if we wanted to abandon the lower base at dawn. Basing my reasoning on the character of the enemy attacks, I calculated that they would leave us a day's respite before trying other manoeuvres; this would allow us to leave quite easily, but we had to take steps to avoid contact and to save most of the things.

Our three sick men, together with Njenje, the man in charge of the base, left by boat for a little village called Mukungo where we thought of organizing resistance; they took with them some of the heavy weapons from Azi's unit — some but not all, because the Congolese element of our own forces had also been affected by dissolution and a lot of things had been scattered around. The Congolese were now making for the Fizi area. At first I planned to attack them but, thinking better of it, ordered anyone who wanted to leave to be allowed to do so, for if it came to an evacuation we would not be able to take everyone with us.

At dawn we set fire to the house that had served as our accommodation for nearly seven months; there was a lot of paper, many documents that could be consigned to oblivion and that it was best to destroy all at once. Shortly afterwards, when it was already daylight, they began to burn the ammunition dumps without consultation; neither Masengo nor I had given any such orders, and in fact I had tried to persuade the Congolese that it was important to take the material with them, if not to the new base then at least to the nearby mountain. Instead, someone put a light to quite a lot of material. As the valuable store burned and exploded, I watched the fireworks from the first hill on the way to Jungo and waited for the many stragglers to catch up. They came with an age-old weariness, an alarming lack of vitality, dropping parts of heavy weapons to lighten their load without a thought for what the weapon might mean in a battle. Virtually no Congolese remained in the units and the Cubans carried everything; I stressed the need to look after those weapons, which would be vital to us if we had to sustain a final attack, and the men set off dragging their feet and making frequent stops, bearing one gun and one machine-gun; they had already left two along the way.

I was waiting for the communications unit; at six o'clock we were supposed to attempt the first contact and I watched the head of the team, Tuma, coming down the hill opposite me from the Upper Base to the lake. It was infuriating; the comrades were spending three hours on a hill that should normally take ten minutes to climb down, and then they had to take a break before continuing on their way. I ordered them to leave anything superfluous and try to walk faster; but among the superfluous things, the telegraph operator forgot the code and someone had to be sent back for it. I had a serious word with the operators, trying to make them see their importance for communications and urging them to make another effort to reach the rendezvous point. We tried to make contact as usual at ten o'clock and failed. We kept moving at the slow pace dictated by the three comrades, who were completely unused to hill walking and marched only with their mind. We had made rather little progress; someone walking normally should take three or four hours from Kibamba (where our base was located) to Jungo. But at three in the afternoon, when we were scheduled to make our second contact with Kigoma, we were still quite a long way from the rendezvous point. At that time we managed to send the following message, which was successfully received.

*Changa:*
*We have lost the base, we are proceeding with emergency equipment, reply urgently whether you can come tonight.*

Then a second message.

*Changa:*
*Today the enemy is not at the lakeside, our position is Jungo, some ten kilometres south of Kibamba. Masengo decided to abandon the struggle and the best thing is for us to leave as soon as possible.*

When the comrades present heard the "understood" from the lake, all their faces changed as if a magic wand had touched them.

Our last message was to ask whether Changa had arrived. The messages were coded and it was necessary to decode them and to encode the reply. The response seemed to be: "No one has arrived here." Then they said they were having difficulties with the apparatus and went off the air.

The precoded message meant that the expected crew had not arrived, but it corresponded to our question. Apparently Changa had had difficulties on the lake (enemy aircraft were flying over it that day) which would imply that the boats had been lost and we could not get away; the faces again clouded over with the weariness and anxiety. At seven o'clock we made another attempt at contact and failed; conditions at the lake meant that our little apparatus could only transmit well at three in the afternoon.

We reached Jungo in time for bed; things were chaotic there, and no food had been prepared for us. When we counted up the men, four were missing: the look-out who had been lost during the guardsmen's advance; the two who had been reconnoitring at Kasima; and a fourth who had come in one of the units from Upper Base and inexplicably disappeared. A comrade had been sent to look for the men at Kasima, but he had returned without locating them. Desperate not to be left behind, he had had a quick look around and come back — as a calculation of the number of hours indicated to me. But I said nothing to him, because there was nothing to be done about it. We organized a unit under Rebocate's command to take the road coming through the mountains from Nganja, so that we would have a commanding view of the two points from which the guardsmen might appear: the heights and the lakeside. As the men were heading for their objective, we heard an explosion at the top of the hill over which the road passed. Since the ground was mined, we thought it was the guardsmen advancing and that we would have no time to organize a defence on the heights. We occupied some slopes, putting together a limited defence, and continued on our way towards Sele, a village quite close to Jungo.

The attempts to make contact at six o'clock and ten o'clock on 20 November were also unsuccessful. The telegraphists walked so slowly that we only reached Sele at midday, whereas that stretch was supposed to have been done in no more than an hour. Most of the men were gathered at Sele and we had something to ease our hunger. Dusk saw the arrival of Banhir, the man who had been left behind on the march. He had sprained his ankle and asked a comrade to let the others know so that they would go and find his rucksack. While waiting, he stayed where he was—but the other man did not do what he had been asked, or did it badly, and in the morning he was still at the place where he had suffered the accident, completely alone. He was at the base until 9.00 a.m. on the 20th, and then he left it believing that he had lost contact with us. The guardsmen had not entered the base; all the roads were deserted, all the houses abandoned.

At 2.30 p.m. we made contact with Kigoma. Our message read:

*Changa:*
   *Total men to evacuate less than 200, will be more difficult each day that passes. We are at Sele, 10 or 15 kilometres south of Kibamba.*

And I received the longed-for reply.

*Tatu:*
   *The crossing is set for tonight. Yesterday the commissioner did not let us cross.*

The men were euphoric. I spoke with Masengo and suggested leaving from that very point at night. As there were a lot of Congolese, the general staff held a meeting at which it was decided that Jean Paulis would remain in the Congo with his men and we and the various leaders would evacuate; the troops who were originally from that area would remain there; they would not be told of our intention to withdraw but would be sent on various pretexts to the nearby village. One of the little boats we still had to ply between various points on the lake arrived and took a large number of the Congolese, but those who were part of our force smelt a rat and wanted to stay. I ordered a selection to be made of those who had conducted themselves best up to that point, so that they would be taken across as Cubans. Masengo gave his authorization for it to be done as I saw fit.

For me it was a critical situation. Two men who had comprehensively fulfilled their mission would now be left behind unless they made their way back within a few hours.[7] The full weight of calumnies—both inside and outside the Congo—would fall upon us as soon as we left. My troops were a mixed bunch, and my investigations suggested that I could extract up to 20 to follow me, this time with knitted brows. And then what would I do? All the leaders were pulling out, the peasants were displaying ever greater hostility towards us. But I was deeply pained at the thought of simply departing as we had come, leaving behind defenceless peasants and armed men whose poor battle sense left them effectively defenceless, defeated and with a feeling of betrayal,

For me, to stay in the Congo was not a sacrifice—not for a year, or even for the five years with which I had scared my men. It was part of a concept of struggle that had fully taken shape in my brain. I could reasonably expect six or eight men to accompany me without furrowed brows. But the rest would do it as a duty, either towards me personally, or as a moral duty to the revolution; I would be sacrificing people who could not muster any enthusiasm to fight. Not long before, I had been able to sense this right here, when I broke into a conversation and they turned to me and in a jocular vein asked about some of the Congolese leaders. I replied sharply that they should first ask themselves what our own attitude had been, whether we could say with hand on heart that it had been of the best; I did not think so. Silence fell, awkward and hostile.

In reality, the thought of remaining in the Congo continued to haunt me long into the night, and perhaps I did not so much take the decision as become one fugitive more.

The way in which the Congolese comrades would view the evacuation seemed to me degrading; our withdrawal was a mere flight, or worse, we were accomplices in the deception with which people had been left on the land. Moreover, who was I now? I had the feeling that, after my farewell letter to Fidel, the comrades began to see me as a man from other climes rather distant from Cuba's specific problems, and I could not bring myself to demand the final sacrifice of

[7]They were rescued a month later by a group of volunteers consisting of Ishirini, Anchali, Aja, Alasiri and Adabu, on Siki's responsibility and with the cooperation of Changa and the group of marines who had arrived at the last hour.

remaining behind. I spent the final hours like this, alone and perplexed, until the boats eventually put in at two o'clock in the morning, with a Cuban crew who arrived and set off immediately that very night. There were too many people for the boats at that late hour. I set three o'clock as the last possible hour for departure, since it would be daylight at 5.30 and we would be in the middle of the lake. Work got under way on organizing the evacuation. The sick went aboard, then the whole of Masengo's general staff—some 40 men chosen by himself—and finally all the Cubans. It was a plaintive, inglorious spectacle; I had to chase away men who kept imploring us to take them too; there was no element of grandeur in this retreat, no gesture of defiance. The machine-guns were in position, and I kept the men at the ready, as usual, in case they tried to intimidate us by attacking from the land. But nothing like that happened. There was just a lot of grumbling, while the leader of the would-be escapees cursed in time with the beating of the loose moorings.

I would like to record here the names of the comrades on whom I always felt I could depend, by virtue of their personal qualities, their belief in the revolution, and their determination to do their duty come what may. Some of them flagged at the last minute, but we will pass over that final minute, because it was a weakening of their belief not of their readiness to sacrifice themselves. There were certainly more comrades in this category, but I was not on close terms with them and I cannot vouch for it in their case. It is an incomplete, personal list, much influenced by subjective factors—may those who are not on it please forgive me and consider that they belong to the same category: Moja, Mbili, Pombo, Azi, Mafu, Tumaini, Ishirini, Tiza, Alau, Waziri, Agano, Hukumu, Ami, Amia, Singida, Alasiri, Ananane, Angalia, Bodala, Anara, Mustafá, the doctors Kumi, Fizi, Morogoro and Kusulu, and the ineffable Admiral Changa, master of the lake. Siki and Tembo deserve a special mention. I often disagreed with them, sometimes violently, about our assessment of the situation, but they always offered me their guileless devotion. And a final word for Aly, a fine soldier and bad politician.

We crossed the lake without any problems, despite the slowness of the boats, and reached Kigoma in daylight in the company of the cargo ship that was making the crossing from Albertville to this port.

A mooring rope seemed to have broken, and the excitement of the Cubans and Congolese rose like boiling liquid over the little container of the boats, affecting but not infecting me. During those last hours of our time in the Congo, I felt more alone than I had done even in Cuba or on any of my wanderings around the globe. I might say: "Never have I found myself so alone again as I do today after all my travels!"

# NO TURNING BACK

## JON LEE ANDERSON

from *CHE GUEVARA: A REVOLUTIONARY LIFE*

1997

I

CHE HAD LAIN low until the final days of his stay in Cuba. Aside from Fidel, the men in his training camp, and a handful of high-ranking revolutionary leaders. Orlando Borrego was one of the few people who knew of his presence. Still only in his late twenties, Borrego was now the Cuban minister of sugar but was keen to accompany Che to the battlefront. When Che sent word that he had selected Jesús Suárez Gayol, Borrego's deputy, to go to Bolivia with him, Borrego asked to go, too. Che refused, but promised he could join at a future stage, when the revolution was more secured.

There was another reason why Che wanted his protégé to stay. After one of Aleida's recent clandestine reunions with Che abroad, she had returned with a special present for Borrego. It was Che's own heavily marked-up copy of *Economía Política*, the official, Stalin-era Soviet manual for the "correct" interpretation and application of the teachings of Marx, Engels, and Lenin in the construction of a socialist economy. With it came a ream of accompanying notations and comments, many of them highly critical, in which he openly questioned some of the basic tenets of "scientific socialism" as codified by the USSR. He also sent an outline on his theory for the "Budgetary Finance System" he favored against the established Moscow-line theories. What Che had had in mind was a new manual on political economy, better applied to modern times, for use by the developing nations and revolutionary societies in the Third World. As for his economic theory, he wanted it expanded into book form. He knew he was not going to have time to finish either project and was now entrusting Borrego with completing the tasks for him.

With Che's package came a personal letter, addressing Borrego by his pet name "Vinagreta" (Sourpuss). Referring to the material he had sent him via "Tormenta" (Storm, a teasing reference to Aleida), Che urged Borrego to "do his best" with it. He also told him to "be patient" about Bolivia, but to "be ready for the second phase."

In Che's critique of the Stalinist manual, he pointed out that since Lenin's writings, little had been added to update the evaluations of Marxism except for a few things written by Stalin and Mao. He indicted Lenin—who had introduced some capitalist forms of competition into the Soviet Union as a means of kick-starting its economy in the twenties—as "the culprit" for many of the Soviet Union's mistakes, and, while reiterating his admiration and respect toward that culprit, he warned, in block letters, that the USSR and Soviet bloc were doomed to "return to capitalism."

When Borrego read this, he was stunned, and thought to himself: "Che is really audacious; this writing is heretical!" At the time, he admitted, he thought Che had gone too far, and wasn't convinced of his dire prognosis. With the passage of time, of course, Che would be proven right.

As Borrego understood it, Che was hoping to have his writings come to light in one fashion or another. "Even if he realized that the new path he was proposing could not be implanted here, for a variety of reasons, he probably hoped he could get something going and try it out for himself if he were able to take Bolivia or one of those countries." In the increasingly Sovietized Cuba of the subsequent years, Borrego never found "the right time" to push for the publication of Che's writings. Reportedly, Fidel considers them highly sensitive even today and has yet to authorize their publication.

While Che had been in the Congo and Prague, Borrego and

Enrique Oltuski had worked around the clock for months on his "collected works"; in the end, they had produced a seven-volume set entitled *El Che en la Revolucion Cubana*, compiling everything from *Guerra de Guerrillas* and *Pasajes de la Guerra Revolucionaria* to Che's speeches and a sampling of letters and articles, including some that were previously unpublished. Che was both surprised and pleased when Borrego showed him the final result, but with characteristic dryness, he looked through the books and cracked: "You've made a real potpourri."

Borrego had two hundred editions printed and gave the first set off the press to Fidel, but the Cuban public never saw them. The books went to the revolutionary *dirigentes* and to individuals on a special list that Che composed, one of the last things he did before leaving Cuba. In the end, only some 100 sets were sent out; the remainder were stored in a warehouse where they presumably remain, if they haven't succumbed to water damage and silverfish.*

**II**

FOR BORREGO, CHE'S impending departure was very hard, and he tried to spend as much time as possible with him in the last days. He made frequent trips to the house in Pinar del Rio, as did Aleida, who stayed for the weekends and cooked up meals for everyone.

Borrego also accompanied Che during his last physical transmogrification. Along with the usual prosthesis in his mouth to give him a puffier look, for his latest disguise, Che was going to have much of his hair plucked out to give him the severely receding hairline of a man in his mid-fifties. As the Cuban intelligence "physiognomy specialist" in charge of the operation plucked Che's hairs one by one, Borrego sat beside him. When Che was unable to bear the pain any longer and yelped, Borrego growled at the barber to "take it easy," only to have Che bark at him to "keep out of it!" The hair had to come out at the roots for it to look naturally bald, and the pain was something he had to bear alone.

One day in October, not long before Che was due to leave, Bor-

*In 1997, in commemoration of the thirtieth anniversary of Che's death, an "abridged" version of Borrego's special edition of Che's works was finally approved by Cuba's government for public consumption.

rego took four gallons of his favorite strawberry ice cream to take to the men in training. A special feast had been prepared, and everyone sat at a long picnic table. When everyone had eaten and served themselves ice cream, Borrego got up, intending to get a second helping. Che called after him in a loud voice: "Hey, Borrego! You're not going to Bolivia, so why should you have seconds? Why don't you let the men who *are* going eat it?"

Che's criticism, heard by everyone, lacerated Borrego; involuntarily, tears began running down his checks. Without saying a word, he got up and walked away, burning with shame and indignation. While sitting on a log, he heard the rough-and-ready guerrillas titter and break into guffaws behind his back, and he knew they were laughing at him. A few moments later, he heard steps behind him. A hand was placed softly on his head and tousled his hair. "I'm sorry for what I said," Che whispered. "Come on, it's not such a big thing. Come back." Without looking up, Borrego said, "Fuck off," and stayed where he was for a long time. "It was the worst thing Che ever did to me," said Borrego.

In a suit and hat, Che now looked something like the Mexican actor Cantinflas, a resemblance first perceived by the late Jorge Ricardo Masetti. That is how Che, as a visiting foreign "friend" of Fidel's, was introduced to a handful of the highest-ranking ministers of Cuba by a complicit Fidel a day or two before Che was to leave. Nobody, according to Fidel, recognized the man in the suit. "It was really perfect," Fidel recalled years later. "Nobody recognized him, not even his closest comrades, who were talking with him the way they would talk with a guest. So we we went so far as to play jokes such as this on the day before he left."

Fidel described his good-bye with Che as a hug, a manly *abrazo* as befitted two old comrades in arms. Since both were reserved men when it came to public displays of emotion, their hug, he recalled, had "not been very effusive." But Benigno, one of the guerrillas present, recalled it as a deeply charged emotional moment at the end of Che's farewell banquet.

The time had finally come: the operation to "liberate" South America was beginning, and all the men present felt the momentousness of the occasion. Special food had been prepared—a cow cooked *asudo* style, red wine, and a roast pig and beer—for Che had wanted it to be an "Argentine-Cuban" meal. But as Fidel talked and talked,

Benigno recalled, giving advice and encouragement to Che, reminding him of past times and moments shared in the sierra, everyone forgot the food and sat listening raptly. Hours passed. Finally, realizing it was nearly dawn and time to go to the airport, Che leapt up.

Che and Fidel met in a quick and short embrace, then stood back looking at one another intently, their arms outstretched on each other's shoulders, for a long moment. Then Che got into the vehicle, told the driver: "Drive, damnit!" and was gone. Afterward, said Benigno, a melancholy silence fell over the camp. Fidel didn't leave, but walked away from the men and sat by himself. He was seen to droop his head and stay that way for a long time. The men wondered if he was weeping, but no one dared approach him. At dawn, they heard him call out and saw Fidel pointing to the sky. There went Che's plane, heading to Europe.

The last few days had been emotional for everyone, but the most poignant were Che's final encounters with Aleida and his children, who were brought out to the *finca* to see him. But Che did not reveal himself as their father. Instead he was "Uncle Ramón." He told them he brought news of their father who had been away for such a long time, that he had recently seen him and was there to pass on his love, along with little pieces of advice for each of them. They ate lunch together, with *tío* Ramón sitting at the head of the table, just like "Papá" Che used to do.

For Borrego, Che's final visit with his three-year-old daughter, Celia, brought separately to see him, was one of the most wrenching experiences he had ever witnessed. There was Che, with his child, but unable to tell her who he was or to touch her and hold her as a father would, for she could not be trusted to keep the secret. And of course, it was also the ultimate test of his disguise: If his own children could not recognize him, nobody would.*

The most Che could do was ask his children to give him a kiss so that he could pass it on to their father. During another visit, five-year-old Aliusha came up to give him a peck on the cheek and then ran back to Aleida's side to exclaim in a loud whisper: "Mama, I think that old man's in love with me." Che overheard the comment, and at that

---

*Hildita was the only one of his children Che did not see. She was ten years of age, old enough to see through his disguise.

instant tears welled up in Che's eyes. Aleida was devastated but managed to contain her own tears until she was out of sight of the children.

On their final visit, *tío* Ramón waved good-bye to his wife and children. It was to be their last sight of one another, and, as he had once predicted in his farewell letter, the youngest of them would retain no memory of him at all.

from # THE COMPLETE BOLIVIAN DIARIES OF CHE GUEVARA, AND OTHER CAPTURED DOCUMENTS

## ERNESTO CHE GUEVARA

### 1968

### may 12

WE WALKED SLOWLY. Urbano and Benigno opened the trail. At 1500 hours, we saw the lake about 5 kms. away, and soon after we found an old trail. Within the hour we came upon a tremendous field of calabash, but there was no water. We prepared a little roast and salted meat with lard and we also had some corn. We also prepared some roasted corn. The scouts arrived with the news that they had stumbled on Chico's house. The same one who is named in the newspaper as being a good friend of Lt. Henry Loredo. He was not home, but there were 4 peons there and a servant girl, whose husband came looking for her and was detained. She cooked us a roast pig with rice, and noodles and squash. Pancho, Arturo, Willy and Darío stayed to look after the knapsacks. The worst of it is, we still have not found any water, other than that at the house.

We left at 5:30, at a slow pace and with almost everybody sick. The owner of the house still had not returned and we left a note giving all the details of the expenses incurred. The peons and the servant were paid 10 pesos each for the work.

Altitude 950 meters

## may 13

DAY OF BELCHING, farting, vomiting and diarrhea: a real organ concert. We remained completely immobilized, trying to digest the pork. We have two cans of water. I was very sick until I vomited, and then I felt better. At night we ate some corn and roasted calabash, and the rest of the banquet from the day before; that is, those who were able to eat. All the radios were insistently broadcasting news about a landing of Cubans in Venezuela which had been frustrated. Leoni's government showed two men, giving their names and ranks. I don't know them, but obviously something went wrong.

## may 14

WE LEFT EARLY, but reluctantly, for Lake Pirirenda, by way of a trail that Benigno and Camba had found while scouting. Before leaving I called everyone together, and gave them a talk about the problems facing us; principally about the food situation. I criticized Benigno for having eaten a can of food and then denying it; Urbano for having eaten a *charqui* on the sly; and Aniceto for his eagerness to eat his share of the food, but for not being so willing to do his share in other matters. During the course of the meeting, we heard the sound of some trucks approaching. In a nearby hiding place, we hid some 50 bags of beans, and two hundred kilograms of corn harvested for our future needs.

When we were off the road, busy picking beans, we heard some shots nearby. Shortly after this, we heard planes searching for us, but they were about two or three kilometers from our position. We continued to ascend a little hill, and spotted the lake. Meanwhile, the police continued their shooting. At nightfall we came upon a house, which appeared to have been abandoned recently. It was well provisioned and there was water. We ate a delicious chicken fricasse with rice, and we remained there until 0400 hours.

## may 15

AN UNEVENTFUL day.

## may 16

WHEN WE STARTED on the march I was ill with the most violent colic, vomiting and diarrhea. They stopped it with demerol, and I lost consciousness while they carried me in a hammock. When I awoke I was much relieved but dirtied all over like a nursing baby. They lent me a pair of pants, but without water my stench extends for a league. We spent the whole day there. I drowsed. Coco explored and found a road running south-north. At night we followed it while the moon was up, and then rested. Message No. 36 arrived, from which our total isolation can be inferred.

## may 17

WE CONTINUED MARCHING until 1300, when we came upon a sawmill which bore signs of having been abandoned some three days ago. It had sugar, corn, lard, cornmeal and water in barrels, which apparently had been transported from a long distance off. Raúl has a sore on his knee which is intensely painful and prevents him from walking. He was given a strong antibiotic and tomorrow it will be lanced. We walked about 15 kilometers.

Altitude 920 meters

## may 18

WE SPENT THE whole day in ambush in case the workers or the troops came. Nothing happened. Miguel went out with Pablito. They found water about two hours away from the camp on a crossroad. We did the operation on Raúl, drawing out 50 cc of purulent liquid. We are giving him general anti-infection treatments. He can hardly walk a step. I extracted my first tooth in this guerrilla band. Unwilling victim: Camba. Everything is going well. We ate some bread made in a small oven and, at night, we had a terrific soup which made me feel great.

## may 19

THE ADVANCE GUARD went out early, taking up position in the ambush at the crossroads. Later, we went out to relieve part of the advance guard while they returned to look after Raúl; and they carried him as far as the crossroads. The other part of the guard went on to the waterhole to leave the knapsacks, and returned to look after Raúl, who is recovering slowly. Antonio made a small exploration down the arroyo and found an abandoned police camp. Here too were found various supplies. The Nacahuasu cannot be too far away and I figure that we should emerge below the Congri arroyo.

It rained all night, surprising the experts. We have food for 10 days and in the nearby fields there are calabash and corn.

Altitude 780 meters

## may 20

NO MOVEMENT TODAY. The center remained in the ambush in the morning; and in the afternoon, the advance guard, which is still commanded by Pombo, who is of the opinion that the position chosen for us by Miguel is very poor. The latter explored downstream and found the Nacahuasu to be a two-hour walk away for a man without a pack. We heard a shot, but didn't know who was shooting. On the banks of the Nacahuasu are traces of another military camp, of probably two platoons. Had an incident with Luis, who protested against my orders not to go near the ambush. However, I think he took it well.

In a news conference, Barrientos denied Debray's status as a newspaperman, and announced that he would ask Congress for the death penalty. All the newspapermen and all the foreigners asked him about Debray. He answered with an incredible smoke-screen of nonsense, the most ridiculous that one could imagine.

• • •

A BLACK DAY for me. It seemed as though everything was going along quietly and peacefully and I had sent 5 men to relieve those in the ambush on the road to Florida, when shots were heard. We went quickly on our horses, and came upon a strange spectacle. In the midst of an intense silence, in the hot sun were the bodies of 4 soldiers lying on the sand of the river bank. We couldn't find the weapons as we didn't know the enemy's position. It was 1700 hours and we waited for nightfall to effect the rescue. Miguel sent word that he could hear sporadic firing on his left. It was Antonio and Pacho, but I gave the order not to shoot without being sure. Immediately, one could hear shots that seemed to come from both sides, and I gave the order to retreat as we could lose under those conditions. The retreat was delayed and news arrived that Pombo had been wounded in one leg and Tuma in the stomach. We took them quickly to the house to operate on them with the instruments that we had there. Pombo's wound was superficial and he only had a headache and was still mobile; but Tuma's wound had destroyed his liver and punctured his intestines, and he died during the operation. With his death I lost an inseparable comrade of many years' standing, whose loyalty survived every test, and whose absence I already feel almost like that of a son. When he fell, he asked that his watch be given to me, but since I was attending him he took it off and gave it to Arturo. That signified his desire that it be given to his son, whom he had never seen, as I had done with the watches of other dead comrades. I shall carry it with me through the war. We loaded the body on a pack animal and took it to be buried far from here.

We took two new prisoners: a *carabinero* lieutenant, and a *carabinero*. We gave them a lecture and we let them go in just their undershorts. Because of a misinterpretation of my orders, they were stripped of everything they had. We came out of it with 9 horses.

**august 7**

AT 11 IN THE morning I had given Miguel and Aniceto up for lost, having instructed Benigno to go up cautiously to the outlet of the Rosita to explore the direction which they took, if they had gone that far. However, at 13 hours the lost ones appeared. They simply had encountered difficulties along the way and it had gotten dark before they reached the Rosita. Miguel certainly had me worried. We remained in the same place, but the explorers found another arroyo and we shall move towards it tomorrow. Anselmo, the old horse, died today and we have only one left; my asthma continues and the medicines are running low. Tomorrow I shall determine whether a group should be sent to the Nacahuasu. On this date it is exactly 9 months since the guerrilla was formed and we arrived. Of the first six men, two are dead, one has disappeared, two are wounded, and I with a case of asthma which I am unable to control.

## august 8

WE WALKED FOR about one hour, which to me seemed like 2 hours because my mare was tired. At one point I stabbed it in the side, making a big gash. The new camp must be the last one in which there is water before arriving at the Rosita or the Río Grande. The *macheteros* are some 40 minutes from here (2 or 3 kilometers). I assigned a group of eight men to carry out the following mission: They will leave from here tomorrow and walk all day. The following day Camba will return to report on their findings. The day after that Pablito and Dario will return to report. The other five will go on to Vargas' house, and from there Coco and Aniceto will return to report on the house. Benigno, Julio and Nato will go to the Nacahuasú to get my medicines. They are to take every precaution to avoid an ambush. We will follow them, and the meeting points will be: Vargas' house or further up according to how fast we can travel; the arroyo which is in front of the cave in the Rio Grande; the Masicurí, or the Nacahuasú. There is a report from the Army that they have discovered an arms cache in one of our camps. At night I got the men together and made the following admonition: We are in a difficult situation; Pacho is recovering but I am a mess and the incident of the mare indicates that there are moments in which I lose control of myself ; that will change, but we must all share alike the burden of the situation and whoever feels he cannot stand it should say so. This is one of those moments in which great decisions must be made, because a struggle of this type gives us the opportunity to become revolutionaries, the highest step in the human ladder and also allows us to test ourselves as men. Those who cannot measure up to these two requirements should say so and abandon the struggle.

All the Cubans and some Bolivians said they would continue to the end. Eustaquio did likewise, but he made some criticism of Mugamga for having the mule carry his pack instead of carrying firewood. This brought about an angry rejoinder from the latter. Julio castigated Loro and Pacho for the same thing, and there was another angry retort, this time by Pacho. I ended the discussion by saying that two things of very different categories were being debated, one of which was whether or not we were willing to continue; the other one deals with small quarrels or internal problems in the guerrilla group, which detracts from the significance of the larger decision. I did not like the statements of Eustaquio and Julio, nor the responses of Moro and Pacho. In short, we had to be more revolutionary and more men of exemplary conduct.

## august 9

THE EIGHT SCOUTS left in the morning. Miguel, Urbano, and Leon, the *macheteros*, proceeded another 50 meters away from the camp. I had a carbuncle in my heel lanced and now I can put my foot down, but it is very painful and I have a fever. Pacho is doing very well.

Altitude 783 meters

## august 12

A GRAY DAY. The macheteros made little progress. Nothing unusual happened and the food supply was low. Tomorrow we shall kill another horse which should provide meat for 6 days. My asthma is in a bearable state. Barrientos has announced the decline of the guerrilla and again threatened with intervention in Cuba. He was as stupid as usual. The radio announced a clash near Monteagudo resulting in the death of one of our men: Antonio Fernández of Tarata. It sounds very much like Pedro's real name. Pedro is from Tarata.

• • •

## august 24

REVEILLE WAS SOUNDED at 5:30 and we headed for the stream we planned to follow. The vanguard began the march and it had gone a few meters when 3 peasants appeared on the other bank. Miguel and his group were called back and we all laid in ambush. Eight soldiers appeared. The instructions were to let them cross the river ford in front of us and to shoot as they approached: but the soldiers didn't cross. They confined themselves to walking around a few times and they passed within rifle range without us shooting at them. The captured civilians said they are only hunters. Miguel, Urbano, with Camba, Dario and Hugo Guzman, the hunter, were sent to follow a trail which heads west but whose end is unknown. We remained in ambush all day. At dusk the macheteros returned with the traps, they caught a condor and a rotten cat. Everything was eaten together with the last piece of anteater meat. The only things remaining are the beans and whatever is hunted.

Camba is reaching the last stages of his moral deterioration. He trembles at the mere mention of soldiers. El Médico is still in pain and giving himself talamonal. I am quite well but ravenous.

The Army issued a partial report to the effect that it had found another cave and that there were two wounded "caused by guerrillas." Radio Havana reported an unconfirmed battle in Taperillas resulting in one wounded soldier.

## august 25

VERY LITTLE NEW. Reveille was sounded at 5 and the macheteros left early. The Army got as close as a few steps from our position but did not try to cross. They seem to be calling the hunters with their shots. Tomorrow we will attack them if the opportunity arises. The trail did not advance sufficiently because Miguel wanted advice and sent a message with Urbano. He transmitted it wrong and at a time when nothing could be done.

The radio announced a battle at Monte Dorado, which seems to be Joaquín's area, and the presence of guerrillas 3 kilometers from Camiri.

## august 26

EVERYTHING WENT WRONG. Seven men came but 5 went down river and 2 crossed the ford. Antonio, who was in charge of the ambush, fired too soon and missed, allowing the two men to beat it back to get more reinforcements. The other five fled and Inti and Coco pursued them but the soldiers barricaded themselves and forced them back. While watching the chase, I noticed the bullets were hitting close, in fact, they were being fired from our side. I broke into a run and discovered Eustaquio had been shooting at them because Antonio hadn't told him what was going on. I was so raving mad that I lost my control and mistreated Antonio.

We left with little speed since the doctor could not keep up the pace well, while the Army was advancing from an island in front of us in numbers of 20 to 30. It wasn't worth it trying to face them. They may have 2 wounded, at most. Inti and Coco distinguished themselves by their decisiveness. Everything went well until the doctor became exhausted and began to hold back the march. At 1830 we stopped without having reached Miguel, who was nevertheless a few meters away and he made contact with us. Moro stayed in a ravine without being able to climb the last stretch and we slept apart in 3 groups. There are no signs that we have been followed.

Altitude 900 meters

## august 31

IN THE MORNING Aniceto and Leon left to explore returning fulfilled their mission would now be left behind unless they made their way back within a few hours.[23] The full weight of calumnies—both inside and outside the Congo—would fall upon us as soon as we left. My troops were a mixed bunch, and my investigations suggested that I could extract up to 20 to follow me, this time with knitted brows. And then what would I do? All the leaders were pulling out, the peasants were displaying ever greater hostility towards us. But I was deeply pained at the thought of simply departing as we had come, leaving behind defenceless peasants and armed men whose poor battle sense left them effectively defenceless, defeated and with a feeling of betrayal.

# CHE

## NECESSARY SACRIFICE

## JON LEE ANDERSON

from *CHE GUEVARA: A REVOLUTIONARY LIFE*

1997

I

IN HIS POSTMORTEM on the Congo fiasco, Che had acknowledged
that one of his greatest mistakes was to attempt a *"chantaje de cuerpo
presente*, or black mail by physical presence, foisting himself unan-
nounced on the Congolese rebels. This had caused animosity and suspicion among the rebel leadership, he noted in "Pasajes de la Guerra
Revolucionaria (Congo)," and it was one of the mistakes he had vowed
to learn from. Yet, when he flew to Bolivia in early November 1966,
he neatly replicated his Congo *chantaje*, once again appearing on alien
turf without an invitation, convinced that the Bolivian Communist
party leadership wouldn't back out of the impending guerrilla war once
he presented it with the fait accompli of his presence. This time, his
mistake would prove fatal.

Things began well enough. When Che—or rather Adolfo Mena
González, a middle aged Uruguavan businessman on a economic fact
finding mission for the Organization of American States—arrived with
Pacho in La Paz on November 3, he was met by his closest aides: Papi,

Pombo, Tuma, and Renan. He checked into a third-floor suite of the comfortable Hotel Copacabana, on the graceful, tree-lined Prado boulevard of central La Paz, overlooked by his favourite old mountain, Illimani, snowcapped and blue.

He took a photograph of himself in the mirror of his wardrobe door. Sitting on his hotel room bed, the pudgy-looking man with a balding pate stares back at the viewer with an intense, inscrutable expression.

The reflective interlude was brief, for Che was not in a mood to waste any time. Two days later, he had descended the bright chill of the altiplano into the dry season dust and swelter of the *chaco*. Accompanied by Pombo, Tuma, Papi, Pacho, and the Bolivian Loro Vázquez-Viaña, he set out on a three-day drive to Ñancahuazú.

During one roadside pit stop to eat lunch, Che finally revealed his true identity to Loro, asking him not to reveal his presence to the party until he had spoken with Monje. According to Pombo. "He told [Loro] his decision to come to Bolivia was because it was the country with the best conditions for a guerrilla base in the Continent." He then added: "I've come to stay, and the only way that I will leave here is dead, or crossing a border, shooting bullets as I go."

## II

BY NEW YEAR'S Eve, Che's hair had begun to grow back and he once more had a sparse beard. His Cuban comrades and a Peruvian guerrilla, "Eustaquio," had arrived at Ñancahuazú, joining the Bolivians who had been in training there. He had an army of twenty-four men, but only nine were Bolivians, among them, Coco Peredo's older brother Inti and Freddy Maymura, a Japanese-Bolivian former medical student. Both had just undergone training in Cuba.

His men had built a proper base camp and a secondary bivouac concealed in the forest above a steep red-stoned canyon several hours' hike upriver from the place they called the "Casa de Calamina"—a tin-roofed brick house, their legal "front" for the future Ñancahuazú "pig and timber farm."

They had a mud oven for baking bread, a meat-drying hut, and a rustic medical dispensary, even crude log tables and benches for eating. They had dug a latrine, and tunnels and cave deposits for their food, ammunition, and most compromising documents. In one cave they had set up their radio transmitter for sending and receiving coded communications from Havana, or "Manila," as it was now referred to. The urban underground in La Paz was taking shape, while Bolivians such as Rodolfo Saldaña, Coco Peredo, and Loro Vázquez-Viaña— the "owner" of the farm—came and went to buy supplies, courier messages, bring newcomers, and transport weapons.

But already Che was worried about the preponderance of foreigners in his "Bolivian army."* What's more, the signs of competitive discord between the Cubans and Bolivians were already showing, which Che tried to remedy with lectures about discipline and by announcing that the Cubans would temporarily be the officers of the little troop, until the Bolivians had gained more experience. This measure, obviously, was not popular with the Bolivians. When Juan Pablo Chang communicated that he wanted to send him twenty Peruvian fighters, Che stalled him, concerned about "internationalizing" the struggle before Monje was involved. What Che needed was a solid base of Bolivian support, and he wanted to have at least twenty Bolivians with him before beginning operations. To do that, he needed Monje.

Despite precautions, the presence of newcomers soon provoked the interest of their few neighbors in this back woods region—just as it had done at Masetti's base near the Río Bermejo farther south. Even before Che had arrived, in fact, his advance men had learned that Ciro Algarañaz, their only immediate neighbor, was spreading the word that he suspected the newcomers to be cocaine traffickers, already a budding profession in this coca-producing nation. Algarañaz's house and pig farm lay at the roadside on the approach to their own *finca*, and they had to pass it to get to their Casa de Calamina; though Algarañaz lived in Camiri during the week, his caretaker lived on the property permanently. Already, on one of their first scouting trips into the bush, Pombo and Pacho had been spotted by the man they called "Algarañaz's driver."

By late December, Che was expecting Monje, and before their guest showed up at camp Che talked to his men about the proposals he would make to the Communist party secretary. First, he would insist that he should be military commander, and in charge of finances; he had no interest in being the political chief, however. For outside support, he proposed asking both the Soviet Union and China for aid,

*In the end, the breakdown of nationalities in Che's guerrilla force excluding the members of his urban network would be as follows one Argentine (Che), one German (Tania), three Peruvians, sixteen Cubans, and a total of twenty-nine Bolivians

and suggested that Moisés Guevara could go to Beijing with a letter from him to Chou En-lai to ask for help with "no strings attached," while Monje could go to Moscow "together with a comrade who could at least say how much [money] he was given."

Che's proposal shows that even at this late date, he could hammer out the differences between the pro-Chinese and pro-Soviet Communists in Bolivia, and use that unity to engage both socialist giants in a common cause. If he could forge a local peace on the ground in South America, then perhaps there was still hope for socialist unity on a larger scale. Finally, he said: "Bolivia will be sacrificed for the cause of creating the conditions for revolution in the neighboring countries. We have to create another Vietnam in the Americas with its center in Bolivia."

From his crude camp in the Bolivian outback, Che foresaw an astonishing, even fantastic sequence of events—and starting the war and spreading it to the neighboring nations were only the first two stages. In the third stage, wars in South America would draw in the Americans. This intervention would benefit the guerrillas by giving their campaigns a nationalistic hue in Vietnam, they would be fighting against a foreign invader. And by deploying forces in Latin America, the United States would be more dispersed and, ultimately, weaker on all fronts, in Bolivia as well as Vietnam. Finally, the spreading conflagrations would lead China and Russia to stop their feuding and align forces with the revolutionaries everywhere to bring down U.S. imperialism once and for all. To Che, what happened in Bolivia was to be no less than the opening shot in a new world war that would ultimately determine whether the planet was to be socialist or capitalist. First, though, he had to deal with Mario Monje.

On December 31, Monje was brought to Ñancahuazú, and at long last the two rivals had their showdown. Che and Monje went together and sat in the forest to talk. Two very poor photographs have survived as visual evidence of that encounter. In one, Che lies on the ground, looking archly toward the seated Monje, who is talking with his legs drawn up defensively.

Monje demanded overall leadership of the armed struggle in Bolivia for himself. He also demanded that no alliance be formed with the *"prochinos."* Che told him he could forswear an alliance with the pro-Chinese Communists, but on the question of command he was unbudging. He would be the military commander because he was better qualified. And he also thought he could handle political decisions better than Monje. But he offered to make Monje the "nominal chief" of the guerrilla operation if that would help him "save face."

Afterward, Monje told the men in camp that he would resign his post as party chief and come and proudly fight with Che—not as party secretary, but as "Estanislao," a simple combatant. He would now return to La Paz and inform the party about the imminent guerrilla war so its members could take precautionary measures, while he himself would resign and return to join the band within ten days.

Either this was a bluff intended to provoke Che into offering him an additional face-saving gesture, or Monje was simply lying. Before leaving the next morning, he assembled the Bolivians and told them the party did not support the armed struggle, they would be expelled if they stayed on, and the stipends to their families would be suspended. Only four men—Coco, Saldaña, Ñato, and Loro—had the party's permission to be there, and that would be honored, but for the rest the choice now was between party and war. They chose the latter; Monje left and did not return.

Rafael Segarra, a Communist party official in Santa Cruz, said that Monje stopped to see him on his return trip from Ñancahuazú and warned: "The shit's going to hit the fan. This thing is going ahead and either we bury it or it'll bury all of us." He urged Segarra to lay low or to disappear, and in the coming days, Monje gave the same advice to party people everywhere.

Monje's actions remain dubious, cloaked in the web of intrigue and suspicion that he helped create. Pombo insists that what Monje perpetrated was an act of "conscious treason," thirty years after the event, Che's widow Aleida still considers Monje—"*ese indio feo*" (that ugly Indian)—as the man who betrayed her husband.

The meeting between Che and Monje had culminated in disaster, and Che's tactlessness had played as great a part in the unhappy ending as had Monje's duplicity and indecision. The die was cast. As of January 1, 1967, Che and his two dozen fighters were, to all intents and purposes, on their own.

**III**

CONTENT THAT A number of young Bolivian Communists had remained loyal to him, and trusting in Fidel's superior powers of persuasion to sort things out with the party hierarchy, Che refused to allow the rupture with Monje to affect his vision of the future. In a coded message to Fidel, or "Leche" (Milk), as he was now referred to, Che told him what had happened in unalarmed tones.*

Indeed, it seemed things were progressing fairly smoothly for Che. Tania had come to Ñancahuazú at the same time as Monje, and Che had dispatched her to Buenos Aires to summon Ciro Bustos and Eduardo Jozami, a young journalist, law student, and the leader of a dissident faction of the Argentine Communist Party—with an eye to getting the Argentine guerrilla movement up and running. Meanwhile, his people were busy organizing his underground network throughout Bolivia.

At his summons, Moisés Guevara came calling. Che told him that that he would have to dissolve his group and join up as a simple soldier, that there could be no more factional activity. At first taken aback, the Bolivian Guevara agreed, and announced he would return to the highlands and recruit some men before returning himself.

At Ñancahuazú, Che's men were now patrolling the vicinity, and a semblance of military discipline had been obtained. The fighters did sentry duty, fetched water and firewood, took turns cooking and washing, while regular porters' missions, or *gondolas*, were organized to carry supplies into the camp. Some men hunted, bringing in turkeys and armadillos for the cooking pot, and Quechua classes began again. There were, of course, the usual discomforts of life in the bush—pernicious insects, cuts and scrapes, men falling all with malaria fever—but Che took it all with aplomb. "Boron day," he wrote on January 11. "Larvae of flies removed from Marcos, Carlos, Pombo, Antonio, Moro and Joaquin."

In the meantime, there were the usual behavior problems, and Che returned to his old strict self in laying down the law. Loro was operating a little too freely, finding time to "*enumorar*" (seduce) women on his supply-buying trips, while Papi was moping around, feeling he had fallen in Che's disfavor. After scolding Papi for what he had called his "many mistakes" in the Bolivian advance work—including making unwanted advances on Tania—Che had ordered Papi to stay with him in the field. The man he had designated his deputy, which she had complained about in Cuba, Marcos, had been abusive with the

---

*A short while later, Fidel wrote him back that Bolivian Communist Simón Reyes was already there, and Jorge Kolle Cueto was on his way for talks to amend the crisis.

Bolivians, and in his Sierra Maestra style, Che publicly upbraided and demoted him, naming the oldest man, Joaquin, in his place.

At the same time, their neighbor, Ciro Algarañaz, was continuing to be an irritation. He and another man had been snooping around, until one day Algarañaz finally approached Loro. He was "a friend." Algarañaz told him, he could be trusted and wanted to know what Loro and his friends were up to, Loro brushed him off, but a few days later some soldiers arrived at the forward camp, questioned Loro, and took away his pistol, warning that he and his friends were under observation and hinting that if they were "up to anything," *they* would have to be taken into consideration. Clearly, the locals believed the guerrillas were contrabandists and wanted a piece of the action. After this incident, Che mounted lookouts to keep an eye on Algarañaz's house.

Then, on February 1, Che left a few men in camp and took most of the others off for what he intended to be a fortnight's conditioning trek into the surrounding *chaco*. The fortnight, however, turned into a grueling forty-eight-day ordeal as the band became lost and endured torrential rain, hunger, thirst, and exhausting marathon hikes. They were reduced to eating palm hearts, monkeys, hawks, and parrots, and with the men worn-out and demoralized, there had been several quarrels. There was also tragedy. Two of the young Bolivians drowned in the swollen rivers, a coincidence Pombo noted as eerily reminiscent of how their stay in the Congo had begun, with the drowning death of Laurent Mitoudidi. For his part, Che lamented the deaths, but also the loss of six good weapons, in the second drowning incident.

Even before returning to camp on March 20, Che knew something had gone awry in his absence: A small plane was persistently circling the vicinity of Ñancahuazú. He soon learned why from an advance party that had come out to meet him.

While he had been gone, some of Moisés Guevara's "volunteers" had arrived, but became rapidly disenchanted with camp life and their relegation to menial chores by the Cubans left in charge. Two had deserted, been captured by the army, and confessed to everything they knew, including stories about "Cubans" and a *comandante* named "Ramón." A few days earlier, Bolivian security forces had raided the Casa de Calamina below the camp; fortunately, nobody had been there at the time, but the army was rumored to be on the move in the area. The aircraft Che had seen circling overhead was obviously a spotter plane; his men told him it had been up there for the past three days.

Walking on, Che was met by runners with more bad news. The army had just returned to their "farm," confiscating one of their mules and their jeep, and capturing a rebel courier—one of Moises Guevara's men—on his way to the camp. Che sped up his pace to reach the camp. When he arrived, he observed "a mood of defeat," some more new arrivals, and "complete chaos" and indecision among his men.

On top of everything else, he had to attend to visitors: Régis Debray, Ciro Bustos, Tania, and Juan Pablo Chang were all there to see him. After bringing Monje to the camp on New Year's Eve, Tania had been busy: after traveling to Argentina on Che's orders, she had ferried Chang and two Peruvian comrades to Ñancahuazú, and had now returned again with Debray and Bustos.

Che dealt first with "Chino" Chang, who had been to Cuba and asked Fidel for help in setting up a new Peruvian guerrilla column; Fidel had told him to get Che's approval. "He wants $5,000 a month for ten months," wrote Che. ". . . I told him I agreed on the basis that they would go to the mountains within six months." Chang's plan was to lead a band of fifteen men and begin operations in the Ayacucho region of Peru's southeastern Andes. Che also agreed to send him some Cubans and weapons, and they discussed plans for maintaining radio contact with one another.

As they spoke, Loro arrived. He had been doing forward sentry duty downriver from the camp and killed a soldier he had caught by surprise. Clearly, the war was about to begin, whether Che wanted it to or not.

He hastened to deal with his other visitors, polishing up details with Chang, then conferring with Debray. The Frenchman, slight and pale, said he wanted to stay and fight, but Che told him that it would be better if he worked on the outside, promoting his cause with a European solidarity campaign. Che would send him out with news for "*la isla*" and write a letter for Bertrand Russell, the champion of international peace, asking for help in organizing an international fund in support of "the Bolivian Liberation Movement."

Then it was Ciro Bustos's turn. Bustos had been awaiting his "contact" in Argentina since his return from Cuba and China the summer before, and after five months it had come in the form of Tania. She had told Bustos to go to La Paz, which gave him the first inkling that Che was in Bolivia. At the same time, he had begun to have doubts about the wisdom of Che's rurally based guerrilla war theory. Bustos sought out the advice of his most trusted comrades in Córdoba, who urged him to express his doubts, which they shared, when he saw Che.

Using a hastily prepared false passport, he had flown off to La Paz in late February. There he was instructed to board a particular bus leaving for the city of Sucre. He spotted another European-looking man on the bus—Régis Debray, he would soon learn—but as the bus was leaving the city, a taxi raced up, and out of it and into the bus came Tania. Bustos thought her actions and their form of transport a reckless public display that could only attract notice. "There we were, the only three foreigners on the bus, like three flies [in the midst of everyone else], looking around, but not talking to one another, and I wasn't very pleased about things."

According to Bustos, the rest of the journey was characterized by amateurish behavior on Tania's part, whom he feared drew undue attention by speaking too loudly, using Cuban slang in the roadside restaurants they stopped in, and driving too fast. (For the final leg, from Camiri, Tanta drove them in her jeep, which she had stashed there after her last trip with the Peruvians.)

At the camp, they found quite a few Bolivian recruits, but Che and most of the Cubans were gone, still out on their trek. Almost immediately, said Bustos, Tania pulled out some packets of photographs she'd taken on her earlier trip and had brought to show everyone. There they were, virtually all of them, posing with their rifles, hamming it up, cooking, reading, or standing around and talking. Incredulous, Bustos spoke to Olo Pantoja, the Cuban left in charge of the camp, and Olo quickly ordered the photos gathered up.

In Che's prolonged absence, discipline had fallen apart, and Bustos found Olo embarrassed about how matters had slipped out of his grasp. The next day, two of Moisés Guevara's "volunteers" went out with their guns to hunt but did not return. Alarm bells rang; the two had seen all the photographs and heard everyone talking openly about "Cuba" and other delicate topics. After sending out a search party in vain, Olo ordered the camp evacuated, and they went to a hiding place farther into the hills. Within a couple of days, when the plane began buzzing the area of the camp, it was clear their worst fears had come true: the deserters had been picked up by the army. It was then that the first men from Che's expedition began returning.

Bustos was stunned when he saw Che. "He was torn apart, practically didn't have clothing; his shirt was in shreds, his knee poked out of his trousers, and he looked really skinny. But imperturbable, he gave me an *ubrazo*, which was really emotional for me; there were no words or anything."

Bustos hung back, watching as Che ate and simultaneously took charge of the situation. He harangued Olo and the other men he had left in charge, using a degree of verbal "violence" that surprised Bustos, and which he had never witnessed before. Later, he would see that it was a pattern in Che's behavior. "Afterward, [Che] would become calm, he would go read, serenely, while the guys he'd punished went around hangdog, turned into shit."

When it came time for Che and Bustos to talk, the first thing Che wanted to find out was why Bustos hadn't come earlier. Bustos told him Tania had not given him a specific time frame. Once again, he observed Che's severity. Calling Tania over, Che tongue-lashed her for having misrepresented his instructions "Damnit, Tania, what did I tell you to tell El Pelao [Bustos]?" he demanded. "What the fuck do I tell you things for!"

"I can't remember exactly what he told her," said Bustos, "but they were strong and violent things, which weren't funny at all, and she started to shake . . . and went away crying." Later, feeling sorry, Che told Bustos to try to comfort her. (He was already unhappy with Tania for having risked exposure by coming to the camp again. After her first visit, he had told her not to return.* What's more, his second Argentine guest, Eduardo Jozami, had come to Bolivia and gone home again when she hadn't shown up for the prearranged rendezvous with him.)

Turning back to his business with Bustos, Che told him: "My strategic objective is the seizure of political power in Argentina. For this I want to form a group of Argentines, to prepare a couple of columns, season them in war for a year or two over here, and then enter. I want this to be your mission. And I want you to hang on as long as possible until you have to join up [in the mountains]. I want you to be the coordinator sending me people."

Che added that the work had to be done well, "not like this shit here, where everyone does what they want." He told him he should work together with Papi on the means of transporting the people, and

*Loyola Guzmán, Che's new "national finance secretary" and a member of his urban network in La Paz, has explained that Tania's initial return trip was really the fault of her group, who had decided to send her along with the Peruvians because they were all busy.

with Pombo on the question of provisions, and reeled off names of others he should liaise with for specific issues. Che said his idea was to form a central command divided into two columns totaling about five hundred men, including Bolivians, Argentines, and Peruvians, who would later split off and take the war to other zones.

As Che talked, Bustos wondered privately how he was going to arrange a food-supply line between Ñancahuazú and Argentina. And how was he supposed to liaise with Pombo, when Pombo was in the bush with Che? For the moment, these details weren't discussed, but already it didn't sound realistic to Bustos. "It was like something magical," he said. "Out of this world . . ."

Che then told Bustos that his first priority was to see him out safely so he could get to work in Argentina, but a dense air of tension and uncertainty hung over everything. The guerrillas' presence had been detected. A soldier had been killed. It was only a matter of time before an army patrol came in looking for them.

## IV

IT CAME TWO days later, on March 23, a day Che recorded in his diary as one "of warlike events." Che had sent ambushes out, creating a defensive perimeter, and at 8:00 A.M. Coco came running in to report that they had ambushed an army unit, killing seven soldiers, and taking twenty-one prisoners, four of them wounded. They had also seized a nice booty of weapons, including three mortars, sixteen carbines, two bazookas, and three Uzi submachine guns. They also captured a document that showed the army's operational plans. Seeing that it called for a two-pronged advance, Che quickly dispatched some men to the other end of the river canyon to lay an ambush. In the meantime, he sent Inti Peredo—whom he was impressed by and was beginning to groom as a leader for the Bolivians—to interrogate the two captured officers, a major and a captain. Che reported later: "They talked like parrots."

Che recorded the victory tersely: he was worried about food supplies now that the approaches to Ñancahuazú were cut off, and they had been forced to leave their camp with their stores behind. Another problem, and a serious one, was that their radio transmitter was malfunctioning: They could receive broadcasts and "Manila's" messages, but they could not send.

The next day brought no new ground troops, but a plane flew over and bombed around the Casa de Calamina. Che sent Inti back to interrogate the officers again, then ordered the prisoners to be set free; the soldiers were ordered to strip and leave their uniforms behind, while the officers were allowed to keep theirs. The major was told he had until noon on March 27 to return and collect his dead.

After the prisoners had gone, Che turned his attention to his men. Marcos had been repeatedly insubordinate, his mistreatment of some of the Bolivians had led to bad blood and open complaints, and Che had already warned him that if his behavior continued, he would be expelled from the guerrillas. Now he stripped him of his role as chief of the vanguard, naming Miguel in his place.

Che's guerrilla "family" had not been very happy to start with, but since the desertions the tensions between the new Bolivians and their Cuban comrades had increased. The *"firmeza,"* or revolutionary fortitude, of the four remaining Bolivians Moisés Guevara had recruited—Paco, Pepe, Chingolo, and Eusebio—was openly questioned, and these men soon found themselves treated with contempt and suspicion and referred to dismissively as the *"resaca,"* or the dregs. On March 25, Che demoted them and told them that if they didn't work, they wouldn't eat. He suspended their tobacco rations and gave their personal belongings away to "other, needier comrades." Another Bolivian, Walter, he criticized for being "weak" on their trek, and for the "fear" he had shown during the previous day's aerial bombardment. To another couple of men, he gave words of encouragement; they had performed well in the last few days. Finally, Che chose that day to name his little army: the "Ejército de Liberación Nacional" (ELN), or National Liberation Army.

Over the next few days, the guerrillas concentrated on looking for food. Scouts came back having sighted groups of soldiers not far away, while others observed a group of about sixty and a helicopter stationed at Algarañaz's house. On March 27, Che wrote "The news exploded, monopolizing all the space on the radio and producing a multitude of communiqués including the [President] Barrientos press conference." He noted that the army was making wild claims of having killed fifteen guerrillas and taken four prisoners, including two "foreigners." He resolved to write up the first guerrilla communiqué to refute the army claims and announce the guerrillas' presence at the same time.

"Obviously the deserters or the prisoners talked," wrote Che. "But we do not know exactly how much they told and how they told it. Everything appears to indicate that Tania is spotted, whereby two years of good and patient work are lost. . . . . We will see what happens."

## V

WHAT HAPPENED WAS a whirlwind of bellicose activity that threw all of Che's plans out the window and forced him to pursue the war he had begun, almost inadvertently, through a cumulative series of errors and and mishaps. He had no choice now but to fight, stay on the move, and try to survive. This imperative would dominate what remained of his life.

The eruption of guerrilla warfare hit Bolivia like a bombshell. Within a few days of the ambush the news reports became more and more exaggerated as the government mobilized its available troops. After first deriding the existence of guerrillas, Barrientos had seized upon evidence found at their camp, including photographs, to decry the foreign invaders as agents of "Castro-Communism," and to call upon the patriotism of his fellow citizens in resisting the outsiders. In this intensely nationalistic nation, the appeal to xenophobia was an effective tool with which to isolate the civilians from the guerrillas; the "foreign" nature of the "Reds" was something Barrientos would now propound ceaselessly, with his army taking up the theme as well.

Right now, there was little Che could do to combat the propaganda except write communiques. More immediately, he and his men needed to avoid being wiped out. Che surmised from the radio reports that the army knew exactly where his band was located. He ordered men to dig new caves to store their weapons in at a smaller camp they had called "El Oso," since an anteater, or *oso hormiguero,* was shot there.

In Cuba, the two dozen — plus guerrillas who were preparing for the "second phase" did not include Borrego, but he and his brother-in-law, Enrique Acevedo, begged Fidel to be allowed to go to Bolivia. They were refused. The guerrillas had been prematurely discovered, Fidel said, and the situation was too volatile: what's more, direct contact with Che had been lost, so there was no way to insert them safely into the field any longer. As the months passed, Borrego and his comrades read the reports from Bolivia with increasing anxiety as the situation of Che and his band seemed to slide irrevocably toward disaster.

In his end-of-the-month summary for March, Che wrote laconically: "This month was full of events. . . ." After analyzing his troops and the current situation, he wrote: "Evidently we will have to get going before I had thought. . . . The situation is not good but today begins a [new] phase to test the guerrillas, which should do them much good once they get over it."

Their days now were spent on the move, alternately looking for or hiding from the army, which seemed to be everywhere in large numbers around them. On April 10 they struck again, firing upon an approaching platoon of soldiers as they came down the river. "Soon the first news arrived, and it was unpleasant," wrote Che, who had stayed at his command post. "Rubio, Jesús Suárez Gayol, was mortally wounded; he was dead on arrival at our camp, a bullet in his head."

Che had lost his first man in action, a Cuban, but three soldiers had been killed, and several others wounded and taken prisoner. After interrogating the prisoners and determining that more enemy forces were on their way, Che decided to leave his ambush in place. By the afternoon, more soldiers appeared and they too fell into the trap. "This time," he wrote, "there were seven dead, five wounded and 22 prisoners."

That night, Bustos recalled, Che did something he found very strange. Rubio's body was placed on the ground in the middle of the camp and remained there all night. It was, Bustos said, like a kind of wake. Nobody referred to the body, but it was right there, unavoidable, a grim reminder of what could await each of them. The next day, after Che made some remarks about Suárez Gayol's bravery—and his carelessness—Rubio was buried in a shallow grave and the prisoners were set free, the captured enemy officer sent off with Che's "Communìqué No. 1," announcing the commencement of hostilities by the ELN, Che noted the motley composition of the men sent in against him. "There are Rangers, paratroopers, and local soldiers, almost children."

Reluctantly, Che was forced to concede that there might be truth to what the news media were reporting: that the army had found their original camp and uncovered photographs and other evidence of their presence. A group of newsmen had been taken there, and on April 11 Che listened to one reporter on the radio describe a photo he had seen in the camp of a man "beardless and with a pipe." It sounded like a photo of Che, but it seemed his identity had not yet been discovered. Two days later came the news that the United States was sending military advisors to Bolivia in a move that it said had nothing to do with "the guerrillas," but was only part of a longstanding military assistance program between the two countries. Che didn't believe it for a second and made a hopeful note: "We may be witnessing the first episode of a new Vietnam." Che was partly right. The United States *was*, of course, sending advisors to help the Bolivians quell the guerrilla threat, but if he thought it would spark off a campaign of national resistance as in "Vietnam," he was wrong. On April 20, his cause suffered a new blow when Debray and Bustos were captured by the army as they tried to exit the *"frente"* by walking into the little village of Muyupampa.

## VIII

NORTH OF THE Rio Grande, the forested land rises massively toward the sky, climbing away in blue mountain eddies toward the brown lunar scree of the Andean highlands in the far distance. Above the tree line, the great denuded hills and chilly plateaus give way to swooping ravines, dotted sparsely with rustic hamlets linked to one another by footpaths and the occasional dirt road. The inhabitants, mostly Indians and mestizos, live by tending pigs or cows, their corn patches and vegetable gardens forming geometric patterns on hillsides around their adobe houses. There is little foliage, and the natives can spot a stranger coming from miles away.

For two weeks, Che's band climbed steadily upward, fording rivers, climbing cliffs, running once or twice into army patrols with tracker dogs. By now, the men were all showing the symptoms of breakdown of one sort or another. They squabbled over things such as who had eaten more food, accused one another of making insults, and, like children, came to tell Che their grievances and accusations. The most alarming symptom of all was displayed by "Antonio"—Olo Pantoja— who one day claimed to see five soldiers approaching; it turned out to be a hallucination. That night, Che made a worried note about the risk this troubling apparition of war "psychosis" might have on the morale of his men.

Che continued to listen attentively to the radio. Barrientos had now put a price on his head—a mere forty-two hundred dollars—while at the same time announcing his belief that Che was dead. Debray's pending trial, which was attracting international media attention, had been suspended until September 17. Another day, he recorded: "A Budapest daily criticizes Che Guevara, a pathetic and apparently irresponsible figure, and hails the Marxist attitude of the Chilean Party for adopting practical stands. How I would like to take power just to unmask cowards and lackeys of every sort and to rub their snouts in their own filth."

Perhaps because of his powerlessness to alter the course of events, his acid humor returned. Radio Havana reported that "a message of support had been received from the ELN" at the recently convened Organización Latinoamericana de Solidaridad conference in Havana, a message, Che noted, that must have been received through "a miracle of telepathy." At the conference, Che's emblematic visage had dominated the proceedings in huge posters and banners, and he was heralded as a hero by Fidel and the attending revolutionary conferees.

In mid-September, news came of the arrest and attempted suicide in La Paz of Loyola Guzmán, the young woman Che had made his Bolivian "national finance secretary" back in the days when everything was just beginning and still held promise. During a lapse in her interrogation session on the third floor of the Interior Ministry, Loyola had hurled herself out of the window to avoid being forced to betray her comrades. She was badly hurt but survived.

On September 21, the group reached an elevation of two thousand meters, or over 6,000 feet, the highest altitude they had yet experienced. Walking along a dirt road under bright moonlight, they headed toward Alto Seco, an isolated hamlet of fifty houses perched on a great rocky dome of mountain. As they marched toward it the next day, Che noticed that "the people are afraid and try to get out of our way." They reached Alto Seco that afternoon, received with a "mixture of fear and curiosity," and discovered that the local mayor, or *corregidor*, had gone off the day before to tell the army they were approaching. In reprisal, Che seized the food supplies in the man's little grocery store and was deaf to his weeping wife's entreaties that she be paid something in return.

Instead of leaving immediately, Che and his men stayed in Alto Seco that night, organizing an assembly in the little schoolhouse, where Inti gave a speech explaining their "revolution" to a "group of 15 downtrodden and silent peasants." Only one man spoke up, the schoolteacher, who asked provocative questions about socialism, and whom Che profiled as "a mixture of fox and peasant, illiterate and guileless as a child."

To such isolated people, the bearded, dirty, and armed guerrillas who appeared in their midst were bewildering. Some even thought they were supernatural creatures. After a visit by the guerrillas, who were looking for food, a peasant woman who lived near Honorato Rojas told the army that she believed they were "*brujos*," sorcerors, because they seemed to know everything about everyone in the area. When they paid her with paper money for her food, she thought their money was enchanted and would turn worthless in her hands.

At the same time, the government had been doing a good job of psychological warfare. In addition to its large-scale military "civic action" program—consisting of road-building, distributing antiguerrilla propaganda, granting land titles to peasants, and handing out school supplies in rural areas—the army and police had been actively ferreting out intelligence from the peasant communities for months. Even before the guerrillas began moving away from Ñancahuazú and operating north of the river, the town of Vallegrande, with its civilian population of six thousand and military garrison, had been put on a war footing. In April, had the military declared the entire province an "emergency zone," imposing martial law and advising the population that "groups of Castro-Communist tendency, mostly foreigners, have infiltrated our country, with the sole objective of sowing chaos and halting the Progress of the Nation, carrying out acts of *bandolerismo*, pillage and assault against private property, especially among the peasantry. . . . The Armed Forces, conscious of its specific obligations, has been mobilized to detain and destroy the foreign invasion, as malicious as it is vandalous."

Since late summer, Vallegrande had become the main base for the army's counterinsurgency operations, and an atmosphere of war hysteria had taken over. A public megaphone blared out antiguerrilla information in the public square, the handful of local leftist students were arrested, foreign-looking strangers detained and questioned. On August 23, according to Lieutenant Colonel Selich's daily log, the entire population of Vallegrande had been "mobilized in the face of a possible Red attack."

On September 1, when the army command in Vallegrande had made radio contact with Captain Vargas Salinas after his ambush of Joaquín's column the night before, there was euphoria—and confusion—at his initial list of "*exterminados*," for it included the name "Guevara." As the assembled armed forces chiefs of staff listened in from La Paz, there was palpable excitement in the voice of army chief General David La Fuente as he pressed Vallegrande for clarification: "Does he mean *Che* Guevara?" They soon discovered that the dead man in question was Moisés Guevara, not the legendary *comandante guerrillero*, but were satisfied the action had been a great success.

What's more, the military now knew that Che Guevara was hungry and sick, with a greatly reduced force of men. A soldier, Anselmo Mejía Cuellar, one of three taken prisoner by the guerrillas for a five-day period in August, told Selich that they walked little and moved slowly, gradually cutting their own path through the bush with machetes—and were "very dirty." He described their weapons and each of the guerrillas' duties, and made some interesting observations about Che. "The jefe travels by horse . . . [and] the others serve him like a God, they made his bed and brought him *yerbu mate*. He smokes a pipe, of silver . . . and travels in the center [of the column] with the wounded man [Pombo, recovering from a leg injury]; he has green trousers and a camouflaged shirt with a coffee-colored beret . . . and wears two watches, one a very large one." Cuellar's fellow ex-prisoner, Valerio Gutiérrez Padilla, said that although Che "never complained," he was obviously "bad off" because his men had to dismount him from his horse.

By the time the guerrillas reached Alto Seco, the army already knew they were coming and had began mobilizing to go after them. On September 24, the garrison in Vallegrande dispatched a regiment of soldiers to establish a forward base of operations at the village of Pucará, some fifteen kilometers (about ten miles) northwest of the advancing guerrillas.

From Alto Seco, the guerrillas moved on, meandering for the next two days through the open landscape at a leisurely pace. Che, sick with what he called "a liver attack," seemed almost in a reverie as he observed "a beautiful orange grove" where they stopped to rest. Approaching the next village, Pujío, he casually noted that he had bought a pig to eat "from the only peasant who stayed home. . . . The rest flee at the sight of us."

Reading these passages, one can't help but conclude that Che had become strangely detached from his own plight, an interested witness to his own inexorable march toward death. For he was breaking every rule sacred to guerrilla warfare: moving in the open without precise intelligence about what lay ahead, without the support of the peasants, and knowing that the army was aware of his approach.

Something Che wrote during his odyssey suggests he knew his time was running out. It was a poem he had evidently written for Aleida in the form of a last will and testament, and he entitled it "Against Wind and Tide."

> This poem (against wind and tide) will carry my signature.
> I give to you six sonorous syllables,
> a look which always bears (like a wounded bird) tenderness,
>
> An anxiety of lukewarm deep water,
> a dark office where the only light is these verses of mine
> a very used thimble for your bored nights,
> a photograph of our sons.
>
> The most beautiful bullet in this pistol that always accompanies me,
> the unerasable memory (always latent and deep) of the children
> who, one day, you and I conceived,
> and the piece of life that remains for me,
>
> This I give (convinced and happy) to the Revolution.
> Nothing that can unite us will have greater power.

As peasants spread the news of their slow approach, the *corregidores* of the villages went ahead to alert the army. On September 26, reaching the miserable little hamlet of La Higuera, located in a bowl of land between two ridges, they found only women and children; all the men had left, including the *corregidor* and the telegraph operator. Che sent his vanguard ahead to scout the way to the next village of Jagüey, but when they reached the first rise of land leading out of La Higuera, they walked straight into an army ambush. Killed instantly were two Bolivians, Roberto "Coco" Peredo and Mario "Julio" Gutiérrez, and the Cuban Manuel "Miguel" Hernández. Camba and Léon, both Bolivians, seized the opportunity to desert Benigno, Pablo, and Aniceto survived and returned to La Higuera, but Benigno was wounded and Pablo had a badly hurt foot.

It had been Vallegrande soldiers who had struck the devastating blow. From his base there, Lieutenant Colonel Selich listed the three dead guerrillas and then crowed proudly that his soldiers "had not suffered a single death, or injury, or even a scratch. A crowning victory won by the Third Tactical Group for the Bolivian Army."

With the smell of victory approaching, the different army units now began to compete to see which would claim the ultimate prize: the final defeat of Che Guevara. Colonel Joaquín Zenteno Anaya, commander of the Eighth Army Division; Colonel Arnaldo Saucedo, his intelligence chief, and CIA advisor Felix Rodríguez had arrived in Vallegrande. Various army units patrolled out of bases both in front of and behind the guerrilla band, in Alto Seco and Pucará. Fresh from their weeks of training, the new U.S.-trained Bolivian Army Rangers now entered the field, reinforcing the soldiers at Pucará.

After the ambush outside La Higuera, Che and the survivors exchanged fire with the army positioned on the heights above them, then withdrew, escaping into a canyon. The next day they tried to find a way out of their predicament, climbing up to a higher elevation, where they found a small patch of woods to hide in. For the next three days, they remained there, anxiously watching the army pass back and forth on a road that cut across the hill just in front of them. Other soldiers were posted at a nearby house. When there were no soldiers in sight, Che sent out scouts to fetch water, gain a sense of the enemy's movements, and find an escape route back down to the Río Grande. For the moment, though, they were surrounded.

In Vallegrande, the three new dead guerrillas had been brought in by mule and jeep and laid out in bloody rows in the Nuestro Señor de Malta Hospital. On September 27, Selich noted that "the astonished people of Vallegrande dared to look at them only from a distance." The next night, the troops who had carried out the ambush returned to base and were "rendered tribute" at a special party thrown by Colonel Zenteno Anaya. After a government commission arrived from La Paz to identify the bodies, Selich once more performed burial duty. At 11:00 P.M. on the night of September 29, he noted: "In absolute secrecy and in some place, the remains of the Red mercenaries killed in the action at [La] Higuera were buried."

On September 30, bringing with him a large retinue of officials and press, President Barrientos returned to Vallegrande to share in the latest triumph. That same night, only fifty kilometers (about thirty miles) away, an exhausted Che and his men stole from cover and began making their way cautiously into the canyon below, careful to avoid contact with any of the peasants whose little farms dotted the area. The radio carried news of the large military mobilization under way; one report said eighteen hundred soldiers were in the zone; another said that "Che Guevara was surrounded in a canyon"; still another gave the news that when Che was caught he would be "brought to trial in Santa Cruz." Then the captures of Camba and León were reported. Both men had obviously "talked," even telling their captors that Che Guevara was sick. "So ends the tale of two heroic guerrillas," Che remarked disgustedly in his diary.

By October 7, the guerrillas were in a steep ravine near La Higuera, where a narrow natural passage leads down toward the Río Grande. Their progress had been slow because Chino Chang, whose glasses were broken, was almost blind at night, he held them back considerably. Still, Che was in a reasonably upbeat mood, beginning his diary entry that day by writing: "We completed the 11th month of our guerrilla operation without complications, in a bucolic mood."

At midday, they spotted an old woman grazing goats and seized her as a precaution. She said she knew nothing about soldiers—or anything else, for that matter. Che was skeptical and sent Inti, Aniceto, and Pablo with her to her squalid little farmhouse, where they saw she had a young dwarf daughter. They gave the woman fifty pesos and told her not to speak to anyone about their presence, although they did so, Che noted, "with little hope that she will keep her word."

There were seventeen of them left now. That night they set off downhill again, under "a very small moon," walking through a narrow stream gulley whose banks were sown with potato patches. At two in the morning they stopped because of Chang, who could not see well enough to walk farther. That night, Che listened to "an unusual" army report on the radio that said that army troops had encircled the guerrillas at a place between the "Acero" and "Oro" rivers. "The news seems diversionary," he observed. He wrote down their present altitude: "2,000 meters [about 6,500 feet]." It was the final entry in his diary.

# PART

### six
## DEATH

"Many shall perish, victims of their errors."

—ERNESTO CHE GUEVARA, APRIL 1967, BOLIVIA

# THE DEATH OF CHE GUEVARA
## BJORN KUMM

*THE NEW REPUBLIC*

NOVEMBER 11, 1967

T HEY BROUGHT CHÉ Guevara at five o'clock in the afternoon of
October 9 to the airfield outside the small town of Vallegrande
in southeastern Bolivia. The fighting had been fierce. Ché had
been among the first casualties and his comrades had been fighting
viciously to recover the body. They failed. Most of them also fell,
among them Ché's Cuban bodyguards Antonio and Pancho. The
remainder, after 30 hours of battle, managed to get away, pursued by
the Bolivian army's tough, US-trained Rangers.

Ché's body was brought in tied to the landing shafts of a helicopter, swirling gently down at the airport one hour before dusk. A car
was waiting at the far end of the field; so were, it seemed, most of Vallegrande's 10,000 inhabitants. Soldiers tried to keep the crowds away,
but as the helicopter touched down, they lost control. Even the soldiers ran toward the helicopter, and behind them came the crowds.
When eventually they came to their senses, the soldiers turned about
and pointed menacingly at the civilians, forcing them to stay where
they were. From the air it must have looked like a gigantic chess game,

with pawns frozen in absurd positions. Meanwhile, the helicopter unloaded the body into the automobile, and the car rapidly took off toward the hospital of Vallegrande.

That is where, a few minutes later, I got my first glimpse of Guevara. They had taken him to an outdoor morgue that looked rather more like a stable on a small hill above the hospital. About 10 persons—doctors, soldiers, nurses—were around the body, working frantically. A nun dressed in white was standing at the body's head. Now and then she smiled gently.

At first, I thought Ché was still alive. It looked as if the doctors were administering a blood transfusion. Through two openings in the neck, they were injecting liquid from a vessel being held by a soldier standing with his legs wide apart above the body. Then I was told they were filling the body with formalin to embalm it.

It was a ghastly sight. Not so much because of the corpse, whose face as the soldiers lifted its head seemed rather peaceful. But there was the white-clad nun, smiling encouragingly; and the laughing soldiers who were slapping each others' backs; and a sturdy man in battledress and an American T-shirt, with a very modern machine-gun, who seemed somehow to be in charge of the whole performance. He saw to it that the fingerprints were properly taken. He waved at the soldiers not to disturb the doctors and nurses at work, and above all he seemed bent on keeping journalists away. Earlier in the day he had ejected two British journalists from Vallegrande's airfield, as they were taking pictures of the troops: He was overheard saying, "Let's get the hell out of here," in a most American way. But at this point he was taciturn, answered questions only in Spanish, and shied away from having his photograph taken. His name is Ramos, one of the Bolivian journalists told me. He is a Cuban refugee, employed, the journalist said, by the Central Intelligence Agency. The Americans brought him and a half-dozen other Cubans here to interrogate guerrilla prisoners.

THIS, THEN, WAS to be Ché Guevara's fate a slab of meat tied to a helicopter, carried from the battlefield in the jungle to a morgue in Vallegrande, laid out in front of the press, and—to top it all—identified and inspected by a refugee *gusano* from Cuba, whose pleasure and satisfaction it was to check, personally that his most hated enemy, next to Fidel Castro, was dead.

As long as they were busy filling the body with formalin, it was rather difficult to see who it really was. The head was thrown back, the long hair was dangling and almost touching the floor. The stench of the formalin was almost impossible to stomach. Suddenly, one of the soldiers grabbed the body by its hair and yanked it into a sitting position.

There was no doubt about it. It was Ché, much slimmer than he used to be in the old photographs, smiling at Punta del Este, cutting cane in Cuba. But that seemed to be a normal consequence of half a year in the Bolivian jungle. He didn't look emaciated, as one had been given to believe by Bolivian army reports that Ché, known as "Ramon" among the Bolivian guerrillas, was a very sick man, suffering from asthma and rheumatism, and finding it impossible to walk.

I recalled a picture that had been hanging in every newsstand in La Paz during the last month. It was originally from *Paris-Match* and showed Ché delightfully stretched out on a sofa like some kind of male model for a female edition of *Playboy*. That picture was supposedly taken shortly before his disappearance from Cuba in 1965. Crowds had stood around that picture in La Paz, reading eagerly every word about the mysterious Number One Revolutionary of Latin America. And now here, in the improvised morgue which had been set up at Vallegrande, the picture had its dreadful counterpart.

They were washing the body. "Show some respect," a Bolivian army sergeant exhorted the journalists, "at least don't take pictures of him in the nude." A captain threateningly showed a film he had grabbed from a bystander's camera and confiscated. The soldiers were trying to dress the body. They got the trousers on, but when they tried to put on the jacket, it turned out that the arms were already getting stiff. And so they had to give up their attempt.

General Ovando, chief of the Bolivian armed forces, was inspecting the ceremony in person. One of the radio reporters, representing a station in Santa Cruz, talked into his tape recorder: "This is Vallegrande. The leader of the Castro communist invasion of our fatherland has fallen here, thanks to the effort of the Bolivian armed forces, commanded by the glorious General Ovando." The general smiled a delphic smile.

How had Ché died? He had been captured Sunday night, the army said; he was mortally wounded and had died early Monday morning. Impossible, the doctors said. Ché died from wounds in the heart and both lungs, around noon Monday, five or six hours before he was brought to Vallegrande. What conclusion must one draw? — that Ché had been coolly executed after his capture.

THE DEATH OF CHE GUEVARA

If the army officials had stuck to one story from the beginning, they would have fared better. But while Colonel Zenteno, chief of the Eighth Division in Santa Cruz, who was directly responsible for the killing of Ché, maintained Ché had died immediately, officials higher up talked freely of what Ché had said and how he had acted after his capture. I flew to Vallegrande in a military transport plane from Santa Cruz, together with Admiral Ugarteche, commander-in-chief of the Bolivian navy, who said: "I have been told that Ché's last words were: 'I am Ché. Don't kill me. I have failed.' I have the impression he wanted to save his life. It's very often like that. In battle, you don't feel fear, but afterwards you become a coward."

The crowd outside the hospital had broken through the gates and were now streaming upwards toward the morgue. The soldiers kept them at a distance, but when finally the body was brought out on a stretcher for the benefit of the journalists, men, women, little girls came forward and the soldiers carrying the stretcher dropped it. For a short while, I thought the crowd was going to tear the body apart. Then the soldiers once again gained control and the body was brought back to the morgue. That's where I threw a last glance at it. "The forehead," I thought; "those very heavy, almost swollen lobes above the eyebrows, that ought to be one of the surest ways to identify Ché."

I looked at the body. The lobes were very heavy, strongly accentuated. If this was not Ché, it was his twin brother.

We went by jeep back to Santa Cruz, and then on to La Paz to tell the world Ché was gone.

# GUEVARA, DEBRAY AND THE CIA

RICHARD GOTT

*THE NATION*

NOVEMBER 20, 1967

## santiago, chile

AT 8:30 IN THE warm evening of Sunday, October 8, I was walking
with an English friend in the main square of Santa Cruz, in eastern
Bolivia, when a man beckoned to us from a café table "I have news
for you," he said. And we said, "Che?" for the possible capture of Guevara had been on our minds for a week. We had been in the small town
of Vallegrande six days earlier and had heard Col. Joaquin Zenteno
Anaya, commander of the Eighth Division of the Bolivian Army, express
confidence that his troops would have Che in their power before the
week was up. He explained that his troops had been reinforced by 600
"Rangers," fresh from the training camp run by United States Special
Forces north of Santa Cruz. He told us how the guerrillas had been
encircled. Escape was possible only on one side, and there the army
had planted soldiers dressed as peasants to report at once if the guerrillas appeared. From the evidence of villagers whom the guerrillas had
met at the end of September, and from that of captured guerrillas, there
was no doubt that Che was the leader of this encircled band.

"Che has been captured," our café contact told us, "but he is severely wounded and may not last the night. The other guerrillas are fighting desperately to get him back, and the company commander is appealing by radio for a helicopter so that they can fly him out." My friend and I hired a jeep and set off for Vallegrande at four o'clock on Monday morning.

We arrived five and a half hours later and drove straight to the air-field. Half the population of the small town seemed to be waiting there, the school children in white dresses and amateur photographers eager to secure pictures of dead guerrillas. Only two weeks before, the bod-ies of the Bolivian leader, "Coco" Peredo, and of the Cuban "Anto-nio" had been landed there. And in the cemetery close to the airfield lies the body of "Tania," the beautiful girl who died with nine other guerrillas on August 31, after being led treacherously into an ambush in the Rio Grande. The inhabitants of Vallegrande had by now become accustomed to the comings and goings of the military.

Suddenly the children began jumping up and down and pointing to the horizon. Within seconds, a speck appeared in the sky and it soon materialized into a helicopter, bearing on its landing rails the bodies of two dead soldiers. They were unstrapped and unceremoniously loaded into a lorry and carted into the town. But as the crowd melted away, we stayed behind, and photographed the crates of napalm that lay around the periphery of the airfield. And with a telephoto lens we took photos of a man in olive-green uniform with no military insignia who had been identified to us as an agent from the CIA. (I shall so refer to him hereafter, for I am convinced that that is what he was.)

Such temerity on the part of foreign journalists—we were the first to arrive in Vallegrande by twenty-four hours—was ill-received, and the CIA agent in the company of some Bolivian officers tried to have us thrown out of town. But we carried credentials to prove that we were bona fide journalists, and after much argument we were allowed to stay. The one and only helicopter then set off again for the fighting zone, some 30 kilometers to the southwest, with Colonel Zenteno aboard. Shortly after one o'clock in the afternoon, it brought him back, triumphant and barely suppressing an enormous grin. Che was dead, he announced. He had seen the body, and there was no room for doubt. Colonel Zenteno is an honest man, not accustomed to reveal-ing more than is absolutely necessary, and there seemed no reason to doubt him. We rushed to the tiny telegraph office and thrust our dispatches to the outside world into the hands of a startled clerk.

Four hours later, at exactly five o'clock, the helicopter was back once more, now carrying a single small body strapped to its rails. This time, instead of landing close to where we were standing, the machine came down in the middle of the airfield, and the onlookers were held back by a cordon of determined soldiers. The distant corpse was quickly loaded into a closed Chevrolet van which sped away. We leapt into our jeep and our enterprising driver followed close. After about a kilometer the Chevrolet turned sharply into the grounds of a tiny hospital, and we were close enough behind to prevent the gates from being closed against us.

The Chevrolet drove up a steep slope, and then reversed toward a small hut with a bamboo roof and one open side, normally used as a laundry. We hurried from the jeep and reached the rear doors of the van while they were still closed. When they were thrown open, the CIA agent leapt out, yelling in English, "All right, let's get the hell out of here." It seemed inappropriate, since he could hardly have been addressing the two British journalists who stood on either side of the door.

Inside the van, on a stretcher, lay the body of Che Guevara. I had seen him once before, four years ago in Havana, and he was not a person whom one would forget easily. Since then, my personal memory of him had doubtless become mingled with the frequent photographs in the press, and I must confess that I had forgotten the blackness of his scanty beard. He seemed smaller, too, and thinner than I had remembered. But months in the jungle had clearly taken their toll. I wanted to reject the evidence of my eyes, but when they carried the body out and propped it up on a makeshift table in the hut, doubt became impossible. The shape of the beard, the design of the face, and the rich flowing hair were unmistakable. He was wearing olive-green battle dress and a zippered jacket. On his feet were faded green socks and a pair of apparently homemade moccasins. Since he was fully dressed it was not possible to see all his wounds. There were two obvious holes at the bottom of his neck, and later when they were cleaning his body I saw another wound in his stomach. I do not doubt that he had wounds in his legs and near his heart, but I did not see them.

Two doctors were probing the wounds in his neck and my first thought was that they were searching for the bullet, but in fact I believe that they were preparing to put in a tube for the formalin that would preserve his body. One of the doctors began cleaning his hands which were covered with blood, but otherwise there was nothing repellent about the body. Che looked astonishingly alive. His eyes were open and bright, and the doctors slipped one of his arms out of his jacket without difficulty. I do not believe that he had been dead for many hours, and at the time I did not believe that he had been killed after his capture. I assumed that he had died of his wounds and lack of medical attention sometime in the early hours of that Monday morning.

The living group around the body was more repellent than the dead: A nun who could not help smiling and sometimes laughed aloud; officers who came with their expensive cameras to record the scene. And, of course, the agent from the CIA. He seemed to be in charge and looked furious whenever anyone pointed a camera in his direction, "Where do you come from?" we asked him in English, jokingly adding, "from Cuba, from Puerto Rico?" But he was not amused, and curtly replied in English, "from nowhere." Later we asked him again, but this time he replied in Spanish, "*Que dice?*," and pretended not to understand. He was a short, stocky man in his middle 30s. He had sunken piggy eyes and almost no hair. It was difficult to tell whether he was a North American or a Cuban exile, for he spoke English and Spanish with equal facility and with no trace of accent.

Fortunately, I was not the only witness of this scene. A correspondent of the news agency, Reuters, was also there and mentioned the CIA agent in his cable. But when his story appeared in *The New York Times*, the crucial paragraphs were missing.

# THE EXECUTION OF CHE BY THE CIA
## MICHÈLE RAY

**RAMPARTS**

MARCH 1968

### [i. the relics of st. che]

FROM ALL PARTS of the world they came to search for relics of St. Che. My role in the hunt was accidental, impulsive. I had just arrived in New York on a reasonably leisurely stopover en route from Paris to Bolivia, where I was to investigate the story of the guerrillas and attempt to unravel the confused accounts of Che's death. But I had hardly gotten out of my taxi when I learned that the vultures were already circling the body of the martyred revolutionary hero.

The news came to me from my friend, Debbie Schabert of Time-Life Editions: "Tomorrow Don Schanche is flying to La Paz as a representative of Magnum. He's going to sign a contract with the Bolivian government for the purchase of Che's diary. . . ."

I didn't even let her finish the sentence; I didn't unpack my bags. Into another taxi and back to Kennedy airport and another jet.

Over Mexico and Lima, across the Andes, over Lake Titicaca, across the barren and arid Altiplano; I made my plans. I knew Schanche. He had been editor of Holiday and was now closing a deal with the corrupt Bolivian generals so that Magnum, the big, U.S.-dominated news consortium, could traffic in Che's literary remains. A kind of romanticism left me repelled at this prospect. I found it bizarre and unjust that the diary of this man who had dedicated his life (and death) to the fight against American imperialism should be exploited, expurgated, perhaps falsified, to the profit of the very political line he abhorred.

I resolved to see the diary before the Americans took it from Bolivia so I could discover just what had motivated this unique rush to publish it. I also resolved to make the deal as difficult for the Americans as possible. I had one card to play, a bluff. When I left Paris, my friend, publisher Jean-Jacques Pauvert, gave me blanket accreditation to negotiate for the purchase of the famous diary. He felt he would have little chance against American money, but told me to try. At least Pauvert would treat Che's remains with the reverence and delicacy they deserved.

Rushing to Bolivia with one thought uppermost in my mind—keep the Americans from getting hold of the diary—I had no idea that weeks later I would leave having reconstructed the last day of Che's life and assured myself that the CIA was responsible for his death.

I landed at La Paz along with Schanche. He didn't know who I was, so I stuck to his trail through customs and checked in at the same hotel, the Copacabana. The project which had brought Schanche to Bolivia, with me at his heels, had been planned and organized by Andrew Saint George, a photographer-journalist from Magnum, which boasts some of the biggest magazines in the world as members. A Hungarian by birth, Saint George was named by Che Guevara in his history of the Cuban Revolution as an agent of the FBI who had been sent to visit the guerrilla band in the Sierra Maestra.

This same Saint George had landed in La Paz just a few days after the press had announced the presence of a diary in Che's saddlebag. It hadn't been much trouble for him to persuade the Bolivian government to abandon its plan to publish the diary and to put it up for sale instead. *The New York Times* had come in on the deal with the Magnum consortium and so Juan de Onís, their Latin American correspondent, had also flown to La Paz. The deal was set. Schanche had only to come to La Paz, take a look at the documents, sign the contract and return to New York.

It was Saturday and Schanche counted on being back home by the next weekend. I didn't have much time. I had arrived too late to find and talk with the intermediaries who are always vital to these sorts of negotiations. So I had to go right to the top: President René Barrientos and General Alfredo Ovando, Bolivia's military strongmen. I already knew them, having interviewed them in August 1965, when they headed the military junta. This made my task easier, and 48 hours after I arrived I had obtained an interview with Barrientos in the presidential palace.

But Schanche had worked even faster: his interview was set for four o'clock, mine for five I was afraid the one-hour difference would be crucial, and that my negotiations could easily be over before they even started. I walked into the President's office expecting the worst.

WHEN I HAD interviewed him two years before, Barrientos was wearing a military uniform covered with all the insignia of his rank. This time the display was gone: the President's attire was ostentatiously conservative.

Stocky and swarthy, his hair cropped short, the President was open and relaxed, even voluble with me. He began by speaking of the circumstances surrounding the death of Guevara. "You know," he told me, "La Paz is far from La Higuera, and I can neither confirm nor deny for you any of the accounts which have been given of the details of Señor Guevara's death. But he died as he wished, fighting for his cause." Was Barrientos trying to imply that he had no idea of what had gone on in La Higuera the day Che died? A difficult position for a chief of state to take, especially in a country as precarious and closely controlled as Bolivia.

As Barrientos came to the end of our interview, I stopped my tape recorder and declared that I had two important things to say to him. 'I am in Bolivia as a journalist," I told the President, "but along with my study of the history of the guerrilla movement, I also represent the French publishing house of Pauvert, which is interested in buying the captured documents, among them, of course, the famous diary."

You could have heard a pin drop. Barrientos, composed as before, said nothing. I went on: "Furthermore, if you negotiate with a non-U.S. firm on equal terms, the international press can't accuse you of being in the hands of the United States. Whatever you decide in the long run, having two competitors in the bidding can only be advantageous to the Bolivian government."

But Barrientos already understood. "I've just seen Schanche and the other," he said. "Everything had been decided, and the business was supposed to be finished by the end of this week. But it's okay with me if you enter the competition. You can appear tomorrow before the Diary Commission."

I had heard of the Warren Commission. Now there was a "Diary Commission!"

Bolivia's grapevine worked even faster than I thought, for Schanche was waiting for me at my hotel; relaxed as ever, he introduced himself, stating he was still sure that "the most important narrative of the last few years" would soon be his. "Who is this Pauvert? Michèle, you're crazy to compete with a trust like Magnum. Don't forget, you're a journalist too. I'm sure we can work things out. This stupid competition is only helping a handful of generals make a killing."

Schanche had a lingering smile for the woman in me, but he had declared war against the competition I represented. Captain Philip Wimset from the American Embassy—a personal friend of Saint George—had obligingly furnished Magnum with very detailed "intelligence reports" on everything that I had written, all my movements and how much I had in the bank. The information was passed through Schanche to the Bolivians.

Schanche made it clear enough what was up when he asked me, "How do you expect the Bolivians to trust you when they know you wrote an article called, 'I'm in Love with the Viet Cong,' and that you seem to be in sympathy with revolutionary movements?" I merely smiled at him in return because through my contacts—I was beginning to have some too—I knew who it was that had sent the "Michèle Ray dossier" to General Ovando's office.

The next day, while Schanche, de Onís and Saint George, accompanied by Colonel Arana from the Bolivian secret service and Captain Wimset, examined the captured documents, I appeared before the "Diary Commission" (whose pompous title, I must confess, intimidated me somewhat). I was still running a long way behind Magnum, but the important thing was to stay in the race.

In reality, the "Commission" was composed of only two members. Hector Mejica, director of information for the President's office, and Jaime Cespedes, director of information for the General Staff. The former represented Barrientos, the latter Ovando.

Mejica seemed open enough to my entry into "the deal," but Jaime's opinion was all too clear. Cespedes (nicknamed "El Gato") is a play-boy, the owner of a fancy Ford Mustang which he drives around and around the Prado, since there are no other roads in Bolivia suitable for this expensive toy. He was also the confidant of Saint George in the negotiations over the documents. For an hour—in a darkened office without a tape recorder, the three of us facing one another with our hands folded in our laps—we tossed around sums amounting to millions of dollars. Finally we agreed that I would make an offer in writing drawn up by a lawyer.

I submitted an initial offer of $80,000, knowing very well that this was too little, but I left the door wide open for further bids. I cabled Pauvert that the documents included not only Che's diary, but also that of Joaquín (one of the guerrillas), a book of Che's poems, the records of the guerrillas' interrogation of various Army prisoners, the photos taken by the guerrillas and the Bolivian Army's filmed reconstruction of the guerrillas' main ambushes. It was really big business.

Naturally, the Bolivian authorities and my competitors had a good look at my cables and the replies. But I have to admit that this tele-graphic espionage was mutual—and Schanche didn't make it any eas-ier by sending a yard of Telex to New York every day. I "borrowed" the key from the hotel desk and visited his room at a time when I knew he had a regular appointment, taking care that I didn't do my "research" at the same time as the agent for the Bolivian secret ser-vice, who came every day to visit my room and those of my "friends."

GENERAL ALFREDO OVANDO, chief of the Bolivian Armed Forces, received my offer—reluctantly. A few days later, he called me to his office.

Unlike Barrientos—who seems the very image of the American Way of Life—the general, with his stiff military uniform and his tiny mus-tache, is a prototype of the South American military man. I began my interview by asking about the different versions of the story of Che's death which were circulating. Also unlike Barrientos, Ovando had a specific answer to the question of how Che died: "Commander Gue-vara, mortally wounded when he was captured, died of internal bleed-ing seven or eight hours after his capture. Some officers were able to speak with him. But of course, you may interview them." (Naturally, I was never able to do this—at least not through official channels.)

Ovando knows he is the strongman of the regime, but he is still waiting to add the presidency to his duties as commander of the Armed Forces. He is patient. The elections will be in 1970 and he has already announced his candidacy. All these Latin American military men who come to power in three-day *coups d'état* dream of one thing only: to be elected 'legally,' even if this means just one more farce.

His eyes darting around the room and coming to rest on everything but me as he spoke, Ovando launched into 15 minutes of abuse against Régis Debray (the French journalist who had been with Che and was captured by the Bolivians) and Che. Then he got down to the point: "Your offer is too low. The Americans have offered $200,000 plus royalties. However, we aren't too happy with a royalty agreement. Make us a better offer in cash. I'll give you a few days."

Because I had seen the Magnum cables, I knew that the figure he quoted as the American offer was correct. Pauvert cabled me: "Stall a little." Since I knew that Pauvert could never beat the Magnum offer, I decided to bluff, and had a lawyer draw up a contract for $400,000. Why not? And I inserted an important escape clause: my offer would hold only after I had seen the documents.

In reality I wasn't fooling anyone. Certainly not the Bolivians, since Ovando had copies of all the cables I had sent to Paris. But it was in his interest for me to stay in the competition. He played the game. Together, we were driving the price up to an indecent level. Of course, our motives were different. He wanted to force Magnum to raise its bid; I wanted to see the documents. Also, as I told him: "The diary in the hands of the United States is like the Koran in the hands of the infidels."

ALTHOUGH THE NEGOTIATIONS for the documents were still nominally secret, by now the matter had become a public duel between France and the United States. The bets were on the table; the Embassies rose to the occasion. And if Andrew Saint George was rumored to be working for the CIA, I became in my turn a dangerous international spy. But for whom was I working? "For the Cubans," claimed Saint George. And he asked his influential friend, Captain Philip Wimset, to take me out of circulation for 48 hours to ask me a few questions. But Ovando, who knew very well that I was bluffing, wouldn't let him. He didn't take these rumors seriously, but only smiled to himself and kept pulling the strings.

As for Philip Wimset, I met him two times in the restaurants of La

Paz. Actually, he was very bad at hiding his feelings: he couldn't keep from fixing a stare on me as if I were Mata Hari returned from the grave. His real hope was to prove that if I succeeded in buying the diary it was for the purpose of giving a copy to the Cubans.

Because I didn't want him to cut my negotiations short with a cable of withdrawal, I never informed Pauvert that I had put "his" $400,000 on the table. But finally, since time was running out, I decided to make all the negotiations public and gave the story to Agence France Presse. Barrientos had declared that very day at Cochabamba that "the diary will be sold to the highest bidder"; my object was to make the destination of the sale money a public issue, which it became when the Agence France Presse story broke.

"It must go to the families of the soldiers killed in the anti-guerrilla campaigns," was a common argument. And a committee was formed in Vallegrande: "The money belongs to 'us,' " it claimed, "we need a highway."

In Paris, Pauvert nearly had a heart attack when he found out just how much money he had "offered." He cabled me to withdraw officially from the bidding.

A few hours after rumors of the impending sale of the documents began to fly all over La Paz, I ran into Schanche on the terrace of the Copacabana. Strangely at ease, he walked up to me and said: "I would like to invite you for champagne this evening."

What had happened? Was he going to sign?

Both of us had interviews with Ovando scheduled for that afternoon. Schanche at five o'clock, myself at four. General Ovando, fingering a cable—which, as I later understood, was Pauvert's withdrawal—said to me: "I assume that you are still in the running. I hope that you have received no negative reply." My competitors were all waiting in the next room: Schanche, Saint George, de Onís and a lawyer recently arrived from New York. Sitting there with a copy of Pauvert's telegram in their hands, they imagined that I had come to announce to Ovando that I was pulling out.

But the original cable was in Ovando's hands, the copy in the hands of my competition—and I had never seen it. Now it was General Ovando who ran the bluff. With a smile he told the gathering in the other office: "*¡Que no!* Michèle hasn't come to withdraw, but to confirm her offer. You had better raise yours, gentlemen."

There was no champagne that evening Instead there was a stormy scene with Schanche. Two days later another cable arrived from Pauvert: "Confirm previous cable withdrawing." This time Ovando obligingly had it sent directly to me.

But Schanche wasn't yet finished with the French. The French members of the Magnum consortium, as well as some of the Americans, took my place in the fray, threatening to leave the trust unless the negotiations were broken off. In New York there were, I found out, doves as well as vultures.

Finally, in Havana, with the news of the bidding now public, Guevara's heirs threatened to file suit against whoever claimed the copyright, for there was every reason to believe that the diary had been altered either in La Paz or by the CIA in Panama. And the prospect for such a legal entanglement was enough to scare off many of the remaining vultures.

Weeks after he had left New York to take a look at the documents and sign the contract, Schanche returned, observing that he regretted that the affair appeared to have been compromising for him. *The New York Times* sent Juan de Onis to greener pastures in Cuba. Only Saint George persisted, conspiring as always with his "intermediaries." The Bolivian government quickly lowered its price, but no serious publishing house would touch the documents now, and Saint George found himself chasing unwilling editors, flying back to New York, cabling Europe, trying to set up another syndicate. Finally he went too far. Making his pitch to Fred Jordan of Grove Press, Saint George claimed: "If you can reach an understanding with the Guevara family in Cuba so that the diary can be published without a risk of a suit, Régis Debray will be a free man." Saint George rather overestimated his influence with Captain Wimset. The CIA was not about to spring Régis out of jail for one book.

Saint George, who had given the diary its commercial value in the first place, failed in his rather desperate overtures to Grove Press and others, but still continues to try to interest publishing houses in the document. Some, like Stein and Day, have shown interest. But in truth, it is hardly the "most important narrative of the last few years," as Schanche called it and others of the vultures believed it to be. It contains no climactic truths about the guerrillas' contacts with other revolutionary movements; there is no theoretical discussion of revolution, no comments on strategy; nor is there anything of a personal nature which mirrors the remarkable legend that was Che Guevara.

The diary is a day by-day, month-by-month record of the guerrillas' personnel, problems, supplies, contacts and movements. Whatever value it might have once had disappeared the moment it fell into the hands of the CIA and the Bolivian secret service. It has spent too much time in hostile hands for its contents not to have suffered.

I had no business left with the diary. I resolved to set out for Camiri, to begin my investigation of the circumstances of Che's death.

## [ii. a ghost of che; a glimpse of debray]

The day before I left La Paz a young journalist came to see me with some information. This wasn't the first time that I had been approached, usually with bad leads, but always for a healthy number of dollars. I asked him how much.

"I don't want any money," he answered, "but I do want to go to France to study. Besides, I have no way of publishing what I know here. And I'm afraid, because they know that I know the whole story of the death of Che. I spent four days in La Higuera *after* he was shot."

If this was true, it was a bombshell. Since the 9th of October no journalist had been able to reach La Higuera; the village had been quarantined by the Army.

Jorge Torrico was the man's name, and I listened to his story with growing interest. "As a journalist for a military magazine," he contended, "I was accredited by the General Staff, by the secret service and by the President's office. Moreover I had followed the anti-guerrilla operations since the very beginning. I had gone on missions with the Bolivian Rangers, and they all knew me. So I had no difficulty in getting to La Higuera and in staying there. Showing my official papers, I told the peasants that I knew the whole story and said I was supposed to write up a secret report I was there for four days; I explored on foot the whole area where Che passed the last weeks of his life. I got back just two days ago. The authorities threw me right out the door and took away my papers."

Why had he come to see me and not Juan de Onis of *The New York Times*, for example?

"I want to go to France. You are the only French journalist in La Paz at this moment except for the representative of Agence France Presse. You are well known and are working for a big magazine."

I was leaving the next day for Camiri and the guerrilla zone and I was still innocent enough to think that I could get to La Higuera myself. So I told Torrico when I expected to be back. "O.K." he replied. "Call me when you get back 20 days from now. I will speak to no one until you return to La Paz. If you go to La Higuera, look for bullet holes inside the schoolhouse in the larger classroom, to the left of the door. One more thing: Che wasn't mortally wounded when he was captured. He had only one wound—in the left leg, nothing serious. He was shot down in cold blood."

Torrico didn't want to say more than this before I'd committed myself to help him get to France. But this was more than enough for me to begin my investigation.

President Barrientos was starting off on a three-day official tour across the country; and since Camiri—where Régis Debray was imprisoned—was included on his itinerary, I obtained permission to accompany him in the presidential airplane a DC-3 that Barrientos insisted on piloting himself. Stopping at Potosi we watched a *Te Deum* and a military parade, which was followed by gangs of Indians brought that morning from the mines. Packed together, marching quickly, all of them seemed grave and vacant. A few naively tried to goose-step as they marched by, carrying with apparent indifference placards whose slogans they probably couldn't read: "Down with the Guerrillas!" and "Long Live President Barrientos." Soon we were back in the DC-3, headed for Camiri.

THE TEN KILOMETERS between the nearest airstrip and the village of Camiri are more than enough for the dust of the countryside to work its way into one's skin and lungs. Stifling, oppressive, the humidity seems to hold a molten sun fixed in the sky. This is no longer the Altiplano; it is the *selva*, the tropical jungle. Before it gained fame because of Debray's trial, Camiri was known primarily as the oil capital of Bolivia. The area of the *yacimientos* (the oil fields), closed off by an electric fence, is only two blocks from the town square. Damply air-conditioned villas, tennis courts, movie theaters, a somewhat muddy swimming pool—this is oil-rich, civilized Camiri. The other Camiri, the real one, has rows of low houses, some with galleries running in front of them along high sidewalks, and unpaved streets where mules and jeeps ignore each other as they pass.

Everyone gathered in the town square in the warm evening: officers, cover-girls in skin-tight dresses, a few teeny-boppers in mini-skirts. Up on the bandstand, Barrientos was making a speech about justice. Clearly visible from where he was speaking is a reddish one-story build-ing, the military prison where Debray and his co-defendants were being held. Loudspeakers were pointed at the cell windows, but the windows were bricked up.

It was in a former library, transformed for the occasion into a court-room, where Debray—looking first at his feet, then at the ceiling—heard his sentence: for him and Bustos, the Argentinean journalist who had likewise lived with the guerrillas, 30 years for "murder and theft." The four Bolivian co-defendants were acquitted.

To prove the charges of murder, the tribunal had considered in detail for two months the ambush at Ñancahuazú on March 23, 1967, the first major contact between the guerrillas and the Army. The pros-ecution tried to prove that the Army, on a routine mission and unaware of the presence of the guerrillas, had been the victim of a vicious sur-prise attack in which seven soldiers had been "murdered."

Because he is an *aficionado* of the movies, and perhaps also to impress the two woman reporters in Camiri (myself and Amelia Baron), Colonel Reque Terán, commander of the 4th Division which covered both Camiri and the area of Ñancahuazú, took us to watch a staged reconstruction of the famous and controversial ambush in which Debray was supposed to have been involved.

In a grey Toyota which had belonged to "Tania"—the pretty girl who had been the guerrillas' supply link with the city before she was killed by the Army—we traversed the road from Camiri to Lagunil-las, and then to Casa de la Calamina where the path takes off towards the Ñancahuazú River, near what had been the main camp of the guerrillas. We went right through Lagunillas, which consists only of a few streets straggling out of a square surrounded by a series of decay-ing buildings. A few miles north is the farm called Pincal which belongs to Ciro Algaranaz, who claims to have been the first to have informed on the guerrillas—in December 1966.

The Casa de la Calamina, a few miles further north, is a small house composed of two rooms held together by a sheet iron roof, which the Peredo brothers, Coco and Inti—Bolivian leaders of the guerrilla band and members of the Communist Party—had purchased in Septem-ber. It was there that Che Guevara, in the company of "Pachunga," another Cuban, arrived on the night of November 1966, after a two-day ride in a jeep from Cochabamba. But he was no longer Che Guevara; clean-shaven, wearing black-rimmed glasses, he had become "Ramón"—Ramón Benitez, his passport read.

We arrived at the Ñancahuazú River with its steep wooded banks and moved towards the passage that led to what had been the central camp. There Colonel Terán deployed the troops brought along for the occasion. One company played the part of the guerrillas, the other that of the Army. Reque Terán directed the show. But suddenly it was no longer the government's version, but Debray's: the guerrillas were on the defensive and the Army on the offensive. The Army, following information from the two men who had deserted on March 11, was attacking the guerrilla camp.

Reque Terán evidently wasn't very interested in the details of Debray's whereabouts as the prosecution's official version had presented them. For him the trial was only an opportunity to revenge himself on the guerrillas: not for killing his Bolivian soldiers, but for having moved the center of their operations north of the Rio Grande into the territory of his rival, Colonel Zenteno, thus taking the glamour of the action away from his area.

Terán had gotten Debray, but it was Zenteno who got Che.

After waiting for ten days I finally obtained permission to see Régis. As I stood in front of his cell, a Bolivian officer flanking me on each side, a microphone dangling inches from my mouth, Debray, on the other side of the bars, started to laugh. "It seems that you are the prisoner," he said. "What they are after," he told me, "isn't justice—it's propaganda. I am guilty of being a revolutionary. Through my person they are trying to judge the guerrilla movement. They've given it 30 years in prison. But I doubt very much that the sentence will stick that long. It is too bad for the prosecutor that he didn't have a more radical punishment in his repertoire to solve the problem once and for all."

As a reward for having transformed Debray's ideology into the crime of "murder and theft," Colonels Guachalla and Iriarte, respectively the president and the prosecutor for the military tribunal, were advanced to the rank of general. They had followed their instructions well.

The Debray trial is over, but notoriety of his unjust imprisonment is very much alive. The Bolivian government has been sadly disappointed if they expected to imprison revolutionary ideas with Régis.

In the same way, the future will show them that insurrection did not die when Che was murdered.

We all left Camiri for Santa Cruz.

## [iii. the mysterious Gringo]

SANTA CRUZ, FOR eight months the center of the anti-guerrilla operations, is the most pleasant city in Bolivia. Its residents are casual, yet at the same time full of the *joie de vivre* which is the heart of the city's charm. And the most beautiful girls in Bolivia, mini-skirted and pony-tailed, live here. Their looks are Spanish rather than Indian, with pale skins and blue eyes. Although the streets are newly paved, Santa Cruz is still infested by dust driven everywhere by the wind.

At the General Staff headquarters I taped an interview with Colonel Joaquín Zenteno, commander of the 8th Division, now famous as the man who captured Che. Elegantly dressed, wearing a small mustache, Colonel Zenteno had another version of Che's death, different from those of Barrientos and Ovando. One month after the event—more than enough time for a common version to be decided upon—Zenteno told me that Che had never spoken at all after his capture; that he had died while being transported from Quebrada del Churo to La Higuera. But Colonel Zenteno was not eager to talk about Guevara's death, although he waxed eloquent on the subject of anti-guerrilla tactics and military strategy in general. He commented with dry humor on the anti-guerrilla training which the U.S. Green Berets had given his Rangers, where the Bolivians spent whole days shouting: "I'm the strongest! I'm the best!" The presumption was that they would begin to believe it.

In Santa Cruz I rented a jeep and, accompanied by Terry Malick from *The New Yorker*, headed towards Vallegrande, the town to which an Army helicopter had brought Che's body from La Higuera. We took the main road out of Santa Cruz, finding it thick with traffic. Four hundred kilometers long, it is the only tarred highway in all Bolivia. We followed it for 90 kilometers, arriving at the village of Samaipata. It was here at 11 p.m. on July 6th that Che and nine of his men audaciously captured the town in a truck they had borrowed nearby.

While they kept the Army officers and government officials holed up in the Hotel Samaipata, one group of the guerrillas ran 150 yards down the highway and entered the local drugstore. There they paid hard cash for provisions, clothing and medicine, asthma medicine for Che. Before leaving Samaipata they stripped nine soldiers of their uniforms. The entire operation lasted about 40 minutes.

Legend has it that Che was giving orders from the top of a nearby hill. But the owner of the Hotel Velocidad, a very talkative woman, knows better. For she shook the hand of Che Guevara in town, telling him: "I am not afraid to shake the hand of a guerrilla." Five months later this event is still the principal topic of conversation. Everyone has his own version of what happened.

For us Samaipata was also a lunch stop. We ate with Colonel Selnich and his wife and daughter. Selnich had been in command of La Higuera when Che was first brought in. He and his family had just come from Vallegrande. Selnich had still another story to tell us: "An Argentine magazine has just claimed that it was Gary Prado who killed Che with a bullet in the heart. But Prado left Santa Cruz just two days ago for La Paz where, without the permission of the General Staff, he stated to the press that he delivered Che to me alive. So you can, see how this matter concerns me. I have to hurry to La Paz."

The circle of fear was closing. The General Staff in the capital had forbidden Selnich to make any statement whatsoever. And Prado's statement, prompted by his fear that Che's friends might revenge themselves on him, cost him his promotion to the rank of major.

Three more hours by jeep over-an almost completely overgrown road and we were in Vallegrande, where two months earlier Che's body had been on display to the press for 24 hours. We could go no further. A roadblock had been thrown across the path leading out of the town towards La Higuera, which was still quarantined. In La Higuera there are 400 *campesinos* who know the truth. And despite all the threats and promises, the Bolivian government still fears that one of them might talk. Besides the authorities, the only person authorized to go there is the Dominican priest, Father Roger Schiller. He was in La Higuera on that fateful Monday of October 9th, arriving just an hour after the death of Che.

About forty-five years old, Father Schiller has been living in the La Higuera area for seven years. I was to see him three times. Our conversation was made more comfortable and secrets easier to keep by the fact that we spoke the same language—Schiller is a French Swiss. Also, the information that Torrico, the young military journalist, had given me in La Paz made it easier for me to broach the topic of the murder of Che. Schiller's testimony corresponded exactly with the little that Torrico had told me. He repeated in detail some of the stories that the peasants told about what had gone on in La Higuera that day. He also told me that a *gringo* had been in the village the day of Che's death. "Who was he?" I asked. "I'm not sure. They called him Gonzales."

I ran into Father Schiller again in Pucara, which I reached with Juan de Onís and a couple from the Peace Corps only by sneaking past the roadblock at the exit to Vallegrande. It was a four-hour trip by jeep across barren mountain ridges. No houses, nothing. The *campesinos* were startled to see us, because since the strange series of events two months before, we were the first strangers who had gotten that far.

But even before we had saddled the horses to push on to La Higuera, Major Mario Vargas stormed onto the scene. Vargas absolutely forbade us to go any further, saying: "I have given orders to my men in La Higuera to stop, and if necessary to shoot down, any journalist, Bolivian or foreign, who tries to get there. We will recognize no papers. And what is more, the *campesinos* will not talk to you. They know that journalists only tell lies. There was one Bolivian journalist there right after the death of Che. But if he comes back, the peasants will lynch him, since they know that he didn't have permission after all and that they were duped."

There could be no doubt that he was referring to my friend, Torrico. And when I asked him to send a soldier with my camera to take a picture of the wall of the schoolhouse to the left of the door where he would find bullet holes, Vargas shouted at me, his voice trembling: "The children can't study any more in that miserable school." He said the Army was thinking of tearing it down and building a new one. We weren't able to gather whether the school had already been destroyed or not. Perhaps the parents didn't want to send their children to a school in which three murders had been committed. Or perhaps the military feared it would become a shrine to the martyr.

To guarantee that we left the area promptly, Vargas began to escort us back to Vallegrande. Just as we parted, he couldn't keep from saying: "Don't tell Zenteno or Ovando that you got as far as Pucara. It's off limits."

On the road back to Vallegrande we suddenly saw a great stir ahead of us. A company of Rangers had just arrived, clambered down from their trucks and spread across the road amid a chorus of shouts and whistles. The remnants of the guerrilla band, commanded by Inti Peredo, had been sighted in the area. Two soldiers, armed with light machine guns, inspected our jeep and verified our papers. We were allowed to pass.

Back in Santa Cruz that evening in the Gran Hotel, a Ranger — whom I vaguely recall having seen at the General Staff headquarters with Major Saucedo, chief of the Second Section (the secret service) — caught sight of me. He said he was part of Gary Prado's company and that for $500 he wanted to tell me what he knew and what he had seen: who was there when Che died, the names of the murderers — for he claimed that several men shot at Guevara — and further information about what the mysterious American "Gonzales" was doing at the scene.

I was interested in his proposal. And because his disclosures should be the most convincing of anyone's, since he had been there, I proposed to him that he leave Bolivia so that his name could be made public without fear of reprisals. (I couldn't keep from smiling as I imagined myself leaving Bolivia followed by a train of Bolivian exiles.) However, he was married and had children; it wasn't possible. This was one lead I could never follow out. But others were rapidly piling up.

BEFORE RETURNING TO La Paz, I had one more visit to make: to La Esperanza, the camp where American Green Berets from the 8th Special Forces in Panama had for 19 weeks trained the battalion of Bolivian Rangers which was to capture Che Guevara. They had set up shop in April in an old sugar factory established by the Alliance for Progress.

World opinion in April still refused to accept the story that the elusive Che was really present in the Bolivian *selva*. But I learned at the Special Forces camp that the CIA, which had pursued Che constantly since his disappearance from Cuba in 1965, no longer had any doubts. This "Ramón" was Guevara, and it was from Bolivia that he had sent the message to the Tricontinental: "Create two, three, many Vietnams, that is the watchword."

It was only after completing my stay at La Esperanza and returning to La Paz to talk at length with Torrico that I was finally able to understand the incredible lengths to which the Americans had gone to get Che. They had begun by sending CIA agents into the area of the guerrillas' ambush; they had been armed with his entire dossier, and their mission was to verify that it was indeed Che who was leading the guerrillas. They were also determined to coordinate the intelligence efforts of the Bolivian military with its secret service. There were two CIA men heading the "get Che" campaign in Bolivia: one was known as "Ramos"; the other was the mysterious "Gonzales"; both are Cubans and members of the CIA counter-insurgency team composed of Cuban exiles operating out of Panama.

Dividing their time between La Esperanza, Camiri and the presumed guerrilla zone, Ramos and Gonzales did not advertise their presence. Both had good covers. The first evidence of Gonzales' presence is contained in Régis Debray's testimony: "Three days after my capture, I was interrogated by a certain Gonzales, the mysterious fingerman for the CIA." In a letter smuggled out of jail, he wrote: "When I was first arrested . . . I was told by the mysterious mastermind of the CIA, Dr. Gonzales, who is probably a Puerto Rican and was in daily contact with both Barrientos and the American Embassy, you interest them more alive than dead."

Ramón-Guevara was the CIA's man, and they did not intend to let him escape because of the incompetence of the Bolivian military. The United States was determined to make Bolivia a model counterinsurgency operation. The Pentagon knows quite well that they cannot afford two or three more Vietnams.

The Americans I saw during my visit to La Esperanza were practically old friends. I already knew "Pappy" Shelton, the camp commander; Dave Wallander, the intelligence officer; and several others. We had dined together in Santa Cruz several times, and they were awaiting my visit. As I arrived, Shelton told me in embarrassment, "I'm terribly sorry, but I've just received orders not to talk about our activities here with you. But please do stay. At least have lunch with us. The order doesn't apply to food and drink."

Since Bolivia was off limits as a topic of conversation, we talked about Vietnam. Every one of the 16 men at La Esperanza had seen action with the Special Forces, and each told his own story about his former pupils, the South Vietnamese ARVN. There was one sergeant, in fact, who had met me briefly on Route Number One less than half an hour before I was captured by the Viet Cong in 1967.

Counterinsurgency looks the same all over the world. I had the sudden impression that I was back in Vietnam, for La Esperanza looks much like any other Special Forces camp. There are always native pupils and American "advisors," inevitable Playboy foldouts on the walls and comic books piled on the tables.

I left La Esperanza and Santa Cruz and returned to La Paz. By now I had most of the threads of the story in my hands: Che was not mortally wounded when he was brought to La Higuera; Prado had handed him over to Selnich alive. I understood the role of the American Green Berets in training the Bolivian Rangers and I was beginning to suspect the presence of the mysterious Gonzales in La Higuera during the hours before Che died. I was anxious to talk to Torrico so that he could confirm what I already knew and pin down some of the missing details.

I found him quickly in La Paz. He was even more anxious to get to France now, and this made him talkative. Soon we found that by combining what each of us knew we could piece together a coherent, if not detailed, account of Che's last 24 hours. Together with insights and details which other sources later provided me, the story, including the crucial role of the American CIA, is reasonably complete.

### [iv. the death of che guevara]

ON THE NIGHT of Saturday the 7th of October, Che Guevara—or rather Ramón—and his men arrive in a canyon called Churo, one of the deep ravines that score the selva in the area to the southeast of Santa Cruz. Their last battle had taken place 11 days before, only a few kilometers away, near the village of La Higuera. That day September 28, Coco Peredo, the Bolivian leader of the guerrilla movement, had been killed. Since then the band has been maneuvering back and forth around the area, passing from canyon to canyon. They choose to stop at a little field of sweet potatoes at the edge of the stream and at the foot of a huge fig tree. It is after midnight and they decide to get some sleep.

A *campesino* who is sleeping nearby to guard his crops hears them coming. He sets out in the direction of La Higuera; the governor had promised a reward of 50,000 pesos for the capture of Guevara. His report reaches La Higuera, where Captain Prado and the 184 men he commands are stationed.

Prado, in a taped interview with the Chilean journalist Augusto Carmona, later said, "The information was transmitted to us by one of our informants who was operating in the area." This may explain why the reward was not paid to the *campesino*, but to the town of La Higuera. To this day, no one knows exactly who that *campesino* was.

While the guerrillas sleep the Army takes up its positions in the Quebrada del Churo. By morning there are four platoons posed on two slopes of the canyon and two units cutting off the exit towards the Rio Grande. The Rangers are armed with mortars and Browning machine guns.

The first contact between the two forces takes place at about one o'clock at the point where the path to La Higuera comes into the gorge. The guerrillas try to escape by this route, but it is blocked, and the only way out for them is to descend the canyon and reach the Rio Grande.

A second engagement 20 minutes later lasts for around a quarter of an hour. Already there are two dead and two wounded among the Rangers. Then comes silence, almost more ominous than the staccato bursts of machine gun fire.

Suddenly, around three o'clock in the afternoon, all hell breaks loose: mortars, machine guns, grenades. Rocks are broken off, boulders come rolling down. The Ranger platoon of Sergeant Huanca ascends the canyon from the Rio Grande to cut off any escape.

Ramón is wounded in the leg. A bullet breaks the barrel of his Garant rifle. His comrade Willy bears him along on his shoulders up about 60 feet of steep climb to a tiny level spot and then up again. They climb by grabbing hold of briars and thorns. Willy helps Ramón, who can't move his leg and is beginning to choke; he is having an attack of asthma. Both of their hands are covered with blood. Below them the firing continues.

Suddenly four soldiers spring up in front of them and surround them. Willy doesn't even have the time to let go of Ramón and raise up his gun. They are prisoners.

"I am Che Guevara," Ramón says simply.

Gary Prado arrives. He takes a photo from his pocket and looks at the scar on Ramón's hand. "It's him all right," he says.

The impossible has happened. Che is in his hands. "I felt a kind of shock," he reported in a later interview, "a sort of elation. But I had no time to talk to him. I had to return to my command. We kept fighting until dusk."

At Vallegrande at about four o'clock, Colonel Joaquín Zenteno, who commands the 8th Division, receives a coded message: "500 *Cansada*." "500" means Guevara. "*Cansada*" (tired), means prisoner. "Pappy" Shelton receives the same message at American headquarters in La Esperanza.

Prado has handed the prisoners over to five of his men with explicit orders not to speak to them. Che is seated next to Willy, racked by another attack of asthma. The soldiers whisper and stare at him.

At dusk the little caravan hits the road. Willy walks by himself with his hands bound and Guevara, limping on one foot, is held up by two soldiers. Behind them mules carry the dead and wounded Rangers in blankets. It is late night when they finally reach La Higuera.

IN THE VILLAGE—which I was never able to reach but where Torrico had spent four days—400 people live in tiny adobe huts with tile roofs. No cars, not even a jeep. A few narrow stone streets, the largest of which, a mule path, widens in the center of town to make a little square. On the square is a school with two low doors; there are two windows latticed with bamboo bars in the two tiny classrooms.

Che is seated in the larger of the two rooms on a bench with his back to the wall, his hands tied. The soldier who brought him has packed and lighted a pipe for him before leaving. He keeps Che's matches as a souvenir. There is no electricity, not even a lantern. The prisoners are alone in the darkness, listening to the babble of voices which reach them from outside.

The parade of commanding officers which will last until noon the next day, begins with Colonel Selnich. He arrives in a helicopter supposedly to bring supplies, but really at Colonel Zenteno's orders to keep the Rangers from talking too much with the prisoners, and to keep things calm while he awaits a decision from his superiors.

In the village square, Prado passes out to his men the belongings of the prisoners. When he was wounded, Che hid the saddlebag full of documents in the brush, to be found by a peasant two days later. But he kept his knapsack.

Around the knapsack the soldiers are grabbing for souvenirs, making trades. Arguments break out. In a little box there are cuff links. (It's hard for them to imagine Che in a white shirt.) Second Lieutenant Pérez roughly shoves open the classroom door: "These are yours?" he asks Che.

"Yes, and I would like them to be given to my son."

Pérez doesn't answer. He leaves.

Another officer, Espinosa, wants a pipe for himself. The one in the knapsack has already been taken. He wants to trade. What to do? He rushes into the school, goes up to Che, takes him by the hair, shakes him and snatches the pipe he is smoking out of his mouth.

"Ha! You are the famous Che Guevara!"

"Yes, I am Che! A minister of state too! And you're not going to treat me like that," answers the prisoner.

And with a quick movement of his foot he sends Espinosa flying into the benches against the wall. Colonel Selnich intervenes at that point. Che knows him—Selnich has already come in once to try to interrogate him. But Che refuses to speak to him or any of the other officers. The soldiers, though, he answers quietly.

Finally a medic is sent to him. "After having passed the entire afternoon in the combat zone and part of the evening with our wounded, I went to examine Che," medic Fernando Sanco told Jorge Torrico. "A single wound in the leg—the left leg. That was all he had. I washed it with a disinfectant."

After having tried vainly to interrogate the prisoner, Selnich decides to leave him alone. He has the guard outside reinforced. On Monday morning Che asks to see the *maestra*, the schoolmistress of the village.

Twenty-two-year-old Julia Cortez told Father Schiller: "I was afraid to go there, afraid he would be a brute. But instead I found an agreeable-looking man, with a soft and ironic glance . . . It was impossible for me to look him in the eye."

"Ah! you are the *maestra*. Do you know that there is no accent on the 'se' of *ya se leer*?" he says as a preface, pointing at one of the drawings that hangs on the wall. "You know that in Cuba there are no schools like this one. We would call this a prison. How can the children of the *campesinos* study here . . . It's antipedagogical."

"We live in a poor country," the schoolmistress replies.

"But the government officials and the generals have Mercedes cars and plenty of other things. ¿*Verdad*? That's what we are fighting against."

"You have come a long way to fight in Bolivia."

"I am a revolutionary and I've been in a lot of places."

"You have come to kill our soldiers."

"You know, a war is either lost or won."

The *maestra* repeated this conversation to Jorge Torrico. "I had to look down while I talked to him . . . his gaze was unbearable. Piercing . . . and so tranquil."

Around noon, Che calls her back again. He knows that he has only a few moments more to live, surely less than an hour. What does he want to tell her? Something important? She refuses to see him.

"I don't know why," she said to Schiller. "I regret it now. Maybe it was because of his eyes, because of the way he looked at me."

SINCE EARLY MORNING on the 9th helicopters have been coming and going. "It's hard to say who came, or when," the mayor of the village told Torrico. "Too much coming and going, too much movement. But I know that General Ovando was there, and General Lafuente, Colonel Zenteno, Rear Admiral Urgateche. And also a *gringo*. Wearing a uniform. Gonzales."

Eduardo Gonzales.

As he climbs out of the helicopter Urgateche rewards the Rangers for getting Che, handing out money to them.

Then all of the high-ranking officers file past this man who does not fear to die. Together and in turn, they try to make him talk. Rear Admiral Urgateche walks up. Suddenly he starts back, purple with anger. Che has spit in his face. Che knows that the interrogation is a mere formality—that the decision about what to do with him has already been made. His wrists bound, seated on his bench, his back to the wall, Che looks at them. He mocks them. Little by little their elation turns into an impotent rage. Who knows whether Che Guevara dead won't be even more dangerous than Ramón alive with the guerrillas? A little before 12:30 the superior officers depart by helicopter, leaving explicit orders.

During the morning another guerrilla, "Benjamín," has been taken prisoner in the Quebrada del Churo by another company of Rangers. He is brought to La Higuera, wounded and exhausted, and thrown into the other room with Willy. Some of my sources claimed that this was not Benjamín, but a man called "El Chino." Torrico and I could not decide on this point.

It is about 1:00 p.m. in La Higuera. Che has managed to make his way across the room and lean up against the opposite wall. The orders have come down to the junior officers. Three of them are competing for the "privilege and honor" of murdering Che. The door to the school opens and Mario Terán enters with his M-2 carbine on his hip. He paces to the other end of the room and turns around. "Sit down," he says.

"Why bother? You are going to kill me," Che answers calmly.

"No—sit down."

Terán makes as if to leave. Suddenly a burst of fire and Che crumples. Behind him, in the wall next to the door, the bullets have made two bloody holes, each as big as a fist.

Terán puts up his gun and calls outside: "That's it. I got him." Then (according to Father Schiller) he goes out to drink a beer.

Che lies on the floor in agony. Pérez comes into the room, a revolver in his hand. He walks over and puts a bullet in Che's neck. "A good hole for the formaldehyde," Doctor Moisés Abraham says the next day to the reporters in Vallegrande.

Two or three men have followed Pérez into the classroom. Now all of them want to fire on the adversary who has so long been invincible. "Okay," reportedly says the officer, "but not above the waist."

So they shoot him in the legs. Among them is the medic, Fernando Sanco, the one who had tended the captive's leg the night before.

In the next room, Willy and Benjamín have heard. When their door opens, they know the fate that awaits them. Sergeant Huanca enters with a gun in his hand; he faces the two men tied together on the floor.

"You have killed him," cries Willy, "I'd just as soon die, along with him."

Another burst of fire; Willy and the other fall to one side. On the wall, around the holes made by the bullets, there is blood mixed with hair.

In her house, 50 meters away, Julia Cortez, the schoolmistress, hears the gunshots. She rushes to the scene. The man she couldn't look at because he gave her a "bad conscience" is spread out in a pool of blood. Now she knows that all her life she will regret not having come back to talk to him.

Peasants come from all sides, mingling with the soldiers who are looking for stretchers to put the bodies on. There is great confusion. Those who know what has happened explain to the people who are arriving. In ten minutes everyone knows. And it is precisely for this reason that two months later the village is still quarantined.

An officer lifts Che's clothing and counts the wounds. Five in the legs, one in the left breast, one in the throat, one in the right shoulder, one in the right arm. Nine wounds, not seven as the doctors at Vallegrande will say.

It is three o'clock and the stretchers are next to the helicopters when Father Roger Schiller arrives on horseback. "As soon as I got the news that morning that Che had been taken alive, I hurried here, hoping to see him before they took him away. But when I arrived they had already shot him down." Then he say, without a great deal of conviction: "If I had been there perhaps they wouldn't have dared.

"I went to the school," continues the father. "It still hadn't been cleaned up. On the ground I found a bullet. Here. Look. It is shattered. I will keep it as a souvenir. The blood was mixed with earth. In the classroom where Willy and Benjamín were, blood was spattered all over. I cleaned it up."

At five o'clock in the evening Che's body arrives in Vallegrande strapped to the runner of a helicopter. Most of the Bolivian officers who had interrogated him in La Higuera have already arrived sometime during the morning. Ramos has been in Vallegrande all day long. Gonzales arrived in the early afternoon, in a helicopter coming from the direction of La Higuera. But when had he left La Higuera? Before Che was killed, or after? Did he stay to supervise the execution? I was never able to find out.

A Chevrolet panel truck is waiting on the airstrip at Vallegrande. Inside it are Ramos and Gonzales. As the helicopter lands, Ramos springs out of the truck and hastily directs the soldiers to load the corpse into the back. The truck races off to the morgue which has been improvised in a nearby shack. It stops. Ramos yells to Gonzales: "Let's get the hell out of here" . . . in English . . . letting down for one telltale moment their carefully maintained anonymity. The disguise is quickly reestablished, however, and Ramos refuses to speak another word of English to the journalists who are arriving on the scene.

Inside the shack, Ramos quietly directs the operations. He helps the doctors inject formaldehyde into the corpse, and he takes the dead man's fingerprints, comparing them with those in the dossier. (The news dispatch sent by Chris Roper of Reuters mentioned the presence of a CIA agent at the morgue. But the paragraph was cut from most American papers.)

After October 10 the traces of the CIA in Bolivia fade out. Ramos was spotted once two days later at a hotel in La Paz, registered once more as a businessman. After this, nothing. Che is dead. They can return to Panama and seal his dossier: mission accomplished. All of the men, money and time used against the small, isolated hand of guerrillas has paid off.

## [v. made in the u.s.a.]

I MUST HAVE asked too many questions while reconstructing the story of how they shot down Che, for the last week of my stay in Bolivia was particularly hectic. The French Embassy and the manager of my hotel received three or four anonymous calls every day threatening my person and advising me to get out of the country as soon as possible.

I arrived at the airport followed by the French consul. He had orders from the ambassador not to leave me until I was safe and sound on a plane out of Bolivia. Before I could board the plane, the Bolivian authorities insisted on painstakingly searching my person and all my possessions. At that very moment, Jorge Torrico, who had given me so much information, was peacefully registering for Lima and Paris, acting as if he did not know me in the slightest.

President Barrientos, on his way to New York, put in the last word for the Bolivian government: "The French señorita has spent a very agreeable and peaceful visit in our country and I don't think she could have had time to inform herself."

But despite the President's certainty, subsequent digging allowed me to "inform" myself in even greater detail about the roles of the CIA men, Ramos and Gonzales.

As the net of American-trained and advised Bolivians tightened around Che, both men arrived on the scene to oversee his capture and execution. On August 5, they came to Santa Cruz, registering at the Hotel Santa Cruz as businessmen. Felix Ramos, aged 26, carried passport No. 0152052; Eduardo Gonzales, 32, carried No. A8093737. They left the hotel on August 12 and were identified by British journalists in Vallegrande some days later—in the company of Major "Pappy" Shelton. At this time they had dropped their cover. No longer posing as businessmen, they wore military uniforms without identifying insignias, with revolvers strapped to their waists.

Ramos and Gonzales were again in Vallegrande at the end of September, making that city the base of their operations and flying periodically to La Esperanza. All the testimony I have gathered has placed

Ramos in Vallegrande all day on October 9 and Gonzales in La Higuera that morning. Whether or not Gonzales ordered the manner and time of Che's murder, it is clear that he flew into La Higuera to make sure that the revolutionary hero died, that his fantastic career was finished once and for all.

The murder of Che was a symbol of the power of the United States throughout Latin America. But as far as the U.S. operations in Bolivia were concerned, it was only a bonus. For in Bolivia the U.S. counterinsurgency campaign has been well-established for years. The United States has pumped $15 million in military aid into Bolivia since 1962 and maintains a permanent military mission in La Paz.

Since 1965 the American "advisors" have trained a number of Bolivian regiments. Many Bolivian officers have been trained in Panama, and some, like Gary Prado, at Fort Bragg by the Special Forces. The operation at La Esperanza, however, dated only from April 1967, and was initiated as a direct result of the first engagement between the guerrillas and government troops at the end of March.

For the guerrillas (although they were not yet contemplating real military operations) hostilities began on March 11, 1967, when two of their men deserted. One of these said later in written testimony that he had come to the guerrillas to gather information, thinking that he could profit by denouncing them. Their statements also included a very schematic outline of the organization of the movement, the names of the guerrillas and, of course, the presence of "Ramón."

As soon as it got this information, the Army began to mobilize the campaign against the guerrillas. On March 16 it seized the home of Coco Peredo. On the 20th, Che, who had come to the central camp from a reconnaissance mission in the neighborhood of Vallegrande, made the decision to defend the area against every incursion of the Army. Although the Army was surprised tactically by the "ambush," strategically the guerrillas remained permanently on the defensive.

The encounter was a setback for the Army—seven soldiers were killed. Less than eight days after the ambush, a group of American military men from Panama, including the intelligence chief of the 8th Special Forces, visited the guerrilla area and conferred with Barrientos.

The first move of the U.S. was to increase the arms shipments to the Bolivians and to secure their supply lines. C-130 transports coming from Panama landed regularly in Santa Cruz, bringing small arms, radio equipment, napalm and medical supplies. At the same time, three-week training courses were hurriedly organized for Bolivian soldiers in the combat zone. Less than eight days after that first ambush on March 23, a photo published in the Bolivian press showed two Green Berets training Bolivians at Lagunillas, a few miles south of Casa de la Calamina, formerly the guerrillas' own training center.

American military operations in Bolivia started in earnest around the 12th of April when a 16-man team of Green Berets arrived from the Canal Zone to set up shop at La Esperanza under the command of "Pappy" Shelton. Their mission, as reported in the Bolivian press, was to train a handpicked battalion of Rangers in counterinsurgency tactics designed specifically for the Bolivian *selva*. "El Soldadito," as the common soldier is called in Bolivia, had to be transformed into "El Ranger." His nationality would remain the same, but his mentality and training were "made in the U.S.A."

The team of Green Berets, according to American Ambassador Henderson—who is anxious to maintain appearances—was under strict instructions not to enter the guerrilla zone itself and not to participate in the fighting. And, for the most part, these instructions seem to have been followed. However, radio contact was maintained between La Esperanza and the staff of the 8th Bolivian Division, and, from September 27th on, with the 2nd Ranger Battalion in the field.

All in all, American military intervention in Bolivia was remarkably "clean." All the dirty work could be left to the CIA agents. And—controlling the operation from the beginning, using a ruthless overkill to make the trap lethal—they were successful. Their plot to see Che Guevara dead worked with machine-like precision from the moment the machinery was put into operation. Their efficiency was almost uncanny. In April the *London Times* correspondent in Bolivia reported that "American military here say it will take six months to turn out a fully trained Bolivian battalion for jungle fighting."

Six months later Che was dead. A model exercise in counterinsurgency. "Create two, three . . . many Bolivias"—that is the watchword at the Pentagon.

But, revolutions are made by conditions, not by men. "This great humanity has said 'enough'": it will not soon forget Che Guevara.

# COMMANDER GUEVARA'S MANY WATCHES

## PACO IGNACIO TAIBO II

from *GUEVARA, ALSO KNOWN AS CHE*

1997

T IS SOMEWHAT surprising that a man who in life showed such detachment from material possessions should have left such a trail of belongings behind in death—things that he lived with, things that belonged to him . . . and things that may have belonged to him.

In Cuba, Che's belongings are venerated as the secular equivalent of saintly relics. In the entrance to the offices of *Verde Olivo*, there is a small display case containing the camera that Che loaned the staff in 1960, and later gave to them. It's an ordinary 35-millimeter Exacta. Visitors invariably stop in front of the display and then raise their eyes to a photo of a smiling Che.

Lina González, an old campesino woman from the Cuban village Lomas del Pedrero, showed journalist Mariano Rodriguez "the stool, the table, and the little cup where he sat and drank coffee."

In Cabaiguán, Cuba, there is a municipal museum dedicated to Che, where visitors can see the plaster cast he had on his fractured left arm during the final days of the battle of Santa Clara. How did it get there? Is it real? As it happens, the cast went with him all the way to the triumphant entry into Havana, and there are photographs that show his arm still in plaster in the La Cabaña fortress. How did the cast find its way back to Cabaiguán?

Several years ago in Cuba, an exhibition of objects related to with the guerrilla campaign in Bolivia was held in the Museum of the Revolution, but "Tania's" jeep was not Tania's, nor did the socks—"thin ones, like those used in Cuban Army dress uniforms"—belong to Che. A survivor of the Bolivian guerrilla campaign told me indignantly: "Che wore thick stockings, bought in France, and those socks [in the exhibit] were nice and new, whereas Che's were torn and stiff, because he never used to wash his feet."

Just like splinters from the True Cross, or good luck charms, Che's belongings inspire a quasi-religious quest among friend and foe alike, a friendly veneration, an unscrupulous traffic and a whole host of ridiculous frauds.

The trade in Che's scant possessions got under way immediately after his capture, between La Higuera (where, as the poet Enrique Lihn said, Che "has set up his posthumous headquarters"), Vallegrande, and La Paz. A mentality that was a combination of looting lust, war booty collecting, and fetishism, which made first the military and then the nearby civilians steal anything they could lay their hands on that had once belonged to Che. U.S. dollars, Bolivian pesos, and Canadian dollars were shared out in La Higuera, behind the backs of the commanding officers. Che's Parker pen found its way into the hands of a sergeant major, who ended up trading it with a journalist for a set of photos. The man who picked up by Che's marriage ring turned his hand to making copies of it, which he was still selling years later. The wrecked M2 rifle landed in Colonel Zenteno's hands; the word is that he gave it to General Alfredo Ovando, to score some brownie points. One of Che's pipes was filched by Colonel Selich, the other by Sergeant Bernardino Huanca. No one, meanwhile, wanted Che's sandals, which were pieces of leather cobbled together with bits of string to replace his lost boots.

Nothing, however, came to have as many simultaneous owners as Che's watch.

When he was captured, Commander Guevara was wearing two Rolex Perpetual Oysters, his own and the one that had belonged to his assistant, Carlos Coello, who gave it to Che moments before he died. The soldiers who captured him took both of them. Che told Captain Prado about this during the latter's first visit to the schoolhouse in La Higuera. Prado summoned the soldiers and retrieved the two watches.

"Here's your watches. Hang on to them, nobody will take them off you."

Che answered that he preferred that they be held in safekeeping for him; if anything should happen to him, he wanted them given to "my folks." Prado asked Che to point out which was his, so he marked the back of one with an "X," using a small stone. Prado hung on to Che's watch, and gave Carlos Coello's to Major Ayoroa.

That was as far as the official version went, but Cortez, the telegraph operator at La Higuera, saw Colonel Selich take Che's watch off his wrist while the prisoner's hands were tied. CIA agent Félix Rodríguez told how he obtained Che's watch by tricking a soldier who had taken it off him; Rodriguez said he placed it on his wrist as the helicopter took off from the town of La Higuera, but in his account the Rolex Perpetual Oyster has turned into a GT Master. The journalist Luis Suárez, meanwhile, maintained that Sergeant Bernardino Huanca came by Che's Rolex by stripping it from his body.

Others attribute ownership to General Alfredo Ovando: in another version, the most fantastic, the watch covers thousands of miles, from the corpse to the doctor who performed the autopsy, and from the doctor to his son, who handed it over to settle a bar debt in the Mexican city of Puebla.

# CHE GUEVARA: "THE BEST WAY TO DIE"

## JOSE YGLESIAS

*THE NATION*

NOVEMBER 6, 1967

L ET US ASSUME that Che Guevara is dead. Simply because of the photographs. A week of news reports made clear only that we are uneasily dependent on Bolivian army generals, backed up in the matter of fingerprint identification, by Argentinian authorities. It is something like having a press release of Sen. Joe McCarthy's confirmed by Senator Eastland. As I write, the Bolivians, who first buried, then cremated Che are saying that they cut off his hands and have kept them. Shocking but perfectly right—like a surprising turn in a Dostoevski novel—and a reminder of the kind of mentality that our special forces are training in the suppression of revolutionary guerrillas. Someone should tell the Bolivian generals—someone steeped in their medieval tradition—that these hands, like Saint Teresa's, may well be with us for a long time: to strengthen the nonreligious but barefoot Order—like Saint Teresa's stoical Carmelites—of the guerrillas of South America.

Responding to a newspaper's nagging need to have an editorial opinion, *The New York Times* began theirs: "If Ernesto Che Guevara *was* really killed in Bolivia, as now seems probable, a myth as well as a man has been laid to rest." The *Times* editorials are usually more prescient about Latin American developments, but this time, after its opening qualifying phrase, the paper threw caution to the winds. Also, its style book. That it accepts Guevara's nickname as a middle name and doesn't surround it with quotation marks is inadvertent evidence of how well Che has captured our imagination. The nickname Che — Argentinian for *fella, buddy, mate* or this generation's *man* — was given to him by the Cubans and accepted by the world: the spirit of this Everyman is going to be difficult to lay to rest.

IT IS A death that Che has often rehearsed, turned over in his mind, gone out to meet. After two years of silence he sent a message to Cuba for publication last April in the first number of the magazine of the Tri-Continental Organization, of which OLAS is a regional group. In it, he analyzed the world political situation and argued for the creation in the Third World of "two, three, many Vietnams." The last paragraphs of the message turn, in a very personal way, to his own role, and end with a perfectly cadenced Spanish sentence: "Wherever death surprises us, welcome be it, so long as this, our battle cry, reaches a receptive ear and another hand stretches out to grasp our arms and other men lend their voices to funeral songs accompanied by the rattle of machine guns and new cries of war and victory."

Two years earlier, when he first left Cuba, he also wrote letter to his mother and father, published in Cuba this year, in which he tells them of his decision. His tone is lighter, but he must tell them that there are real dangers he may not survive. He recalls, however, that when he embarked on the *Granma* from Mexico to invade Cuba he was an untried doctor and soldier. Now, he adds, he is no longer interested in the first and is "not a bad soldier." Then carefully, without sentimentality, he tells them how much he loves them, for he fears that as a young man he was rigid in his ways and difficult to understand and may not have made his feelings clear.

The story of how he became "not a bad soldier" is also the story of how he became a man who could make his feelings clear. (Only by never quoting him have newspaper men been able to give him a reputation for toughness.) When the eighty men of the *Granma* came ashore in Cuba, late and off-course, they were forced to march through swamps, where they lost their equipment, and arrived at a cane field the next day, hungry, their feet a mass of sores. A peasant guide betrayed them and, in the open, they were attacked by the Batista army and air force. Che was wounded and only twelve of the eighty were to survive. During that moment, when everything seemed lost, I started to think of the best way to die," he wrote in *Episodes of the Revolutionary War*. "I remembered an old story by Jack London in which the protagonist, leaning on the trunk of a tree, tries to face death with dignity . . . It's the only image I remember."

In his letter to Fidel Castro two years ago, Che said: "Other lands claim my modest efforts." Last winter, in the section of northern Oriente Province where I spent three months, Cubans used to repeat it to me, and then ask: "What do you think of our Che?" It was a rhetorical question, one that they asked when they wanted the conversation to take an agreeable turn. It was not simply that they knew him personally but that he symbolized the whole revolutionary stance of Cuba: in Fidel Castro's words, that the duty of a revolutionary is to make the revolution.

IT WOULD HAVE surprised those people who lived near or worked in the nickel processing plant at Nicaro or the manganese plant at Moa that Guevara had in the *Times* editorial's words, "soured in the more sober responsibilities of helping to build a post-revolutionary Cuba." They knew that it was while he was Minister of Industry that Nicaro was brought to full production and that Moa, built by the U.S. Government and never operated, became without even a blueprint for guidance, the most lucrative industry in the country. He tramped up and down the hills where the minerals were mined; every truck driver and railroad man knew him. At Nicaro, later they put up a sign at the entrance to the plant: "The only way to leave the country with dignity is to take the path that Che took." I understand that the same statement can be read at the airport in Varadero, at the other end of the island, where the daily plane load of exiles leaves for Miami.

On Monday, April 17, it was difficult to find a newspaper in Cuba, for they carried the full text of his message and the photographs of him with his beard shaved off, in shirt and tie, in fatigues but still clean-shaven and finally, in fatigues with his new beard. None of it disappointed my friends in Oriente; the photographs delighted them, the text reminded them of his straightforward truth telling. "There is a sad reality," he wrote. "Vietnam, this nation that represents the aspirations, the hopes of a whole disinherited world, is tragically alone. . . . The solidarity of the progressive world with Vietnam resembles the bitter irony that the cheers of the plebes held for the gladiators in the Roman arenas."

"Isn't that just like Che!" everyone said.

The *Times* editorial also said that Che's effort "was doomed to fail because he violated a basic revolutionary tenet—that a successful guer-rilla movement requires strong indigenous roots and leadership. . . . Che Guevara's death should shatter the illusions of those who, like Fidel Castro, still think revolution is for export." The *Times* might have remembered Simon Bolívar, but it should have known that Che had considered this point in his message:

> There is so great an identity among the classes of these coun-tries that they achieve an identity of an "international American" type . . . Language, customs, religion, a common boss, unite them."

He proposed a guerrilla war that would openly fight for socialism, for he was certain that the national bourgeoisies of Latin America are incapable of fighting for national independence. He was aware that among Communists there are enormous differences world-wide about tactics and strategy, and said it was useless to try to end them with words; only when they weaken the tactics of struggle should they be analyzed and discussed. However—"About the grand strategic objec-tive—the total destruction of imperialism—we must be intransigent."

There is a somber tone, and many terrible prophecies in this last section that leads to his final, personal statement:

> Many shall die victims of their errors, others shall fall in the hard combat that draws near; new fighters and new leaders will rise from the heat of the revolutionary fight.
>
> And the combats shall not be mere street fights of rocks against tear gas, nor peaceful general strikes; nor will it be the fight of an enraged populace that in two or three days will destroy the repressive organs of the governing oligarchies it shall be a long, bloody struggle, whose fronts will be in the guerrilla hide-outs in the cities, in the homes of the fighters—where the repression will seek out easy victims in their families—in the massacred

peasant population, in villages and cities destroyed by enemy bombings.

And, I repeat it once more, a cruel war. Let no one have any illusions when he starts it and let no one hesitate to start it for fear of the results that it can bring to his people. This is almost our only hope of victory.

It is a strange voice to hear so far from the world of which it speaks. A voice repellent to our comfort and our common sense—thank God, he looks for no recruits amongst us. His is a revolutionary ideology in which death and tragedy occupy, close in the foreground, an unwanted, redemptive place. For a moment one draws close to the *Times* editorial writer and to the news stories that immediately told us that the guerrilla movement has failed.

But wait—in that day's batch of meager news that said all that remains of Che is his hands, there was one item that reported a new clash had occurred in the mountains of Bolivia between the army and a band of guerrillas.

# PART

## seven
## ICON

"You know how much I admire Che Guevara. In fact, I believe that the man was not only an intellectual but also the most complete human being of our age: as a fighter and as a man, as a theoretician who was able to further the cause of revolution by drawing his theories from his personal experience in battle."

## —JEAN-PAUL SARTRE

# MAGICAL DEATH
# FOR A MAGICAL LIFE

## EDUARDO GALEANO

from *WE SAY NO: CHRONICLES 1963–1991*

### 1992

"I BELIEVE ARMED STRUGGLE is the only solution for peoples who are struggling to be free, and I live in accordance with my beliefs. Many will call me an adventurer, and I am. Except I'm an adventurer of a different sort, one who risks his skin to test his beliefs. This adventure might be the definitive one. I'm not looking for it, but it falls within the logical calculation of probability. If that is the case, here is a final embrace. I've loved you very much. I just haven't known how to express my affection. I'm extremely rigid in my behavior and I think sometimes you did not understand. It wasn't easy to understand me. But if only for today, believe in me. I've polished my will with the delight of an artist, and it should sustain these flaccid legs and tired lungs. I will do it. . . . Remember every so often this little twentieth-century *condottiere*."

Che Guevara wrote these lines to his parents a short time before he dropped out of view. By the time the letter arrived in Buenos Aires, his mother, Celia, had already died without seeing her son. She did not receive this "final embrace," this goodbye that foretold the news that has just shaken the entire world. "In the laborious work of revolutionaries, death is a frequent accident," Che once wrote regarding the death of an intimate friend. His letter to the Tricontinental Congress ends with a salute to impending death, as long as death announces "new cries of war and victory." A thousand times he said dying was so very possible, yet so insignificant. He knew well: after his successive deaths and resurrections, he himself claimed to have seven lives. He used up the seventh as he had planned. *He entered into death asking neither permission nor forgiveness*: he led his men forth to face the bullets of the surrounding army in the dusty ravine of Yuro. Machine-gun fire pierced his legs but he kept shooting for a while, seated, until a well-placed blow blasted his M-I from his hands. A large group of soldiers captured him alive, despite the efforts of the few surviving guerrillas who from the middle of the afternoon until nightfall found the courage to fight hand to hand for the wounded man. Later they were exhibited at his side, their heads destroyed by gun butts, their bodies slashed open by bayonets. After the battle, after a full night and day in the Higueras Valley military camp, the wait grew unbearable. Finally, the order arrived from the government palace to kill the prisoner.

STILL WARM, THE body was tied to the runners of a helicopter and carried up through a cloudless sky over the inhospitable sun-beaten terrain where the mountains open toward the Amazon Basin. In the Lord of Malta Hospital in the village of Valle-grande, Che's body was shown to a group of journalists and photographers. Later it disappeared, along with a chubby bald man who gave orders in English. He had injected the body with a liter of formaldehyde. Bolivia's President Barrientos said Che had been buried, while General Ovando said he had been cremated—in a place without the means to do it. They announced that they had cut off his hands. The Bolivian government ended up with a few embalmed fingers and a photocopy of the guerrilla's diary; the destination of the body and the original diary is secret or legend.

So filled with hallucination and mystery were his life and death that innumerable legends have been woven about this hero of our times. Several legends, a few, are the fruit of the boundless capacity for infamy of certain fools who threw themselves like crows on the memory of dead Che, although they would never have withstood the gaze of Che alive. Others, nearly all, grew out of the people's imagination, which celebrates the immortality of the fallen hero on the infinite and invisible altars of our Latin America.

"AT THAT MOMENT, when everything seemed lost, I started thinking about the best way to die. I remembered an old story by Jack London in which the protagonist, leaning against a tree trunk, prepares to end his life with dignity." Che wrote this remembering a decisive moment amid the butchery that followed the landing of the Granma on the coasts of eastern Cuba. Eleven years have passed since that first brush with death. Now I look at the wire-service photos one by one. They present the body from all angles, the holes where the lead penetrated his flesh, the ironic and tender smile, proud and full of compassion, which more than one fool confused with a rictus of cruelty. I can't help but stare at that wonderful face of a Jesus from the River Plate. And I want to congratulate him.

The day of his baptism by fire, in a place called Alegría de Pío in Cuba, Che made a decision that would forever mark his destiny: "I had a knapsack full of medicines and a case of bullets. Together they weighed too much to carry. I picked up the bullets, leaving the knapsack behind as I crossed the clearing to the canefield." In the farewell letter to his parents, Che himself wrote that "almost ten years ago I wrote you another farewell. As I remember it, I regretted not being a better soldier or a better doctor. I'm no longer interested in the latter. As a soldier I don't do badly."

He chose to be on the front lines of the revolution, and he chose it for keeps, without even allowing himself the benefit of the doubt or the right to repent. *This is the unheard-of case of a man who abandons a successful revolution he made along with a handful of crazies, to throw himself into launching another.* He didn't live for victory, but for the struggle, the ever-necessary unending struggle against indignity and hunger. And he didn't even turn his head to look back at the lovely fire rising from the bridges he had burned.

His asthma wasn't the cause, as one Buenos Aires daily claimed, nor was it the oblique and sophisticated resentment of an impoverished patrician, as a widely read magazine insinuated: Che's embrace of solidarity can easily be traced in his life. And that word, *solidarity*, offers the only key to understanding him, even though it is absent from the dictionaries used by the scribes of the system.

An infinite number of possibilities lay before the eyes of young Ernesto Guevara when he came down from the sierra of Córdoba to the asphalt of Buenos Aires. He worked twelve hours a day, six to support himself and another six as a volunteer. He was a brilliant medical student, but at the same time he read treatises on advanced mathematics, wrote poetry, and began ambitious projects of archaeological research. When he was seventeen he started writing a "Dictionary of Philosophy," because he found that he and other students needed one. In 1950, a photograph of Che, who at that time signed his name Ernesto Guevara Serna, appeared in an advertisement in *El Gráfico*. The ad quoted a letter he had written to Micrón, a company that made motors for bicycles. In it, Che reported that he had traveled four thousand kilometers through twelve of Argentina's provinces, and that the motor had worked well. Now Armando March, a union leader and boyhood friend of Che's, recalls that while Ernesto was a student, his mother had an operation — they suspected a tumor on her breast. Ernesto set up an improvised laboratory in his home and experimented feverishly with guinea pigs and pipettes and oil solutions to try to save her life. Che and March had wanted to go to Paraguay to fight against the dictator Morínigo. Intelligent and multifaceted, with an innate seductive power that his life would only confirm and augment, young Ernesto Guevara was not a coddled and resentful kid. He was a young man open to adventure, with no clear political ideas and with a marked inclination to prove to himself that *he could do everything he could not do*. The continuous asthma attacks, which for years obliged his father to sleep sitting up so that his son could spend the night leaning on his chest, did not keep him from playing soccer and rugby, though at the end of the game his teammates would often have to carry him from the field. Asthma kept him from going to school after the fourth grade, but he managed to take his exams on his own, and later on in high school he got excellent grades. The war against asthma was the first war Che fought and won: he won it insofar as he never let asthma make any decisions for him.

This great warrior of Latin America was rejected as unfit for military service by the Argentine army. That was when Che crossed the Andes on a motorcycle and, drawn by the legend of Machu Picchu, reached Peru by foot. The residents of a leper colony then built a raft for him and his friend Alberto Granados, which they rode from the heart of the Brazilian jungle to Colombia. In Iquitos they worked as soccer coaches. Che got deported from Bogotá and ended up on a plane carrying thoroughbred horses to Miami. Some time later he made a second trip through Latin America, to Bolivia, to the streets of La Paz, where miners were marching triumphantly with dynamite caps in their belts — and later to Guatemala. "We couldn't see Che in Ernesto Guevara," Guatemalan revolutionaries who had known him told me years later. He was nothing more than a bureaucrat in the agrarian reform ministry, or an Argentine lying sick in his bed in a rooming house full of Peruvian exiles from APRA, Peru's eternal opposition. However, in Guatemala, Ernesto Guevara discovered Che. He discovered himself in the euphoria and defeat of the Guatemalan revolution, in the achievements and mistakes of a process of reform in progress, and in the helpless rage that accompanied the fall of Arbenz. Paradoxically, it was a ship of the United Fruit's White Fleet that took Guevara to Central America, where his true passion for socialism emerged.

He could have been a distinguished doctor in Buenos Aires' elegant Barrio Norte, or a prestigious specialist in blood or skin disease, a professional politician or a highly esteemed expert in any technical field. He could have been a fascinating café charlatan, as brilliant as he was derisive and excessive, or a jaded adventurer for adventure's sake. Years later, he could have remained the idolized leader of a revolution consecrated by success. The right always loves to put revolutionaries on the psychoanalyst's couch, to diagnose rebelliousness by reducing it to the clinical analysis of some original frustration, as if militancy and commitment were nothing more than the result of some bottle not being served on time, or the impossible love for Mommy. But Che was a living example of how revolution is the purest form of fraternity and human dignity, and also the hardest, the most difficult. His was not the pathological catharsis of a lad from a wealthy family in decline, but an act of continuous generosity: very few people in the history of our time have renounced so much so often, in return for one or two hopes, and he asked nothing for himself but to be the first at times of sacrifice and danger, and the last at the moment of recompense and security. Very few men have had such good alibis with which to soothe the conscience: the asthma that harassed him ceaselessly or the very important role he played in the construction of socialism in Cuba. Even he admitted how hard it was for him at times to climb a mountain during the days in the Sierra Maestra. "At those moments, I remember how hard the peasant Crespo worked to get me to walk. When I couldn't go on and I'd ask them to leave me behind, he would use that special vocabulary of our troops: "Shitty Argentine, walk or this gun butt will make sure you do." Despite the asthma, Che became a minister of the revolution capable of cutting cane or driving tractors with his face swollen from cortisone and an inhalator tied to his belt. In the same way, he was the revolutionary instructor Colonel Bayo's best student in Mexico, when Fidel Castro's men were training for the invasion. (In Mexico, Che earned a living taking children's pictures in the plazas and selling little stamps of the Virgin of Guadalupe; when the government tried to deport him, he fled from the airport and made contact with his comrades again.)

Before Mexico, he had already begun another secret war, the struggle against cynicism and the inability to believe which seems inherent to the excessive spirit of the people of the River Plate, particularly the *porteños* of Buenos Aires. When he heard a loud bunch of Cuban youths in a café in Costa Rica talk about the attack on the Moncada and the coming revolution against Batista, Che commented, "Why don't they tell another cowboy story?" In Mexico some time later, those same young people introduced him to a big man who had just been released from Isle of Pines prison. His name was Fidel Castro.

Recently, in Buenos Aires, I had the unwarranted privilege of reading the letter that Che's mother tried to send him shortly before her death, and that never reached him because Che had already disappeared. As if sensing her own impending death, in that letter the mother announced that she would tell him what she had to as naturally as she could and that he ought to answer the same way: "I don't know if we have lost the frankness with which we used to speak, or if we never had it, and we've always spoken in that somewhat ironic tone characteristic of everyone who lives on the shores of the River Plate, aggravated by our own family code that is even more closed. . . ." Che must have insinuated something about his next destination, because in the other paragraph Celia says, ". . . Yes, you would always be a foreigner. That seems to be your destiny."

A CLOSE FRIEND of Che's mother defined it this way: "Che's intimates and girlfriends in Córdoba are now a legion, if you are to believe them. At two kisses a doorway, it would have taken him his entire life. But the truth is that he had tremendous magnetism. You know what I mean?

That boy who listened to Vivaldi, read Heidegger, and set off to see America was tempted by practically every path. I think it was Trotsky, I'm not sure, who said that the most revered revolutionary is he who could have chosen something else instead of the revolution, and yet *prefers it.* Ever since then, solitude somehow became an obligation. The only profound relationship he could accept was with the revolution itself. He always had a deep need for completeness and purity."

This man who had all the doors of professional and personal success open to him became the most puritan of Western revolutionary leaders. In Cuba, he was the Jacobin of the revolution: "Watch out, Che's coming," Cubans would say in jest, but meaning it. That need for completeness and purity became, then, an incomparable capacity for personal sacrifice. He was intransigent with himself to the extreme of not allowing himself a single weakness, a single step in the wrong direction, so as to be able to demand as much from others. He didn't have the flexibility of Fidel Castro, who proved his aptitude for political negotiations by dealing with God and the Devil long before he took power. After he became a guerrilla, Che seemed to live according to the motto *All or nothing.* It's not hard to imagine the exhausting battles with the temptations of doubt this refined intellectual must have fought to achieve at last that steely certainty, that astonishing rigor.

"HE IS PERHAPS the most fascinating Latin American legend since El Dorado," writes the *Times* of London. A Falangist daily in Madrid compares him to the conquistadores in the huge scale of his undertaking, and *Azul y Blanco*, the organ of right-wing nationalism in Argentina, affirms that he was "a hero of the nineteenth century." Fidel Castro says he never will be able to speak of him in the past tense, and General Ovando himself admits that he was "a hero in any part of the world." Bolivia's President René Barrientos, wisely termed "an idiot" by Che in his war diary, declares that "an idealist has died." The priest Hernán Benítez, who was Evita Perón's confessor, exalts the figure of the fallen leader in these terms: "Like the Jews of the Old Testament who believed the prophet Elijah to be alive, the Spaniards of the Middle Ages and El Cid, the Galicians and Artús, it is also possible that in years to come the guerrilla soldiers of the Third World will believe they feel the hallucinating presence of Che Guevara amid the clamor of battle."

The pens for hire, meanwhile, have not lost the opportunity to exhibit their capacity for infamy. One Argentine magazine suggests that Che was the assassin of Cuban revolutionary leader Camilo Cienfuegos; another affirms that he's better dead than alive, since that way it's clear that terror is not the road to progress for Latin America; a third expresses surprise that guerrillas are not the product of the West, but of "communist countries." I imagine Che, with a slightly bitter smile, setting aside all this luxuriously printed verbiage that offends both one's intelligence and one's sensibilities.

I think of those true words of Paul Nizan: "There is no great work that is not an accusation of the world." The life of Che Guevara, so perfectly affirmed by his death, is, like every great work, an accusation of our world.

# DEATH AND INFLUENCE
## ANDREW SINCLAIR

from *CHE GUEVARA*

1970

N DEATH, CHE has had more influence than when he was alive. Dead men may tell no tales, but they can make a legend. Che was not only one of the more heroic men of his age; he was also one of the more intelligent, more original, more ascetic, more radical, more human, and most beautiful men of his age. His face has launched a thousand turmoils, his words a hundred revolts. He has provided the Marxists with their first saint, who has dedicated his life and death to the poorest of men without help from God. The walls of the student halls of the world are chalked with the words, CHE LIVES. His martyrdom has been the condition for his inspiration of the young. He may have died for the poor, but he also died for the future.

More immediately, Che's death coincided with the full fury of the Red Guard movement in Mao's China. With Che as their personal symbol and the Red Guards as their general model, many of the students of the world revolted in 1968. The events of 1968 were curiously similar to those of 1848, when a wave of insurrection swept through most of the capital cities of Europe and ended in the victory of the powers that were. The chief difference between the student revolts of 1968 and the middle-class revolts of 1848 lay in the form of the new inspiration. For both Che and the Red Guards were inspired by the concept of a rural revolt that would sweep up out of the countryside to purge the corruption of the cities. The middle-class students who fought in the streets of Paris during the May Revolution, or of Chicago during the Democratic Convention, or of Berlin or London or Buenos Aires or Tokyo or Mexico City or twenty other cities during the year after Che's death came from an urban or suburban setting. They did not want to know of their misconception of Che's and Mao's thought. Yet Mao was to remind them, when he sent off twenty million of the Red Guards back to labor in the countryside. As the *New China Daily* told the parents of Chinese youth, "The greatest love one can give one's sons and daughters is to encourage them to go to the front line of production and to temper themselves in the countryside . . . through re-education by the poor peasants."

The governments of the world won in 1968. In Latin America, nearly all the guerrilla risings were suppressed. In communist and capitalist countries, in developed and in underdeveloped countries, the protest of the young was defeated by the power of the old. Harsher measures were taken in Kenya as well as in Czechoslovakia, in Mexico as well as in France, in China as well as in the United States. It was a global reaction against a global revolt, partially inspired by Che's death. But just as Bolívar failed five times before succeeding in Latin America, and Che himself failed three times in Guatemala and the Congo and Bolivia for his one success in Cuba, so the failure of the revolts of 1968 did not mean the end of revolts. For Che's most explosive idea was that the revolution is permanent and that it creates itself. Authority has not sat safe in its seats since that heresy reached the minds of the young.

The reasons for the cult of Che Guevara are both personal and cultural. In himself, he came from a bourgeois, white, prosperous, educated, suburban background, as do so many of the new middle-class student revolutionary leaders of our time, who despair of the capacity of the old-style Communist parties and labor unions to lead any sort of revolution at all. These new radicals find it easy to identify with Che. What he did and tried to do makes the impossible for them possible. He was not a product of historical necessity. He was a revolutionary who chose to be so. Thus his example gives hope to all those, such as Régis Debray, who wish to work for the poor and the lost of the world without having been born black or oppressed or under-privileged. Birth did not make Che. He was self-made.

While the revolutionary remains the hero of our times, no other revolutionary hero will supplant Che. The rapid development of his cult after his death was the logical outcome of the end of his life, which had been spent in an atmosphere of secrecy, mystery, potency, and combat. Che's cowardly murder brought him instant consecration, because his death made certain all the qualities ascribed to him. His choice to leave Cuba and his martyrdom for his cause set him above Fidel Castro or Ho Chi Minh or Mao Tse-tung as a symbol of revo-lution, even though his talents as a guerrilla leader may have been inferior. If Che had remained in Cuba or had died accidentally like Camilo Cienfuegos, his portrait would not be paraded by students all over the world, his example would not be quoted everywhere, his works would not be so widely read. Not only Marxists, but almost all pro-gressives, and even pacifists who qualify their admiration for Che by warning that they disagree with some of his methods, would agree with Fidel's praise of Che's qualities as a man: "If we wish to express what we want the men of future generations to be, we must say: 'Let them be like Che.' "

In every cult there is an element of the untrue and the irrational. In the cult of Che, that element is his identification with Christ. Because he fought for the poor and because he chose to be sacrificed in his prime, he gives a mystical feeling that he died for *us*, for all humanity. Clearly, he killed other men. Clearly, he hated his enemies. Clearly, his beliefs stemmed from political doctrines loathsome to many. Clearly, he advocated and used tactics that were sometimes dubious or inhuman. Clearly, he was a man who lived in his muck and sweat like a beast in the jungle. Yet clearly, he transcends all these facts. He appears as larger than a human being, as somebody approach-ing a savior. When all is said and done, when his words and acts have been coldly seen and sometimes condemned, the conviction remains that Che was always driven by his love for humanity and for the good in mankind. The ideals expressed in his writings, his whole life and his passion and his death, transcend ideology. The photograph of his corpse now is pinned as an icon in many country homes across Catholic Latin America.

Sartre was correct when he called Che "the most complete man of his age." There was a Renaissance quality about Che; he had more careers in thirty-nine years than a whole squad of men have in their lives, and he had more lives than any litter of cats. He tried to be professional in everything he did, as a doctor, a diarist, a political and military theorist, a guerrilla fighter, an economist, a tactician, a banker, a planner, an industrialist, an ambassador, a propagandist, and as the doer of all his other duties. But he was complete in more than his work. He was all in one piece. He seems to have had hardly any contradictions or inner conflicts. He was amazingly consistent in all he said and thought and did. The professional administrator who discussed the economy of Latin America was no different from the guerrilla hero in Bolivia who had decided that combat was the only way of solving his continent's social and economic problems. The difference between Che and other men was that Che did not let other men put his ideas into practice. He practiced them himself.

There was no duality between Che's actions and his words. The writer practiced what he preached and put other intellectuals to shame. The man of action set down his experiences and analyzed them to draw practical and moral conclusions from them. The dreamer applied his skills in trying to make his dreams concrete. Che was an absolutist. He wanted to pursue everything to its just conclusion. His consistency was almost maddening in its effortlessness. There was no trace of hypocrisy in him. When he said that working for one's fellow men was the greatest joy a man could have, it was true for him. He thought it was fit for a revolutionary to go and die under the flag of a nation not yet born, and he did just that, not making a great display of courage, but being courageous and cheerful as if he were doing the most natural thing in all the world. He said that no one was irreplaceable and really felt that this applied to him as much as to anyone else. So he exposed himself and died. He was a complete man.

History will probably treat Guevara as the Garibaldi of his age, the most admired and loved revolutionary of his time. The impact of his ideas on socialism and guerrilla warfare may be temporary: but his influence, particularly in Latin America, must be lasting. For there has been no man with so great an ideal of unity for that divided and unlucky continent since Bolívar. The young will find new heroes, but not more inspiring. And the consequences of his death are only beginning to be seen in the social upheavals and changes around us. When the general in *Viva Zapata!* looks down at the riddled corpse of the dead guerrilla leader, he says, "Sometimes a dead man can be a terrible enemy." For the rich nations of the earth, and for the corrupt governments that rule many of the poor nations, the dead Che is a terrible and a beautiful enemy.

# THE SPIRIT OF CHE GUEVARA

## I. F. STONE

from *GUERRILLA WARFARE*

**1967**

THE WORD THAT first came to mind on meeting Che Guevara was simplicity. I had been waiting to see him for some time late at night in the Cuban National Bank building in Havana. It was in 1960, during my first visit to Castro's Cuba. Che was then Economics Minister, a heady post for a wandering Latin-American revolutionary. Waiting with me in the anteroom of his office on the top floor of the building were several members of the old oligarchy—suave, plump, cynical and smooth. Guevara greeted me with a warmth I found puzzling until I learned that, a few years earlier, the U.S. Embassy in Mexico had accidentally touted me to him and his fellow revolutionaries. Che told me the Embassy had bought up every copy it could find of my *Hidden History of the Korean War* when it appeared in Spanish translation. The remaining copies were all the more widely read and appreciated, perhaps too highly. Che greeted me as a fellow rebel against Yanqui Imperialism.

He was the first man I had ever met whom I thought not just handsome but beautiful. With his curly reddish beard, he looked like a cross between a faun and a Sunday-school print of Jesus. Mischief, zest, compassion and a sense of mission flashed across his features during our interview. But what struck me most of all was that he seemed in no way changed, corrupted or intoxicated by the power which had suddenly fallen into his hands. I met his lovely dark-eyed Cuban wife for a moment before we sat down with an interpreter to a midnight supper. He spoke with that utter sobriety which sometimes masks immense apocalyptic visions. His were beginning to be nothing less than a hemispheric showdown with the Colossus of the North, and its final overthrow. He was already pictured in the U.S. press as the foremost communist in the Castro entourage. Talking with him, this soon seemed another reflection of our simplistic North American political universe. There were no communist clichés in his conversation. What might have been taken for them by an American reporter was his deep distrust of the U.S. This had multiple roots. He was an Argentine, i.e., a citizen of that Latin country which regards itself as our chief rival in the hemisphere. He had seen at first hand how crudely and brutally we had dealt with Latin aspirations in Guatemala, after the long night of a dictatorship whose horrors we had regarded with equanimity so long as no hand was laid on the United Fruit Company; in Guatemala as in Cuba, land reform had set the alarm bells ringing in Washington. As a doctor in self-imposed exile from Peronist Argentina, he had begun by practicing medicine among the Indians in Bolivia and knew the misery of the continent at first hand.

Men become revolutionaries for diverse, often surprising and sometimes unworthy motives—rancor, dislike of themselves, greed for power, or a hatred of stupidity which easily becomes contempt for humanity itself, since stupidity is its most salient characteristic. In Che one felt a desire to heal, and pity for suffering. It was out of love, like the perfect knight of medieval romance, that he had set out to do combat with the powers of the world. This was Galahad, not Robespierre. The focus of his political concern was not Moscow but his America—from the Mexican sierra to the Argentine pampas, the America we forget when we ethnocentrically use the word in the U.S. Of our talk on that first visit I remember the vivid relic of a fragile hope soon dissipated. "We are going to be the Tito of the Caribbean," Che said of the Castro regime. "You get along with Tito and you will gradually reconcile yourself to getting along with us." But accommodation with a rebel from the Russian empire was quite different from accommodation with a rebel from the American empire. American policy soon demonstrated that Castro would have to be Khrushchev's protégé if he were to survive our animosity.

On my second visit some weeks before the Bay of Pigs there was no more talk of Titoism. Now Che spoke with enthusiasm of what he had seen in his grand tour of the Soviet bloc. What impressed him most was the reconstruction of North Korea and the quality of its industrial output—here was a tiny country resurrected from the ashes of American bombardment and invasion. Perhaps he saw this as a preview of Cuba's fate.

I was not surprised when the news broke that Che had suddenly disappeared and it was said that he had set out on a wider mission. He was not made for a desk. He was a permanent revolutionary. Even Cuba may have become too sedate for his taste. In the early years of the Castro regime, when heretical communist and anticommunist works could still be seen in Havana's bookstores and there was still some faint hope of a peaceful settlement with the U.S., Latin exiles who had come to Cuba for support already began to complain that there was a palpable cooling off of revolutionary ardor. Like the Polish Jacobins came fruitlessly for aid to revolutionary Paris, they began to feel that the interests of the new state in the international order had begun to blur revolutionary fraternity. For the revolution, as for the Church, the world is full of snares and pitfalls: the unavoidable minimum of intercourse with things-as-they-are, the need for trade to earn one's bread, the necessity for some diplomatic relations, the lure of friendly hands in ideologically repugnant places (like Franco's to Castro), and the logic of statecraft which demands weapons, technology, compromise and duplicity. With the assumption of temporal power, the Revolution, like the Church, enters into a state of sin. One can easily imagine how this slow erosion of pristine virtue must have troubled Che. He was not a Cuban and could not be satisfied with building freedom from Yanqui Imperialism in one Latin country only. He thought in continental terms. In a sense he was, like some early saint, taking refuge in the desert. Only there could the purity of the faith be safeguarded from the unregenerate revisionism of human nature.

Che will live with Bolívar and Juárez among the heroes of the Latin hemisphere. His little book on guerrilla war has become not only a bible for revolutionaries but the anti-bible of the Green Berets of Fort Bragg where John F. Kennedy initiated the training of Special Forces as the Janissaries of the counter-revolution. But few in our own country pay much attention to those sober reflections with which Che begins his practical and unrhetorical little handbook. He says that where there is some hope of peaceful change, even if only the simulacrum of democracy, the conditions are not yet ripe for successful guerrilla action. This is in perfect accord with the ideology of 1776, but everywhere, out of politically mindless military logic or anti-communist panic, we ourselves—as most recently in Greece—lay down the welcome mat for our adversaries.

I have always felt there was something anachronistic in Castro's Cuba and in Che's mission to build a new and bigger Sierra Maestra in the Andes. The musical accompaniment of the Castro revolution was Chopin and the spirit of Garibaldi hung over it. It had all the naïve hopefulness and humanitarian faith of the 19th century. It had not heard of Hiroshima or of IBM's new Sinai, the computer. The hard realities of the hemisphere are very different from the revolutionary clichés of Castroism. How to create new managerial and scientific cadres to replace the old oligarchies and American aid? How do you inspire and organize for hard work over many hungry years an illiterate mass quite different in its conditioning and past from, let us say, the immemorially productive people of China? For after the music of the revolution dies down, everybody still has to go to work.

There are riches at hand easily seized, but how do you cash in the swag? If you expropriate U.S. oil in Venezuela, how do you sell it in a world where the cartel controls the tankers and the outlets, and the Soviet bloc has surpluses of its own to sell? If you expropriate U.S. copper in Chile, how do you refine and sell it under U.S. blockade or attack? How many Cubas can Moscow support in a style to which they would otherwise never hope to become accustomed? How do you persuade to the revolutionary course men of good will appalled by the harvest of hatred in our time—the crematoriums, the liquidation of the kulaks, Hiroshima and Nagasaki? These mass murders were committed under the influence of some vision that this was the way to the earthly paradise. How convince us that a New World can only be built after another outburst of bloodshed?

I recognize the Shelleyan purity of Che's intentions. I mourn the prospect that he may be dead. I welcome the fact that new Che's will spring up to carry on his work—for without the fear of revolutionary challenges neither the Latin oligarchy nor Washington will make peaceful change possible. But I believe their success would be out of all proportion to the terrible cost, and I believe this romantic handful underestimates the power, flexibility and intelligence of the American colossus. Yet when I see the follies our beloved country commits in Vietnam and elsewhere, the billions we spend on "defense," while hate, misery and despair build up to volcanic proportions in our black slums, I wonder whether Che's long-range estimates may not prove more realistic than mine. Lyndon Johnson may precipitate what Che Guevera alone could never accomplish.

# A MEMORY AND A HOPE

## GONZALEZ and SALAZAR

from *THE GREAT REBEL: CHE GUEVARA IN BOLIVIA*

### 1969

**P**OPULAR INSURRECTION COMES into being as a spontaneous response of peoples who have suffered foreign oppression. As an instrument of national liberation the phenomenon is not new, but today it is proving to be a historical constant in the four corners of the world because exploitation by imperialist powers has created an intolerable climate. Peoples in all five continents are taking up arms because they can no longer exist within the infrahuman scheme of life that has been imposed on them.

Guerrilla warfare is not foreign to Latin American history. In the colonial period the precursors of guerrilla insurrection were first the native chiefs; later, the mestizos and criollos were most active in rural areas. The leaders led agrarian communities to the mountains, where rebels with inferior materiel could have a chance to counter-balance the regular forces of the Spanish metropolis. The Indian rebels created what we would call today "free territories." The Royalist armies often put down these patriotic uprisings, crowning their campaigns with cruel and bloody reprisals. But they did not succeed in putting down the indomitable forces of rebellion, and they managed only to secure armistice until the next uprising.

At certain times during this period, the guerrilla factions grew stronger, created liberated zones, and tried to function as regular groups. Repression, failure of their efforts, and transitory pacification of the country were the immediate results. But it was the peace of the tomb, and lasted only as long as it took the guerrillas to get back up into the mountains and reorganize their cadres. Months or years later, after constant announcements by the Spanish generals that "the country is pacified," the country rose up in arms again. Thus, after a succession of bright days and dark and bitter days, the political emancipation long hoped for finally came about.

Alto Perú — today Bolivia — had to go through fifteen years of guerrilla struggle and civil uprising to consolidate the Republic in 1825, but it did not attain complete independence until our time. The Argentine historian and statesman, General Bartolomé Mitre, in his book on *The War of the Small Republics*, describes the struggle in Alto Perú succinctly and accurately:

> This was one of the most extraordinary wars because of the genius with which it was waged, one of the most tragic because of its bloody reprisals, and one of the most heroic because of its hidden, deliberate sacrifices. The lonely and isolated theater in which it took place, the multiplicity of interests and situations outside of the horizon of history, the humility of its leaders, its combatants, and its martyrs, has long hidden its true grandeur and prevented a real knowledge of its political scope.

And he adds farther on: "Each valley, each mountain, each town, is a little republic, a local center of insurrection, which has its independent leader, its flag, and its neighborhood Thermopylaes; their isolated efforts nonetheless converge toward a general result, which is produced without previous agreement of the parties."

The first guerrilla *focos* in Alto Perú were born in the native communities around Lake Titicaca, but the ideals they upheld were capable of being expanded, with blood and the death of their martyrs, to every corner of the country. The Universidad Mayor Real y Pontificia de San Francisco Xavier de Chuquisaca provided the ideology, the cities molded the political leaders, and guerrillas sprang up in the mountains, fields, and valleys. Chuquisaca, La Paz, Cochabamba, Oruro, Santa Cruz, and Tarija contributed the political principles and set the revolutionary keynote, while Lípez, Ayopaya, Aroma, Tarata, Pocona, Chayanta, Porco, Cinti, Valle Grande, Florida, and La Tablada are like so many flags representing the conquests of the stubborn ideal of emancipation. Its names are engraved on the history of the country like paradigms for eternity. Its ideologies, its protomartyrs, and its leaders mingle to form the common base of nationality. The list is long, and without special favoritism we may cite as examples Tupac Amaru, Tupac Katari, Julian Apaza, Murillo, Arze, Camargo, Muñecas, Zudañez, Lemoine, Monteagudo, Padilla, Warnes, Lanza, Méndez, Uriondo. Yesterday, as today, the enemy was the enemy of the social community and there was no discrimination of race, nationality, or creed in the defense of freedom. Mestizos from other regions of the continent and men from far-off places fought for this freedom: Frenchmen, Irishmen, Russians, Poles. And at their sides were the brave heroines, among them the outstanding trio Juana Azurduy de Padilla, Bartolina Siza, and Manuela Gandarillas.

Along with the inalienable patrimony of a free land, the guerrillas of the nineteenth century bequeathed to us a sentimental and romantic legend, accessible only to the sensibility of our Indo-mestizo people. Perhaps for that reason, even though they do not approve of any form of violence, a large part of the intellectual sectors of the nation did not condemn the guerrillas of Ñancahuazú with sectarian vehemence. If they did not sympathize openly with them, they at least tried to understand the reasons for their sacrifice, which from the beginning gave promise of being sterile, insofar as an immediate victory was concerned. Outwardly, at least, there was an attitude of general indifference, for people could not understand how a handful of men could disturb the stability of the nation and its historic continuity. It is possible that this attitude was due to the fact that the most vigorous nuclei opposing the government were in the mining centers and in the cities, among intellectuals, workers, and middle-class people, who have a definable influence on public opinion. It is also possible that this indifference, which resulted in only limited support for the guerrillas, was primarily rooted in disaffection toward the government in power rather than in genuine sympathy with the insurgents. The truth is that the majority of national opinion was convinced that the government was wrong in its policy toward the guerrilla problem, wrong to limit itself to liquidating it by force of arms without attacking its real cause: social injustice. This at least was the opinion expressed in the parliament by punctilious representatives of the nationalist parties (the FSB and the MNR). These legislators wanted it shown on the record that they recognized the existence of two different situations in the war against the guerrillas—that of the government and that of the armed forces—and emphasized that "they were with neither the guerrillas nor with the government, because both are negative factors contrary to [the interests of] the great national majorities." Only the conservative political parties and economic and social sectors, whose interests coincided with those of the government, mobilized votes in its favor and held lukewarm and indecisive demonstrations in the capitals of *departamentos* and some of the cities of the provinces, but the forced chauvinist speeches during these demonstrations did not impress the indifferent audiences. The women's committees and the committees for defense did not succeed in convincing people that the guerrilla movement might destroy the foundations of the nation.

The armed forces indirectly marshaled opinion against the guerrillas. Commanders of divisions and groups from the Acción Cívica Militar working in rural areas were generally represented in the committees for national defense.

Peasants, who have been a significant factor in elections since 1952, were easily manipulated by the authorities so that the shifts of opinion in this group were always led from higher up.

As one of the most important pressure groups, the Catholic Church maintained a cautious attitude. In accordance with its traditional position, it officially came out against Communism, but it abstained from marshaling support for the government in its fight against the guerrillas. Young laymen and post-Vatican II priests in some cases fully approved of the appearance of guerrillas, though this is not to say that they supported them fully.

The one who best summed up this state of collective consciousness in these days was the Bishop of Cochabamba, Monsignor Armando Gutiérrez Granier, who in part of his Pastoral Letter on the Guerrillas of August 1, 1967, stated:

Although in the present historical circumstance the legally constituted government has the right and the duty to answer force with force, and in an emergency to defend itself, let it be remembered that lasting peace is not conquered by force of arms alone but the restoration of justice, for as Pius XII said, following Isaiah: "Peace is the work of justice."

It is only right that we reflect that as long as our people live in misery with wages too low to provide for their human and family necessities; as long as their jobs are not secure, and therefore they are in a state of permanent anxiety, not knowing whether tomorrow they will have bread for themselves and their family, there will always be people who will listen to agitators and even commit themselves to the tragic adventure of the guerrillas.

To attain the lasting peace to which our people aspire, it is indispensable to propose to them an immediate economic and social political program that will open perspectives allowing Bolivians to possess the necessary material goods and the minimum comfort compatible with the dignity of the human person; guarantee them job security through the creation of sources of work that will avoid unemployment and support union rights; a more equitable distribution of national income, avoiding the glaringly obvious inequality of wages and salaries between those most favored and those who are poorest; a politics of austerity in the daily lives of the ruling classes that will help the poorest to bear their previous sacrifices and those consequent upon the launching of a development program—all this within an Integral Development of "the whole of man and the whole of men," as Paul VI proposes in the encyclical *Populorum Progressio*.

And the distinguished prelate, one of the most brilliant minds of the Catholic hierarchy in Bolivia, concluded his document with this exhortation: "We will celebrate the mass of August 6, the anniversary of the Independence of Bolivia, in the cathedral church, in this intention, and I ask all priests to join with me in this intention by celebrating the 'sacrifice for the Peace of the Fatherland, the reconciliation of all Bolivians, and the eternal rest of the fallen guerrillas.' "

ERNESTO GUEVARA WAS neither the standard-bearer of a Utopian messianism nor a borrower of concepts for confronting what happened to be the historical problems of his time. Nor were his actions during his life the consequence of resentment or unjust personal or family pretensions. He understood that the revolution is not a collection of schematic principles or an interpretive formula, but a historico-social phenomenon. For this reason he refused to cling to any theoretical dogmatism outlining revolutionary orthodoxy. Though he did not completely reject Lenin's postulate that "there is no revolutionary movement without a revolutionary theory," he understood that theory "as an expression of social truth, is above any enunciation of that theory; that is to say, that there can be a revolution if the historical reality is interpreted correctly and the forces intervening in it are used correctly, even without an acquaintance with theory."

It may be that he was wrong in his choice of means to transform the stiff mechanism of present-day society, but no one ever denied the noble sincerity of his ultimate aims since he always placed himself on the firing line, ready to give his life in the service of his ideals. He was not an imperturbable noisemaker but the revolutionary combatant par excellence. For this reason, his most recalcitrant enemies and even those who fought against him in the last campaigns respected his person and his sacrifice at the hour of his death, with rare exceptions that are lost in the thick shadows of hatred.

His death had world-wide repercussions and deeply touched collective sensibilities. Statesmen, politicians, thinkers, and men of eminence, without regard for ideology or personal creeds, emerged from the silence they maintained during his lifetime to express their grief. But it was among the most humble all over the world that the impact of his death was most painfully felt. We were the witnesses of the anguish experienced by the people of Cochabamba the night of Wednesday, October 11, 1967. The local newspapermen had been in Valle Grande that morning. Anxious knots of people crowded around the journalists and radio broadcasters, impatient to find out the latest details on the battle that was drawing to its close. And when the daily *Los Tiempos* scooped the world by putting out an edition around midnight with the latest news and the first photographs of Guevara's death, an invisible cloud slowly descended on the city.

Guevara was a combination of warrior and apostle, adventurer and prophet. He was a lay missionary for social justice. His personality was not shaped in gambling dens or aristocratic clubs, as he himself once said. He was a down-to-earth creature with deep human sensibilities, in spite of having imposed a severe Jansenist discipline upon himself. He demanded things from himself so as to demand them from others. He spontaneously gave up all comforts that life might offer him and only accepted and adapted himself to his ruling standards. When he decided to burn his bridges behind him, he drew a line between his past and his future destiny and flung himself into the fight. He has illustrious predecessors along the path of American freedom that he chose to take: Tupac Amaru, Bolívar, Esteban Arze, César Augusto Sandino, Emiliano Zapata, and Gualberto Villarroel showed him the way. And like Camile Torres, he made himself worthy of following in their footsteps. He sowed and we shall reap. The seed will germinate and other generations will taste the new vintage in the wine-press of time.

His life and his death do not represent a truncated parabola, but a circle that connects the beginning and the end with mathematical precision. A life and a death that will have permanent continuity that no force will be able to trick us out of. His physical body may have been converted into rotting flesh or scattered ashes, but his spirit will endure throughout eternity because he entered the hearts of the humble.

So be it, leader of this continent!

IN BOLIVIA IT *is traditional for markets of regional fairs to be held on certain days of the week in provincial towns and, on occasion, in the capitals of the departments. Aside from being an occasion to buy and sell goods, they are also rite and festival, and draw people from all over the region who have faith in magical cures. The fair is similar to the Moroccan marketplace, where contraband goods are sold as though they were legal, where people eat, drink, buy and sell everything, from pigs to nylons, from aspirins to the latest-model sewing machines, from rusty nails and tin cans to short-wave radios.*

*In Valle Grande the fair falls on Sunday. Since Guevara's death, peasants have come from the most remote corners of the province and formed lines to buy Che's photograph, which they take to the church to have blessed. This is in accord with their simple and innocent ancestral belief that those who have died a tragic death have the power to answer requests for miracles. A kind of legend has already grown up around the miracles of "Saint Che," whose portrait can frequently be found in peasant huts in the midst of Catholic images. Many people have even had masses said in his memory.*

*A rapid "Gallup poll" in the locality revealed the following statistical information: up to October 22, 1967 — twelve days after his death — some 6700 photographs of Che had been sold.*

# IMAGES AND GHOSTS

## PACO IGNACIO TAIBO II

from *GUEVARA, ALSO KNOWN AS CHE*

**1997**

THE ARGENTINE POET Paco Urondo, who died years later at the hands of the Argentine military, wrote when he heard of Che's death:

It will rain without stopping for a week, and the unbelieving, or those who are not superstitious, will think it is just a coincidence, that what is happening is somewhat exceptional but pure chance. Friends come along wetter each time and now this shitty weather has gone on longer than ever. But this time the guesses will not be done à la Buenos Aires; people will not speak of the damp and the calamities that plague them — no, not even about their livers: this time they will guess some other way; there is no peace, just silence.

Celia, Che's fourth daughter, was born in 1963, during her father's next-to-last year at the Cuban Industry Ministry, a year and a half before he left for the Congo, and can only see her father through other people's memories. She has tried many times to read the Bolivian diary, but has not been able to bring herself to do so.

Fidel Castro says he has often seen Che in his dreams in recent years. He confessed to Italian journalist Gianni Miná that Che speaks to him and "tells me things."

Ana María, Che's sister, told a Spanish journalist at the beginning of the seventies: "At times I feel that someone is looking at me but beyond me, as if I were somehow he, and I feel as if I am no one and I do not know what to do. I have had to learn to live with these events."

This is not unusual. We all know the strange and amazing way that dead people leave a huge void, a gaping hole in the lives of those who survive them. Ernesto Guevara has acquired a magical aura over all these years, however; it has not been dimmed by his death, and has touched many people who never knew him.

After the guerrilla campaign passed near the town of La Higuera, whose school sheltered Che in last hours and then as a corpse, the town was devastated by a terrible drought. Plants and animals died and the peasants were forced to emigrate. Popular wisdom, hushed rumors, and folk tales had it that the weather was a divine punishment for allowing Che to die at the hands of the soldiers.

In La Higuera, locks of hair and bloodstained scraps of Che's pants are exhibited like a saint's relics. In Lagunillas, a street photographer has had a good business of selling photos of Che's corpse, and many of the town's inhabitants have made it a point to place a photograph of the dead Che on top of the stone slab in the laundry at the Malta Hospital, the photo of a secular Christ.

The peasants of Cochabamba have evolved a litany, a strange kind of prayer: "Little soul of Che, by your leave please work the miracle that will make my cow well again. Grant me that wish, little soul of Che."

The Vallegrande nurse who stripped Che's corpse admits: "At times I dream about Che and I see him as if he were alive, and he tells me that he's going to take me away from the wretchedness in which I live."

The La Higuera schoolhouse was torn down and a health clinic built in its place. The clinic never opened, and no doctors or medicines ever appeared. Eventually another school was built. The Uruguayan journalist Ernesto González Bernejo visited it in 1971:

"What do you know about Che?," he asked a campesino boy when the teacher wasn't paying attention.

"That's him there," the child answered, pointing to a portrait of Simón Bolívar.

Francisco Rivas, a sixty-year-old campesino who lived near La Higuera and had fourteen children, said: "I didn't realize it then. Now I know that I have lost a lot."

In a church in Matanzas, Cuba, Ernesto Guevara can be found in an altarpiece, one of a heavenly host; at another church, in the Mexican state of Tamaulipas, he shares the corner of a mural with the devil.

Che's death left thousands of men and women dumbstruck, disconcerted, astonished, unsettled. After eleven short years on the political scene—and without meaning to—Che had become a living symbol of the much postponed, much betrayed Latin American revolution; the only thing of which we may be sure is that such stuff as dreams are made of never dies. Nonetheless, Ernesto Guevara had died in Bolivia. The Uruguayan poet Benedetti wrote:

*There we are*
*shaken*
*enraged,*
*though death might be*
*another foreseeable absurdity*

In Santa Clara there is a twenty-one-foot bronze statue of Che by Jose Delarra, the same person who gave a porcelain sculpture of Che's face to a Cuban astronaut, so that Che could travel to the stratosphere. The statue is a stocky, almost fat Che Guevara, who has a Santa Claus–like beard and does not smile. That's the trouble with statues: bronze reproduces the smile badly.

I interviewed Dariel Alarcón at his home on the outskirts of Havana. He is a witty, smiling man, but toward the end of the interview, when he remembered that Inti Peredo, Harry Villegas, Leonardo Tamayo, and he might have been able to rescue Che that October afternoon, a shadow fell across the room. It is one of those things a person cannot live with.

I spoke with Che's former secretary, José Manuel Manresa, in the dark, as there was a power cut in the Havana district in which he lives. At times he broke down, and he wore his emotions on his sleeve.

"You Guevara men, the ones who lived alongside Che, give the impression of being marked, branded, with a Z on your foreheads like Zorro used to make."

"We were poor benighted souls who were going who-knows-where in life and just waiting to meet a man like Che."

There was a long silence: then a sob could be heard. One did not know what to ask next.

That sense that they have been abandoned, that Che has gone without them, kills them. Joel Iglesias entered a severe crisis that drove him to drink, Alberto Mora committed suicide. Díaz Arguelles could never forgive Che for having taken his bosom pal Gustavo Machín rather than him, and did not forgive Che even when he himself died years later in Angola facing South African armored cars, in an epic event not at all unworthy of Che himself. Efigenio Ameijeiras wavers between saying he could have kept Che's enthusiasm at bay, and feeling pain at not having been there to keep it at bay. For many years Victor Dreke wondered what he had done wrong in Africa for Che not to have taken him to Bolivia. And although the answer is "Nothing," the question gnaws at him. The Acevedo brothers ask themselves the same question, as does Che's friend Oscar Fernández Mell, as does Emilio Aragonés, who was struck by a terrible illness that nearly killed him when he returned from Africa. As does Ulises Estrada, whom Che sent away in Prague because he was very visible. As does Orlando Borrego, his deputy at the ministry of industry. As does Enrique Oltuski, who has yet to write the book that will say that they did not agree on so many things . . . And when I speak to them I could bet my head and not risk losing it, by wagering that in Cuba today, almost thirty years after his death, there are almost a hundred men and women who would have sold their souls to the devil in exchange for being able to die with Che in Bolivia.

I was to find one last photograph of Che. In Theo Bruns's house in Hamburg is a poster with the caption "Comrades: I have a poster of all of you at home, Che." I was thankful for a respite, and for the return of the biting wit that was so much his in life.

My neighbor and friend Juan Gelman wrote some time ago:

*But*
*the serious thing is that Che*
*really did enter into death*
*and wanders thereabouts, they say*

*beautiful*
*with stones under his arms*
*I am from a country where now*
*Guevara must die other deaths*
*each of which will atone for his death now*
*he who laughed is dust and food for worms now*
*may he who cried think of this*
*and may he who forgot forget or remember.*

Memories.

There is a memory. Out of thousands of photos, posters, T-shirts, tapes, records, videos, postcards, portraits, magazines, books, phrases, accounts—all ghosts haunting an industrial society that does not know where to put its myths in the sobriety of memory—Che is watching over us. He is our secular saint. Despite all the paraphernalia, he comes back. Thirty years after his death, his image cuts across generations, his myth hovers over neoliberalism's delusions of grandeur. Irreverent, a joker, stubborn, morally stubborn, unforgettable.

# THE HARSH ANGEL:
# THE REVOLUTIONARY WHO COULD
# FIND NO REVOLT TO PLEASE HIM

## ALMA GUILLERMOPRIETO

*THE NEW YORKER*

OCTOBER 6, 1997

S O MANY INCINERATED lives: the would-be guerrillas who starved to death in northern Argentina, the young men drowned in vats of excrement in Brazil, the eviscerated martyrs of Guatemala, the sociology student in Argentina whose severed hands were delivered in a jar to her mother: the children of Che. The slogans that defined those furious and hopeful times—"Two, three, many Vietnams!" and "The first duty of a revolutionary is to make the Revolution"—were Che's slogans. They sound foolish and empty now, but because it was Ernesto (Che) Guevara, the guerrilla hero, who pronounced them they were heard and followed around the world. The range of his influence spans almost the entire latter half of the twentieth century.

He was the century's first Latin-American: an astonishing fact, given that hundreds of millions of people in the hemisphere are joined by the same language, the same Iberian culture, the same religion, the same monstrously deformed class system, the same traditions of violence and rancor. Despite those essential bonds, Latin America's

**THE HARSH ANGEL**
431

twenty-one nations lived in determined isolation and a common mistrust until Che came along and, through his acts, proclaimed himself a citizen of them all. He was an artist of scorn, heaping it on the sanctimonious, the officiously bureaucratic, the unimaginatively conformist, who whispered eagerly that the way things were was the best way that could be arranged. He was a living banner, determined to renounce all the temptations of power and to change the world by example. And he was a fanatic, consumed by restlessness and a frighteningly abstract hatred, who in the end recognized only one moral value as supreme, the willingness to be slaughtered for a cause.

Another astonishing fact is that so many members of my generation, who were just coming of age at the time of his death, wanted to be like him, and to obey him, even while we knew so little about him. It was only after he was hunted down by Bolivian Army forces, on October 8, 1967, and the unforgettable picture of his corpse — emaciated torso, tousled hair, and liquid, vacant eyes — was displayed on the front pages of newspapers around the world that Che became familiar to young people. It was in death that he became known. Three biographies have come out this year. Two of them — "Che Guevara: A Revolutionary Life," by Jon Lee Anderson (Grove; $35), and "Compañero: The Life and Death of Che Guevara," by Jorge Castañeda (Knopf; $30) — are groundbreaking: they take on the difficult task of demolishing the Che legend, as it was created and nurtured over the decades by the Cuban regime he had helped found. The third, "Guevara: Also Known as Che," by Paco Ignacio Taibo II (St. Martin's; $35), hews too closely to the official myth. Taibo, best known outside Mexico as the author of a number of inventive detective novels, is an engaging and lively writer, but his hagiography is intended only for the true believer.

Anderson's book is an epic end run around the guardians of the Che legend. A journalist who has made a career writing about wars and guerrillas, Anderson lived in Cuba for three years in order to do this project, and he persuaded Che's second wife, Aleida March, to let him read Che's private diaries. He also seems to have talked to everyone else still alive who ever knew Guevara, and one of the things that such dogged reporting has enabled him to do is to tell us, in wonderful new detail, about the hero as a youth.

Ernesto Guevara de la Serna was born in Argentina in 1928, the son of an intellectually curious, high-strung mother and a debonair, womanizing father who ran through his wife's fortune and never quite managed to get any of his own business schemes off the ground. The couple fought constantly, and the father slept sometimes on the living-room sofa, sometimes in another house. At the age of two, Ernestito, the firstborn and favorite of the Guevaras' children (they had five), developed asthma, and for long stretches throughout his childhood he was bedridden. Spurred on by his mother, Celia, he became a pre-cocious and methodical reader and a stoic patient. As with Teddy Roosevelt, physical hardship and endurance became a habit, and Ernesto seems never to have succumbed to the invalid's temptation to engage in complaint and self-indulgence.

In adolescence, and at least partly as a response to his handicap, Ernesto emerged as a full-fledged macho, having his way with the family maids (once literally behind the back of his favorite and very strait-laced aunt, who was then sitting primly at the dining-room table); refusing at the age of fifteen to attend a protest demonstration because he did not have a revolver; making it a point of pride never to bathe. (His upper-middle-class schoolmates remember his nickname, Chancho, or Pig, not so much because it was ugly as because he was so proud of it.) Before his machismo destroyed him, it served him well: it tempered his will and spurred him to become an athlete — one who, despite the crippling asthma, always made a point of outracing, out-kicking, and outhiking his less exigent peers. (Machismo also gave him style: in the midst of his physical exploits, he would stop and suck on his inhaler for a few moments, or give himself a quick adrenaline injection through his clothes, and then return to the field.)

At twenty-two, when he was studying medicine in Buenos Aires, he discovered that the life of a wanderer suited him. Interrupting his studies, he left home and motorbiked alone through northern Argentina. The following year, he and his best friend embarked on an eight-month hitchhiking adventure: it took them through northern Argentina again and then on to Chile, Peru, Colombia, Venezuela, and, finally, the United States. He was already a disciplined diarist, and a few years later, when he was no longer signing himself "Pig" but, rather, "Che," he took his notes from that trip and turned them into a book. It was translated into English in 1995 and became a brisk seller for the British publishing house Verso, under the title "The Motorcycle Diaries."

The diarist is an idealistic young medical student who has chosen his profession as a way of doing good in the world but otherwise does not think much about politics. The living conditions of the people he travels among shock him, but he is just a susceptible to the wonder of Machu Picchu. He comes across as high-spirited—jumping into a cold lake to retrieve a downed duck—endlessly curious, amusing, and very likable: "Allergic as I am to the cold, swimming . . . made me suffer like a bedouin. Just as well that roast duck, seasoned as usual by our hunger, is an exquisite dish."

By his own account, this jolly and enthusiastic young man was buried forever at the expedition's close. The last section of the "The Motorcycle Diaries" is eerie. In a dreamlike, utterly different voice, he recounts a meeting with a mysterious prophet, who tells him that revolution will come to Latin America, and that it will destroy those who cannot join it. After recounting this conversation, Guevara writes:

> I knew that when the great guiding spirit cleaves humanity into two antagonistic halves, I will be with the people . . . Howling like a man possessed, [I] will assail the barricades and trenches, will stain my weapon with blood and, consumed with rage, will slaughter any enemy I lay hands on.

We will probably never know when Guevara tacked this final entry onto the original, beguiling text, or what circumstances provoked it. We do know that his discovery of the revolutionary faith transformed him, as a writer, into a hopeless termagant. And we know something more remarkable: that the words he wrote were not simply a young man's posturing, for from the time of his final departure from Argentina the following year, 1953, to the moment of his death, in 1967, the asthmatic, footloose, irreverent diarist sought to become the iron-willed avenger of his prophecy. Another idealistic and enterprising young man, upon being confronted with the poverty, racism, and injustice that Guevara sees and records in "The Motorcycle Diaries," might have strengthened his commitment to medicine, or thought of ways to give Latin America's poor the weapon of literacy. For reasons that even the most ambitious biographer can only speculate on—rage against his father, love of humanity—Guevara decided instead to spend his life creating Che, the harsh angel.

GUEVARA REMAINED A pilgrim for another three years, waiting for a cause to find him. During that time, he floated northward again, read Marx and Lenin, and decided that he was a Marxist. In Bolivia in 1953, he was a skeptical witness of Victor Paz Estenssoro's populist revolution, whose limited—but hardly insignificant—achievements included the liberation of the Indian peasantry from virtual fiefdom and the establishment of universal suffrage. For his part, Guevara never considered any alternatives to violence and radicalism, and perhaps it is true that in the Latin America of those years it required more self-delusion to be a moderate reformer than to be a utopian revolutionary. At any rate, a nine-month stay in Guatemala was cut short by the 1954 coup against the reformist government of Jacobo Arbenz—a coup sponsored by the Central Intelligence Agency. This monumentally stupid event not only set Guatemala on the road to decades of bloodshed but confirmed Che's conviction that in politics only those willing to shed blood make a difference.

In late 1954, Guevara arrived in Mexico, and he spent two years there that would have been listless and inconsequential but for two events. He made an unhappy marriage to a Peruvian radical he had first met in Guatemala, Hilda Gadea, and he had a child with her. (Guevara and women is a nasty subject. Anderson, ever attentive to his subject's sex life, quotes from Guevara's unpublished diary on the courtship: "Hilda declared her love in epistolary and practical form. I was with a lot of asthma, if not I might have fucked her. . . . The little letter she left me upon leaving is very good, too bad she is so ugly.") And he met Fidel Castro, who arrived in Mexico in 1955, fresh from a two-year imprisonment in Cuba, following his disastrous assault on the Moncada Army barracks.

There is no record of Ernesto Guevara's ever before, or subsequently, expressing unrestrained admiration for a fellow-being. Fidel, with his natural bonhomie, energy, and boundless faith in his own leadership, was the exception. The chemistry was mutual: Fidel trusted him, relied on him, and, on the evidence, loved him more than any of his other comrades, with the possible exception of Celia Sánchez (Fidel's closest companion until her death, in 1980). Guevara's relationship to love, whether it involved his parents, his comrades, or his women, was uneasy, but his love of Fidel was wholehearted and transforming, because it opened the path to the life he was seeking. Within hours of their first meeting, Guevara signed on as a medic for Fidel's harebrained plan to land an expedition on the eastern end of Cuba and start an insurrection against the dictator Fulgencio Batista.

In November of 1956, the creaky yacht Granma set sail from Veracruz, bound for Cuba and glory. By then, the Argentine Guevara, who, like all his countrymen, interjected the word *che*—roughly, "man," or "you"—at least once in every sentence (as in "Hey, *che*, is that the way to clean a rifle, *che*?"), had been rebaptized. He would be, forevermore, *el Che*—the Argentine. It was a term that underlined not only the affection and respect his comrades felt for him but also their intense awareness of his differentness, his permanent standing as a foreigner in the revolution he had adopted as his own.

He was keenly aware of his outsider status as he sailed for Cuba. Other portents must have been harder for him to see. There was his medical training, for example, which had drilled into him the universality of the principle of the scientific cure (that is, that penicillin, say, will get rid of pneumonia in both a French peasant and a Mexican socialite). A central flaw in his thinking for the rest of his life was to assume that what he learned about guerrilla warfare in the process of overthrowing Batista amounted to a prescription—a necessary remedy for every form of social disease. Another flaw was that he was inescapably committed to a certain definition of virility and to the code of conduct it implied: a macho definition, not unusual among Latin-Americans of his generation. As a result, he found it unbearably humiliating ever to lose face, back down, admit defeat. He could not see that Sancho Panza might be as heroic as Quixote. And he was as blind to nuances of character as he was tone-deaf: for all the painful insights into his own nature which he reveals in his diaries, and for all his astute observations in them on landscape, warfare, and political dynamics, there are no credible portraits of his fellow-men. There are only revolutionaries, who are full of virtue, and counter-revolutionaries, who are worthless.

The next chapter in Che's life coincides with one of the century's most startling military triumphs. Having landed as disastrously as was to be expected on Cuba's shores, Che, Fidel Castro, Fidel's brother, Raúl, and a handful of others survived Batista's ferocious assault and went on to forge the beginnings of a revolutionary army in the Sierra Maestra. By 1958, Che's military intuition and daring, his organizational skills, and his outstanding personal bravery had won him the undisputed title of Comandante and a leading role in the revolution. Sharing his life with Cubans, who have always held ablutions and nattiness to be almost supreme virtues, Guevara still refused to bathe, or even tie his shoelaces, but now that he was Che his odorous aura was part of a mystique. He was roughing it in the great outdoors, planning strategy with Fidel, sharing his camp cot with a stunning *mulata*, risking his life and proving his manhood on a daily basis. His days, as he narrates them in "Reminiscences of the Cuban Revolutionary War" (again, reworked pages from his diary turned into a book), read blissfully like an adventure out of *Boys' Life*. And yet it is at this point, according to Anderson, that Che wrote in his unpublished diary:

> A little combat broke out in which we retreated very quickly. The position was bad and they were encircling us, but we put up little resistance. Personally I noted something I had never felt before: the need to live. That had better be corrected in the next opportunity.

Happiness and the desire for it — "the need to live" — were, in a revolutionary, symptoms of weakness.

CHE'S LIFE FOLLOWING the revolution's triumph was a slow accretion of wreckage, and it is in the narration of this collapse that "Compañero," Jorge Castañeda's beautiful and passionate biography, is most lucid. We turn the pages hoping that the trouble will end soon, that Guevara may be spared, or spare himself, if not from failure, then from ludicrous defeat; if not from hideous physical suffering, then from death; if not from death, then from ignominy. But Castañeda is as unflinching as his hero: he has searched C.I.A. records and the recollections of Guevara's closest comrades in order to prise away layers of after-the-fact justifications and embellishments of the Che legend. In the process, he makes Ernesto Guevara understandable at last, and his predicament deeply moving.

Castañeda's Che is a man who could not bear the natural ambivalence of the world, and found relief from it (and, curiously, from the torment of asthma) only in the unequivocal rigors of battle and radicalism. Appointed first to the National Agrarian Reform Institute and then to head the central bank in Fidel's revolutionary regime, he was, like so many other battle heroes, before and after him, flummoxed by the day-to-day realities of governance. Why should Cuba have a monetary policy that sought to placate imperialism? Why was it necessary to compensate exploiters and oppressors for their sugar-cane haciendas instead of merely expropriating the land for *el pueblo?* Why corrupt workers by offering them more money to work harder? Che nearly killed himself accumulating "volunteer work hours" of his own, cutting cane and stacking sacks of sugar after the gruelling hours he put in at his desk, in order to prove that moral incentives could beat lucre as a stimulus to productivity. He may have begun to suspect toward the end of his stay in Cuba that other mortals liked to put their free time to a different use. He certainly believed that the revolution's leadership was tacking dangerously toward pragmatism. "The New Man"—a new type of human being that the revolution was to manufacture—was not being turned out swiftly enough.

Che was unable to deal with his disapproval of the course that Fidel was taking and his simultaneous love for the man; with his disillusionment with the Soviet Union and the self-satisfaction of the burgeoning Cuban bureaucracy; with the palace intrigues of the new regime (particularly those of Fidel's brother Raúl); and, probably, with the gnawing awareness of his own failings as a peacetime revolutionary. It seems reasonable to interpret his decision to leave Cuba as Casteñeda does—as the result of his need to get away from so much internal conflict. (In the course of explaining this decision, Castañeda provides an extraordinary account of the ins and outs of Cuban state policy, Cuban-Soviet relations, and Castro's dealings with the United States.) Che was leaving behind a second wife, six children, his comrades, his years of happiness, and the revolution he had helped give birth to; none of these were enough to convince him that he belonged.

Guevara's original intention was to return to his homeland and start a guerrilla movement there. A 1965 expedition to the Congo, where various armed factions were still wrestling for power long after the overthrow and murder of Patrice Lumumba, and his last stand in Bolivia, Castañeda writes, followed improbably from Fidel's anxious efforts to keep Che away from Argentina, where he was sure to be detected and murdered by Latin America's most efficient security forces. Castro seems to have felt that the Congo would be a safer place, and the question of whether it was a more intelligent choice doesn't seem to have been addressed either by him or by the man he was trying to protect. (In Cairo, Jon Lee Anderson notes, Gamal Abdel Nasser warned Che not to get militarily involved in Africa, because there he would be "like Tarzan, a white man among blacks, leading and protecting them.")

As things turned out, the Congo episode was a farce, so absurd that

Cuban authorities kept secret Che's rueful draft for a book on it—until recently, that is, when one of his new biographers, Taibo, was able to study the original manuscript. Guevara was abandoned from the beginning by Congolese military leaders, like Laurent Kabila, who had initially welcomed his offer of help. He was plagued by dysentery and was subject to fits of uncontrollable anger, and emerged from seven months in the jungle forty pounds lighter, sick, and severely depressed. If he had ever considered a decision to cut bait and return to Cuba, that option was cancelled weeks before the Congo expedition's rout: on October 5, 1965, Fidel Castro, pressed on all sides to explain Che's disappearance from Cuba and unable to recognize that the African adventure was about to collapse, decided to make public Che's farewell letter to him: "I will say once again that the only way that Cuba can be held responsible for my actions is in its example. If my time should come under other skies, my last thought will be for this people, and especially for you."

Guevara was sitting in a miserable campsite on the shores of Lake Tanganyika, bored, frustrated, and in mourning for his mother, when he was told that Fidel had publicized the letter. The news hit him like an explosion. "Shit-eaters!" he said, pacing back and forth in the mud. "They are imbeciles, idiots."

GUEVARA'S FINAL TREK began at this moment, because once his farewell to Fidel was made public, as Castañeda writes, "his bridges were effectively burned. Given his temperament, there was now no way he could return to Cuba, even temporarily. The idea of a public deception was unacceptable to him: once he had said he was leaving, he could not go back." He could not bear to lose face.

A few months later, having taken full and bitter stock of his situation, he made the decision to set up a guerrilla base—intended as a training camp, really—in southern Bolivia, near the border with Argentina. From there, he convinced himself, he would ultimately be able to spark the revolutionary flame in Argentina and, from there, throughout the world.

He knew, of course, that his death would fan that flame. One wonders if he had any sense in the final awful weeks of how badly things would end, not just for him but for everyone involved in the ubiquitous attempts at armed radical revolution that followed upon his death. I am thinking now of Guatemala, which, more than any other country in the hemisphere besides Cuba, formed Guevara's view of the world and was a testing ground for his ideas about class warfare and the struggle for liberation, and which paid the price. And I am thinking of the Guatemalans I knew, like the poet Alaíde Foppa, a feminist editor, art historian, and critic, who was a great friend of my mother's. Alaíde had lived in exile in Mexico with her husband, Alfonso Solórzano, since the 1954 coup against Arbenz. They had five children, including Mario, who returned to Guatemala in the late seventies to found an opposition newspaper. The youngest, Juan Pablo, joined a Guatemalan guerrilla organization. The group's founders, who had trained in Cuba and been directly encouraged by Che, shared his faith that a small group of steel-willed men could win the people's support and overthrow an unjust regime, no matter how large or well trained the enemy's army might be, or what foreign powers might decide to intervene. In 1979, Juan Pablo was captured by the military, and killed. In Mexico City two weeks later, his despondent father died when he walked into oncoming traffic.

Just before Christmas of the following year, 1980, I arrived in Mexico from Central America, expecting to spend Christmas Eve with my mother at Alaíde's house. That did not happen, however, because when I walked into my mother's apartment I found her holding the phone, silent with shock. Alaíde, following her son's death, had apparently made the decision to match his sacrifice: she travelled to Guatemala City on a courier mission for the guerrillas, and there, the caller on the phone had just told my mother, she was almost instantly detected and "disappeared" by the security forces. According to her relatives, she was kept alive and tortured for months. Her corpse has never been found.

And then Mario was killed. I had last seen him the previous year. We had had dinner in Mexico City, and he had listened joyfully to my account of the Sandinistas' overthrow of Anastasio Somoza in Nicaragua—a spectacularly unforeseen event, which I had covered as a reporter, and which had revitalized flagging guerrilla forces everywhere. I had no idea that within weeks of my meeting with Mario he himself would go underground, joining the guerrillas' urban infrastructure in the Guatemalan capital. He learned in clandestinity of his mother's disappearance, and then he, too, was betrayed. Someone revealed the location of his safe house to the Army (probably under torture, which true revolutionaries, unlike other human beings, were supposed to resist to the end, but rarely did), and Mario was ambushed and killed. This occurred during a period of weeks when the military regime unleashed a campaign of systematic massacre directed against Mayan campesinos who had joined the guerrilla group that Mario belonged to. Because the campesinos were poorly trained and poorly armed, and the Army troops were not, and because support for the guerrillas was only substantial, and not overwhelming, thousands of impoverished men and women paid with their lives for their revolutionary beliefs. It was only last year, after twenty years of brutal struggle, that peace was signed in Guatemala.

Alaíde and Mario appear in my memory whenever I try to make sense of those fervid times. I remember my mother, too, who, having been forced at last out of her distrust of politics, stood timidly in a crowd in front of the Guatemalan Embassy and whispered slogans against the dictatorship (she hated crowds and slogans, and did not know how to shout), because something had to be done even though there was nothing left to do. Alaíde was exceptional only in that she was sixty-seven when she responded to the call issued in Havana by Fidel on the day he told Cubans that Ernesto Guevara was dead. "Be like Che!" Fidel cried, and the exhortation gave purpose to an entire generation that desperately needed a way of being in the modern world, a way to act that could fill life with meaning and transcendence. But, in the end, Che, who, unlike Fidel, was quite uncurious about how the real world worked—why people supported or failed to support a cause, how General Motors turned out cars, what accounted for the Mexican ruling party's longevity—could offer only one course of action, and this was his tragedy, and that of Alaíde and her children: the only way to be like Che was to die like him, and all those deaths were not enough to create the perfect world that Che wanted.

I THINK OF Che, starving and thirsty in Bolivia, hardly able to walk, because of weakness and asthma, and lost, wandering in circles with a handful of comrades through the scrubby Bolivian highlands while the Army and its C.I.A. advisers drew their noose tighter. (Perhaps, Castañeda speculates, he and his hopeless cause had been abandoned at this stage by the support network in Cuba.) His companions on this dismal trek were men who had signed on, out of devotion to him, for what was evidently a suicide mission, but he would deprive them of what meagre rations there were as punishment for the smallest act of indiscipline, and call them trash. Che, who loved animals, wrote in his diary that he had stabbed his skinny mare in a fit of rage and frustration. One can see from his account how diminished and stilted were the emotions he dared allow himself three months before he was killed, and how very stubborn he was:

I am a human wreck and the episode with the little mare proves that at moments I have lost control; this will be rectified but the situation must weigh evenly on all of us, and whoever doesn't feel capable of bearing the load must say so. This is one of those moments in which large decisions must be made: this type of struggle gives us the opportunity to become revolutionaries, the highest rank in the human species, but it also allows us to graduate as men. Those who are incapable of achieving either of these two stages should say so and abandon the struggle.

Guevara was born in Latin America's hour of the hero. So many of our leaders have been so corrupt, and the range of allowed and possible public activity has been so narrow, and injustice has cried out so piercingly to the heavens, that only a hero could answer the call, and only a heroic mode of life could seem worthy. Guevara stood out against the inflamed horizon of his time, alone and unique.

There is, however, a problem with the heroic figure (as the Cubans, who kept Che's diaries and documents secret all this while, perceived), and that is that the hero can have no faults, and is answerable, as Che was, only to his own exalted sense of honor. This picture of the hero is still satisfying to large numbers of Latin Americans who are not in a position to exact an accounting from their leaders but do, on the other hand, demand that their leaders act grandly and provoke fervor and states of rapture, as the dead Che now does. But the living Che was not the perfect hero for his time and place: he demanded that others follow his impossible example, and never understood how to combine what he wanted with what was achievable. It remains forever a matter of debate whether Che's life and example speeded the advent of the present era, in which there are no perfect causes, and where men like him are more than ever out of place.

# GOODBYE TO ALL THAT

## CHRISTOPHER HITCHENS

*THE NEW YORK REVIEW OF BOOKS*

JULY 17, 1997

### 1.

WHEN, SHORTLY AFTER the triumph of the Castro revolution, Ernesto Guevara took over the direction of the Cuban National Bank, it became his duty to sign the newly minted ten-and twenty-peso notes. This he did with a contemptuous flourish, scrawling the hold *nom de guerre* "Che" on both denominations. By that gesture, which made those bills a collectors' item in some quarters of the left, he expressed an ambition to move beyond the money economy and what used to be termed "the cash nexus." It was a stroke, at once Utopian and puritanical, that seemed to sum up his gift both for the improvised and the determined.

Revisiting Havana recently, for the purpose of making a BBC documentary on the thirtieth anniversary of Guevara's murder, I discovered that there are now four legal currencies in circulation. The most proud and salient of course, is the United States dollar. Nowhere outside the Panama Canal Zone has any Latin American economy capitulated so utterly to the usefulness of this green symbol. Once the preserve of the Cuban *numenklatura* and of those with access to special diplomatic "dollar stores," the money of *Tio Sam* is now the preferred street-wise mode of exchange, and also the essential legal tender in hotels and newly privatized restaurants. Next in importance is the special "INTUR" money, printed by the Cuban Ministry of Tourism for the exclusive use of foreign holidaymakers. Large tracts of Cuba, especially the Varadero beach section outside Havana, have been turned into reservations for this special breed of "internationalist." Third comes the *peso convertible*, a piece of scrip with a value pegged to that of the dollar. And last we find the Cuban peso a mode of exchange so humble that windshield-washers at intersections, when handed a fistful will wordlessly hand it back.

ON THIS LAST currency appears the visage of Che Guevara. It certainly, if somewhat ironically, demonstrates the regime's fealty to his carelessness about money. Meanwhile, under stylized poster portraits of the heroic Comandante, and within sight of banners reading—rather gruesomely perhaps—*Socialismo o Muerte*, the youth of Havana sell their lissome bodies as they did in the days of the Sam Giancana and George Raft dispensation. Junk tourist artifacts are sold from stalls outside Hemingway's old Bodeguita. The talk among the liberal members of the writers' union, as also among the American expatriate veterans, is all of the surge in street crime and delinquency. With unintentional comic effect, these conversations mimic their "deprived or depraved?" counterparts in Los Angeles and New York. Is it the lack of jobs and opportunities? Or could it be the decline in the moral basis of society? After all, it's not that long since Martha Gellhorn instructed her readers that mugging in Havana was unknown. The old "moral versus material" debate continues in a ghostly form, as if there were a pentimento of Che concealed behind the partly gaudy and partly peeling façade.

Leaving Cuba and landing in Cancún, Mexico, I buy *The Miami Herald* and *The New York Times*. On the front page of the *Herald* is the news that Hector Silva, candidate of the Farabundo Martí Liberation Front, has been elected mayor of San Salvador. The paper mentions that many of Silva's enthusiasts "still sport" lapel buttons bearing the likeness of Guevara. When I interviewed him in 1987, the brave and eloquent Señor Silva was a much likelier candidate for assassination than election.

The front page of *The New York Times* reports from Zaire, and carries the claim of Laurent-Désir Kabila that his rebel forces will be in the capital city by June. The paper's correspondent, citing the inevitable "Western diplomatic sources," quotes them as saying that they will be surprised if it takes as long as that. One of Guevara's first acts, after the overthrow of Batista, was to extend hospitality and training to the embryonic forces of the Sandinista and Farabundo Martí fronts. And one of his last acts before embarking for Bolivia, was to spend some time on the shores of Lake Tanganyika, attempting to put a little fiber and fervor into the demoralized anti-Mobutu guerrillas. (At this time, he formed a rather low opinion of M. Kabila, whose base and whose tactics were too tribal, who demonstrated a tendency toward megalomania, and who maltreated deserters and prisoners.) Still, Mobutu had been the jewel in the CIA's African crown. So perhaps not all the historical ironies turn out to be at Guevara's expense.

THE SUPERFICIAL ACCOUNT of Che's significance is narrated chiefly in symbols and icons. Some of these constitute a boutique version: Antonio Banderas plays a sort of generic Che in the movie rendition of Sir Andrew Lloyd Webber's *Evita*. As photographed by Alberto Korda with an expression of untameable defiance, Che became the poster boy of the vaguely "revolutionary" generation of the 1960s. (And of that generation's nemesis: the Olivetti conglomerate once used a Che poster in a recruiting advertisement with the caption "We would have hired him.") The Cuban government recently took legal steps to stop a popular European beer being named after its most popular martyr.

Much of the attraction of the cult has to do with the grace of an early and romantic death. George Orwell once observed that if Napoleon Bonaparte had been cut down by a musket ball as he entered Moscow, he would have been remembered as the greatest general since Alexander. And not only did Guevara die before his ideals did, he died in such a manner as to inspire something akin to superstition. He rode among the poor of the *altiplano* on a donkey. He repeatedly foresaw and predicted the circumstances of his own death. He was spurned and betrayed by those he claimed to set free. He was by calling a healer of the sick. The photographs of his corpse, bearded and half-naked and lacerated, make an irresistible comparison with paintings of the deposition from Calvary. There is a mystery about his last resting place. Alleged relics are in circulation. There have even been sightings. . . .

The CIA and its Bolivian military allies chopped off Guevara's hands in order to make a positive fingerprint comparison with records in Argentina: the preserved hands were later returned to Cuba by a defector from La Paz. We may be grateful that the Castro regime did not choose to set up an exhibit of mummification on the model of Lenin's tomb. Though I did discover, during my researches in Havana, that the pictures of Guevara's dead body have never been shown in Cuba. "The Cuban people," I was solemnly told at the national film archive, "are used to seeing Che Guevara alive." And so they do, night after night on their screens—cutting cane as a "volunteer," greeting parties of schoolchildren, orating at the United Nations or the Alliance for Progress, posing in a clearing in the Sierra Maestra or the Bolivian uplands.

One of the special dramas of the Latin American region is that of the *desaparecido*, or "disappeared person." From Buenos Aires to Guatemala City, there are still committees of black-draped *madres* who demand to know the whereabouts of their sons and daughters. And there are also "Truth Commissions" which have come up with the most harrowing evidence of what did happen. Che Guevara is the most famous "disappeared person" in the hemisphere. When Jon Lee Anderson, the author of this intelligent and intriguing biography, published his findings last year on the probable burial site of Guevara's remains (still undetermined, but very probably underneath the runway of a military airport at Vallegrande in Bolivia), he had the incidental effect of igniting a movement of relatives of the *desaparecidos* in Bolivia itself.

Another way of describing, and incidentally of de-trivializing, the legacy of Guevara is to place him as a founding figure of "magical realism." In his *Motorcycle Diaries*, an account of a continental road trip he took as a young medical student in the early 1950s, we read in Guevara's own youthful prose about his fact-finding tour of the leper colonies of Latin America. He celebrated his twenty-fourth birthday at one such colony in the Peruvian Amazon. The patients threw him a party at the conclusion of which, flown with locally distilled *pisco*, he made a speech and said:

> The division of America into unstable and illusory nations is a complete fiction. We are one single mestizo race with remarkable ethnographic similarities, from Mexico down to the Magellan Straits. And so, in an attempt to break free from all narrow-minded provincialism, I propose a toast to Peru and to a United America.

As he later described the same occasion in a letter home to his mother:

> Alberto, who sees himself as Peron's natural heir, delivered such an impressive demagogic speech that our well-wishers were consumed with laughter. . . . An accordion player with no fingers on his right hand used little sticks tied to his wrist, the singer was blind and almost all the others were hideously deformed, due to the nervous form of the disease which is very common in this area. With the light from lamps and lanterns reflected in the river, it was like a scene from a horror film. The place is very lovely. . . .

The boy "Che" drunkenly spouting pan-Americanism to an audience of isolated lepers in a remote jungle — here is a scene that Werner Herzog might hesitate to script, or Gabriel García Márquez to devise. (Márquez once said in the hearing of a friend of mine that in order to write about Guevara he would need a thousand years or a million pages. His non-fiction book *Operation Carlotta*, a straight-forwardly not to say panegyrically Fidelist account of the Cuban expedition to Angola, does deal briefly with Guevara's earlier foray into the Congo.) But writers as diverse as Julio Cortázar and Nicolás Guillén[1] have taken Guevara as an inspiration and indeed one of his more lasting memorials may be in the regional literary imagination.

## 2.

IF WE TAKE this as Anderson does — as a chronicle of a death foretold — then it may be related as an intelligible series of chapters and parables. First we have the rebel: the James Dean and Jack Kerouac type. The young "Che" — the nickname is distinctively Argentine and translates roughly as *copain*, or pal — came from an Irish-Spanish family of impoverished aristocrats with the patronymic of Lynch. He was always a charmer and a wit, and always a troublemaker and heartbreaker. His period of youthful sexual repression seems to have been

---

[1] The imagery of these texts tends to be nationalist-heroic rather than socialist or revolutionary. Though a highly orthodox Communist himself, and a contemporary of Neruda, Nicolás Guillén composed an ode in 1959 comparing Guevara to Martí and San Martín. Julio Cortázar wrote a death-paean for Che, offering his own hands and pen as a replacement for the hands chopped off by the killers.

short: an appealing candor about the physical and libidinous runs through all his writings as it does with very few professional revolutionaries. His family was anti-Nazi and anti-Peronist during a time when this could be perilous in Argentina.

Ernesto took an active if rather theatrical part in local youth and student activism, helping out refugees from Republican Spain and cheeking pro-Nazi teachers and professors. The boy is not yet the father to the man except in two respects: he does not dislike Peron as much as his family does, because Peron is at least a nationalist and a foe of the *Yanqui*. And he is gravely debilitated by asthma, an affliction which he refuses to allow to incapacitate him. The story of his bodybuilding, sporting enthusiasm, and outdoor effort, all aimed at putting strength into a feeble frame, reminds one of nothing so much as (of all people) Theodore Roosevelt. From this derives an emphasis on the will which is essential to the story.

PARABLE TWO CONCERNS his resolve to become a physician. Not only did this expose him to encounters with veteran socialist doctors, but it also gave him a first-hand experience of the misery of the region. The *Motorcycle Diaries*, which reinforce the Dean-Kerouac scapegrace image at one level, also contain some very moving and detailed accounts of this part of his education. A monograph could easily be written on the "radicalizing" effect of medical training on young idealists of the middle class. Guevara was much influenced, on his rattling around the southern cone, by an encounter with the Peruvian leprologist and Marxist Dr. Hugo Pesce. This man, the author of a book on Andean underdevelopment entitled *Latitudes del Silencio*, was the recipient ten years later of an inscribed copy of Guevara's first book, *Guerrilla Warfare*. Clearly its author was interested in more than socialized medicine. (Another attentive reader of that first edition was President John F. Kennedy, who had it rapidly translated for him by the CIA and who then ordered the setting-up of the "Special Forces"—materializing Regis Debray's thesis that "the Revolution revolutionizes the Counter-Revolution.")

Parable three brings us to the consummate-internationalist. Of mixed nationality to begin with, Guevara married a Peruvian woman and took out Mexican citizenship for his children. He was awarded, and later renounced, Cuban nationality. He died in a country named for Simon Bolívar and near a town named for one of Bolívar's lieutenants. His favorite self-image was that of Don Quixote, the rootless wanderer and freelance righter of wrongs. "Once again," as he wrote on quitting Cuba, "I feel Rosinante's ribs creaking between my heels." (It was Alisdair Macintyre who first compared this observation to one made by Karl Marx, who drily noted that "knight errantry is not compatible with all forms of society.") Indeed, Guevara came late to Marxism. For him, the great personal and political crux occurred as a result of his stay in Guatemala in 1954, where he was a direct witness to the ruthless and cynical destabilization of the Arbenz government by the CIA.

THIS STORY HAS been well told before, notably by Stephen Schlesinger and Stephen Kinzer in their book *Bitter Fruit*. Our knowledge of the coup, of the complicity of the United States, and of the hellish consequences for all Guatemalans but especially for the descendants of the Mayan *indigenes*, has recently been sharply enhanced by disclosures from the archive of the Central Intelligence Agency, and by the excavation of an archipelago of unofficial mass graves across the Guatemalan countryside.[2] In the Kinzer-Schlesinger narrative, Guevara rated only a glancing mention. Jon Lee Anderson has reconstructed his part in the events with punctilious detail.

Guevara arrived in Guatemala in December 1953, at the end of his long period of bumming around the continent. He decided to stay, and resolved to become more serious about himself, because he could scent both revolution and counterrevolution in the air. Nor were his instincts at fault. The election of the reformist Jacobo Arbenz had set in motion the two things that the reformists most feared—namely the rising expectations of the revolutionaries and the poor, and the direst forebodings on the part of the United States. (The febrile atmosphere of the place and the moment is well caught in Gore Vidal's novel *Dark Green, Bright Red*.) Guevara decided to offer his credentials as a physician to the new regime, and hoped to be employed as a "barefoot doctor" among the peasants. Discouraged by the bureaucratic response to this proposal, he mingled at first rather ineffectually with the milieu of stateless rebels and revolutionaries who had converged on Guatemala City: the losers in the battles with Somoza and Trujillo and Batista. As he was arriving, Guevara had written home to say that:

[2]See, especially, Peter Kornbluh, *The New York Times*, Op-Ed page, May 31, 1997, on the CIA's published plans to assassinate the Guatemalan then-leadership, and Larry Rohter, "Guatemala Digs Up Army's Secret Cemeteries," *The New York Times*, June 7, 1997.

Along the way, I had the opportunity to pass through the domin-
ions of the United Fruit, convincing me once again of just how
terrible these capitalist octopuses are. I have sworn before a picture of the old and mourned comrade Stalin that I won't rest
until I see these capitalist octopuses annihilated. In Guatemala
I will perfect myself. . . .

Fidel Castro's failed but already legendary attack on the Moncada
barracks in Cuba had taken place the preceding July, and Guevara
fell in (initially as a doctor for one of their number) with some of his
exiled comrades. The talk was all of a coming confrontation with the
colossus to the north, and its local octopus clientele. And indeed, the
script for the events reads like a primer in elementary Leninism. The
Dulles brothers and their corporate friends did embark on an armed
destabilization of the elected Arbenz government. They did engage
the support of neighboring oligarchs such as General Anastasio
Somoza. They did find and pay a military puppet named Castillo
Armas. And they did invade Guatemala with a mercenary force. Guevara and his "internationalist" friends watched all this with a mixture
of shame and incredulity, convinced that their predictions about the
uselessness of gradualism were being confirmed, so to speak, before
their very eyes. But they were impotent.

Chased into the sanctuary of the Argentine embassy by the coup
he had long foreseen and tried vainly to resist, Guevara spent some
very concentrated time with desperate militants who would, in the succeeding decades, become guerrilla commanders in El Salvador,
Nicaragua, and Guatemala itself. Together, they reviewed the lessons
of the defeat. Chief among these, they felt, was Arbenz's failure to dis-
tribute arms to the people. Next came his refusal to take action against
the CIA's clever manipulation of the local press. It was a crucible
moment: a young man receiving an indelible impression at a forma-
tive age. Up until then, Guevara had even by his own account been
playing at revolution. Henceforth he would not joke about Stalin.
Rather he would school himself in the intransigence of the "socialist
camp," and begin to study the canonical work of us lately deceased
but and not yet disowned General Secretary.

IN THE SUCCEEDING parable, Guevara decides that he has found a
mission in life. Guatemala must be avenged. Imperialism must pay

for its arrogance and cruelty. To a friend he writes an agonized letter, saying that the Arbenz government was defeated and betrayed just like the Spanish Republic but without the same courage and honor in its extremity. Indignantly, he repudiates the stories about atrocities committed by pro-Arbenz forces, adding ominously: "There *should* have been a few firing squads early on, which is different. If those shootings had taken place the government would have retained the possibility of fighting back."

Chased from Guatemala to Mexico, when he encounters the young Fidel Castro he needs no persuading that this meeting was meant to happen. Before long he is pursuing a more intensive study of Communist literature and a rigorous training as a guerrilla fighter.[3] (Iconographic note: When the rebel-bearing vessel Granma beaches on Cuban shores and runs straight into an ambush all later accounts stress that this left the nucleus of revolutionary disciples at the numinous number twelve.)

Trotsky once remarked that what distinguished the revolutionary was not his willingness to kill but his readiness to die. The anti-Batista war conducted by Castro, Guevara, Camilo Cienfuegos, and Frank Pais was, by most standards a near-exemplary case of winning "hearts and minds" and recruiting popular enthusiasm. Some informers and deserters and backsliders were executed out of hand, but Guevara seems at first to have shown no relish for such work. Indeed, he cashiered one of his deputies in Camaguey province a bizarre American freebooter named Herman Marks, because of his undue eagerness to take part in reprisal killings or off-the-spot battlefield punishments. Yet Anderson has unearthed a suggestive detail. Once in power in Havana and immediately charged by Castro with purging and punishing Batista's police apparatus, Guevara set up an improvised drumhead tribunal at the harbor fortress of La Cabana, where he sent for Marks again and re-employed him as an executioner.

Some justified this kind of "people's court" as utilitarian Herbert Matthews of *The New York Times* had a go at defending them "from the Cuban's perspective." (The paper wouldn't print his efforts.) But other foreign correspondents were appalled by the lynch trials ordered by Fidel Castro himself, that were held in the Havana sports stadium

[3]According to Aleksandr Fursenko and Timothy Naftain in *One Hell of a Gamble: Khrushchev, Castro, and Kennedy, 1958–1964* (Norton, 1997), which is based on recently released Soviet archives, Guevara went to the length of becoming a formal member of the Cuban Communist Party as early as 1957.

Raul Castro went even further in the city of Santiago machine-gunning seventy captured Batistianos into a ditch dug by a bulldozer. When challenged by friends and family, Guevara resorted to three defenses. First he claimed that everybody at La Cabana had had a hearing. The speed at which the firing squads operated made his argument seem exiguous. Second its reported by Anderson, "he never tired of telling his Cuban comrades that in Guatemala Arbenz had fallen because he had not purged his armed forces of disloyal elements, a mistake that permitted the CIA to penetrate and overthrow his regime." Third, and dropping all pretense, he told a protesting former medical colleague: "Look, in this thing either you kill first, or else you get killed."

Methods and rationalizations of this kind have a way of establishing themselves, not as "emergency measures" but as administrative means of dealing with all opposition. That was the point made by Rosa Luxemburg in her original criticism of Leninism. The Luxemburg example was brought up in a fascinating interview given by Guevara to the American socialist academic Maurice Zeillin on September 14, 1961. In this discussion, the new minister came out firmly for "democratic centralism," praised the Soviet example, and flatly opposed the right of factions or dissidents to make their views known even within the Communist Party itself. Asked by Zeitlin about Luxemburg's warnings on this score Guevara replied coolly that Luxemburg had died "as a consequence of her political mistakes" and that "democratic centralism is a method of government, not only a method of conquering power." It was clear, in other words, that his authoritarian stance was taken on principle and not in response to "tactical" considerations. Huber Matos and other allegedly "bourgeois" supporters of the original revolution who were imprisoned had already found this out, as had the Trotskyists who dared to criticize Fidelism from the "left."[4]

THE FINAL PARABLE is the one in which Guevara recognizes that in a sense his kingdom can never be of this world. Those who sympathized with the Cuban revolution at the time very often did so because

[4]The entire interview, which is replete with the most lugubrious orthodoxy can be found as an appendix to Robert Scheer and Maurice Zeitlin, Cuba: An American Tragedy (Penguin 1964). Until relatively recently it was the custom among certain apologists for Castro to say that United States policy was "driving him into the arms of the Soviet Union." Now that the Cuban one-party state has outlived the Soviet one this excuse is at least no longer vulnerable to the charge that the embrace of the Soviet Union had been the preferred destination in any case.

they explicitly hoped for a non-Soviet model. In the figure of "Che," some of them, at least, thought they had found their exemplar. And they were, in one unintended sense, not mistaken. Guevara was privately critical of the Soviet bloc, already well into its post-Stalinist phase, on the grounds that it was too soft. It wanted "peaceful coexistence" with the American imperium abroad, and a system of capitalist emulation at home. There is a good deal of evidence that he privately sympathized with the emerging position of the Maoists — especially for the "countryside versus city" theses of Lin Piao, where the immiserated peasants of the world were supposed to surround the debauched metropoles and overwhelm them by sheer force of numbers and might have done so more openly if not for the close yet surreptitious friendship between the Castro brothers and Moscow.

It is certain that he was enraged by Khrushchev's compromise with Kennedy over the missiles and by the generally lukewarm attitude of the Warsaw Pact toward revolution in the Third World. In February 1965, while addressing an "Afro-Asian Solidarity" meeting in Algiers, he went so far as to describe the Kremlin as "an accomplice of imperialism" for its cold-cash dealings with impoverished and insurgent states. This, and the general chaos arising from his stewardship of the Ministry for Industry made him an easy target for inner-party attacks by the unsmiling elements among the Cuban Communist Party: people for whom the very words "romanticism" and "adventurism" were symptoms of deviation. His dismissal from the ministry followed immediately on his return from Algiers, and he soon afterward set off for Africa with no very clear, mandate or position.

The word "romantic" does not make a very good fit with his actual policies as industry minister. The French economist René Dumont, one of the many well-meaning Marxists who advised Cuba during this period, recalls making a long study of the "agricultural cooperatives." He told Guevara that the workers in these schemes did not feel themselves to be the proprietors of anything. He pressed him to consider a system of rewards for those who performed extra tasks in the off-season. As Dumont records, Guevara's reaction was tersely dismissive. He demanded instead:

A sort of ideal vision of Socialist Man, who would become a stranger to the mercantile side of things working for society and not for profit. He was very critical of the industrial success of the

**GOODBYE TO ALL THAT**
453

Soviet Union [!] where, he said, everybody works and strives and tries to go beyond his quota, but only to earn more money. He did not think the Soviet Man was really a new sort of man, for he did not find him any different, really, than a Yankee. He refused to consciously participate in the creation in Cuba "of a second American society."

It's worth noting at this point that Guevara made almost no study of American society, scarcely visited the country except as a speaker at the United Nations and evinced little curiosity about it in general. When asked once again by Maurice Zeitlin, what he would like the United States to do he replied, "Disappear."

IN VIEW OF the resemblance of Guevara's Spartan program to other celebrated fiascos and tragedies like the Great Leap Forward, it deserves to be said that he was unsparing of himself. He worked unceasingly, was completely indifferent to possessions, and performed heavy lifting and manual labor even when the cameras were not turning. In the same way, he wanted to share in the suffering and struggle of those, in Africa and elsewhere, who were receiving the blunt end of the cold war. The murder of Patrice Lumumba in the Congo, for example seems to have affected him in very much the same personal way as did the overthrow of Jacobo Arbenz. He was perhaps one of those rare people for whom there is no real gap between conviction and practice.

And he did have a saving element of humor. I possess a tape of his appearance on an early episode of "Meet the Press" in December 1964, where he confronts a solemn panel of network pundits. When they address him about the "conditions" that Cuba must meet in order to be permitted the sunshine of American approval, he smiles as he proposes that there need be no preconditions: "After all, we do not demand that you abolish racial discrimination. . . ." A person as professionally skeptical as I. F. Stone so far forgot himself as to write: "He was the first man I ever met who I thought not just handsome but beautiful. With his curly reddish beard, he looked like a cross between a faun and a Sunday-school print of Jesus. . . . He spoke with that utter sobriety which sometimes masks immense apocalyptic visions."

Those whom the gods wish to destroy they probably begin by calling "charismatic." The last few years of Guevara's life were a study in diminishing returns. He drove himself harder and harder relying more and more on exhortation and example, in order to accomplish less and less. In the case of the Cuban economy, the argument over "moral" versus "material" incentives became muddied with the system eventually resolving itself into one of material non-incentive, periodically prodded by slogans along Eastern European lines.

ON THE FRONT of the "world revolution," which is more fully treated by Anderson, Guevara's tricontinental activity (Asia, Africa, Latin America) was sometimes ahead of its time and sometimes behind, but never quite on target. For example, he lent his support to a catastrophic guerrilla operation in the wilds of his native Argentina—catastrophic in the sense that it was an abysmal failure and led to the deaths of most of its members as well as of a few civilians but catastrophic, too, in that it began the quasi-bandit phase of radical politics in Argentina. Like Trotsky in exile, his guesswork sometimes allowed him to make important predictions, or even to compose moving post mortems. But he could do no more than dream of a new "international."

He was among the first to appreciate the central importance of the war in Vietnam: a place where the hated American empire had made itself morally and militarily vulnerable. But his most celebrated speech on the subject which called for replicating the Vietnamese experience across the globe, sounded bombastic at the time and reads even more so today. His voyage to Africa to combat Mobutu and his white mercenaries in the Congo and to open a second front against apartheid and colonialism, was conducted on a moral and material shoestring. He was humbled on the battlefield as well as sabotaged by the anti-Ben Bella coup in Algeria and an outbreak of second thoughts by the Tanzanians. As Guevara scuttled his last positions on Lake Tanganyika in 1965, he did not try to delude himself:

A desolate, sobering and inglorious spectacle took place. I had to reject men who pleaded to be taken along. There was not a trace of grandeur in this retreat, nor a gesture of rebellion . . . just some sobbing as if [I] the leader of the escapees, told the man with the mooring rope to let go.

GUEVARA'S HEALTH—ANOTHER subject on which he did not delude himself—had deteriorated further in Africa, and his fortieth birthday was looming up. It was evident to him that he had only one more chance to deal a decisive stroke at the detested imperial power. He had had Bolivia in mind for a long time, because its *altiplano* abutted several other countries and a guerrilla foco properly inserted there might act as a lever on an entire region. The extreme altitude, desolation and under-development of the area do not seem to have struck him as a disadvantage until far too late, although it was at this time that he began to recur to the subject of his own death which he always prefigured as a defiant one in the face of hopeless odds.

Anderson's reconstruction of the Bolivian campaign is exhaustive and convincing. It is clear that the Bolivian Communists regarded Guevara's adventures as an unpardonable intrusion into their "internal affairs," and that they had the sympathy of Moscow in so doing. The persistent rumor that Castro too, was glad to be rid of a turbulent comrade is rated by Anderson as less well founded. A successful revolution or even upheaval in Latin America would have strengthened his hand and perhaps helped end his isolation and dependence: Havana kept in touch with the doomed expedition for as long as it could.

But of course it also had, in the case of a defeat, the option of declaring an imperishable martyrdom. Since 1968, the "Year of the Heroic Guerrilla," Cuban children have been instructed in almost Baden-Powell tones that if they seek a "role model," they should comport themselves *como el Che*. This strenuous injunction only emphasizes the realization that Guevara's Cromwellian, ascetic demands on people bordered on the impossible, even the inhuman. The grandson who is said most to resemble him—a young man named Canek—has quit the island in order to pursue the vocation of a heavy-metal guitarist in Mexico, and it is a moral and material certainty that many of his generation wish they could do the same.

Having been captured in the first days of October 1967, Guevara was killed in cold blood. The self-serving account of his last hours given by Felix Rodriguez, the Cuban-American CIA agent on the scene, at least makes this clear. Rodriguez wastes a lot of time explaining that he was full of doubt and remorse, and that he had no authority to overrule the Bolivian military but succeeds only in drawing a distinction without a difference. The Bolivian Special Forces would have done what they were told and it seems that, Rodriguez notwithstanding, they knew what was wanted of them. As always in these cases, a "volunteer" executioner was eager and on hand. Che's surviving disciples managed to escape in a wretched state across the Chilean border, where they were met by a then obscure physician named Salvador Allende and given by him a safe-conduct to Easter Island and home.

GUEVARA'S EXEMPLARY FINAL days which Rodriguez describes as suffused with "grace and courage," demonstrated yet again and conclusively that he was no hypocrite. The news of his murder somehow helped to inaugurate the "hot" period of the 1960s, in which, however much the image of "Che" was to the fore, it was the hedonist Utopians rather than the rigorous revolutionary puritans who made the running. Thus, in a slightly bizarre manner, the same Che was able to achieve the impossible or at least the incompatible, by simultaneously summoning an age of chivalry and an age of revolution. That posthumous accomplishment was necessarily brief.

Our own age of sophists and calculators has thrown up some of the surviving actors in secondary roles. Felix Rodriguez for example, having gone on to serve the CIA in Vietnam and El Salvador, surfaced again as George Bush's embarrassing underling in the Iran-contra scandal. He was stunned while being questioned on other matters by Senator John Kerry's committee of investigation into illegal drugs and guns to be asked from the chair why he had not tried to save Che Guevara's life.[5]

As Jon Lee Anderson's work serves to remind us, when Che Guevara first spurred Rosinante into the field the world was a radically different place. Most of South and Central America was in the safekeeping of military *caudillos*. The Portuguese empire was secure in Africa. Vietnam was still (just) a French colony. The Shah of Iran had been crammed back on his throne. Nelson Mandela was a semiclandestine human rights lawyer. Algeria was French and the Congo was Belgian. The Suez Canal zone was British. In the processes that overturned his situation, Guevara was a nebulous and elusive but nonetheless real presence. The very element that gave him his certainty and courage—his revolutionary communism—was also the element that condemned him to historical eclipse. In setting down the whole story in such a respectful but objective manner, Jon Lee Anderson has succeeded in writing for himself and I suspect for many others, a nuanced goodbye to all that.

[5]*Shadow Warrior: The CIA's Hero of a Hundred Unknown Battles,* by Felix Rodriguez with John Weisman (Simon and Schuster, 1989).

# TEN THOUSAND REVOLUTIONS: THROUGH SOUTH AMERICA, IN SEARCH OF CHE GUEVARA

## PATRICK SYMMES

**HARPER'S MAGAZINE**

JUNE 1997

## buenos aires, argentina, january 4, 1996

ON THE WAY down to the port, we drive behind the Casa Rosada, the presidential palace. The taxi is moving fast (in Buenos Aires, they all do), and I catch a sudden glimpse of a tiny crowd, some banners, and a cloud of smoke drifting through the air.

"Tear gas," the driver announces. "Roll up your window."

We barrel along toward the port, passing a dark green beast lumbering the other way up the avenue. It is an armored truck topped with a comically tiny spout for shooting water at the *delincuentes*. I ask my driver what cause has brought peaceful Argentina back to the brink of civil unrest.

"Well," he says, meditating for a moment while cutting off a bus. He looks in his mirror—at me.

"What day of the week is it?" he asks. Thursday, I say. "Well," he says, "I think on Thursday it's the teachers."

The shipping agent has called: after three days my motorcycle has at last been located deep within a warehouse. I pay off the cabbie and follow a dock foreman who eventually and with great flourish presents me with a Honda chopper. Unfortunately, it is not mine. Mine is a BMW dirt bike. It takes only a few more hours to find it in yet another building behind some pallets of shrink-wrapped VCRs.

The saddlebags are still attached, which astonishes the foreman. Like every Argentine I have met, he takes his countrymen for thieves. Perhaps my luck is due only to the poverty of the enclosed possessions: a sleeping bag, a tent, and a copy of *The Motorcycle Diaries*, a road journal written long ago by that disinherited son of Argentina, Ernesto "Che" Guevara. Before he was famous as Fidel Castro's right-hand man, before he seeded revolutions across Latin America and appeared on a million North American dormroom posters, the young Che Guevara had set off to see the Americas by motorcycle. It was January 4, 1952, exactly forty-four years ago; he was just twenty-three. My plan is to retrace the journey described in his diary, going where he went, seeing what he saw.

Che changed Latin America because this trip changed him. Departing Buenos Aires an aristocratic rake, he returned eight months later a revolutionary. His new credo traveled with him, first to Bolivia, then Guatemala, and eventually Mexico, where he joined forces with Fidel Castro. By the time Castro overthrew the Cuban government in 1959, Che was more than a master of guerrilla warfare; he was its guru. Tens of thousands of young men and women then followed either him or his example. They besieged Brazil, Peru, Bolivia, Colombia, Chile, Argentina, Nicaragua, and El Salvador with cycle after cycle of guerrilla assaults, each one met with brutal countermeasures by armies uniformed or secret and the whole process descending into the generation-long bloodbath that was Latin America in the '60s, '70s, and '80s.

Now, but for the clockwork motions of the If-it's Thursday-then-they-must-be-teachers variety, the left has gone silent across the hemisphere, its old logic short-circuited by the end of the Cold War, its vocabulary inadequate to the challenge of NAFTA, GATT, and MERCOSUR, globalization, privatization, liberalization. The victory of free-market thinking is not without benefits or without costs. This morning's newspaper reports above the fold that stocks on the Argentine Bolsa are again climbing; below the fold an intrepid reporter has solved the mystery of Argentina's missing cats. As a rather gory photo shows, the children of the new shantytowns are roasting them for dinner.

Fertile ground for new revolutionaries once, but now the ground seems tired and produces only old ones: Che himself, missing for almost thirty years, has reportedly been traced to a small town in rural Bolivia. Back in 1967 he was killed there leading a dismal guerrilla column and then stuffed into an anonymous grave sometime before dawn. Now, spurred by the confession of a military of officer, a team of Argentine forensic experts has descended on Bolivia, trailed by some sixty journalists from all over the world. Che's imminent exhumation has sparked an absurd, necrophiliac dispute: the Argentines want his body brought here as a symbol of reconciliation with their lost son; the Cubans want Saint Che taken to Havana to breathe life into the dying revolution; the Bolivians want to keep him for the tourist revenues.

I could ride to Bolivia right now and be there before his bones are divided among the wolves, but I have arranged this trek not merely to see Che's body; I would understand something of his soul as well. And so I must approach Bolivia as he did, via Patagonia, Chile, and Peru. By the time I reach him, he may be gone.

I repack the saddlebags and kick the motorcycle to life. I turn left or right at random and throw the bike from side to side on the straightaways, relearning its balance. After a while I look up and see I am in La Boca, the Brooklyn of Buenos Aires. Tough, working-class Italians live here, guarded against outsiders, believing only in the invincibility of the Boca soccer team and the divinity of Eva Duarte de Peron, she of haute couture and Andrew Lloyd Webber. She, too, has been exhumed a time or two, but it is always dangerous to tamper with old myths. Someone has spray-painted a message on the corrugated fencing of a construction sight: MADONNA PUTA.

## departing buenos aires, january 6

AT NOON, 229 MILES outside of Buenos Aires, I run the tank dry and coast to a stop at a blank spot on the map of the empty, flat pampas. Trees here are a sign of man, so I walk toward a distant clump and find a tattered shack, careful to clap loudly, twice, as I approach. This is a gaucho greeting: on the enormous plain, being close enough to knock is considered rude. After a few minutes a sleepy, shirtless cowboy emerges, scratching himself and offering greetings in archaic, formal Spanish. We spend ten minutes exchanging pleasantries at pistol range before he leads me to another shed in back, pushes aside enough tackle to outfit a cavalry regiment, and begins sucking mouthfuls of gasoline from the tank of his Ford Falcon. Sputtering away on this mixture of fuel and spit I am able to reach Miramar at sunset.

In 1952, Che stopped here to say goodbye to the life he was leaving—the relatives, friends, and most of all his beautiful girlfriend, Maria del Carmen "Chichina" Ferreyra, an heiress from one of the most prominent families in Cordoba. Miramar was then an exclusive resort of the rich, a white city on the South Atlantic coast where people from "good family" idled away the summer in quiet splendor. Che spent eight days here, much of it necking with Chichina in her family's car. "[I]n the great belly of the Buick," he wrote with evident irony, "the bourgeois side of my universe was still under construction."

But Chichina doesn't come to Miramar much anymore. As with the rest of Argentina, an impoverished but striving middle class has taken over, thronging the white city with blaring radios and surfboards and stripping away the old elegance. To see her I must ride north, to Cordoba.

I find her waiting for me on the steps of Cordoba's cathedral; she is in her sixties now and strikingly beautiful. For four hours she strides purposefully through her city, showing me old churches, interesting bookstores, chic cafes, art galleries, houses of the nobility, squares with elegant fountains, and plazas. She talks charmingly about religious art, the latest news from Washington, her life during the Dirty War, the cult of Evita Peron, economic globalization, the fate of Africa, the Internet, Cuba's health-care system, Greenwich Village, the publishing industry, race relations in Peru—everything but Ernesto Guevara. She is unwilling to become a footnote to his story. I pry, though, and by the time we step into an old courtyard at the law school, a well-preserved gem of colonial architecture, I have clearly worn out her courtesy. She begins to fume, and I can see that the tour is over.

We turn to leave and her step falters. Behind us, unseen as we walked in, is a huge portrait of Che, his scowling visage topped by the familiar red-starred beret. The students at the law school have been protesting something; it isn't clear what. VENCEREMOS, the poster shouts—"We will win!"

Chichina stares for a moment at the face she once kissed, a myth she has been fleeing across a lifetime. She mutters something so quiet that I have to lean forward to hear her: "It's just an icon that has nothing to do with him," she says. She walks beneath the poster and into the dark passage that leads to the street. "They don't even know who he was."

## san martin de los andes, argentina, february 4

COMING OUT OF a Patagonian rainstorm into the lakeside town of San Martin, I have to thaw my fingers over a coffee-shop cortardo before I can even flip through the local phone book, looking for a name that doesn't exist.

Che's diary mentions staying outside San Martin with a family of "very welcoming Germans" named Von Putnamer. The name isn't listed here or in nearby towns. No doubt time will have wiped away much of Che's trail.

The waiter sees me closing the book and asks who I am looking for. I give him the name.

"Puttkamer," he corrects. "25250, I think."

Oscar Von Puttkamer answers the phone on the first ring. "How soon can you come over?" he says. "I'll tell you all about it."

The Von Puttkamers were Prussian nobility in previous generations, and the estancia that Che mentioned was a suitably huge ranch where dozens of poorly paid peones labored to enrich the owners. Time, hyperinflation, and political chaos have changed things somewhat, and Oscar now lives on just a fraction of the old land, in a small, sturdy house that he built with his own hands. He has only two peones — both of them ancient — who later admit to me privately that their boss is a fair man.

"I was only one or two when he was here," Oscar says, sitting me down in front of a big plate of food. He doesn't remember anything about the visit, naturally, but five years ago a friend told him of Che's diary and the entry mentioning the "don Putnamers." I show him a passage that even mentions "one of the owner's sons" who found the filthy and famished traveler "a bit odd."

"Just think," Oscar says with a great belly laugh, "Che Guevara probably looked into my crib!"

"Of course," he says, the smile dying on his face, "I hate everything that son of a bitch did to us."

Oscar begins ticking off the "Guevarist" guerrilla groups that began to appear in Argentina as early as 1961. The Uturunco, the Revolutionary Popular Army, the Montoneros—no matter how many times the army wiped out one cell another appeared, until bombs were roaring in the cities and policemen were gunned down routinely on street corners. Like most of the Argentines I've met, Oscar remembers this public madness better than the silent terror that followed the military coup of 1976, when secret death squads killed more than 10,000 Argentines. The great majority of the killing was done by the right, not the left, but Oscar can't help blaming Che.

"He provoked the greatest national conflict in our history," Oscar says. "Look at us now," he adds, a remark explained only by his sad tone.

When the young Guevara peered into Oscar's crib, revolution could not have been further from his mind. "Maybe one day when I'm tired of wandering, I'll come back to Argentina and settle in the Andean lakes," he wrote. He fantasized about commuting to his future medical practice in a helicopter. He wrote a self-mocking sketch of the peones rising for work in the early morning while he indolently sips his tea and spends the day trout fishing.

Later, rod in hand, I wade into the same river below the estancia that Che fished in. One by one the trout slip from their hidden lies beneath the willow branches and hook themselves. I make a fire and eat under the stars.

## futaleufu, chile, february 6

I CROSS THE Andes on a dirt road in the rain, clear customs, and push on toward the Carretera Austral, the only north-south road in these remote parts. This road is somewhat famous in Chile: it was pushed through the deep forests of the south allegedly on the personal orders of General Augusto Pinochet and is constantly cited as an example of his good works. Having overthrown Chile's elected president, Salvador Allende, in 1973, killed 3,000 of his own citizens, and ruled Chile despotically for seventeen years, the General needs all the credit he can get, I suppose. Unfortunately, the road proves to be the exact same mixture of mud and gravel as the roads that civilian governments build in South America. The only difference is that on the Carretera Austral, the bridges are named after military officers martyred at the hands of leftist guerrillas. Since the guerrillas were few and inept during Pinochet's rule, there are actually more bridges than officers, and thus even sergeants and a few privates end up honored.

I'm busy composing a metaphor about Chile as a land of holes in the ground, of anonymous graves and buried secrets, when I strike an actual hole in the General's road, fly first left and then right, and finally shoot sideways into the bush at thirty miles an hour, shattering the windscreen, snapping off various bits and pieces of the motorcycle, and cracking a rib.

Lying on the ground in the rain with the motorcycle on top of me, I hear a truck drive by. Five minutes later it comes slowly beeping backward down the road and stops. The driver ties a rope to the back of the truck, pulls the bike up the embankment, and we bang on various bent pieces with hammers until he has to hurry off. I stand in the middle of the road, in the rain, in the emptiest quarter of South America, surrounded by my broken and muddy possessions. Che had crashed thirteen times by this point, but this knowledge is of no comfort. I press the starter button and the bike comes back to life. I go on.

## caleta gonzalo, chile, february 9–11

AFTER A FEW days the pain in my side has grown unbearable, and I am given shelter by an American millionaire. For his past sins as head of a retail-clothing empire, he has purchased an indulgence in the form of 700,000 acres of precious old-growth forest. The millionaire is going to give this land back to Chile as a national park, preserving it forever from the clear-cutting on which Santiago now depends for hard currency. For three days I recuperate in his compound at the end of an isolated fjord, surrounded by trackless wilderness. The buildings were made by local craftsmen, using local wood and local techniques. There are no phones or faxes, and everything is heated with wood stoves. The food is grown in a vast garden; the shellfish, taken from the fjord by area skin divers. The millionaire wears a sweater that was woven in the village across the fjord. For all this he pays handsomely— a way of assuring that the indigenous people can remain here, doing what they have always done. It is a form of modern leftism, topdown, money-driven, and entirely post-politics. The millionaire refers to this arrangement as "deep ecology." The locals call it a miracle.

On my last night there some boats arrive bearing folk musicians from all over southern Chile, nearly one hundred of them, the finest and most traditional players in the land, all lured here with healthy paychecks to put on a grand concert in the airplane hangar. The audience consists of myself, the millionaire, his wife, and a few local boys who wander in, drawn by the thrumming of the generator in the darkness. At one point the millionaire stands up and gives a short and thoughtful speech in heavily accented Spanish on global economics. He stumbles a bit pronouncing monoculturizacion.

The next morning I sail down the fjord on a fishing smack with twenty of the musicians, wondering whether Che would be an environmentalist by now. When we are out of sight of the compound, some of the players put on tiny headphones and start listening to rap music. They all say that the millionaire—whom they call patron, or boss—is a wonderful man, the very best.

But still, one guitarist says as we lurch up the fjord on thick seas, he is being very stubborn about not buying a satellite dish and some TV sets.


### chuquicamata, chile, march 4

WE AREN'T ALL that broke, but explorers of our stature would rather die than pay for the bourgeois comfort of a hostel.
— From Che's letter to his mother, July 6, 1952

At last, a hero I can believe in. The young Che is a brilliant moocher, and in Chuquicamata I employ a routine he proudly describes in his diary for getting free food and drink I talk my way into the local fire station, and soon I am entertaining the caretaker with stories of my world travels. Naturally, he provides a glass of Chilean red to accompany such talk, but I steadfastly refuse to touch it until he grows insulted. "Well," I say, repeating Che's line, "no offense, but in my country we're not used to drinking without some food to wash it down."

In no time at all the caretaker has whipped up a vast meal. And he throws in a free bed for the night. How well Che knew how to lead men.

In the morning I stand, slightly hungover, at the lip of the Chuquicamata copper mine. It is an astoundingly large hole in the desert, two miles long and a mile and a half wide, all of it dug out by the 10,000 men who have labored here over the course of the century. The pit has hardly changed since 1952—it was the largest open-pit mine in the world then, and still is—but the political terrain has shifted back and forth around it. When Che stood here the mine belonged to Anaconda, the Montana copper giant. The miners were paid a dismal wage and lived in dismal conditions: collapsing shacks, no health care. In 1964 the mine was partly nationalized, and not by a Marxist like Salvador Allende but by President Eduardo Frei, a conservative. In his turn, Allende expanded state control and gave the miners a social contract unprecedented in Latin America: housing allowances, a subsidized canteen, free medical care, and guaranteed employment. Even the country's laissez-faire dictator, General Pinochet, was careful to preserve this public ownership of the means of production, which is why some Chileans called his economic policy "right-wing socialism."

Now President Frei—that is, the son of the earlier President Frei— is talking about "efficiency" and "new times" for Chile, which the miners interpret to mean selling the mine back to the gringos. The men Che called the "blond, efficient, arrogant managers" are already back in the desert: Australian, South African, and American firms are operating a new, highly automated mine not far from here.

At the lip of the pit, I approach the only miner in sight, a short fellow in a dusty orange jumpsuit and a blue hard hat. He is staring at a suitcase at his feet from which two wires run to a disk resembling an upside-down dinner plate. "He pe ese," he says: GPS, the Global Positioning System. He works for the mine's surveying office, which tracks on a daily basis the constantly changing shape of the hole. He is testing the new GPS system, and if it works the surveying office will be reduced from ten men to five. "They will find a job for me somewhere else," he says, probably with one of the private subcontractors the mine is relying on more and more to cut costs. The miners are keenly aware of the ground shifting under their feet. This fellow looks over the hole and discourses on globalization, added-value production, and the price of Indonesian copper.

There is a great cloud of dust over the digging operations to the left, which are close to some buildings that he points out. "El pueblo Americano," he says. The American town. It is the former residence of the Anaconda engineers, a village of fine New England-style clapboard houses. The digging, he notes, must follow the copper vein wherever it goes, and right now that is toward the American town. It will take years to cover the last few hundred yards, according to the surveyors' calculations, but eventually the iron rule of profit means that the copper must be taken out and the town must fall.

"In 2005," the miner says, "pfft." And he undercuts the clapboard village with a sudden slice of his hand.

### chacaluta, chile, march 9

HOUR AFTER HOUR I follow smooth blacktop through the desert, a waste land interrupted only by the occasional roadside whorehouse or the distant ruins of old mining camps. I leave the pavement twice to bounce over the packed soil and investigate these wrecks. The first is a small town of collapsing huts surrounded by barbed wire, and my engine rouses the caretaker from a drunken slumber. This place, he explains, was a concentration camp during the 1970s, and one can still find graffiti left on the barracks walls by imprisoned Allende aides.

The other ruin proves to be a lonely cemetery. A sign identifies it as the Rica Aventura nitrate mine. Rich Adventure: the name rings a bell, and digging in Guevara's diary I find a brief note that he spent a couple of nights here, observing some of the same miners now buried in front of me. Since even plastic flowers wilt in this heat, the tombs are decorated only with scraps of iron—wreaths made from barrel hoops, metal flowers blooming with rust, vines of barbed wire. The whole boneyard rattles in the wind like an untuned orchestra.

Back on the road, three more hours of emptiness and then what seems at first a mirage: a lone figure walking by the side of the road in a dust storm. But he is real: a sunburned madman patrolling the desert with ten liters of water in his backpack. For twenty minutes I tape-record him babbling about Masonic conspiracies, the secret languages of mountains and trees, and other nonsense. I give him some bread.

"In Chile, there are only two kinds of people," he says by way of thanks. "The innocent and the living."

### lima, peru, march 20

I WAKE UP late and hungry, find some carryout, and as I'm walking back to my hotel I pass in front of the Palestinian Consulate. A pair of pudgy policemen jump out of the bushes and demand that I surrender the dangerous parcel bomb I'm carrying. They argue about who should open it and settle on me. I untie the ominous string, unwrap the suspicious brown paper, and open the disturbing cardboard box. We all look at the three empanadas inside. "One chicken, two beef," I say. But I am grateful for their care. There are two guerrilla groups in Peru, and both of them mix bombs with diplomats. The more deadly of the two is the infamous Shining Path, unique among Latin guerrillas in that it despises Che as just another "revisionist dog" like Fidel Castro or Leonid Brezhnev. The Shining Path are Maoists, cold killers who use machetes in highland villages and car bombs in urban areas. Their rivals, the MRTA, are a more traditional group—what the academics call "Guevarist" in orientation. They worship Cuba and try to kill mostly soldiers and policemen. It is the MRTA, of course, who will in a few months take more than 400 hostages during a party at the Japanese ambassador's residence. Such sieges were once standard in Latin America and often were followed by terrifying massacres (at the Colombian Palace of Justice, 1985) or large ransoms (at the Nicaraguan National Palace, 1978). Yet the party raid will be different from the moment MRTA guerrillas slip inside disguised as waiters carrying canapes. The inevitable commando assault will follow a truly postmodern siege in which the guerrillas watch soap operas and release statements via their Web page while the hostages hold self-improvement seminars on topics such as the benefits of kidnapping insurance. A pollster—himself a captive—will be allowed to survey his fellow hostages and publish the results: surprisingly, only 87 percent of those held on the first floor will feel that security at the party was "inadequate." In the end, the inept guerrillas will be playing a game of indoor soccer when Peruvian commandos finally burst in and kill them all.

No wonder they still can't locate Che's body in the Bolivian mud. Perhaps he is too embarrassed to be found.

## lima, march 28

I RIDE UP the Avenida de Garcilaso de la Vega into the city's choked and choking center. Weaving among the stalled traffic, I slip past the collectivo taxis and their "door boys" shouting destinations; past the inevitable Volkswagen Beetles spewing black smoke, the inescapable taste of Lima; past the teenage soldiers with Galil rifles clouding the sidewalks around important buildings; past the vendors who flood the intersections selling lottery tickets, cigarettes, gum, windshield wipers (I no longer have a windshield to wipe), key chains, old magazines, statuettes of Jesus Christ, and soccer balls.

In 1952 Lima was still the "city of the viceroys," as Che called it. The old city center was Spanish in appearance and manner, "the perfect example of a Peru which has never emerged from its feudal, colonial state. It is still waiting for the blood of a truly liberating revolution."

The R word at last. Che believed that a revolution would be "truly liberating," but I can't say that the bloodshed so far has done Peru any good. The old Lima has indeed been replaced, but by a new order that swings into view once I pass the presidential palace and ride up onto the bridge over the filthy Rio Rimac: shantytowns as far as the eye can see. They are filled with the poor who have been driven from their old lives by innumerable revolutionaries, by drug traffickers, by army massacres, by the globalization of agriculture and the lure of city lights. For forty years they have flooded down from the hills, an army of peasant millions, surrounding Che's city of viceroys with a belt of shabby homes, each wave of migrants climbing higher up the stony hills until the old Lima lives surrounded by the sullen gaze of its mestizo bastards.

Navigating these "New Towns" is impossible for a stranger. There are few landmarks and fewer street signs, so I follow vague instructions like "go past the tower" and "left in five minutes" and "look for the restaurant" until, after half an hour of circling, I find the leper colony. The gate is open and I drive straight in, kill the engine, dismount, and am immediately overwhelmed by children.

Their questions, in order:

"Is it true in your country you can rent Nintendo games?"

"What kind of cargo do you carry?"

"Is America the last country?"

"Would you like to see where Che Guevara lived?"

Before Che ever conceived of world revolution, he believed in the untouchables. In medical school he developed an interest in leprosy, and in Peru he visited three leper colonies, including this one. In those days the lepers were forced to live here. Now, although the walls remain, the gate is open and the only lepers still living here are the twenty or so who chose to stay. They get medical care, some food, and crude houses that are nonetheless far superior to the shanties outside the walls.

Che noted that one of the most powerful treatments for leprosy was a firm handshake: when he sat with the lepers, took their hands confidently, played soccer and ate with them, they saw that he had no fear. "This may seem pointless bravado," Che wrote to his father, "but the psychological benefit to these poor people—usually treated like animals—of being treated as normal human beings is incalculable . . ."

I'm no Che. The first adult I meet is named Serafino, and when we shake hands I blanch visibly at his thumbless grip. Like many lepers, Serafino has a slightly "crazy" expression, the result of nerve degeneration in his face. Even in Che's day there were medicines to arrest the disease, but poverty is its own illness, and Serafino grew up untreated. Born sometime in the 1950s—he doesn't know when—he was exiled to his first leper colony in 1967.

Serafino raises fighting cocks and corn and Chinese onions, all of which he shows me. He wasn't here in 1952, of course, but Che is a vast myth in Latin America, and lepers have their own channels of communication. While irrigating his corn, Serafino tells me that Che "lived here for about two or three months. In the daytime he worked in the laboratory inventing new treatments, and at night he went into the city and organized his groups." Eventually, Serafino explains, Che launched his world revolution in Peru, was defeated in battle, and fled to his death in Bolivia.

Every detail of this story is wrong—Che was here a couple of weeks, he spent his days touring museums, he wasn't a guerrilla then, and he never fought in Peru—but in the minds of Serafino and millions of the dispossessed the story is entirely true. Across the continent there are a hundred such tales, and the point is always as powerful as it is simple: Che lived and died for us.

Serafino shows me the little blue shack where Che supposedly lived. There was a photo of him on the wall inside for many years, but they had to take it down in the 1970s. Yes, I say sympathetically, it wasn't safe to keep a photo of Che during those reactionary times.

"No," Serafino says, "they had to paint the place."

On the way back to my motorbike I notice, gleaming up on a hillside in neon splendor, a statue of Jesus looking down upon the city.

UP INTO THE Andes, the poison of Lima dropping behind as I climb from sea level to 8,000 feet in ninety minutes and then stop at a police post to adjust my wheezing carburetor. The policemen ask about the bike, about where I have been and where I am going. They talk about how nice it would be to drive a motorcycle across America one day, and I nod, hating these moments. We all know that they will live in these cold mountains for the rest of their lives. Only a few nations are allowed to dream.

Climbing another hour I top the road at 15,400 feet and enter the rugged altiplano that will carry me down the spine of the Andes and into Bolivia. Days crawl by in a series of miserable and precious moments: driving through a snowstorm without gloves, fording seven rivers in a single day, a "highway" that loses its pavement and eventually its sanity in ever narrower twists, a landslide that erases the road from a cliff face for thirty-six hours, a band of peasant pilgrims who take me for a priest and begin kissing my hands (having lost my modesty a thousand miles back, I bless them gladly and send them on their way), soldiers looking for "a few bandits" just ahead, peasant dancers in blue-eyed masks reenacting the Conquest for fifty drunken Indians and one suddenly nervous blue-eyed boy, and always the precious gasoline spooned into my dry tank with coffee cans.

Ten days later I touch pavement again in Cuzco. Che wrote pages about the "impalpable dust of other ages that covers" the city, but now the ancient capital of the Incas is a tourist trap. Suddenly I am surrounded by Gore-Tex, guitar-playing hippies, and beautiful French-Canadian girls. I have a kind of nervous breakdown while eating pizza in a 500-year-old palace and have to lie down for a day. Possibly this is altitude sickness.

### cuzco, april 11

THIS PLACE IS crawling with guerrillas, but they've all retired. I spend a morning in the office of a municipal bureaucrat who admits vaguely to having been "in the movement" during the 1960s. At one point he stands behind his desk, thundering out memorized sections of Che's famous 1961 speech in Uruguay.

"He was a symbol," the man says, slumping into his chair again to catch the breath he has lost over the last thirty years, "a symbol of a new type of leader, of a new era. He wasn't a bureaucrat or a union leader or a politician"—three terms that could describe this man himself—"but a romantic type. He crossed from country to country, traveling by foot or horse or motorcycle like you, getting to know all of Latin America."

In a coffee shop, another aged guerrilla tells me about training under Che in Cuba in 1961. He flips over the syllabus of the economics course he now teaches and draws a crude sketch of Latin America. Working fast, he begins filling the map with the span of guerrilla history: the years and locations (Cuba 1959, Peru 1963/65, Bolivia 1967), the forgotten acronyms (NOL, ELN, MTR, JPC, COB, MIR, MNR), the names of fallen leaders (El Che, Mario Monje, Hugo Blanco). He draws arrows slicing along the paths of influence, the lines of escape, the clandestine missions. After thirty minutes, the outline of the continent itself is obscured by this spirograph of failed revolutions, and at last he pauses. He says nothing for a while, rapping the pen furiously against the table, a drumbeat of disillusion, death, disaster.

"We failed," he says. "He sent us. We failed."

"We were young," he says.

## la paz, bolivia, april 19

THE TRANSPORT WORKERS are on strike, and they plan to shut down La Paz to emphasize their demands for higher wages. They've asked the poor of the city to descend from the surrounding hillsides and join the demonstrations. All morning the breeze has carried a faint whiff of pepper gas and distant "pops" that sound like shotguns.

I follow the sound of cheering down an alley until I see twenty-odd men hiding behind the corner of the old San Francisco Cathedral. They are giggling and watching nearly a hundred policemen in motorcycle helmets strolling down the big avenue. The giggling intensifies, and finally the men stop into sight, twice chant, "The people united/will never be defeated," and then start running past me. The riot policemen come steaming up the alley after them, the shopkeepers slam their doors shut—this is obviously a practiced routine—and gas canisters are gracefully overhead in pursuit of the escaping delinquences. I spend a few minutes rolling around on the cobblestones, choking and crying, my eyes welded shut, listening to the dull crump of the gas grenades and the crisp reports of the shotguns.

More giggling, though this time it is the riot policemen who are laughing at their out-of-shape sergeant huffing to catch up with them. By the time I can breathe again, both sides have vanished, and little boys are scampering around the alley collecting Winchester 12-gauge casings, marveling over the bright green plastic and sniffing at the lingering cordite.

### la paz, april 20

IN THE MORNING, small items in the newspapers report that the transport workers failed to block a single avenue, let alone shut down the city. At first light I drive up and out of the city, passing beneath a series of bridges and overhead walkways. They are already lined with blue, green, and gray uniforms, shotguns, rifles, pepper-gas guns. Dawn at 10,000 feet is cold, and the men are blowing on their fingers and stamping their feet, waiting for the game to begin again. I roll south all day, toward Che's burial ground.

### somewhere near mataral, bolivia, april 22

THE FIRST, SECOND, third, fourth, and fifth flat tires of my journey. A displaced spoke is to blame. I spend a night on a mountainside lying in a field of quinoa. I wake up covered with ice.

### la higuera, bolivia, april 25

YESTERDAY I SPOKE on a provincial radio station about the purpose of my trip, my itinerary, and my frank opinion of Che's guerrilla tactics here in Bolivia. Today I am bouncing over a dirt road toward La Higuera, the tiny village where Che died, and when I get to the sole intervening town I find the schoolteacher, the mayor, and the postmaster standing in the square waiting for me. They are one man.

"First of all," he says, "take this letter up to La Higuera." He hands me the weekly mail run. "Second of all, I heard what you said on the radio about Che and you're wrong." We spend half an hour in his office, drinking moonshine and debating socialism, the New Man, and Che's mountain-guerrilla-base strategy. I used to never drink and ride.

I'm hardly down the road when an old man in a straw hat flags me down. "You must be the gringo on the radio," he shouts toothlessly. "I talked to Che Guevara right on this spot thirty years ago!" We chat; I promise to eat dinner with him on my way back this evening. I never see him again.

Onward, riding ridge lines through country without a line of smoke or a visible house. In 1966, at the height of his reputation as the prince of guerrillas, Che calculated that this desolate, empty quarter of Bolivia was the perfect place to launch his world revolution—brutally poor, inaccessible to conventional troops, ideal for guerrilla ambushes. Reality proved the reverse: Che's band of Cuban army officers and Andean intellectuals wandered aimlessly through the countryside, lost and hungry, while the army picked them off one by one over the course of eleven months. The peasants constantly betrayed them, and eventually Che and a few survivors were trapped in a ravine right below this road. Badly wounded, the rifle literally shot out of his hands, Che was captured, taken to La Higuera, and executed.

There are only twenty-two families in this desperate village. Many of them ratted on Che to the army, but the Cuban government has forgiven them and sent a doctor to work here in Che's honor. I interview this man as he pulls teeth from an old woman's mouth and rhapsodizes about *la guerrillero heróico*. Then I deliver the mail and leave for Vallegrande, the provincial capital where twenty-nine years ago Che's corpse was taken for public display.

About three kilometers outside La Higuera I see Che himself striding down the road and pull over to give him a ride. The fellow's real name is Jans van Zwam, and he is a fortyish Dutch tourist who has kitted himself out to look as much like Che as possible: a black beret with a red star, a Che T-shirt, a neat (though red) Che beard. He even has a tattoo of a fiercely defiant Che on his left arm.

"For twenty years I dream of coming to Bolivia," he says. He has passed through four airports in thirty-six hours, landed in southern Bolivia, jumped in a taxi, and come straight to La Higuera—where, by his own account, he burst into tears. Like all Che fans, Jans explains the man's greatness with a personal parable. "I didn't have no education," he says from behind me as we roll along. "At fourteen I am going to work. After much time I pick up a book. It is about Che Guevara. I see he is a doctor, from good family. He have everything, he could be a good life, but he give it up to fight for the poor. So I think he is a good fellow, and I read another book." End of parable.

Between navigating and listening to Jans talk about the various designs he considered for his Che tattoo, I miss a true milestone: somewhere on this stretch I complete the ten thousandth revolution of my odometer since leaving Buenos Aires.

At dusk we strike the outskirts of Vallegrande and stop at the hospital shed where Che's body was put on display twenty-nine years ago. Jans unsheathes an enormous knife and carves his name and, in Dutch, a message—YOU ARE MY LIGHT—on the wall among hundreds of similar messages of devotion left by tourists from all over Latin America. As dusk deepens, we ride down to the airfield to look at the excavation.

They never did find Che's body. The retired army officers pointed, the forensic scientists dug, the journalists watched, but day after day the shoveling produced nothing. The search expanded, old peasants were interviewed, ground-imaging radar was brought in to scan the dirt, and eventually even a bulldozer went to work. After a few weeks the journalists went home. After three months, the Argentine excavators went broke.

Beneath the planets and stars of the blue night, the only signs of this fantasy are the coffin holes scattered around the field. Jans peers into several of them, takes some pictures, then bursts into tears again.

I'm speechless, road sick, uncompassed by this moment of arrival. Ten thousand miles is a long way to come to see emptiness. There never was any revolution here, not the kind Che believed in. From Argentina to Mexico, there were so very many attempts and so very many, very costly failures, until the earth swallowed up all the ideals, all the blood, all the bodies.

Like La Higuera with its doctor, though, Vallegrande did get one inadvertent benefit from Che's efforts. Because of tourists like Jans, the government decided some time ago to install electricity. Up on the hillside now, the town glows in the night, basking in its privilege of light amid so much darkness.

# EL CHE GUEVARA:
# CUBA AS SHOWCASE OR SPARK

## EDUARDO GALEANO

from *WE SAY NO: CHRONICLES 1963–1991*

### 1992

#### *THE INCOMPARABLE GLORY*

I ask him if he is a member of the Communist Party. No, he is not. Would he like to be?

"Oh! The title of Communist is a most noble title. I am still very far from attaining that incomparable glory. I still have a lot of studying to do. I must finish changing my ideas if I am to reach such an elevated goal. It would be a great honor for me."

The emperor insists on my having a fourth cup of jasmine tea.

The dragons on the porcelain surface are fighting.

*(1963)*

#### TRANSLATED BY ASA ZATZ

### 1

"**T**RAITOR," I TOLD him. "You're a traitor." I showed him the clipping from a Cuban newspaper: he had on a baseball uniform, he was pitching. I remember that he laughed, we laughed; if he said something, I don't know what it was. The conversation bounced like a Ping-Pong ball from one subject to another, from one country to another, from one memory to another, from nostalgia for home and experiences of the revolution, to jokes: "What's happening to my hand? It's cursed." Damned? "Of course. It shook Frondizi's hand and Frondizi [Argentine president, 1958–62] fell; it shook Janio Quadros's [Brazilian president, 1961] hand and the same thing happened to him." It's a good thing I have no place to fall from, I responded with a worried look, and he laughed, furrowed his brow, sat down, stood up, walked about the room, let the ash fall from his *cazador* cigar, and pointed at me with it, at my chest. He'd go to the blackboard to explain a complicated thought, more like a debater than a teacher, scribbling it out with chalk: the polemic on economic calculations and the validity of the law of value in socialist society, or the system of paying people by production norms. He was caustic like people from the River Plate, aggressive, and at the same time fervent like a Cuban, sincere: generous with the truths he had discovered, but on guard, ready to bare his teeth to defend them. A profound and lovely strength flowed from inside him incessantly; as with everyone else, his eyes gave him away. He had, I recall, a pure, clean gaze, like the dawn: the look of a true believer.

## 2

HE BELIEVED, ALL right: in Latin America's revolution, in its painful evolution, in its destiny. He had faith in the new human condition that socialism *ought* to engender. When he talked about such subjects, one got the impression that the temperature of his blood rose, but whenever I started jotting down notes he kept his enthusiasm on a short rein. Then, his eyes fixed on the Bic dancing on the paper, he'd blow out two or three dense lungfuls of blue smoke between thick mustache and scraggly beard, and, smiling, he'd make some mischievous and cutting comment. Being a journalist was awful. Not because I had to go to work after so many incoherent nights and days of vertigo without sleep, nor because of how nervous all that made me, but because the flow of communication that burst forth spontaneously every so often would always get cut off. "We're talking among Cubans and Uruguayans," Che would then lie, to avoid an indiscreet question. Yet everything about him showed that the passion vibrating in him, shining throughout him, had broken down the borders others had invented for Latin America, and that he of course did not believe in them. Talking with that man you could not forget that he had come to Cuba after a pilgrimage throughout Latin America. He had been—and not just as a tourist—in the whirlwind of the nascent Bolivian revolution, and in the convulsive agony of the Guatemalan revolution. He carried bananas in Central America and took photos in the plazas of Mexico, to earn life; and to risk life, he threw himself into the adventure of the Granma.*

## 3

"ONE DAY THEY came by," he wrote in his farewell letter to Fidel, "asking who they should notify in case of death, and the real possibility that it could happen hit us all. Later on we discovered that it was true, that in a revolution (if it's real) either you win or you die." In search of new victories, or of his own end, he left Cuba. Yes, there in the middle of the tempest and the fight, you win or you die: "under other skies" now. Others, friends, so many friends had fallen along the way: they would continue to fall. El Patojo, for example, who had been on the run with him during the rough times in Mexico and ended his days shot full of lead in the Guatemalan jungle. (Don't trust, don't trust, Che had advised him: he died betrayed by a high school friend.) Another one was the Argentine Masseti who got lost, badly wounded, in the woods of Salta.

Che was not made for a desk job: he was a *creator* of revolutions, and it was obvious; he was not, or he was in spite of himself, an *administrator*. In his words and gestures under his apparent calm, you could sense the tension of a caged lion that would have to spring free.

## 4

HE MISSED THE mountains. I don't mean to imply that he was of no use in the peaceful rebuilding that follows armed victory. Very much to the contrary, Che was also an exemplary revolutionary in this sense, a worker who never tired in any of his posts of great responsibility. People suspected that he, like Fidel, never slept: day and night there were

---

*The Granma was the yacht that carried Fidel Castro, Che Guevara, and eighty other revolutionaries from Mexico to the coast of Cuba to begin the guerrilla war.

complicated matters to be resolved, and difficult tasks to be undertaken, above all in the struggle to industrialize the country. At the end of each workday, and each workday lasted an entire week, he would go on Sunday to cut cane as a volunteer. He would still find time, inexplicably, to read, write, and debate. And to fight with the relentless asthma that had plagued him during the guerrilla war. ("The order to set off," he told us, "arrived suddenly, and we all had to leave Mexico just as we were, in groups of two or three. We had a traitor among us, and Fidel had ordered that once the order was given we should leave with whatever we had in hand, to get away before the traitor had a chance to notify the police. That traitor . . . we still don't know who it was. So that's how I ended up leaving without my inhalator, and during the crossing I had a ferocious attack. I thought I would never arrive.")

He was totally committed, "as it should be," to the difficult task of building socialism in Cuba. Of all the leaders, he was the most austere and, because of his capacity for sacrifice, the most like the image of a Christian in the catacombs. Obsessed with the notion that the mystique of socialism, the faith in the new world being born, should spur development, he refrained from the excessive use of material incentives or systems of payment that might give someone hopes of "becoming a Rockefeller." The possibility that upholding the law of value—in which he did not believe—might lead to a return to capitalism ("other cases prove it") made him indignant. In this regard he was inflexible. "The gentlemen of the INRA [Agrarian Reform Institute]," he would say, referring to those who wanted to carry out a different revolutionary economic policy. His famous article answering Charles Bettelheim ends, for example, "Those who defend economic calculations fit the old saying 'I'll take care of our enemies, I hope God will protect us from our friends.' " On the next page of the same issue of *Cuba Socialista*, the first paragraph of an article by Joaquín Infante warns that "economic calculation is the method of economic policy used in socialist companies in the USSR and in other socialist countries and in popular democracies. . . ."

Criticized perhaps correctly by certain economists for "idealizing" the revolution, Che Guevara always used his biting capacity for polemics to illuminate *Cuba's* problems. It had nothing to do with the Sino-Soviet split, as some erroneously believed. "We're not going to get involved in that," he told us to explain why Cuba didn't publish a text by Paul Baran that referred to the conflict between Moscow and Peking. Any analogy could only be made by extension, but Cuba, its destiny as the advance guard of the Latin American revolution, was at the center of his concerns. "I'm not interested in discussing these things outside Cuba," he warned us when he referred to the controversial issues of the rhythm of the revolution, the keys to its development, the interdependence of domestic and foreign policy, issues on which the leaders took different positions. Che was the outspoken leader of one side, with clearly defined stances not only on economic calculation and the law of value, but on the relative importance of industrialization, the conflict between the budget system and decentralization, and Cuba's role in the broader scope of continental revolution.

As much as he was prone to argue, he did not hesitate to admit his own mistakes, which were the mistakes of the revolution itself: lowering sugar production, or "attempting to substitute for too many imports by making finished products with all the tremendous complications that importing intermediate products brings."

## 5

CHE, NOT BORN of their land but vitally involved in the challenge of their revolution, touched the Cuban people with his example. He lived just as he preached; everyone knew it, and on top of loving him, they admired him. Candela, the driver who took us through Cuba at the wheel of a luxurious expropriated Cadillac, liked to call him "horse." This supreme praise *a la cubana* was applied to only three people from Candela's mouth: Fidel, Che, and . . . Shakespeare. The efforts to bring theater to the people bore fruit in this unexpected way: every so often, Candela would go into a trance and out would rush a torrent of comments on the Elizabethan playwright ("It is pronounced several ways; the Americans say Chéspir") and of his work: "Oh, yeah. That was a real horse, chico. A horse: very philosophical his writing, and very didactic, yes sir."

All down the length of Cuba, wherever we went, Reina Reyes, Julio Villegas, and I, we met peasants, workers, technicians, students, officials, all quoting Che as frequently as they quoted Lenin or Fidel:

"Monoculture means underdevelopment; Che explained it clear as could be."

"The revolution is won by sacrifice, chico, like Che says. Or do you think everything is a party?"

Cuba was like an enormous resonating box for his essential message, the most important of all, heard by all, understood, incorporated, spread: the revolution is a force that purifies people, pushes them beyond selfishness. And purity earned must be defended, with bullets, study and work, as if it were life itself.

## 6

IN SANTA CLARA, which a poet once called the city "of red and multiple roofs," Candela showed us the walls still bitten by lead, the exact place where Batista's armored train had been derailed and attacked, the police station besieged by Vaquerito who fell once and for all at the head of a suicide squad. He told us about improvised alleys through garden walls, Molotov cocktails, blood and fire; Che Guevara, his wounded arm held by a rag, was the hero of the stories. "It's going to be six years," Candela said. "And it hasn't rained here since then." But the images were still alive in the retinas of the witnesses and protagonists, and the scars were visible, they still burned: history, which had no need for the passage of time to turn this into legend, was still occurring, the enemy attacking, the revolution battling on, and death was still something that could touch anyone at any moment.

## 7

CHE'S IRREVERENCE WAS the irreverence of the revolution. But in another style, more like ours in the River Plate, sober and sarcastic. Perhaps it was nostalgia for his lost home, half vengeance and half homage, that made Argentines the butt of his most acid comments: he would remind them that revolutions are made and not said, that the mission of communist parties is to be at the vanguard of the revolution (a satisfied smile) . . . but lamentably in almost all of Latin America they are in the rear guard (indignant silence). When a well-known Peronist got mad because he had been kept waiting more than a month for an appointment, Che patted his back: "But you've waited eight years to make the revolution. . . ." And other wicked comments:

once he suggested that to raise money for the revolution, they buy certain people from Buenos Aires for what they were worth and sell them for what they *thought* they were worth.

**8**

THE IMAGE OF the guerrilla Che in Santa Clara foreshadowed that of Che struggling in the inhospitable Bolivian jungle, and it got confused with the memory of Che at the Punta del Este conference, brilliant statesman, economist, somber prophet: that refined intellectual, who read poetry anthologies in the Sierra Maestra, knew by heart much of Neruda's *Canto General*, spoke admiringly of the novels of Carpentier, and laughed at socialist realism. But through all the images, or adding them together, one emerges. It was Che at a press conference, answering the question of some idiot who wanted to know if he was Argentine, Cuban, or what:

"I am a citizen of America, sir," he said.

When we spoke in Havana, I told him. "The destiny of Cuba is intimately linked to that of Latin America's revolution. Cuba can't get confined within its borders; it works like an engine of continental revolution. Right?" And he answered:

"There was a chance that wouldn't be the case. But we have eliminated such chances. If Cuba agreed to stop being an example for the Latin American revolution, then the Latin American revolutionary movements would not be directly linked to Cuba. The simple fact of being alive does not make one an example. In what way is it an example? The way the Cuban revolution approaches its relations with the United States and the spirit of struggle against imperialism. Cuba could become a purely economic example."

"A sort of socialist showcase."

"A showcase. That would safeguard Cuba up to a point, but would divorce it from the Latin American revolution. We are not a showcase."

"And how can you spread the strength of an example and not end up simply contemplating your achievements? Through solidarity? How far can that reach? What are the limits? How would you define what's needed for solidarity between Cuba and the liberation movements of Latin America?"

"The problem of solidarity—yes, yes, of course you can write this down—consists of doing all that's feasible for the Latin American revolution within a legal framework, and that framework is the relation between countries on the exchange of ideology or politics, on the basis of mutually respected accords."

"A situation which only exists with three countries."

"With two. Bolivia broke off relations this afternoon."

He took it for granted that it would not be long before Uruguay would do the same.

I had the impression, I said, that Chile's decision to break relations surprised the Cubans. "What do you mean it surprised us? It did not surprise us a bit." But the people in the street seemed truly astonished. "The people, maybe. The government, no. We knew what was coming." I asked him what he thought of certain statements of Chile's FRAP [the leftist Popular Action Front] on Cuba, shortly before Frei's victory.* "Well, we thought they were terrible," he said. I suggested that it could be the result of the circumstances: the inevitable zigzags on the electoral road to power. He declared: "Power in Latin America is taken by force or it is not taken." He shook his head and added, "Put it down as 'generally speaking.' " So let's say the road to the government, not to power, I said. To confuse one with the other could have serious consequences, right? That happened in Brazil, didn't it?

But then Che remembered that he was with a journalist: spontaneity and caution chased each other without respite during three hours of conversation.

## 9

"SUPPOSE NEW REVOLUTIONS occurred in Latin America. Would that produce a qualitative change in Cuban—U.S. relations? The possibility of a coexistence accord has been mentioned. But if the fire spreads and imperialism is forced to throw water on the flames, what will happen to Cuba, the spark?"

"We define the current relationship between Cuba and the United States as an automobile and a train moving more or less at the same speed. The car has to cross the tracks. As the crossing gets closer, so

*Chile's Popular Action Front (FRAP) was an alliance of six leftist parties formed in 1956, a precursor to Allende's Popular Unity (UP).

does the possibility of a crash. If the car—which is Cuba—crosses before the train, that is, if the Latin American revolution acquires sufficient depth, then we'll already be on the other side: Cuba will no longer matter. Because imperialism is attacking Cuba not out of spite, but because it is important. I mean that if the Latin American revolution gets to the point where a large number of U.S. troops have to be deployed, then a number of territories will no longer matter. We will have already passed the railroad crossing. We deepen our confrontations with the United States every day, objectively and fatally as the situation in Latin America worsens—and the best of it is how bad it is. Now if the situation gets so bad that the United States has to send in lots of troops and equipment, by its own weight Cuba's importance will disappear. The fundamental issue will not be Cuba as a catalyst, because the chemical reaction will have already occurred. The unknown is whether we will cross before the train. We could step on the brakes, but that is unlikely."

"From this perspective, is coexistence possible?"

"The point isn't about Cuba, it's about the United States. The United States is not interested in Cuba if the revolution doesn't gel in Latin America. If the United States manages to dominate the situation, what will it care about Cuba?"

## 10

"AND SUPPOSE THE Latin American revolution doesn't get off the ground. Would it be possible for Cuba to continue moving forward?"

"Of course it's possible."

"In the long run?"

"In the long run. The worst of the blockade is over."

"I'm not only referring to physical survival. I mean, couldn't cutting off Cuba from its source of Latin American nourishment cause other sorts of problems—internal deformations, ideological rigidity, ever stronger ties of dependency? A Latin American revolution would undoubtedly enrich Marxism: it would allow for the theory to be best applied to our particular reality. And if the revolution becomes Latin America-wide, it would allow Cuba to resume its natural, framework of existence. This isn't a statement; it's a question."

"It sounds a bit idealistic to me. We can't speak of sources of nourishment. The sources of nourishment are Cuban reality, no matter what that may be, and the correct application of Marxism-Leninism to the Cuban people's way of being, under given conditions. Isolation may cause many things. For example, we might fail to understand the political situation in Brazil; but distortions in the march of the revolution, no. Of course, it's much easier for us to speak with a Venezuelan than a Congolese, but we would definitely understand the Congolese revolutionaries perfectly, even though we have yet to speak with them. There is an identity in the struggle and in the ends pursued. A revolution in Zanzibar could also give us new things, new experiences; the union of Tanganyika and Zanzibar; the struggle in Algeria, the struggle in Vietnam. We have the Indian apron of our American mother, Martí liked to say, and that's fine, but a long time ago our American mother went through successive changes. And these are becoming more and more worldwide: a world capitalist system and a world socialist system. The fact that Algeria is free strengthens Cuba. We keep one thing always clear: Cuba's identity with revolutionary movements. In spite of the racial, religious, historic relationships, Algeria is closer to Cuba than to Morocco."

"And closer to the USSR than to Morocco?"

"That's one the Algerians will have to answer."


## 11


"WHEN YOU REFERRED to the 'world socialist system' you mentioned countries that are not part of the socialist bloc. Nationalist movements inclining toward socialism have placed their own stamp on those countries."

"The final result will necessarily be either a move toward socialist integration or a return to the capitalist camp. The Third World is a world in transition. It exists because dialectically there is always a camp between opposites where contradictions sharpen. But it cannot remain there isolated. Algeria itself, as it deepens its socialist system, little by little leaves the Third World."

"Couldn't we speak of a Third World that cuts across the socialist bloc? The conflict between the Chinese and the Soviets, no longer silent, was analyzed by some Marxist thinkers like Paul Baran as a consequence of the contradictions between socialist countries with different levels of development and different degrees of confrontation with imperialism."

"The death of Paul Baran left me deeply moved. I held him in great esteem; he was here, with us."

Imperturbable, he moved his Havana cigar in silence; he watched my pencil as if it were an intruder taking part in our dialogue; I decided to put it away. From then on, Che Guevara answered a shower of questions on economic issues. From the Geneva Conference ("Some people have the answers, others have the things") to the mistakes made in the domestic economic process, Che Guevara spoke patiently and at length.

Until an enemy broke into the room to remind the minister of industries that his rival had been waiting for twenty minutes by the chessboard on the floor below. And he wasn't about to lose the tournament just like that.

# PERMISSIONS

"The Making of a Revolutionary: A Memoir of the Young Guevara" by Dolores Moyano Martin. Copyright © 1968 by The New York Times Company. Reprinted with permission. Originally appeared in *The New York Times*, August 18, 1968.

Excerpts from *The Motorcycle Diaries* by Ernesto Che Guevara, translated by Ann Wright. Copyright © 1995 by Ann Wright. Reprinted by permission of Verso Ltd.

Excerpts from *Back on the Road: A Journey Through Latin America* by Ernesto Che Guevara, translated by Patrick Camiller. Copyright © 2001 by Patrick Camiller. Used by permission of Grove/Atlantic, Inc.

Excerpt from *My Friend Che* by Ricardo Rojo, translated by Julian Casart. Copyright © 1968 by Doubleday, a division of Random House,